INTRODUCTION

The History of British Women's Writing, 700–1500

The History of British Women's Writing

General Editors: **Jennie Batchelor** and **Cora Kaplan**

Advisory Board: Isobel Armstrong, Rachel Bowlby, Carolyn Dinshaw, Margaret Ezell, Margaret Ferguson, Isobel Grundy, and Felicity Nussbaum

The History of British Women's Writing is an innovative and ambitious monograph series that seeks both to synthesise the work of several generations of feminist scholars, and to advance new directions for the study of women's writing. Volume editors and contributors are leading scholars whose work collectively reflects the global excellence in this expanding field of study. It is envisaged that this series will be a key resource for specialist and non-specialist scholars and students alike.

Titles include:

Liz Herbert McAvoy and Diane Watt (*editors*)
THE HISTORY OF BRITISH WOMEN'S WRITING, 700–1500
Volume One

Caroline Bicks and Jennifer Summit (*editors*)
THE HISTORY OF BRITISH WOMEN'S WRITING, 1500–1610
Volume Two

Mihoko Suzuki (*editor*)
THE HISTORY OF BRITISH WOMEN'S WRITING, 1610–1690
Volume Three

Ros Ballaster (*editor*)
THE HISTORY OF BRITISH WOMEN'S WRITING, 1690–1750
Volume Four

Jacqueline M. Labbe (*editor*)
THE HISTORY OF BRITISH WOMEN'S WRITING, 1750–1830
Volume Five

Forthcoming titles:

Mary Joannou (*editor*)
THE HISTORY OF BRITISH WOMEN'S WRITING, 1920–1945
Volume Eight

History of British Women's Writing
Series Standing Order ISBN 978–0–230–20079–1 hardback
(*outside North America only*)

You can receive future titles in this series as they are published by placing a standing order. Please contact your bookseller or, in case of difficulty, write to us at the address below with your name and address, the title of the series and the ISBN quoted above.

Customer Services Department, Macmillan Distribution Ltd, Houndmills, Basingstoke, Hampshire RG21 6XS, England

---

The History of British Women's Writing, 700–1500

Volume One

Edited by

Liz Herbert McAvoy and Diane Watt

First published 2012 by
PALGRAVE MACMILLAN

Palgrave Macmillan in the UK is an imprint of Macmillan Publishers Limited,
registered in England, company number 785998, of Houndmills, Basingstoke,
Hampshire RG21 6XS.

Palgrave Macmillan in the US is a division of St Martin's Press LLC,
175 Fifth Avenue, New York, NY 10010.

Palgrave Macmillan is the global academic imprint of the above companies
and has companies and representatives throughout the world.

Palgrave® and Macmillan® are registered trademarks in the United States,
the United Kingdom, Europe and other countries.

ISBN 978–0–230–23510–6

This book is printed on paper suitable for recycling and made from fully
managed and sustained forest sources. Logging, pulping and manufacturing
processes are expected to conform to the environmental regulations of the
country of origin.

A catalogue record for this book is available from the British Library.

A catalog record for this book is available from the Library of Congress.

For our grandmothers:

Doris Mary Dodson,
Florence Hilda May Eriksson,
and Mary Ellen Whiles,
and
Annie Sophia Butler,
and Mary Denness McIntosh

Contents

Series Preface

One of the most significant developments in literary studies in the last quarter of a century has been the remarkable growth of scholarship on women's writing. This was inspired by, and in turn provided inspiration for, a postwar women's movement, which saw women's cultural expression as key to their emancipation. The retrieval, republication, and reappraisal of women's writing, beginning in the mid-1960s have radically affected the literary curriculum in schools and universities. A revised canon now includes many more women writers. Literature courses that focus on what women thought and wrote from antiquity onwards have become popular undergraduate and postgraduate options. These new initiatives have meant that gender – in language, authors, texts, audience, and in the history of print culture more generally – are central questions for literary criticism and literary history. A mass of fascinating research and analysis extending over several decades now stands as testimony to a lively and diverse set of debates, in an area of work that is still expanding.

Indeed so rapid has this expansion been, that it has become increasingly difficult for students and academics to have a comprehensive view of the wider field of women's writing outside their own period or specialism. As the research on women has moved from the margins to the confident centre of literary studies it has become rich in essays and monographs dealing with smaller groups of authors, with particular genres and with defined periods of literary production, reflecting the divisions of intellectual labour and development of expertise that are typical of the discipline of literary studies. Collections of essays that provide overviews within particular periods and genres do exist, but no published series has taken on the mapping of the field even within one language group or national culture.

A History of British Women's Writing is intended as just such a cartographic standard work. Its ambition is to provide, in ten volumes edited by leading experts in the field, and comprised of newly commissioned essays by specialist scholars, a clear and integrated picture of women's contribution to the world of letters within Great Britain from medieval times to the present. In taking on such a wide-ranging project we were inspired by the founding, in 2003, of Chawton House Library, a UK registered charity with a unique collection of books focusing on women's writing in English from 1600 to 1830, set in the home and working estate of Jane Austen's brother.

JENNIE BATCHELOR
UNIVERSITY OF KENT

CORA KAPLAN
QUEEN MARY, UNIVERSITY OF LONDON

Acknowledgements

A book such as this one necessarily reflects the labours of many people, for all of which we, as editors, wish to extend our gratitude. First and foremost we are indebted to our contributors, not only for their production of interesting, informative, and frequently ground-breaking essays but also for the professionalism and cooperation displayed in the tasks of revising, amending, and supplementing contributions during the editing process. Special thanks are also due to those contributors who stepped in at very short notice to fill a void or another contributor's withdrawal. We are also grateful to Liz Cox and Lisa Schaffnit, research postgraduates at Swansea University and Aberystwyth University respectively, for the careful compilation of the bibliography over many months, and also to Liz for her hard work on the chronology. We would also like to proffer our thanks to areas of our respective current and previous institutions for financing the research assistance for this project: namely the Research Institute of the College of Arts and Humanities at Swansea University, the Institute of Medieval and Early Modern Studies at Aberystwyth and Bangor Universities, and Aberystwyth University Research Fund. Without such support, this project would have been much more fraught an endeavour than it proved to be. Patricia Watt kindly read through the manuscript prior to submission to the press. Finally, thanks go to Cora Kaplan and Jennie Batchelor, the series' editors, for their willingness to negotiate on content and rationale, and to Palgrave Macmillan more generally for their helpful advice and support during the volume's production.

Notes on the Contributors

Amy Appleford is Assistant Professor of English at Boston University. She has published on Julian of Norwich's *Revelation of Love*, the 'Dance of Death', and other topics in fifteenth-century pastoral theology and literature, as well as on Shakespeare's *Henry VIII*. She is currently working on a monograph on late-medieval death culture called *Learning to Die in London, 1350–1530*.

Alexandra Barratt is Professor Emeritus at the University of Waikato, New Zealand. She has worked extensively on medieval writings for and by women. A second, enlarged edition of her widely used anthology, *Women's Writing in Middle English*, appeared in 2010, and her monograph, *Anne Bulkeley and her Book: Fashioning Female Piety in Early Tudor England*, in 2010. She continues to research Dame Eleanor Hull and her translations from Anglo-Norman.

Catherine Batt is Senior Lecturer in Medieval Studies at the School of English, University of Leeds. Her research interests include translation, material culture, gender studies, poetics and the representation of women, Anglo-Norman literature, Arthurian literature, early and later Middle English romance, saints' lives, devotional literature, and twentieth-century medievalism. She has published on, *inter alia*, Clemence of Barking, Caxton, the *Gawain*-Poet, Thomas Hoccleve (including *Essays on Thomas Hoccleve*: ed., intro., and contr. [1996]), Thomas Malory (including *Malory's Morte Darthur: Remaking Arthurian Tradition* [Palgrave Macmillan, 2002]), and Sylvia Townsend Warner. Her most recent project is a translation of Henry, duke of Lancaster's *Book of Holy Medicines* (forthcoming), and she is currently researching medieval Sloth.

Anke Bernau is Senior Lecturer in Medieval Literature and Culture at the University of Manchester. In 2007 she published *Virgins: A Cultural History* and in 2009 the co-edited volume *Medieval Film*. Other recent publications include articles on medievalism, medieval historiography, and origin myths. Her current book project is on the representation of memory, forgetting, and emotion in imaginative literature of the fifteenth and sixteenth centuries.

Jennifer N. Brown is Assistant Professor of Language and Literature at Marymount Manhattan College. Her book, *Three Women of Liège: A Critical Edition of and Commentary on the Middle English Lives of Elizabeth of Spalbeek, Christina Mirabilis, and Marie d'Oignies*, was published in 2008. She has also published articles in both journals and edited collections on Marie d'Oignies and Jacques de Vitry, Catherine of Siena, and Edward the Confessor. Her co-edited collection on Barking Abbey is forthcoming. She also writes the Medieval Women's Writing and Middle Scots Poets chapters for the annual bibliographic review, *The Year's Work in English Studies*.

Jane Cartwright is Reader in Welsh at the University of Wales Trinity Saint David and former Head of the Department of Welsh at the University of Wales, Lampeter. She specializes in Middle Welsh poetry and prose and her particular interests include women's history, religious texts, and saints' cults. She is the author of *Y Forwyn Fair, Santesau a Lleianod: Agweddau ar Wyryfdod a Diweirdeb yng Nghymru'r Oesoedd Canol* (1999) and *Feminine Sanctity and Spirituality in Medieval Wales* (2008), as well as the editor of *Celtic Hagiography and Saints' Cults* (2003).

Catherine A. M. Clarke is Senior Lecturer in English and Associate Director of the Centre for Medieval and Early Modern Research at Swansea University. Her research centres on earlier medieval literature and culture, with particular attention to questions of place, power, and identity and an emphasis on interdisciplinary approaches. Her publications include the monograph *Literary Landscapes and the Idea of England, 700–1400* (2006), the edited collection *Mapping the Medieval City: Space, Place and Identity in Chester, c.1200–1600* (2011), and a forthcoming book on writing power in Anglo-Saxon England.

James Daybell is Professor of Early Modern British History at the University of Plymouth, and Fellow of the Royal Historical Society. He is author of *Women Letter-Writers in Tudor England* (2006) and editor of *Early Modern Women's Letter-Writing in Early Modern England, 1450–1700* (Palgrave Macmillan, 2001), *Women and Politics in Early Modern England, 1450–1700* (2004), and (with Peter Hinds), *Material Readings of Early Modern Culture: Texts and Social Practice* (Palgrave Macmillan, 2010). He has published more than twenty-five articles and essays on the subjects of early modern women, and letters, and his new monograph, *The Material Letter: Manuscript Letters and the Culture and Practices of Letter-Writing in Early Modern England, 1512–1635*, will be published with Palgrave in 2012. He is also editor (along with Adam Smyth, Birkbeck College, University of London) of the Ashgate book series, Material Readings in Early Modern Culture.

Mary C. Erler is Professor of English at Fordham University in New York. She is the author of *Women, Reading, and Piety in Late Medieval England* (2002) and of 'Devotional Reading' in *Cambridge History of the Book in Britain*, Vol. III: *1400–1557* (1999). She edited *Ecclesiastical London: Records of Early English Drama* (2008) and, with Maryanne Kowaleski, *Women and Power in the Middle Ages* (1988) and *Gendering the Master Narrative: Women and Power in the Middle Ages* (2003).

Lara Farina is an Associate Professor of English at West Virginia University. She has published on medieval women's reading practices in her book, *Erotic Discourse and Early English Religious Writing* (Palgrave Macmillan, 2006), and in the collections *Women, Wealth and Power in Medieval Europe* (2010) and *The Lesbian Premodern* (Palgrave Macmillan, 2011). She is currently researching the history of sensation, particularly the sense of touch, and is editing (with Holly Dugan) a special issue of *Postmedieval* devoted to the 'intimate senses' of taste, touch, and smell.

C. Annette Grisé is Associate Professor in the Department of English and Cultural Studies at McMaster University. Her research on manuscripts and early printed books for and by women religious in late-medieval England includes work on the cult of continental female mystics in England, women's reading and devotional practices, and the texts associated with Syon Abbey. She has recently published chapters in the *Blackwell Companion to Medieval Poetry*, *Syon Abbey and its Book*, and *After Arundel: Spiritual Writings in Fifteenth-Century England*, and is co-editing a collection of essays on devotional reading in late-medieval England.

Shari Horner is Professor of English at Shippensburg University. She is the author of *The Discourse of Enclosure: Representing Women in Old English Literature* (2001), as well as numerous articles on Anglo-Saxon poetry and saints' lives, including 'The Vernacular Language of Rape in Old English Literature and Law: Views from the Anglo-Saxon(ist)s' and 'The Violence of Exegesis: Reading the Bodies of Ælfric's Female Saints'. Her current work focuses on intersections of the material and the textual in early medieval hagiography.

Clare A. Lees is Professor of Medieval English Literature at King's College London where she also directs the Centre for Late Antique and Medieval Studies. She has published widely on early medieval literature and has particular interests in gender studies, religious culture, and landscape. With Gillian R. Overing, she co-authored *Double Agents: Women and Clerical Culture in Anglo-Saxon England* (2001, repr. 2009) and co-edited *Gender and Empire* (for the *Journal of Medieval and Early Modern Studies*, 2004) and *A Place to Believe In: Locating Medieval Landscapes* (2006). Her other work includes *Tradition and Belief: Religious Writing in Late Anglo-Saxon England* (1999), *Gender in Debate from the Early Middle Ages to the Renaissance*, co-edited with Thelma S. Fenster (2002), and *Fragments of History: Rethinking the Ruthwell and Bewcastle Monuments* (with Fred Orton and Ian Wood, 2007). She is currently editing *The Cambridge History of Early Medieval English Literature*.

Liz Herbert McAvoy is Reader in Medieval Literature and Gender Studies at Swansea University where she is also Associate Director of the Centre for Medieval and Early Modern Research. She has published widely on medieval women's writing and female anchoritism, including *Authority and the Female Body in the Writings of Julian of Norwich and Margery Kempe* (2004) and *Medieval Anchoritisms: Gender, Space and the Solitary Life* (2011). She has also edited a number of essay collections, including *Rhetoric of the Anchorhold: Space, Place and Body within the Discourses of Enclosure* (2008), *A Companion to Julian of Norwich* (2008), and *Anchoritic Traditions of Medieval Europe* (2010). Her current work focuses on a number of late-medieval anonymous texts known to have been written by women.

Carol M. Meale is currently Senior Research Fellow at the University of Bristol. As Reader in Medieval Studies there she co-founded and directed the Centre for Medieval Studies. Her particular interests are the lives of individual women (especially in East Anglia), late medieval literature, and codicology, on all of which subjects she has published widely. She is editor of *Women and Literature in Britain, 1150–1500* (2nd edn., 1996) and *Readings in Medieval English Romance* (1994), and, amongst other collaborations, she has co-edited *Medieval Women: Texts and Contexts in Late Medieval Britain: Essays for Felicity Riddy* (2000). She is currently working on the issues of language and gender in relation to patronage.

Laura Saetveit Miles is currently at the University of Michigan, Ann Arbor as a Fellow at the Michigan Society of Fellows and Assistant Professor in the Department of English. She received her PhD in English Literature from Yale University, and an MPhil in Medieval English from the University of Cambridge. Her book project is titled *Mary's Book: The Annunciation in Medieval England*. Recent articles include the winning essay of the Society for Medieval Feminist Scholarship 2010 Prize for Best Article by a Graduate Student, 'Looking in the Past for a Discourse of Motherhood: Birgitta of Sweden and Julia Kristeva', *Medieval Feminist Forum*, 47 (2012), and 'Richard Methley and the Translation of Vernacular Religious Writing into Latin', in *After Arundel: Religious Writing in Fifteenth Century England*, ed. Vincent Gillespie and Kantik Ghosh (2011). Laura is a co-founder of the Syon Abbey Society (www.syonabbeysociety.com).

Sue Niebrzydowski is Lecturer in Medieval Literature at Bangor University, Wales. Author of *Bonoure and Buxum: A Study of Wives in Late Medieval English Literature* (2006), she has published late-medieval women's writing, and on the dialogue between this literature and the cultural texts that attempt to construct paradigms of medieval womanhood. She has also edited *Middle Aged Women in the Middle Ages* (2011) and contributed to a number of essay collections. Her current work focuses on the impact of ageing on women's reading and writing practices.

Gillian R. Overing is Professor of English and co-director of Medieval Studies at Wake Forest University. She has published widely on gender, culture, and landscape in the early medieval period, including *Language, Sign and Gender in* Beowulf (1990), *Landscape of Desire: Partial Stories of the Medieval Scandinavian World* (with Marijane Osborn, 1994), and *Double Agents: Women and Clerical Culture in Anglo-Saxon England* (with Clare A. Lees, 2001, repr. 2009). She has co-edited several essay collections including *Class and Gender in Early English Literature: Intersections* (1994), *Gender and Empire* (2004), and *A Place to Believe In: Locating Medieval Landscapes* (2006). Her recent work focuses on perceptions of the body in Anglo-Saxon England, and on critical reassessment of *Beowulf* in essays for *New Medieval Literatures* (2010) and the forthcoming *Cambridge History of Early Medieval Literature.*

Elizabeth Robertson is Chair of English Language at the University of Glasgow where she is also co-director of Centre for Medieval and Renaissance Studies. Formerly Professor of English Literature at the University of Colorado, she is also founding editor of *Medieval Feminist Forum* and the Society for Medieval Feminist Scholarship. She has published a large number of essays on gender and religion in medieval literature in journals and collections of essays including *Speculum* and *Studies in the Age of Chaucer*. With Stephen Shepherd, she co-edited the Norton Critical Edition of *Piers Plowman* (2006) and is currently completing a monograph: *Chaucerian Consent: Women, Religion and Subjection in Late Medieval England*. She is working on a new project on representations of the soul in medieval literature called *Souls that Matter.*

Michelle M. Sauer is Professor of English and Gender Studies at the University of North Dakota (Grand Forks, ND). She specializes in Middle English language and literature, especially women's devotional literature, and publishes regularly on anchoritism, mysticism, asceticism, hagiography, and church history. Her recent publications include the co-edited volume, *The Lesbian Premodern* (Palgrave Macmillan, 2011), and *How to Write about Chaucer* (2009), as well as *The Companion to Pre-1600 British Poetry* (2008). Her current projects include an edition of the Wooing Group, an anchoritic guidebook, a book on gender in the Middle Ages, and several edited collections as well as articles and essays, most focusing on the intersections of gender and space and same-sex relations in religious writing.

Corinne Saunders is Professor in the Department of English Studies at Durham University, and currently Head of Department. Her research interests focus on medieval romance literature and history of ideas, particularly related to gender, the body, and medicine. She is Associate Director of Durham's Centre for Medical Humanities. She is author of *The Forest of Medieval Romance* (1993), *Rape and Ravishment in the Literature of Medieval England* (2001), and *Magic and the Supernatural in Medieval Romance* (2010). In addition, she has published over thirty essays and articles on a wide range of literary and cultural topics, as well as editing and co-editing a number of essay collections, including *A Blackwell Companion to Romance: from Classical to Contemporary* (2004), *Cultural Encounters in Medieval Romance* (2005), *A Concise Companion to Chaucer* (2006), and *A Blackwell Companion to Medieval Poetry* (2010). She is the English editor of the international journal of medieval studies, *Medium Ævum*.

Myra J. Seaman is Associate Professor of English at the College of Charleston. She has published on Middle English romance, textual studies, dream visions, medievalisms, and posthumanisms medieval and modern. She co-edited the essay collection *Cultural Studies of the Modern Middle Ages* (2007) and is at work on another essay collection of medievalists considering humanism, then and now. In addition, she is an editor of the journal *postmedieval: a journal of medieval cultural studies* and a founder of the scholarly collective known as the BABEL Working Group. She is currently working on an extended project that investigates affective literacy among the late-medieval English gentry through an object-oriented ontological approach.

Nancy Bradley Warren is Professor of English and Head of the English Department at Texas A&M University. She has published extensively on medieval and early modern female spirituality, including *Spiritual Economies: Female Monasticism in Later Medieval England* (2001), *Women of God and Arms: Female Spirituality and Political Conflict, 1380–1600* (2005), and *The Embodied Word: Female Spiritualities, Contested Orthodoxies, and English Religious Cultures, 1350–1700* (2010). She is currently co-editing collections of essays on Christine de Pizan and St Colette of Corbie, and she is guest editor of a forthcoming special issue of *JMEMS* on 'Monasticisms Medieval and Early Modern'.

Diane Watt is Professor of English Literature and Head of the School of English and Languages at the University of Surrey. She was formerly Professor of English Literature at Aberystwyth University. She has published widely on women's writing and medieval literature. Her books include *Secretaries of God: Women Prophets in Late Medieval and Early Modern England* (1997), *Amoral Gower: Language, Sex and Politics* (2003), and *Medieval Women's Writing: Works by and for Women* (2007). She has also edited *Medieval Women in the Communities* (1997), and translated *The Paston Women: Selected Letters* (2004). Her most recent co-edited collection is *The Lesbian Premodern* (Palgrave Macmillan, 2011), with Noreen Giffney and Michelle Sauer.

Chronology

c.487–500	St Non reputedly gave birth to St David, patron saint of Wales. St Non is referred to in the late-eleventh-century Latin *Life* of David, the fourteenth-century Welsh *Life* of David and the late-medieval Breton *Life* of Non.
c.500–700	The 'Age of the Saints' when various Welsh female saints reputedly founded abbeys and nunneries, e.g. Gwenfrewy, Melangell, Dwynwen, Non, San Ffraid.
c.597	The Mission of Pope Gregory to convert Anglo-Saxons began with the arrival of Augustine in Canterbury.
c.657–80	Hild, abbess of Whitby flourished; Cædmon composed the Old English 'Hymn'.
c.675–85	Barking Abbey was founded.
c.685–700	Aldhelm of Malmesbury composed the prose *De virginitate*, dedicated to Hildelith and others.
716	The date of Boniface's first mission to the continent, to Frisia.
731	Bede finished *Ecclesiastical History of the English People*.
c.732	The nun Leoba sent a poem to Boniface.
782	Abbess Leoba died.
c.836/7	Rudolph composed the *Life of Leoba*.
c.838	Osburh, mother of Alfred the Great, flourished.
848/9–899	The life of Alfred the Great.
c.900–50	Hywel Dda, King of Wales, reputedly began the process of formalizing Welsh law which, by the thirteenth century, would include a tractate known as the Welsh Law of Women outlining the legal status, rights, and privileges of Welsh women.
c.975–1000	The major collections of Old English poetry were compiled including the Vercelli Book (including *Elene*) and Exeter Book (including *The Wife's Lament*, *Wulf and Eadwacer*).
978–88	The *Chronicle of Æthelweard* was written for Abbess Matilda of Essen.

c.998	Ælfric wrote the *Lives of Saints* and *Colloquy*.
c.1000	The *Beowulf* manuscript was compiled.
c.1010	Ælfric Bata wrote the *Colloquies*.
c.1035–1123	Marbod of Rennes flourished.
1041 or 1042	*Encomium Emmae Reginae* was written for Queen Emma (widow of Cnut).
1045	Edith (of Wessex) married Edward the Confessor.
1066	Edward the Confessor died; the Battle of Hastings marked the beginning of Norman rule in Britain.
1066–1070	*Vita Ædwardi Regis* was commissioned by Edith, widow of Edward the Confessor.
c.1080–3	Goscelin of Saint-Bertin's *Legend of Edith* was commissioned by the Wilton community, and the *Liber confortatorius* was written for the recluse, Eve, a former nun of Wilton.
1086	Cnut IV of Denmark was murdered (marking the end of the threat to Norman rule).
c.1096	Christina of Markyate was born.
1100	Henry I acceded to the throne.
1100–18	*Life of St Margaret of Scotland* was written for Queen Matilda, first wife of Henry I.
c.1100–*c*.1285	The Poets of the Princes flourished in Wales.
Before 1102	Baudri of Bourgeuil's *To Countess Adela* was written for William the Conqueror's daughter, Adela of Blois.
1106	*The Voyage of St Brendan* by Benedeit was dedicated to Edith-Matilda (later re-dedicated to Henry I's second wife, Adeliza of Louvain).
1119–31	St Albans Psalter was produced for Christina of Markyate.
1121–35	Philippe de Thaon's *Bestiare* was dedicated to Adeliza of Louvain, second wife of Henry I.
c.1131	Christina of Markyate made her profession at St Albans.
c.1135	Richard de Clare settled Benedictine nuns at Usk Priory.
1139–70	Hywel ab Owain Gwynedd flourished, renowned for his courtly love poetry.
1145	Markyate was established as a priory.
1146	Geoffrey of St Albans died.
c.1155	*The Life of Christina of Markyate* was written by a monk of St Albans.
c.1155–66	Christina of Markyate died.
c.1160s–90	Marie de France composed the *Fables*.

c.1160–1200	Marie de France composed the *Lays* (*Lais*).
1161	Aelred of Rievaulx wrote *De institutione inclusarum* for his sister.
1163–1189	The Nun of Barking's *Life of Saint Edward the Confessor*, was written at Barking Abbey.
c.1175–1200	Clemence of Barking wrote *The Life of St Catherine*.
c.1177	Marie d'Oignies was born in Nivelles, Brabant-Liège.
c.1180	Denis Piramus wrote *La Vie Seint Edmund le Rei*; Chrétien de Troyes flourished.
1187	Augustinian canons established themselves in Oignies.
1190	Marie de France composed the *Saint Patrick's Purgatory*.
c.1190–1220	Oxford, Bodleian Library, MS Bodley 34 was written (containing *Lives* of Saints Margaret, Katherine and Juliana; *Sawles Warde* ['The Guardianship of the Soul'] and *Hali Meidenhad* ['Holy Virginity']).
c.1197	The Lord Rhys founded the Cistercian house for women at Llanllŷr.
c.1200	'Marie' composed the *Life of Saint Audrey*.
c.1200–30	The 'AB texts' (*Ancrene Wisse*, 'Wooing Group' prayers, 'Katherine Group' texts) were composed for anchoritic readers.
1213	Marie d'Oignies died; Jacques de Vitry left the community at Oignies.
c.1215	Jacques de Vitry wrote the *Life* of Marie d'Oignies.
c.1225	*King Horn* was composed.
c.1229–35	Robert Grosseteste preached to the Franciscans at Oxford about the piety of the beguines.
c.1231	Thomas of Cantimpré wrote the Supplement to the *Life* of Marie d'Oignies.
1240	The *de Brailes Hours* was produced for a female patron (Susanna?) in Oxford.
c.1250–*c*.1275	Efa ferch Gruffudd ap Maredudd commissioned Brother Gruffudd Bola to translate the Creed of Athanasius from Latin into Welsh because she wished to read it in her native tongue.
1267	Llywelyn ap Gruffudd was recognized as Prince of Wales.
1284	The Statute of Wales was enacted by Edward I.
c.1285–*c*.1525	The Welsh Poets of the Gentry composed a vast corpus of Middle Welsh poetry including large numbers of love poems and praise poems to specific named women.

*c.*1289–1327	The life of Elizabeth de Burgh (m. Robert I of Scotland).
1293–4	The foundation of London house of Franciscan Minoresses.
Late 13th century	*The Thrush and the Nightingale* was composed.
*c.*1300	*Sir Orfeo, Guy of Warwick,* and *Sir Beves of Hamtoun* were all composed.
*c.*1300–1400	London, British Library, MS Harley 4725 was produced (an English manuscript with the *Life* of Marie d'Oignies).
1302/3	St Bridget of Sweden was born.
1310	Marguerite Porete was born.
1337	The 'Hundred Years War' began when Edward III of England, nephew of Charles IV, claimed the title 'King of France'.
*c.*1342	Julian of Norwich was born.
*c.*1343	Geoffrey Chaucer was born.
1347	St Catherine of Siena was born into a Sienese wool-dyer family.
1348–9	Richard Rolle wrote the *Form of Living* for Margaret Kirkby.
1348–50	The first major outbreak of the Black Death in England.
1349	St Bridget travelled to Rome.
*c.*1350	The White Book of Rhydderch was commissioned by Rhydderch ab Ieuan Llwyd of Parcrhydderch, Llangeitho. It includes Welsh versions of the *Lives* of Mary Magdalene, Martha, Mary of Egypt, Katherine, and Margaret, as well as the Mabinogi legends (depicting strong female characters such as Rhiannon, Branwen, Aranrhod, and Blodeuedd); *The Good Wife Taught Her Daughter* was composed.
1358–1417	The life of Margery de Nerford, a London vowess.
1359–99	The life of Eleanor de Bohun, married to Thomas of Woodstock.
1363–76	Katherine Sutton, abbess of Barking, and the first recorded English woman playwright, flourished.
1365	Christine de Pizan was born in Venice, Italy.
1366	St Catherine of Siena underwent a spiritual espousal with Christ.
Before 1368	Chaucer composed 'An ABC' or *La Priere de Nostre Dame*.
1370–80	St Catherine of Siena began her public ministry.
*c.*1370–1449	The life of John Lydgate.

1371	St Bridget made a pilgrimage to the Holy Land; The Knight of La-Tour Landry composed *The Book of the Knight of La-Tour Landry.*
1373	The death of St Bridget of Sweden; the birth of Margery Kempe; Julian of Norwich received her primary visions.
1375	The first Brigittine house, at Vadstena, was founded.
c.1375–90	Walter Hilton composed the *Scale of Perfection* (addressed to a 'ghostly sister').
1377	Oxford, Bodleian Library, MS Bodley 240 was produced containing the *Life* of Marie d'Oignies; the canonization process for Bridget began under Pope Gregory IX.
1377–8	St Catherine of Siena wrote the account of her revelations, *Il Dialogo* (*The Dialogue*).
1380	Christine de Pizan married Estienne de Castel; Catherine of Siena died.
1381	St Katerina of Sweden, Bridget's daughter and first abbess of Vadstena, died; date of the English Rising (also called the Peasant's Revolt).
c.1384	The Bible was first translated into English.
1384–95	Raymond of Capua composed the *Legenda Major*, the most significant account of the life of Catherine of Siena.
Mid-1380s	Julian of Norwich completed the short text (*A Vision*).
Late 14th century	Middle English *Ipomadon* was composed.
c.1385	Chaucer's *Troilus and Criseyde* was composed.
c.1387–1400	Chaucer's *The Canterbury Tales* was composed.
1388	Julian of Norwich received a further revelation.
1389	On the death of her husband Christine de Pizan began writing to support herself and her three children; the will of Sir Bartholomew Bacon of Erwarton, Suffolk, bequeathed a book of 'Romaunce' to his wife.
1390s	*Sir Gawain and the Green Knight* was composed.
1390s–1416	Julian of Norwich's long version (*A Revelation*) was composed.
1391	St Bridget of Sweden was canonized.
1392	The date of the first surviving vernacular English letter written by a woman.
c.1393	Margery Kempe married.
c.1394	Eleanor Malet, later Hull, was born.

Late 1300s	The 'Vernon Manuscript' was composed for a female readership.
1400	Chaucer died.
*c.*1400	Christine de Pizan wrote the *Letter of Othea to Hector*.
1400–15	Owain Glyndŵr led the revolt against English rule in Wales.
1401	William Sawtre, the first Lollard in England to be killed for his beliefs, was executed in Norwich.
1405	Christine de Pizan composed *Book of the City of Ladies*.
*c.*1405	Agnes Berry (later Paston) was born.
1406–7	Christine de Pizan composed the *Book of the Body Politic*.
1409	Thomas Arundel, Archbishop of Canterbury, issued the Constitutions of Oxford.
1410	Christine de Pizan composed the *Book of the Deeds of Arms and Chivalry*.
*c.*1410	Archbishop Arundel authorized Nicholas Love's *Myrrour of the Blessed Lyf of Jesu Christ*.
*c.*1412	Joan of Arc was born at Domrémy.
*c.*1413	Margery Kempe visited Julian of Norwich.
1413–15	Margery Kempe travelled on pilgrimage to the Holy Land and Rome.
1415	Syon Abbey was founded by Henry V; shortly thereafter Catherine of Siena's *Il Dialogo* was translated into English as *The Orchard of Syon* for nuns at Syon Abbey.
1415–26	Lydgate wrote the *Legend of St Margaret* for Anne Stafford, married to Edmund Mortimer.
After 1416	Julian of Norwich died.
1417/18	The date of the will of Elizabeth Wolferstone of Campsea Ash, Suffolk, book owner.
1419	St Bridget's canonization was reconfirmed by Pope Martin V.
1420	The *Gilte Legende*'s version of the *Life* of St Catherine was probably composed; Agnes Berry married William Paston I.
*c.*1420	Margaret Mautby (later Paston) was born.
*c.*1420–38	Margery Kempe dictated her book.
1420s	Eleanor Hull translated the *Meditations Upon the Seven Days of the Week*.
1421	Lydgate composed *Siege of Thebes*; the Earl of Warwick twice consulted the anonymous Winchester anchoress.

1421–2	John Lydgate composed the *Life of Our Lady*; Hoccleve dedicated his *Series* manuscript to Joan of Westmoreland.
1421–3	Eleanor Hull purchased plenary indulgences for herself and her husband John Hull.
1422	The vision of Winchester anchoress ('A Revelation of Purgatory').
*c.*1425–50	Oxford, Bodleian, MS Douce 114 was produced, owned by Beauvale Charterhouse in Nottinghamshire, which contains the *Life* of Marie d'Oignies in English.
After 1425	*The N-Town Plays* were written down.
1429	Elizabeth Paston was born; Joan of Arc raised the siege of Orléans; Christine de Pizan composed the *Ditié de Jehanne d'Arc*.
*c.*1430	Gwerful Fychan was born.
1431	Joan of Arc was executed.
1436–8	*The Book of Margery Kempe* was revised and completed.
1438	The Sinful Wretch (possibly Eleanor Hull) completed the *Gilte Legende*.
1440	Margaret Mautby married John Paston I.
*c.*1440	The 'Findern manuscript' was possibly produced for a female readership.
*c.*1440–50	*Knowing of Woman's Kind in Childing* was composed.
1443	Margaret Beaufort was born.
1443–7	Osbern Bokenham's *Legendys of Hooly Wummen* was compiled.
1445	John Talbot, earl of Shrewsbury, presented Margaret of Anjou with MS British Library Royal E VI, which includes Christine's *Book of the Deeds of Arms and Chivalry*, as a wedding gift.
1450	Stephen Scrope translated Christine de Pizan's *Othea* into English and William Worcester wrote the *Book of Noblesse*, based on Christine de Pizan's *Book of the Deeds of Arms and Chivalry*.
Mid-15th century	*The Good Wyf Wold a Pylgremage* was composed.
1451–1504	The life of Isabella Queen of Castile.
1455	The Battle of St Albans took place (traditionally seen as the start of the Wars of the Roses).
1456	Joan of Arc was rehabilitated.

1456 or 1457	Eleanor Hull and Roger Huswyf presented a copy of Nicholas of Lyra's commentary on Scripture to St Albans Abbey.
1458	The date of the will of Margaret Wetherby of Norwich, widow and monastic benefactor; Eleanor Hull made her will at the Benedictine priory of Cannington, Somerset.
1459	The date of the will of Alice Foster of Norwich, widow and monastic benefactor.
1460	Eleanor Hull died.
*c.*1460	Juliana Berners flourished; Gwenllïan ferch Rhirid Flaidd flourished.
*c.*1460–*c.*1502	The life of Gwerful Mechain.
1461	Catherine of Siena was canonized.
*c.*1463–74	Oxford, St John's College MS, 182, was produced, copied by the confessor of Henry VI, the Carthusian John Blacman; it contains the *Life* of Marie de Vitry.
1466	Beatrice (Beatrix) Balle of Norwich, widow and book owner died; John Paston I died.
*c.*1470	Sir Thomas Malory composed *Le Morte d'Arthur*; *The Floure and the Leafe* was composed.
1475	William Stonor married Elizabeth Rich (née Croke), widow of wealthy merchant; date of the will of Thomasin Gra of London and Norfolk, widow and book owner; *Book of Noblesse* was revised in connection with Edward IV's efforts to retake territory in France.
*c.*1475	*The Assembly of Ladies* was composed.
*c.*1475–1500	Oxford, Bodleian, MS Ashmole 61 was composed.
1476	William Caxton set up a printing press in London, the first in England.
1479	Agnes Paston and Elizabeth Stonor died.
1484	Caxton's translated the *Book of the Knight of La-Tour Landry*; Margaret Paston died; George Cely married Margery Rygon, widow of wealthy merchant.
1485	Henry Tudor defeated Richard III at Battle of Bosworth and ascended the throne as Henry VII, thus ending the Wars of the Roses; Caxton printed the *Morte d'Arthur*.
1486	The St Albans Schoolmaster-Printer published *The Boke of Hunting*, attributed to 'Dam Julyans Barnes'.

1487	The date of the will of Alianore Nicholson of East Dereham, Norfolk, widow and book owner.
1489	George Cely died.
c.1493	The *Lyf of Saint Katherin of Senis* was printed in English by Wynkyn de Worde.
Late 15th century	*Thewis [Customs] of Gud Women* was composed.
c.1500	Alis ferch Gruffudd ab Ieuan ap Llywelyn Fychan was born.
c.1500	*The Life of Catherine of Siena* (printed c.1439) was reissued; Eleanor Percy married Edward Stafford, 3rd Duke of Buckingham.
c.1500–55	Catrin ferch Gruffudd ap Hywel flourished.
1501	Wynkyn de Worde printed extracts from *The Book of Margery Kempe*.
1503	Margaret Beaufort's translation of *De Imitatione Christi*, Book IV, was published.
1506	Margaret Beaufort's translation of *Speculum Animae Peccatricis* was published.
1509	Margaret Beaufort died.
1519	*The Orcharde of Syon* was printed in England by Wynkyn de Worde.
1521	Henry Pepwell published Brian Anslay's translation of the *Book of the City of Ladies*; Pepwell reprinted extracts from *The Book of Margery Kempe* and excerpts from Catherine of Siena's *Life* alongside other devotional treatises.
c.1530	Elsbeth Fychan flourished.
1534	Elizabeth Barton, the Holy Maid of Kent, was executed.
1536–43	The English Parliament passed a series of laws known as the Acts of Union.
1539	Syon Abbey was dissolved.

Writing a History of British Women's Writing from 700 to 1500

Liz Herbert McAvoy and Diane Watt

How can a history of British women's writing be written? Such a project must necessarily be collaborative if it is to attempt to be comprehensive, but even then any claim to comprehensiveness has to be qualified: paradoxically the more expansive the history, the more partial it will be. The challenges of writing such a history are perhaps even greater for scholars working in the early periods because we are forced to confront and to rethink many deeply ingrained assumptions about women's writing. This volume focuses on a period of literary history that is often marginalized in accounts of women's writing in English: the Middle Ages. It is a widely accepted view that there are only two women writers in English in the period before 1500, and therefore there is little to be said for an age (or ages) when women writers were so much an exception. Furthermore, the two medieval English women writers whose names are widely known, Julian of Norwich (1342/3–after 1416) and Margery Kempe (c.1373–after 1439), did not think of themselves as writers or authors. Nor were they responsible for literature as it is thought of today – they did not compose poetry, or romances, or fiction of any sort. Even these two 'named' women writers do not comfortably fit established evolutionary models of women's literary history over the *longue durée*, with their emphases on the spread of literacy, the bias towards print culture, and the emergence of the woman poet, and ultimately of the professional author of drama or fiction.[1] Yet the difficulty of locating how the medieval period fits into literary history is not unique to women's writing: medieval understandings of authorship, literature, and national identity, and the contexts and processes of writing and textual circulation were quite distinct from later periods and therefore deemed problematic more generally.

Throughout the medieval period, God was considered the ultimate *auctor* or *author*, and the Bible was the source of all *auctoritas*, or written authority. *Author* could also mean 'writer' but the idea was associated with classical writers and patriarchs of the church, in other words with writers and thinkers of long ago, who were inevitably male.[2] Writings that we might now think of as literary works were often read not solely for entertainment, but for moral edification, and the distinction between the literary and the didactic was not one that was widely recognized. Before the introduction of the printing press in England in 1476, texts were written and copied by hand, and therefore could not be mass-produced, at least according to modern standards. Furthermore, most 'English' or indeed 'British' writers, male or female, have to be understood, at least in part, in relation to continental rather than simply insular traditions.

The period before 1500 stands apart, then, for a whole range of reasons. Catherine Clarke, in her essay in this volume, asks us 'to question the very notion of "Britishness" in relation to literature' (p. 41). In the Middle Ages, the political, linguistic, and cultural boundaries of what we now think of as Britain were drawn along different lines from the later periods. Furthermore, the picture of women's writing in Britain for the period before 1500 is a very complex one. Britain was, then as now, multicultural and multilingual. French, Latin, Scottish Gaelic and Scots (in Scotland), and Welsh (in Wales) were often the literary and religious languages of choice, and the degree of contact with other linguistic forms and cultures, including those of Ireland, Scandinavia, the Low Countries, and continental Europe more generally, was significant. If we include just some of these languages in our consideration, then suddenly there are more famous names to add to our list of women writers, including Clemence of Barking (*fl.*1163–*c.*1200), Marie de France (*fl.*1180), and Gwerful Mechain (*fl. c.*1460–*c.*1502). Pushing back the period boundary into the more distant past, and including works from before the so-called 'Norman Conquest', enables us to take into account even more women, such as the famous circle of eighth-century women who corresponded with St Boniface, including Leoba, Bucge, Eangyth, Ecgburg, Eadburg, Cyneburg, and Berhtgyth. These women were Anglo-Saxon by birth and education, but travelled to Germany as early Christian missionaries. Indeed, throughout the Middle Ages, Britain enjoyed close links to the continent, and by the fifteenth century a number of continental women writers, secular and religious (Christine de Pizan (1365–*c.*1430), Marie d'Oignies (1177–1213), Bridget of Sweden (1303–1373), Catherine of Siena (1347–1380)), had had their works and/or lives translated into English and/or circulated in England. As will be seen in some of the essays in Part IV of this volume, Marie d'Oignies, Bridget of Sweden, and Catherine of Siena provide partial models for *The Book of Margery Kempe*. Indeed it is striking that an early-sixteenth-century reprinting by Henry Pepwell of a very short abridgement of *The Book of Margery Kempe*, places the extracts of that text alongside a selection of other English and continental mystical texts, including a short *Life* of Catherine of Siena.[3]

One pleasing consequence of including in this volume the works of 'British' women (the term 'British' is, of course, anachronistic in this context) not written in English, is that the range of genres under consideration becomes more recognizably 'literary' to an educated twenty-first-century readership: saints' legends, romances, fables, erotic poetry. Marie de France is so important, and so *exceptional*, because she seems to have written in *all* of these genres, because contextual and manuscript evidence suggests that some of her poetry may have circulated fairly widely in her lifetime and thereafter. For these reasons, Marie de France corresponds much more closely to modern definitions of authorship than either Julian of Norwich or Margery Kempe. And if our working definition of writing is extended to include functional, practical texts, such as personal and business letters never intended for anything but a narrow familial readership, then yet more names appear, amongst the most well-known of whom today are Margaret Paston (*c*.1420–1484), her mother-in-law Agnes (*c*.1405–1479) and daughter-in-law Margery (d. 1495), her daughter Elizabeth (1429–1488) and friend Elizabeth Clere (d. 1493). Dismantling the boundaries between translation and authorship and acknowledging the importance of the former as a legitimate form of cultural creativity provides still more names: most notably Dame Eleanor Hull (*c*.1394–1460) and Lady Margaret Beaufort (1443–1509). Yet, as all undergraduates of Middle English know, names are not really all that important in the period before Chaucer (who did write *Sir Gawain and the Green Knight*?). If, as already noted, authority was God-given, and the true author was God Himself, how did any individual, male or female, have the confidence to write in his or her own name? Most works were in fact anonymous, and while men may have produced the vast majority, arguments can be, and have been, made for female authorship of some. In the case of at least one anonymous text considered in this volume, the fifteenth-century *Revelation of Purgatory*, which is written as a letter to a confessor, the author is unambiguously female. Nevertheless, by the end of the Middle Ages, authors increasingly *did* append their names to their texts: Geoffrey Chaucer (1343–1400) is the most famous example, of course. Sometimes when continental texts by women were transmitted to England, their female authorship was overlooked, or they were re-ascribed to male writers. This happened when Christine de Pizan's *Book of the City of Ladies* was translated into English by Brian Anslay and published by Henry Pepwell in 1521.[4] More radically than simply making the case for female authorship of anonymous texts, however, we would insist that any consideration of medieval women's writing calls for greater attention to be paid to processes of collaboration in the production of texts and a rejection of the idea that a single 'author' can have ownership of a text. At a most basic level, this collaboration may be between woman 'author' and a trusted male secretary. Margery Kempe's principal secretaries were her son (almost certainly) and a priest who acted as her confidant. Margaret Paston relied on a range of individuals, including her sons, her family chaplain, and some of the higher status family servants. However, if the model of literary production is complicated still further, the idea of collaboration can be extended to take into account the roles played by patrons, readers, and sometimes even subjects. A surprising number of medieval texts enjoyed female patronage, from the Anglo-Saxon period onwards: famous examples of women patrons include Matilda of Essen (979–1025) and Queen Edith (*c*.1029–1075). A whole range of texts were of course aimed, at least in part, at a female audience, including the early thirteenth-century *Ancrene Wisse* or *The Guide for Anchoresses*, and its related and associated texts. *The Book of Margery Kempe* illustrates very clearly the ways in which author and subject can become blurred in hagiographical and visionary texts in particular.

To write a history of British women's writing for the medieval period, then, is to write a different sort of literary history – a more expansive, inclusive, contextualized, nuanced history that defies established teleologies, pushes against traditional boundaries and limitations, and challenges accepted categories and terminology. Any attempt to write about the medieval period as the starting point for a history of British women's writing has to be flexible in its definitions of (literary) history, British, women's writing, and even writing itself.

Critical History

Such a flexible understanding of literary production, however, has not always been accepted within literary historiography which has tended, until recent times, to render women's contribution to medieval 'English' literature all but invisible. Except for a cursory and, frequently, 'token' allusion to those safely 'named' female authors, Julian of Norwich and Margery Kempe, mentioned above, traditional accounts have by default promoted the written word within medieval culture as emphatically male. Such a radical misconception was, of course, famously berated by Virginia Woolf as early as 1928 in a pivotal essay, later published as *A Room of One's Own*. In this work, Woolf set out to critique the foundations of an all-male literary canon and establish a rationale for what would later become an attempt to uncover and recuperate women's literary production, in which context she adds somewhat disconsolately, 'But these are difficult questions which lie in the twilight of the future.'[5]

Even in that futuristic 'twilight', however, critics have continued to be seduced by the myth of women's lack of literary productivity in the Middle Ages. In his preface to *The Cambridge History of Medieval Literature* published in 1999, for example, David Wallace defended the absence of any chapters on women's writing in this extensive volume thus: 'A single chapter on medieval women writers might be disproportionately brief, since nothing by a female mendicant or nun (so far as we know) survives in Middle English', adding by way of *caveat* that women, like religious writing, were nonetheless 'everywhere at work'.[6] Such claims, of course, by a commentator whose mission was ostensibly to 'defamiliarise [...] present accounts of medieval and Renaissance literature',[7] are rendered all the more extraordinary in the light of the attempts of an already established twentieth-century feminist imperative to uncover for women 'a literature of their own'; indeed, the book by the same title, *A Literature of their Own*, written by Elaine Showalter in 1977, joined other concerted endeavours to demonstrate the ways in which the history of women's writing within a specifically English context had long been beset by its own political problems.[8] During the same period, works such as *Literary Women* by Ellen Moers (1977), Kate Millett's *Sexual Politics* (1977), and, of course, *The Madwoman in the Attic* by Sandra M. Gilbert and Susan Gubar (1979) not only attempted in their different ways to recover a lost literary history for women, but in places seethed with barely concealed anger at the sexual and cultural politics that had ensured that loss in the first place.[9] Later, this same baton was taken up by feminist commentators such as Janet Todd in her *Feminist Literary History* (1988), Margaret J. M. Ezell in *Writing Women's Literary History* (1993), Laurie Finke in *Women's Writing in English* (1999), Jennifer Summit in *Lost Property* (2000), and, in the specific context of medieval women's writing, Joan M. Ferrante in *To the Glory of her Sex* (1997), and Carole M. Meale in her edited collection, *Women and Literature in Britain, 1150–1500* (1993), all of whom attempted to further identify and theorize this loss, as well as pointing towards additional questions needing to be confronted in order to ensure some kind of valid recuperation.[10] Ferrante, in particular, did much to identify women as very often occupying positions at the centre of public life – within political, religious, and cultural arenas – whilst Meale had some years previously already offered nuance to definitions of what constitutes 'women's writing', extending the term to include writing produced for, and read by, women. Both commentators, therefore, offered weight to the maxim articulated by Ferrante in the introduction to her book: 'history in any form from the Middle Ages to the present which does not include the role of women is not true history'.[11]

Such a statement has clearly gone on to become a given within more recently produced work on medieval women's writing, particularly *The Cambridge Companion to Medieval Women's Writing*, edited by Carolyn Dinshaw and David Wallace in 2003.[12] Modifying Wallace's own claim made in 1999 regarding the lack of medieval women's writing, this volume takes up Ferrante's mantle, drawing upon a cultural materialist analysis to complement literary analysis and concentrating on the literary activities of women in a number of public, private, and institutional contexts: the 'estates' of women, for example; women in enclosed spaces, both religious and domestic; women in the church; women's participation within literary debate. As such, it makes a valuable contribution to our understanding of the material conditions which generated opportunities for women's literary activities – or which militated against them, although its primary focus is again on the later period, with relatively little examination undertaken of what we term here the female-focused 'pre-texts' of the Anglo-Saxon period.

An additional contemporaneous enterprise has been to make available for a modern audience some of the hitherto less readily accessible and frequently anonymous female-authored texts from the past, excerpted and collected together in anthologized format. Even this act of recovery, however, has been misleading, more often than not as a result of problematics generated by the selection process itself, but sometimes because of attitudes and opinions which have been internalized by even the most feminist of scholars. Of particular note in this context is the extensive – and highly worthy – collection, *The Norton Anthology of Literature by Women* (1985), also compiled by Gilbert and Gubar. Indeed, the first edition of this work famously categorized the perceived 'lack' of medieval women's writing as being the result of a retreat by the female imagination into the 'Dark Ages' of creativity.[13] Such a statement, of course, threatens to tip over into essentialist assumptions of ontological invisibility rather than acknowledging that invisibility's being a result of politico-cultural imperatives or deeply entrenched reading practices both within the premodern and modern periods. Such misconceptions self-evidently call out for a careful unpicking of the fabric which has long occluded the visibility of women's contribution to literary production in the early period and for our need to look at the past in radically different ways.

The production of further anthologies subsequent to *The Norton Anthology*, ones which include a selection of hitherto more obscure medieval texts written by women, or those clearly associated with female authorship, has certainly widened access to the debate. Notably, Alexandra Barratt's anthology, *Women's Writing in Middle English* (1992) and Carolyne Larrington's *Women and Writing in Medieval Europe: A Sourcebook* (1995) have helped to fill some of the lacunae formed by the literary absence of women and left underexamined by Gilbert and Gubar,[14] although Barratt's collection begins with thirteenth-century texts and Larrington's includes considerable material written *about* rather than by women. Larrington does, however, attempt to open windows on the Anglo-Saxon period by including, for example, a range of Old English pregnancy charms, not normally considered but very likely composed by women.

Such recuperative endeavours have also been accompanied by a proliferation of survey volumes intent on similar enterprise, although many of them have also glossed over or ignored the 'lost property' of the Anglo-Saxon period. For example, Summit's study, mentioned above, focuses only on the fifteenth and sixteenth centuries, although her work remains extremely valuable for its suggestion that the developing sense of a homogeneous national and linguistic identity which was characteristic of the period led to a gendered construction of the literary canon, the legacy of which still resounds loudly today. Such analyses, which focus on the later Middle Ages, are not necessarily applicable to the Anglo-Saxon period, however. Nevertheless, it remains the case that, from Anglo-Saxon times onwards, anxieties regarding national identity and the various vernaculars were commonplace, albeit manifesting themselves in different ways within different epistemological climates, but inevitably including a gendered dimension which served to occlude the role of women's relation to literary production. The much overlooked Anglo-Saxon period, therefore, in which women are even less visible, has continued to generate its own problems for contemporary feminist scholarship and the recuperation of female authorship, problems which were first recognized by Clare Lees and Gillian Overing in a pivotal essay published in 1994. In this essay, the authors argued that twentieth-century Anglo-Saxon historiography had inadvertently conspired with the Venerable Bede himself to exclude the role of Hild, abbess of Whitby, in the so-called 'birth of English poetry' generally attributed to the *Hymn* apparently written by the abbey's former herdsman, Cædmon.[15] Reprinted as the first chapter of Lees and Overing's *Double Agents* (2001),[16] this essay constituted a rousing attempt to redress the marginalization of Anglo-Saxon women by traditional scholarship, best summed up, perhaps, by the somewhat poorly informed but widely held assumption articulated by Gilbert and Gubar that there are 'no texts in the Old English period that have been definitively identified as composed by women'.[17] Indeed, this type of misapprehension was also promulgated by Dale Spender in her1986 work, *Mothers of the Novel: A Hundred Good Writers before Jane Austen*. In this study, Spender finds no 'good' female authors whatsoever before Mary Wroth in the early-modern period, in spite of the book's main thesis that women's letter-writing was eventually to give birth to the novel as we know it today. Here, Spender overlooks entirely the considerable epistolary activity of medieval women, both during the later Middle Ages and the Anglo-Saxon period, although she does acknowledge that she may have left herself 'open to the charge of not having looked hard enough'.[18]

Lees and Overing's *Double Agents* substantiates fully such a lack of 'looking' which was clearly based on an internalized assumption that there was nothing to find. Instead, they sought to push out the methodological boundaries traditionally set within Anglo-Saxon scholarship, pulling together for scrutiny both Latin and Old English texts from a wide and varied range of genres, including that of letter-writing. As a result, they began the necessary problematizing of notions of women's authorship and, indeed, what constitutes *English* writing more widely during the period, paving the way for later examinations such as Diane Watt's recent *Medieval Women Writers* (2007).[19]

In her book, Watt extends the critique of Lees and Overing to cover the later period from Christina of Markyate (1096–after 1155) to the Paston women, mentioned above, and similarly uncovers different models for what constitutes women's writing, English writing, or, indeed, 'writing' more generally. Importantly, Watt establishes the concept of collaboration as key to the uncovering of how women most effectively contributed to textual production in the Middle Ages: whether as patrons, sponsors, visionaries with amanuenses, or translators of previously circulated texts. In this she also draws upon and further develops Laurie Finke's important call in 1999 for a 'heteroglossic' approach to medieval women's literature and a dismantling of all of the terms normally associated with it in order to pursue the act of recovery. As Finke asserts: 'In manuscript culture, book production is a much more obviously collaborative art', pointing out, too, that authorship was also made complex by issues of patronage, and that books were sometimes produced on demand.[20] Moreover, as mentioned, it should not be forgotten that named authorship was not an imperative for the medieval text as it was from the early modern period onwards. Thus, within a context where even male authorship fails to fit the 'pure' and 'monolithic' author-centred paradigms established since the eighteenth century, it was inevitable that the female author would drop from visibility within what Summit terms the 'key sites at which "English Literature" was invented'; for Summit too, the female author was always already 'constructed as absent from the literary tradition' because of such considerations.[21]

If, then, we follow the calls of these commentators, and (re)consider what constitutes female authorship, writing, or the concept of 'literature' more generally, we find ourselves in a far better position to begin answering the much-debated question raised by Sheila Delaney in 1987 in her then controversial essay on the tradition of women's writing, ' "Mothers to Think Back Through": Who are They?'[22] Here, Delaney takes exception to the over-exposure of the few named women writers from the medieval period, arguing that it is misleading for us to concentrate our critical efforts on such writers merely because they appear to fit post-Enlightenment configurations of named, and therefore 'closed' authorship – Christine de Pizan, for example. As mentioned, such women were, of course, by any stretch of the imagination unusual and an idealizing approach to them therefore fails to produce a balanced or comprehensive picture of women's relationship to literary production more generally. Moreover, this type of effort also guarantees perpetuating the invisibility imposed upon other perhaps less exceptional women who were nevertheless also important to contemporary literary culture. The notion of literary collaboration, then, as the essays collected in this present volume fully attest, whether through patronage, translation, the *ars dictaminis*, conversation, charismatic influence, or even readership, offers us a plethora of women writers to 'think back through' within a much widened 'British' tradition. It also opens up and helps us reassess the important role, whether overt or covert, played by women within literary history, allowing a more nuanced set of answers to Delaney's still pressing question – and certainly refuting Wallace's claim that there are too few medieval writers to fill a chapter of a book.

Pre-texts and Contexts

The first section of the volume, entitled 'Pre-texts and Contexts', provides an essential historical, linguistic, and cultural background to the history of British women's writing in the medieval period, from women's participation in the very earliest English writing and the subsequent marginalization of their contribution, to the vilification of women and women's claims to authority in the later Middle Ages. It is important, however, to pause and to reflect on the connotations of the section title. To start with the latter term first, according to the *Oxford English Dictionary*, the noun 'context' can mean 'The whole structure of a connected passage regarded in its bearing upon any of the parts which constitute it; the parts which immediately precede or follow any particular passage or "text" and determine its meaning'.[23] Here, of course, we are considering the context not of a passage or text but of women's literary history in the Middle Ages. The risk taken by a contextual approach to women's literary history is that it can seem to relegate certain texts, and groups of texts, and indeed periods of history to the category of background, and effectively bracket them off from the primary focus of the volume. This is explicitly not our intention. The areas of women's writing addressed in the first four chapters of this section – pre- and post-'Conquest' writing, writing in Old English, Latin, French, and Welsh – are seen as crucial to our understanding of medieval women's literary history in its entirety, and thus, by providing a bigger picture of British women's writing, as playing a significant part in, as the *Oxford English Dictionary* puts it, 'determin[ing] its meaning'. By placing these chapters at the start of the volume, we are not simply following a rough chronological order (which is not strictly followed throughout the rest of the volume, where thematic ordering prevails) but we are deliberately giving precedence to this important material. Only the last chapter in the section, on antifeminist writing, might be seen to be contextual simply in the sense of providing crucial background information necessary for understanding women's writing.

Turning to the noun 'pre-text', according to the *Oxford English Dictionary*, this can be defined as 'the literary, historical, or biographical material which informs or contextualizes a literary text', although it can also mean 'the events imagined to precede those portrayed in a fictional work'.[24] Clearly our use of 'pre-text' here adapts the former meaning, although in this case we are adapting it to consider how literary, historical, and linguistic material might inform and contextualize not simply a text, but medieval women's literary history *per se*. Nevertheless, our use of 'pre-text' also deliberately draws on aspects of the second meaning of the word as provided by the *Oxford English Dictionary*, because to some extent the act of reconstructing the very earliest history of British women's writing does involve using the imagination. Judith M. Bennett has recently published an important defence of expansive historical narratives of gender: *History Matters: Patriarchy and the Challenge of Feminism* (2006). In a chapter entitled 'Who is Afraid of the Distant Past?' Bennett provides compelling evidence that within the discipline of women's history there has been a strong movement away from studying the premodern era and a 'creep toward the present'.[25] As Bennett explains, the study of the distant past is often neglected because it is *challenging* in all sorts of ways. In taking issue with the dominant focus on what she calls 'the short view', she concludes that 'the passage of time provides new perspectives, clearer understandings, and more measured analyses'.[26] Bennett's arguments are of equal relevance to the study of medieval women's literary history. As we have already seen, the distant past of medieval women's literary history is all too often overlooked in recent studies, and there are a number of reasons for this: the prevalence of unhelpful stereotypes about women's illiteracy and lack of education; the prevalence of mistaken assumptions about the sort and amount of evidence that exists, or about the forms that literary production and circulation took in the Middle Ages; the linguistic and historical inaccessibility of surviving material; and scholarly discomfort about the challenge that the distant past makes to existing paradigms of women's literary history. In order to understand this distant past, scholars need to come armed with specialist knowledge and tools, but, in the face of more limited evidence of women's engagement in literary culture, in pushing back the historical boundaries of our understanding and in constructing a new narrative, they need to be willing to make a leap of faith, or of the imagination. This is exactly what the first three essays in this volume do.

These first three essays are all concerned with the early Middle Ages. The volume opens, appropriately, with a chapter by Lees and Overing, in which they revisit and develop further parts of their argument in *Double Agents*, and set out an agenda for future scholarship. Lees and Overing argue that the omission of women's writing pre-1066 by both mainstream literary history and women's literary history demands a new analysis of women's apparent absence together with new assessment of their contribution and agency. The examples of Hild, abbess of Whitby, the nuns of Barking Abbey, and the Anglo-Saxon missionary Leoba, illustrate that once we understand fully how conditions for and evaluation of artistic production, patronage, and literacy work against a paradigmatic model of sole male authorship, a far richer and more nuanced picture of women's participation in literary culture pre-1066 becomes visible. Catherine A. M. Clarke adopts a similar approach to that of Lees and Overing in the following chapter, in which she too argues for a reconsideration of modern assumptions about authorship and agency. For Clarke, the contribution of women to literary production in Britain not only before but also after the Conquest is prominent and pivotal. Attention has to be paid to female patronage, textual communities, and collaborative networks which enable literary production. The vital roles played by figures such as Matilda, abbess of Essen, Emma of Normandy, Edith of Wessex, Adela of Blois, and Matilda and Adeliza (wives of Henry I) demonstrate the importance of female figures in fostering the vibrant multilingual literature of the tenth to the twelfth centuries. In the next chapter, Catherine Batt turns to writings in French and in what is now referred to as 'the French of England'. Batt makes the compelling case that the French of the English should be viewed not in isolation, but as culturally of a piece with other media of literary expression. Her chapter, as part of its survey of the nature of women's contributions, in French and the French of the English, to the literary and cultural landscapes of the twelfth and thirteenth centuries, attempts, then, to reconceptualize the integral nature of that landscape. That is, even as it considers the work of authors such as the enigmatic figure of Marie de France (whose actual identity is still rather mysterious) or Clemence, a nun of Barking Abbey, this chapter re-addresses assessments of the nature and function of insular French (along with the nature and status of translation), and argues for women's engagement with literature in that medium as paradigmatic of the dynamic of medieval culture in general.

This volume not only pushes against the limits of women's writing in historical terms, but it also does so in geographical terms, as is illustrated by Jane Cartwright's essay on medieval Welsh women writers in particular. The inclusion of this Welsh material (and indeed the Latin and French material discussed by Clarke and Batt) reflects in part a recent emergence in literary scholarship of what has been termed by Sarah Prescott 'women's "archipelagic" literary history'.[27] As Philip Schwyzer and Simon Mealor explain in *Archipelagic Identities*, an archipelagic approach goes beyond tracing literary and cultural influences and instead challenges the very 'silencing or co-optation of non-English voices'.[28] Archipelagic scholarship entails a greater emphasis on a British, and Irish, rather than a more limited *English* literary history. John Kerrigan argues in his study *Archipelagic English*, that 'to devolve is to shift power in politics or scholarly analysis from a locus that has been disproportionately endowed with influence and documentation to sites that are dispersed and skeletally understood'.[29] One of the potential advantages or side-products of such an approach is that it can bring to light previously unknown writers, including women writers. Jane Cartwright's survey of Welsh writing in the period 1430–1555 dramatically illustrates this point as it focuses on poetry by a surprising number of women. The most famous, in contemporary terms at least, Gwerful Mechain, is discussed alongside Gwerful Fychan (b. *c.*1430), Gwenllïan ferch Rhirid Flaidd (*fl. c.*1460), Alis ferch Gruffudd ab Ieuan (born *c.*1500), Catrin ferch Gruffudd ap Hywel (*fl. c.*1500–55), and Elsbeth Fychan Fychan (*fl. c.*1530). Here we find the evidence of an established tradition of late-medieval women poets that is missing for, or less developed within, other parts of the British Isles. Gwerful Mechain is best known today for her 'Cywydd y gont' or 'Cywydd [ode] to the cunt', and the importance and unique nature of this poem should not be understated, but the breadth of topics covered in Gwerful Mechain's poetry in particular sheds fresh light on the experiences and attitudes of women in

medieval Wales, providing valuable insights into not only female sexuality and humour, but also religious devotion, bardic education, and women's interaction in literary circles. That women were writing such a range of poetry in medieval Wales, even if they did not do so elsewhere in Britain at the same time, is fascinating. Cartwright's chapter incidentally illustrates a further limitation of conventional women's literary histories – the tendency to accept unquestioningly traditional periodization and teleologies in categorizing writing as 'medieval', 'early-modern', 'eighteenth-century', 'Victorian', 'modern', 'postmodern', or 'contemporary'. We have already seen that in the second chapter Clarke questions the existence of a significant divide between women's engagement in literary culture pre- and post-Conquest. Here Cartwright illustrates that within Wales, at least, the artificiality of setting an absolute endpoint of 1500 for medieval women's writing. Interestingly, a similar point might be made about Scottish women's poetry in Gaelic where continuities exist from the late fifteenth century through to the sixteenth and seventeenth centuries. The earliest examples of verse by 'named' women were composed by educated women from the upper echelons of society: Aithbhreac Inghean Corcadail's (*fl.*1460) 'A Phaidrín do dhúisg mo dhéar' ['Oh rosary that woke my tears'] and Iseabail Ní Mheic Cailéin's (*fl.*1500) 'Atá fleasgach ar mo thí' ['There's a young man in pursuit of me'] and 'Is mairg dá ngalar an grádh' ['Woe to the one whose sickness is love'].[30] While insufficient medieval Scottish women's writing exists to justify devoting a chapter of the volume to the topic, it is important to note the emergence of this poetry at the very end of our period.

The final chapter in the first section provides a bridge to the second section, entitled 'Bodies, Behaviours, and Texts'. As opposed to the previous four chapters, Anke Bernau's study of the medieval antifeminist tradition is consciously conceived as contextual in the sense of sketching out in detail a background for understanding women's writing in the Middle Ages. Bernau provides an overview of the kinds of traditions and sources that influenced and provided the basis for medieval misogynist writing, and traces the dispersal of antifeminist discourse in a range of different but often overlapping genres, from conduct literature and romance to satire, hagiography, devotional literature, Marian writings, drama, and sermons. The pervasiveness of medieval misogyny is indeed extraordinary, as is its virulence, although an alternative counter-tradition of defences of women did also exist. At the end of her extensive survey of antifeminist texts, Bernau asks how medieval women (and men) might have responded to the ideas contained within them. Geoffrey Chaucer, in the Wife of Bath's Prologue, offers one famous fictionalized female response in which the Wife tears up her husband's book of wicked wives, and is beaten for her pains, but the other chapters in this volume reveal some of the more subtle and complex ways in which women negotiated the restrictions imposed upon their scholarship and literary engagement and replied to the misogyny of their time.

Bodies, Behaviours, Texts

If a misogynistic imperative was explicit within a great number of medieval texts directed at women, and implicit in a large proportion of those which were not, it is possible to argue that an inbuilt fear of or, at the very least, an antipathy towards women, was fundamental to the body of the medieval text itself, a body which, of course, necessarily reflected the epistemological climate of its day. Subject to multiple discourses inherited from classical philosophy, medicine and astronomy, biblical commentary, patristic argumentation, and cultural practice, for example, by the Middle Ages the body had taken on a role as a visceral, female signifier: whilst maleness and masculinity were characterized as warm, dry, rational, and stable, equating with the human soul, femaleness and femininity were cold and wet, irrational and readily changeable, forever locked in synecdochal unity with humanity's fallen flesh. Thus, the unruly female became irrevocably subject to policing by a 'superior' male authority, the legacy of which continues to reverberate today. Moreover, this policing was both physical and discursive, dovetailing most conveniently with the grand narrative of Christian origins which characterized Adam the first man as namer and quantifier and Eve the first woman as named and quantified. In this way, women became the subject of – and subjected by – language and discourse, rather than being the originators of them, leaving questions resonating loudly as to how they could ever aspire to represent themselves in writing or respond actively and dynamically to their representation by men. Moreover, with God as the ultimate authority – the *auctor* – and man made in God's own image, his authorial interlocutor, how then could a woman presume to usurp the divine role and what misrecognitions would arise should she impose her troublesome body upon the authoritative text? Such questions are central to any consideration of medieval women's writing and are ones taken up concertedly in all of the essays collected in Part II of this volume. Here the contributors seek to explore the role played by bodies and the behaviours they generate, both prescribed and proscribed, within female literary production. As such, they build concertedly on Bernau's argument that, whilst antipathy towards the female body was rife within medieval culture and its artefacts, and whilst such views may also have been replicated and accepted, they were also nevertheless manipulated, mocked, undermined, and critiqued in their own time, by men as well as women in individual literary endeavours.

The chapters in this section therefore address texts authored by both men and women, although all of the works examined have close associations with women, if not as authors, then as patrons or readers. Whilst not necessarily written for the consumption of women exclusively, nevertheless many genres and texts did appear to resonate with them in very specific ways. This is particularly true of medieval romance and conduct literature, for example, and of accounts of the virgin martyrs, devotional and

Marian literature – texts which, in spite of their often antifeminist tenor, proved perennially popular for a woman readership. In this context, the case of medieval romance can, perhaps, be offered as a paradigm. Although not typically fashioned especially for women, nevertheless some of those recurrent subjects which we find in medieval romance contained widespread possibilities for women's engagement in both their textual production and dissemination, as Corinne Saunders argues in her essay. Set against the stereotypical damsel-in-distress and virgin as object of desire, for example, are a plethora of far more proactive female roles redolent with a range of imaginative possibilities for the woman reader or female patron: the wooing woman, woman as helper or handmaid, woman as enchanter or faery other, woman as dynastic stalwart, the calumniated queen, to mention just a few representations which may well have resonated in very specific and empowering ways for the woman reader. Indeed, as Myra J. Seaman argues in her own essay, in later medieval manuscript anthologies, such romance tales frequently appeared alongside behaviour-enhancing conduct literature aimed at both men and women, texts which shared a common didactic purpose and frequently containing intertwining themes and motifs. Such diversity of representation not only suggests an extensive authorial engagement with topics directly relevant to women's interests and the cultural work they undertake, but also reveals how their concerns, desires, and interests may ultimately have served to shape the genres themselves. In this way, both Saunders and Seaman demonstrate the clearly collaborative nature of medieval romance production and its impact upon the lived lives of women, both inside and external to the text, within that collaborative process.

Such collaborative practices of production are also testified to by both hagiographic and devotional narratives, in which female – or feminized – bodies and behaviours again take up centre stage. Within the virgin martyrologies, for example, the saint is frequently rendered naked, her body undergoing the threat of, or actual sexual assault in an attempt to regulate what is (mis)read as its unruliness. Whilst some commentators have seen such treatments as fetishistic and delimiting, others have suggested that this is too simplistic a reading and that, in fact, a reader may well have taken pleasure and strength from the saint's resolute resistance to torture and her refusal to recognize pain. In her essay on the subject, however, Shari Horner takes such an argument further, pointing out that the textual matrix – and system of response – surrounding such saints' lives extends far beyond their medieval readers. Indeed, these lives document copiously a widespread community in which the tortured women repeatedly produce texts written with and upon their own bodies, texts which are then exposed to the eye of subsequent generations of readers/viewers for their own 'reading', interpretation, or rewriting. As such, the saint's body acts as a collaborative text itself, which the saint herself writes and offers up for continual reading and rereading, regardless of whether the life in its original form had been male authored, as many seem to have been. We must remember, too (and here, Bernau's argument is again relevant), that female reading practices were not necessarily ideologically obedient ones; and, as Horner also asserts, the power of the female saint's body is that her immediate audience of pagans and oppressors consistently misread the text written upon it, only able to understand it literally, rather than perceiving its spiritual or symbolic meaning. In this way, the hagiographic text opens up a means for women to write themselves, their bodies, and bodily behaviours into the body of text itself – and especially for readers who may understand its encoding in female-specific ways. Such a complex dynamic between the internal and external workings of the hagiographic text and the body of its protagonist thus provides a clear example of how the space of its textual culture itself may be expanded to include not only the female subject and readership but also those women who owned such hagiographies, passed them on to other women in their wills, acted as patrons for their production, or appeared within the manuscripts as dedicatees.

This textual and collaborative community, then, resists and decries the type of 'systematic amnesia'[31] which has long kept women out of the frame of our understanding of literary production in the Middle Ages, something which Michelle M. Sauer expounds in her focus on the role played by women within the genre of devotional literature, a particularly bodily form of literary production in which abject bodies, both internal and external to the text, form the primary focus and intentionality. One of Sauer's primary concerns here is to destabilize the Cartesian notion of the single-authored, male, 'rational' text which, so she argues, has occluded the extremely important contribution made by women to devotional literature in particular, a genre which developed out of a late-medieval concern for the corporeal reality of biblical events and the Christian's duty to experience and re-experience them through and with their own bodies. Such a response, which in the later Middle Ages looked often to women and the cipher of their emotion-driven and reactive bodies as its paradigm, encouraged a cultural preoccupation with incarnational theology, over which the human Christ with his passive, vulnerable, fleshly, open and feminized body presided alongside Mary, whose flesh he had taken on in his humanity. Women, of course, deemed equally passive, carnal, fleshly, and feminine, were well placed to excel within such affective approaches to God and, as such, were closely associated with such texts, whether by means of the deeply feminized discourses within them, or else by the affinity generated between the texts and their own responses to them. Taking the form of didactic prayers and treatises, rules for living, and mystical texts (and, as Seaman argues, conduct literature too) written primarily for the laity of both sexes, women in particular were encouraged to respond to these texts in imaginative and physically affective ways. This, perhaps, is realized most literally in the liturgical dramas thought to have been composed by Katherine Sutton, abbess of Barking (d. 1376).

In these devotional dramas not only are women's contemporary social practices incorporated and foregrounded, such as the laying out and washing of the body of the dead Christ during the deposition scene, but some of the dramatic roles, both male and female, were evidently undertaken by the nuns or even the abbess herself. As such, the devotional text becomes, in many ways, the 'performance' text and, in so arguing, Sauer unlocks its multiple functions and the plethora of ways in which it may have been 'read' and (re)produced within a gendered context. Like the hagiographic narrative, then, such texts were clearly not meant simply to be read literally and understood in conventional ways. On the contrary, by means of the performative responses which they generated, the texts were themselves imprinted upon the bodies of their women readers to be read culturally by the rest of the community.

If, within hagiographic writings, conduct literature, and devotional texts, meaning is produced via the scripts of both internal and external bodies, then the multiplicity of possibilities for more traditionally feminine bodies within such texts is key to offering wider access to women in terms of literary production. This is particularly true of the Marian text, which proliferated alongside devotional treatises in the later Middle Ages. Here, as Sue Niebryzdowski demonstrates, the reader is presented with the iconic figure of the Virgin Mary in a plethora of guises: like the Lady of romance literature, she is multifaceted and, like those narratives attached to the virgin martyrs, the text of her body runs in several directions at once, her behaviour not necessarily consistent or readable through a single lens. Amongst her most common guises are those of mother, teacher, intercessor, and queen. She was, however, also Empress of Heaven and Empress of Hell, able to harrow the devil with her heel, as Eve harrowed the serpent with hers. Moreover, in the development of apocryphal accounts of her life to embellish the few details yielded by the Gospels, Mary was also revered as child, as maiden, as mother, as mourner, and as matriarch, all of which aspects are celebrated alongside her divine attributes in those Marian texts under scrutiny here. As Niebryzdowski points out, Mary formed the ideal for women in every part of the life-cycle; indeed, female-associated Marian texts demonstrate that women responded to Mary as a malleable symbol, aspects of whose marriage, childbirth, and motherhood were sufficiently similar to their own to inspire a very personal identification which, on occasion, was transferred to textual practice. Late-medieval Marian texts associated with secular women in particular should be considered, therefore, in terms of their constituting an act of *translatio* [translation] in that they formed female-mediated acts of interpretation and appropriation that served, like affective responses to devotional works more widely, to reveal the significance of the Virgin Mother to her earthly adherents. As such, the Marian text, like the conduct manual, not only taught the woman reader how to become a good Christian, but also offered instruction on how to be the good woman called upon to inscribe her own body with the text of a perfect Marian piety to be read as such by others. As Seaman argues, such inscriptions or *translatio* also work to point the way forward to social advancement and the encourage-ment of reading networks for women who could share the advice proffered in such books, share the books themselves, and open further avenues for their own literary participation. Such an approach, therefore, also expands our understanding of the functioning of women's literary networks, both synchronic and diachronic: not only how they functioned as authors but what they read, when they read it, and, most importantly, how they read it. After all, even Margery Kempe was able to readily inscribe upon herself the discourses of wifely obedience, devoted motherhood, Marian imitation, and self-sacrificial minister to the poor whenever the engine of the church apparatus moved in to threaten her attempts at autonomy, an inscription which ultimately led to the production of a material literary endeavour. Clearly, many medieval women were fully cognizant of the disjunction between discourse and practice, between ideologically obedient reading and creative response and how both bodies and behaviours could be usefully manipulated in the service of literary production and its cultures.

Literacies and Literary Cultures

The third part of the volume, 'Literacies and Literary Cultures' focuses directly on the range of women's literary activities, considering in detail key issues already identified in earlier chapters, including women and manuscript production, circulation and ownership; women's literary and religious networks; women's literacy and education; women as readers, as translators, and as letter-writers; and the question of anonymous female authorship. Again, we know from the famous example of *The Book of Margery Kempe*, that even a woman who could not read or write had access to books, and was part of a 'textual community',[32] in so far as Kempe records how a supportive priest read to her from mystical and devotional works from the English and continental traditions, and also how one of her own main scribes was encouraged in his support of Kempe after reading a book that had been lent to him, as well as other treatises.[33] Books were clearly of great importance to pious laypeople, women as well as men, who wished to strengthen and to share their religious practices. While we do not know if Margery Kempe or her reader owned or borrowed the books which she had read to her, evidence does survive for some of her contemporaries in England, including in her own locality of East Anglia, which was of course a centre of religious enthusiasm, orthodox and heterodox, in the last centuries of the Middle Ages. Women's manuscript ownership in the later Middle Ages is the focus of Carole M. Meale's essay, which builds upon and develops her own previously published research in this area, and also upon key stud-ies by scholars such as Felicity Riddy and Mary C. Erler.[34] A key source of information about ownership of codices is testamentary: manuscripts were valuable assets, and as such, they were often specifically mentioned in individuals' wills. Such testamentary evidence has to be treated with caution, as Meale observes, not least because it is limited predominately to the gentry and mercantile classes, and survives in limited geographical areas, and furthermore, because most wills by women are by widows. Furthermore, the amount of information given about the nature of the books mentioned in a will is sometimes minimal. Nevertheless, as Meale demonstrates, wills can be extremely revealing about such women's reading tastes, and about their literary, religious, and social networks. It is clear that, like Margery Kempe, many late-medieval laywomen saw themselves as part of a circle of piety and devotion, and that their books and shared reading experiences reinforced this sense of belonging. However, whereas in the case of Margery Kempe it is possible to establish a connection between book ownership (or borrowing) and book production because we can see the influence of at least some of the books read by Kempe and her secretary on *The Book of Margery Kempe* itself, how typical is this? In what ways might women's book ownership have shaped the types of works being written and copied? The exploration of the connection between women's book ownership, women's reading, and textual production, circulation, and reception, is developed further by Lara Farina, who shares with Meale a concern that scholarship on women's reading is skewed by the surviving evidence against women in the lower range of the social spectrum. Farina offers a broad survey of medieval women's reading in Britain which looks back to the literary productions associated with monastic houses for women of the twelfth century discussed by Clarke and Batt, and considers, *inter alia*, the sort of romance, hagiographic, and devotional texts discussed by Saunders, Horner, and Sauer. The evidence presented by Farina reveals that women as patrons, readers, and book owners had a far more significant effect on late-medieval literary culture than has previously been recognized. Elizabeth Robertson, nevertheless, sounds a note of caution in her consideration of women and their literary and religious networks. Robertson, like Farina, addresses material produced over several hundred years in order to provide a wide-ranging picture. Robertson's approach is to consider more specifically what the evidence of the production and subsequent transmission of manuscripts of some key texts associated with women (focusing initially on two texts also discussed by Farina: *The Life of Christina of Markyate* and *Ancrene Wisse*) reveals about such networks. Robertson points out that (as is the case with the networks of transmission of the only surviving manuscript of *The Book of Margery Kempe*) these appear to be predominantly male. Nevertheless, Roberston's final case-study, the showings of Julian of Norwich, does confirm the importance of women's agency: as Robertson states 'this extraordinary early example of women's writing survives primarily because of the writing of women' (p. 158).

In the final three essays in this section, Liz Herbert McAvoy, Alexandra Barratt, and James Daybell turn our attention away from manuscript production, transmission, and ownership, and from readership, audience, and reception, and back, once again, to the vexed and extremely complex question of medieval women's authorship. It is worth noting that considerably more doubt is cast on whether specific medieval women writers (such as Marie de France) ever even existed than on whether their male counterparts did. In the chapter on women's writing in Wales in Part I of the volume, Jane Cartwright discusses some of the problems surrounding the attribution of works to the Welsh women poets whose names are recorded. As Cartwright rightly states, 'Accurately establishing authorship is one of the first problems encountered in any study which involves discussing the work of a particular medieval or early modern poet' (p. 61). The canon of even that most famous of English medieval poets, Geoffrey Chaucer, is still a subject of debate even after centuries of scholarship – and, interestingly, Bernau, in her essay, discusses a poem formerly (but no longer) attributed to Chaucer. How much more difficult is it, then, to establish whether an anonymous text was authored by a man or a woman? Certainly the gender of the narrative voice (whether masculine or feminine) should not be assumed to be indicative of the gender of the author. Yet anonymous texts are so prevalent in the Middle Ages that it would be naive to assume that none was composed either partially or entirely by women. Liz Herbert McAvoy, in her essay, deconstructs the patriarchal assumption that anonymous was a man.[35] In order to do this, McAvoy does not set out to prove female authorship in a conventional sense of particular works, but rather to consider what is meant by authorship, and why, or whether, it really matters. Beginning with some of the earliest English poetry (the Anglo-Saxon poems, 'Wulf and Eadwacer' and 'The Wife's Lament', poems also considered by Lees and Overing in their essay), and moving on to consider some key early and later Middle English works, including devotional texts and courtly dream visions, McAvoy argues that because these texts either adopt a female subject-position or demonstrate a clear affinity with female subjectivity, female agency and voice should be attributed to them. For McAvoy, the fact that histories of women's writing tend to be populated by *named* women, with very little attention being given in the construction of these histories to anonymous work, is a serious limitation. But Alexandra Barratt, in the next chapter, raises a further problem: what to make of women such as Dame Juliana Berners (*fl.*1460) whose names have come down to us, but about whom very little is known. As with her predecessor, Marie de France, doubt has been cast on whether Berners really was a historical person. Barratt makes the convincing case that Berners, to whom the poetic work *The Boke of Hunting* has been attributed, should be seen as part of a tradition of women translators into the vernacular that goes back at least as far as Clemence of Barking and the anonymous nun of Barking, and, arguably Marie de France – all discussed by Batt in

Part I. Yet whereas the early medieval writers were translating works into Anglo-Norman or French, Berners was translating from Anglo-Norman into English. As such, Berners should be compared to her better-known late-medieval counterparts, Dame Eleanor Hull and Lady Margaret Beaufort, both of whom, however, translated religious rather than secular works, and neither of whom translated into verse. Barratt's chapter introduces in detail one genre of medieval literature – works in translation – that might not be associated with 'authorship' according to modern classifications, but that certainly fits medieval definitions of writing. After all, many of Chaucer's works, including some of his most famous (such as *Troilus and Criseyde*, or the Knight's Tale), were effectively creative translations and adaptations.

The final chapter in this section, James Daybell's extensive overview of medieval letter writing, invites us to consider another such genre often marginalized in literary histories. As mentioned earlier in the context of Dale Spender's work, letters are crucial to women's literary history because they provide some of the earliest surviving examples of writing by medieval women: the correspondence of Leoba and the other English missionary nuns in Boniface's circle, mentioned by Lees and Overing in Part I. They are also crucial because one of the most prolific women writers of the late-medieval period, Margaret Paston, was a writer of letters. Furthermore, as Daybell points out, a case can be made that there are more examples of letters by women in this period than there are of any other form or genre of female-authored writing. Rather than focus exclusively on Margaret Paston, or the other women letter writers in her family and wider circle in fifteenth-century East Anglia, Daybell looks at the correspondence of the Pastons, alongside that of the Plumptons, Celys, Stoners, and Lisles, as well as the letters of numerous other late-medieval women. This detailed examination of the evidence of such a range of women's writing enables a full and detailed analysis not only of women's style, but also of lay literacy in the mercantile and aristocratic classes at the end of the Middle Ages. In summary, female subjectivity and agency might be asserted in anonymous texts, or even in texts authored by women but re-ascribed to men, and some women found their voice in the media of translation and letter-writing. Nevertheless, as we will see in the final section, it was as mystics and visionaries that female authority found its fullest expression.

Female Authority

The issue of female literary authority is, as we have seen, central to an understanding of the complexities of women's relation to writing throughout the premodern period and has been discussed in some considerable detail by a number of the authors of those works surveyed at the start of this introduction. As recounted earlier, in strictly theoretical terms, a woman could not be an *auctor*, since, as we have also seen, this was a role reserved for men within culturally approved discourse. If women were to be involved in text-making, it was as objects of that discourse, not as producers. However, the essays collected in this volume make it patently clear that, from the very earliest of times, medieval women were inextricably involved in the production of texts and that 'writing' was a complex and multivalent concept bearing little relation to our own contemporary notions of single authorship and originality. Authority, therefore, was not gained by the uniqueness of the text, or by single authorship. Nor was it gained by attaching an authorial name to an individual text as an act of ownership: to reiterate, most medieval texts were anonymously produced and many authorial attributions came about either serendipitously or by later attribution, sometimes even erroneous. The fact is that the human author failed to signify in the light of God as divine author and, in many ways, writing, as the Word of that same God, anticipated by some one thousand years the attempts of Roland Barthes to kill off the author in favour of the text,[36] and an even more recent call for a new type of 'surface reading', one which will 'accurately depict the truth to which a text bears witness' within literary studies.[37] Such an ideological position, of course, worked both for and against medieval women: whilst ontologically unable to author a text, their authorship could, in theory, remain hidden behind anonymity, or else could be imbricated in the writing of a male scribe or collaborator, as many of the essays collected here demonstrate. In fact, it is not until the later Middle Ages that we see women actively moving from behind such screens into the open daylight as writers, a time when, as discussed above, the female body had transmuted into a paradigm for devotion to the human Jesus, the site for an identification with the Virgin, and synecdoche for the good regulation of all those other bodies which made up a newly urbanized society.

The final section of this volume therefore examines the ways in which late-medieval women writers negotiated their own authority, to varying levels of success, and the ways in which subsequent generations of readers manipulated that authority on their behalf. Foremost among these are still the two 'named' writers, Julian of Norwich and Margery Kempe, mentioned earlier in this introduction. As Amy Appleford points out, however, although Julian is the earliest woman writer in the English language for whom we have a name, her entire work steadfastly attempts to erase her own visibility from her texts. If the twelfth century saw the rise of the individual, as Caroline Walker Bynum famously argued,[38] this was deeply resisted by Julian who insists at every point in her writing that it is for her fellow Christians whom she writes and that God speaks through her for them. Of course, Julian here is both defining herself as a mere lowly vessel filled by the word of God as a result of visionary experience; yet she also constructs herself in terms of the traditional male *auctor* similarly inspired by the word of God and constituting his authoritative mouthpiece. As a result, she works with, instead of against, her own sex and gender constraints, manoeuvring them into a position whereby they also become synonymous with textual authority. As Julian rhetorically asks her reader: 'Botte for I am a woman shulde I therfore leve that I shulde nought telle yowe the goodenes of God, sine that I sawe in that same time that it is his wille that it be knawen?'[39] For Julian, it is her duty as a human being to impart her special insights to other human beings, a duty which, as Appleford argues, continued to be executed in various manifestations long after her death up to the present day. Indeed, also in Appleford's estimation, Julian may now well be the second most widely read Middle English writer after Chaucer.

There is also little doubt that Julian's authority was contributed to during her own day by the fact that she adopted the life of an anchorite during the course of her writing, taking up the life of a religious recluse in a locked cell attached to the church of St Julian in Norwich for the final twenty-three years or so of her life. From the twelfth century onwards, English anchoritism had become a predominantly female vocation and was particularly popular amongst laywomen of the gentry and aristocratic classes. It is not without significance, too, that another of our known women writers from the late Middle Ages was also an anchorite: the author of *A Revelation of Purgatory*, discussed here by Mary C. Erler, was a Winchester anchorite whose influence and text penetrated to the heart of the fifteenth-century Lancastrian dynasty to levels just below the king himself. This visionary anchorite's text details an account of purgatory, to which she has recently gained visionary access by means of her deceased friend, Margaret. It is also Margaret who instructs the anchorite to take her experiences to a circle of highly influential churchmen both verbally and in the form of a letter, and the resultant text, which documents with some authority the pains of purgatory to be expected by every Christian soul, is clearly conceived of as a collaborative effort between the two women. The fact, too, that the men who make up the text's immediate audience comply with the holy women's wishes in praying for Margaret's soul, suggests the success of the visionary's collaborative strategy for achieving textual authority.

In her instructive and prophetic mission, the Winchester visionary forges clear correlations with her close contemporary, Margery Kempe, although there is no evidence beyond the circumstantial to suggest that they knew of each other. We do know, however, that Margery was acquainted with Julian whom she tells us she met in 1314 and upon whom she clearly drew for her own authority. Furthermore it is significant that Kempe would also be defined as an anchorite after her death in a printed redaction of her writing,[40] although again there is no evidence to suggest that she ever embraced this particular expression of the holy life. She does make much of anchoritic authority within her book, however, frequently shielding herself behind its religious orthodoxy. Her own brand of late-medieval spirituality is nevertheless eclectic, to say the least, demonstrating in her chameleon-like practices some of the increased opportunities available to women within a late-medieval urban context, as well as ways in which a woman writer might negotiate the excesses of Archbishop Arundel's early fifteenth-century proscriptions against vernacular writings and his drive to counter religious heterodoxy. Whilst Kempe's interpretation of female spiritual practices may remain ultimately indefinable, her promotion of close female relationships in her writing (including the one forged briefly with Julian) to counterbalance those less successful relationships discussed by Diane Watt in her essay on Kempe, echo closely those of the Winchester visionary and Margaret. This in turn points towards Kempe's own determined construction of a suitable methodology for gaining literary authority through her female and feminine status. Such a methodology, so Watt also argues, is based in part on the biblical example of Martha and Mary, a highly prevalent motif within anchoritic and associated literature especially. Characteristically, Kempe literalizes into prevalent hermeneutics this sisterly relationship, playing the active Martha to Julian's contemplative Mary and, in so doing, carving out a space for safe and vouched-for female spiritual practices and their textualization within her own contemporary culture.

By the time these three women writers were operating, the writings of other religious women from the continent had also begun to circulate in England, women whose reputations had already been established abroad and endorsed by church authority. Both Erler and Watt argue for the influence of some of these women upon the Winchester visionary and Kempe respectively, particularly Bridget of Sweden (d. 1373), examined in this final section by Laura Saetveit Miles. Not only was Bridget a visionary and holy woman of some repute, she was also a social activist, noblewoman of considerable influence, and, ultimately, a revered saint. Widely disseminated throughout Europe, her writings were particularly popular in England where they were read in both Latin and Middle English and closely associated with the reform movement within which both Kempe and the Winchester visionary were also inextricably caught up. It was as a result of this reform movement, too, that Henry V founded the nunnery of Syon Abbey in 1415 for the Brigittine nuns in England who provided the first female audience for Bridget's writings within an insular context. As Miles points out, both Kempe and the author of *A Revelation of Purgatory* had close associations with Syon Abbey, arguing too that Bridget provided a widespread model of writerly authority for women in England and a model for female collaboration via her multiple female audiences. Similar arguments can be made too for Catherine of Siena and Marie d'Oignies, both earlier precursors to the other women writers examined in this section. Like the writings of Bridget, the works of or about these women first gained influence and popularity on the continent before being translated into Middle English for a lay audience in the fifteenth century. Catherine's work had long had a following on the continent and she had herself become subject to cult status. Not only did she leave behind accounts of her exemplary life written about by others in order to support her cult, accounts which, as C. Annette Grisé argues, she closely supervised herself, but she also authored her own autobiography, numerous letters, and a popular cycle of prayers. Her writings reached England in the fifteenth century and, perhaps because the socio-religious climate was then able to accommodate them, had a major impact upon women's devotional and reading practices, again within a Syon Abbey context, before extending their range to reach an audience of educated and pious lay women beyond the nunnery walls.

Unlike Catherine, Marie d'Oignies did not leave behind any writings of her own. Nevertheless, as Jennifer M. Brown demonstrates, her *Life* as written by her confessor, Jacques de Vitry, presents Marie clearly as the driving force behind the narrative. This text can thus be read as a compendious collection of Marie's own discourse, her voice permeating the entire work. It was the Middle English translation of this text to which, by her own account, Kempe was given access via her priest and scribe, and it is certainly a text which encouraged her in her own religious practices and helped to imbue her writings with textual authority. Indeed, as Grisé and Brown argue in the context of Catherine of Siena and Marie d'Oignies, these literary women from the continent should be regarded as influential precursors – foremothers, even – to both Julian and Kempe (and, we could add, the Winchester visionary), who participated in the larger continental female visionary traditions of which Bridget, Catherine, and Marie were an integral part and upon whom these English women writers drew overtly for their literary rationale and authority.

Also influential in fifteenth-century England in her ability to mobilize and combine elements of hagiography, social critique, and visionary or prophetic registers for political ends was the French writer, Christine de Pizan, who, as Nancy Bradley Warren argues, provides perhaps the most telling paradigm for what this introduction has been arguing for here. In her poetic eulogy for the newly executed Joan of Arc, *Ditié de Jehanne d'Arc*, Christine explores issues surrounding the female authorial voice, drawing poetic comparisons between patriarchal attempts to silence Joan's voice and the difficulties she herself faces as a woman writer. In a type of hermeneutic collaboration between Joan, her subject, and herself, the writer, Christine, forges a poetic narrative which anatomizes many of the thorny issues of voice and authority which are central to the enterprises of all the woman writers considered in this volume. In this text, too, as in so many of her other writings, Christine fearlessly inserts herself into the heart of her own writing, beginning the poem with the self-assertive and tradition-defying *'Je, Christine'*, a self-assertion which, in its simplicity, outdoes even Margery Kempe's relentless self-presentation as subject. Nor is it merely the use of the first-person pronoun 'I' which is at stake here, for other women writers at other times have similarly made use of this same subject-positioning. It is the use of Christine's forename in apposition to the self-defining 'I' which categorically stamps upon the late-medieval female-authored text the *right* to an authorial subject-position and ownership of a text's initiation. Christine's *'Je'* is therefore freighted with all those elided and invisible selves whose contributions to literary production remain unaccounted for and who, at least within an English context, this present volume now attempts, in part, to make visible.

Notes

1. For such an example of women's literary history, see Janet Todd, *Feminist Literary History: A Defence* (Cambridge: Polity Press, 1988). For an influential critique of traditional teleologies of the women's writing, see Margaret J. M. Ezell, *Writing Women's Literary History* (Baltimore: Johns Hopkins University Press, 1993).
2. See Jennifer Summit, 'Women and Authorship', in *The Cambridge Companion to Medieval Women's Writing*, ed. Carolyn Dinshaw and David Wallace (Cambridge: Cambridge University Press, 2003), pp. 92–3.
3. See Diane Watt, *Secretaries of God: Women Prophets in Late Medieval and Early Modern England* (Cambridge: D. S. Brewer, 1997), p. 157.
4. *The boke of the cyte of ladyes* (London: Henry Pepwell, 1521), fol. Aa4r.
5. Virginia Woolf, *A Room of One's Own* (Harmondsworth: Penguin, 1945), here at p. 101.
6. David Wallace (ed.), *The Cambridge History of Medieval Literature* (Cambridge: Cambridge University Press, 1999), p. xx.
7. Ibid., p. xiv.
8. Elaine Showalter, *A Literature of their Own: From Charlotte Brontë to Doris Lessing* (Princeton: Princeton University Press, 1977).
9. Ellen Moers, *Literary Women: The Great Writers* (London: W. H. Allen, 1977); Sandra M. Gilbert and Susan Gubar, *The Madwoman in the Attic: The Woman Writer and the Nineteenth-Century Literary Imagination* (New Haven: Yale University Press, 1979); Kate Millett, *Sexual Politics* (London: Virago, 1977).
10. Todd, *Feminist Literary History*; Ezell, *Writing Women's Literary History*; Jennifer Summit, *Lost Property: The Woman Writer and English Literary History, 1380–1589* (Chicago: University of Chicago Press, 2000); Laurie A. Finke, *Women's Writing in English: Medieval England* (London: Longman, 1999); Joan. M. Ferrante, *To the Glory of her Sex: Women's Roles in the Composition of Medieval Texts* (Bloomington: Indiana University Press, 1997); Carole M. Meale (ed.), *Women and Literature in Britain, 1150–1500* (Cambridge: Cambridge University Press, 1993).
11. Ferrante, *To the Glory of her Sex*, p. 3.
12. See n. 2 above.
13. 'Introduction' to *The Norton Anthology of Literature by Women: The Tradition in English*, ed. Sandra M. Gilbert and Susan Gubar, 1st edn. (New York: W. W. Norton, 1985), p. 15.
14. Alexandra Barratt (ed.), *Women's Writing in Middle English* (London: Longman, 1992); Carolyne Larrington (ed.), *Women and Writing in Medieval Europe: A Sourcebook* (London: Routledge, 1995).
15. Clare A. Lees and Gillian R. Overing, 'Birthing Bishops and Fathering Poets: Bede, Hild, and the Relations of Cultural Production', *Exemplaria*, 6 (1994), 35–65.
16. Clare A. Lees and Gillian R. Overing, *Double Agents: Women and Clerical Culture in Anglo-Saxon England* (Philadelphia: University of Pennsylvania Press, 2001; reprinted with a new preface Cardiff: University of Wales Press, 2009), pp. 15–39.

17. 'Introduction' to *Norton Anthology*, ed. Gilbert and Gubar, p. 1.
18. Dale Spender, *Mothers of the Novel: A Hundred Good Writers before Jane Austen* (London and New York: Pandora, 1986).
19. Diane Watt, *Medieval Women's Writing: Works by and for Women in England, 1100–1500* (Cambridge: Polity Press, 2007). See also Watt's essay, 'Literature in Pieces', in *The Cambridge History of Early Medieval Literature*, ed. Clare A. Lees (Cambridge: Cambridge University Press, forthcoming).
20. Finke, *Women's Writing*, pp. 58 and 73.
21. Summit, *Lost Property*, p. 5.
22. Sheila Delaney, '"Mothers to Think Back Through": Who Were They? The Ambiguous Example of Christine de Pizan', in *Medieval Texts and Contemporary Readers*, ed. Laurie A. Finke and Martin B. Shichtman (Ithaca: Cornell University Press, 1987), pp. 177–97.
23. *Oxford English Dictionary*, s.v. 'context', n. 4(a).
24. *Oxford English Dictionary*, s.v. 'pre-text', n.
25. Judith M. Bennett, *History Matters: Patriarchy and the Challenge of Feminism* (Manchester: Manchester University Press, 2006), p. 42.
26. Ibid., p. 52.
27. Sarah Prescott coins the phrase 'women's "archipelagic" literary history' in her article 'Archipelagic Orinda: Katherine Philips and the Writing of Welsh Women's Literary History', *Literature Compass*, 6.6 (2009), 1167–76.
28. 'Introduction' to *Archipelagic Identities: Literature and History in the Atlantic Archipeligo, 1550–1800*, ed. Philip Schwyzer and Simon Mealor (Aldershot: Ashgate, 2004), pp. 3–4. See also Jeffrey Jerome Cohen (ed.), *Cultural Diversity in the British Middle Ages: Archipeligo, Island, England* (New York: Palgrave Macmillan, 2008).
29. John Kerrigan, *Archipelagic English: Literature, History, and Politics, 1603–1707* (Oxford: Oxford University Press, 2008), p. 80.
30. Catherine Kerrigan (ed.), *An Anthology of Scottish Women Poets*, with Gaelic translations by Meg Bateman (Edinburgh: Edinburgh University Press, 1991), pp. 52–5 and 60–1; Anne C. Frater, 'The Gaelic Tradition up to 1750', in *A History of Scottish Women's Writing*, ed. Douglas Gifford and Dorothy McMillan (Edinburgh: Edinburgh University Press, 1997), pp. 1–14. See also Sarah M. Dunnigan, C. Marie Harker, and Evelyn S. Newlyn (eds.), *Woman and the Feminine in Medieval and Early Modern Scottish Writing* (Basingstoke: Palgrave Macmillan, 2004); and Elizabeth Ewan and Maureen M. Meikle (eds.), *Women in Scotland, c.1100–c.1750* (Edinburgh: Tuckwell, 1999).
31. David Aers, 'A Whisper in the Ear of the Early Modernists; or, Reflections on Literary Critics Writing "The History of the Subject"', in *Culture and History, 1350–1600: Essays on English Communities, Identities and Writing*, ed. David Aers (Michigan: Wayne State University Press, 1992), pp. 177–202 (pp. 180–1).
32. On textual communities see Brian Stock, *The Implications of Literacy: Written Language and Models of Interpretation in the Eleventh and Twelfth Centuries* (Princeton: Princeton University Press, 1983), especially pp. 88–92.
33. *The Book of Margery Kempe*, ed. Sanford Brown Meech and Hope Emily Allen, EETS o.s. 212 (Oxford: Oxford University Press, 1940), pp. 142–4 and 152–4.
34. Carol M. Meale '"...alle the bokes that I haue of latyn, englisch, and frensch": Laywomen and their Books in Late Medieval England', in *Women and Literature in Britain, 1150–1500*, ed. Carol M. Meale, 2nd edn. (Cambridge: Cambridge

University Press, 1996), pp. 128–58; Felicity Riddy, ' "Women Talking about the things of God": A Late-Medieval Sub-culture', in *Women and Literature in Britain*, ed. Meale, pp. 104–27; Mary C. Erler, *Women, Reading and Piety in Late Medieval England* (Cambridge: Cambridge University Press, 2002).

35. Virginia Woolf famously surmised 'that Anon, who wrote so many poems without signing them, was often a woman': *A Room of One's Own*, pp. 50–1.

36. Roland Barthes, 'The Death of the Author', in *Authorship from Plato to the Postmodern*, ed. Sean Burke (Edinburgh: Edinburgh University Press, 2005), pp. 125–30.

37. Stephen Best and Sharon Marcus, 'Surface Reading: An Introduction', *Representations* 108 (2009), 1–22.

38. Caroline Walker Bynum, 'Did the Twelfth Century Discover the Individual?', *Journal of Ecclesiastical History*, 31 (1980), 1–17.

39. *The Writings of Julian of Norwich: 'A Vision Showed to a Devout Woman' and 'A Revelation of Love'*, ed. Nicholas Watson and Jacqueline Jenkins (Turnhout: Brepols, 2006), *Vision*, Section 6, ll. 40–3, p. 75.

40. This redaction was first printed by Henry Pepwell in 1521 and reprinted by Wynkyn de Worde. For an edition of the text see *The Book of Margery Kempe*, ed. Meech and Allen, pp. 353–7.

Part I
Pre-texts and Contexts

1
Women and the Origins of English Literature

Clare A. Lees and Gillian R. Overing

Literary history rarely associates women with writing and cultural production in the earliest period of English literature (*c*.600–1150). More commonly this Anglo-Saxon period is ignored even by historians of women's literature. In consequence, as scholars and teachers of this early culture we are often asked the following questions. What, women and the origins of English literature? Were women writing? What were they writing? This chapter, however, demonstrates that early medieval women are vital to the production and reception of literary culture. It's all a matter of rethinking the evidence.

This chapter begins by addressing the problems and possibilities that arise when we write women into early medieval literary history. Let us start with the problems. First, no named woman writer is known to have been working in the vernacular language of Anglo-Saxon, or Old English, in the British Isles before 1150. This perceived absence has resulted in the period of Old English vernacular literature being routinely ignored in histories of literature and in histories of women's writing.[1] In early medieval writing in general, however, the concept of the author is radically different from that of more modern periods. Literary production in this period is often anonymous, spoken rather than written, and communally produced and received. Yet critics still habitually refer to Old English texts as the literate products of individual male authors. The anonymous author is, after all, most often 'he'. Literary history, we argue, needs to take account of the fact that orality is in many ways central to cultural production of all kinds in this period and that it is deeply intertwined with issues of literacy, status, gender, and collaboration. Those writers whose names we do know are mostly male and mostly associated with the religious orders, with the possible exception of King Alfred: they include Ælfric, Alcuin, Aldhelm, Bede, Boniface, Byrhtferth, Cynewulf, Cædmon (the so-called first poet in English literature) and Wulfstan.[2] These figures are not 'authors' in the modern sense of the term, however: in prefaces and in concluding materials they identify themselves or are described as clerics, translators, dreamers, patrons, penitents, and kings. As this list of writers in Latin and English also indicates, literature in this period is not monolingual. Texts are written in Latin or Old English or both; they may also draw on Scandinavian, Irish, Welsh, Scottish, or continental linguistic forms and influences (such as Flemish). Scholars are only now working out the extent of multilingualism and inter-lingual exchange between the languages of Ireland, the British Isles, and the continent, and their impact on the meaning of 'English' literature.[3] Furthermore, to consider writing before the historical codification and classification of written texts as literary means addressing many different genres including those which might seem to modern readers to be didactic or functional as well as those which are self-consciously aesthetic: poetry, prose, hagiography, riddles, sermons, aphorisms, histories and chronicles, law codes and tracts.

Looked at differently, however, these problems become opportunities to revise the scholarly paradigms of how we think about and identify women's agency as writers, readers, and participants in the production of literature and of culture. To take a simple binary view of how texts work – literate or oral, heard or read, by a single author or in collaboration, Latin or English, poetry or prose – obscures and undervalues the complexity of cultural production in this period. The historical conditions for textual production, patronage, and literacy work against a paradigmatic model of sole male authorship and in consequence we can point to a far richer and more nuanced picture of women's cultural work.

This chapter explores three scenarios of women's participation in textual production in order to challenge assumptions that literary history routinely makes about women, agency, collaboration, and authorship in this period. These are the story of Hild and Cædmon and the canonical 'origins' of Old English poetry; the evidence of Barking Abbey for seventh-century female Latin literacy and literary production; and the account of Leoba and her reading nuns in eighth-century Germany. These early medieval scenarios help us to indicate the wide purview of women's sphere of literate activity in English poetry, Latin prose and poetry, and to measure its geographic reach across the British Isles and in continental Europe.

Hild was a highly educated, politically influential aristocrat. She was a well-connected, well-known figure in the pre-eminent seventh-century kingdom of Northumbria, the most northerly of the Anglo-Saxon kingdoms. Abbess of the famous dual abbey of Streoneshalch, usually identified with Whitby, Hild was an acclaimed mentor and teacher, who advised kings and educated bishops and was part of a network, even dynasty, of royal religious women who were central players in the conversion of the Anglo-Saxons to Christianity and in the subsequent political and religious conversionary mission of the Anglo-Saxons to the continent. Hild's story, however, is not configured with the story Bede tells us about Cædmon the poet, one that is rehearsed in every discussion about the 'origins' and history of English literature.[4] In Bede's *Ecclesiastical History of the English People*, Cædmon is a lonely farm labourer, who is embarrassed at his inability to participate in poetry-making after dinner in the monastery at Whitby and so one night retires to the cattle shed. Visited in his sleep, he is commanded to produce a poem or rather, as the idiom of the day puts it, he is asked to sing a song. Reluctant even in his dream, after three insistent promptings from his spiritual visitor from the other world, Cædmon then dutifully sings the nine-line poem that is known to us today as Cædmon's 'Hymn' and is ubiquitous in accounts of the origin of English literary history. Apparently the first poem in English, the 'Hymn' is extant in Latin paraphrase as well as several Old English versions, and is one of the most glossed and overwritten texts in the corpus of Anglo-Saxon manuscripts.[5] But Cædmon also goes on to produce many more English poems, Bede tells us, based on Scripture. This later poetry is now lost but we do know that it was engineered and facilitated by Hild at her monastery at Whitby. When we think of Cædmon, however, do we think of Hild?

Critics have examined Bede's story from many viewpoints, from celebrating Cædmon as the 'father' of English poetry to appraising rather more critically its Christian appropriation of 'native' Germanic traditions of song-making. We too have analysed it elsewhere, looking at the gendered assumptions in Bede's account of English literary production whereby the 'birth' of English poetry becomes an all-male affair.[6] For the purposes of this history of women's writing and in order to reformulate women's relation to literature in the Anglo-Saxon period, let's put the following facts back into this familiar scenario. The 'origin' of English literary history would not have been possible without Hild's patronage in particular or the more widespread general practice of female leadership of dual monasteries in the early period of Anglo-Saxon Christianity. Female patronage is not separate from masculine authorship in Cædmon's story; on the contrary, one is the function of the other and both are creative literary practices. For Cædmon's 'Hymn' is not simply a singularly authored text by a divinely inspired yet lowly male lay labourer who moved up to become a poet-monk and then on into history; it is better understood as part of a system of Christian education and cultural production governed and enabled by female religious patronage. The poem the inspired Cædmon sings is about the Christian creation; it is worth pausing too on the creativity and inspiration of its makers, Hild and Cædmon. When Cædmon wakes up from his dream, he reports it verbally to the estate manager or reeve who in turn reports it to Hild. It is by Hild's authority that Cædmon is subsequently instructed in the stories of Scripture and given the task of turning them into English poems. Orality and literacy are as much a part of this account of the beginnings of English literary history as are patronage and authorship.

Meanwhile in another seventh-century double monastery in the southern kingdom of the East Saxons, Essex, we find more highly educated, well-connected, wealthy religious women associated with the community of Barking Abbey.[7] Often older, perhaps formerly married, widowed, or separated, these women offer a slightly different – or at least slightly better known – female demographic for the seventh century than that of Hild's Whitby. And, indeed, it is in part because of this demographic that these women occasion a paradigm-shift in early medieval definitions of virginity that has major consequences for the doctrine and practices of monasticism in the Middle Ages subsequently. Virginity is a spiritual practice prized because of its emulation of the chaste body of Christ, but from this period on it will not be exclusively the prerogative of intact females or males. Barking Abbey is also part of the history of learning and literature written in Latin in the Anglo-Saxon period because of its association with the singly authored, highly sophisticated, and stylistically ornate prose text, *De virginitate* [*On virginity*] by Aldhelm (abbot of Malmesbury, bishop of Sherborne from 705).[8] The prose *De virginitate*, together with its poetic counterpart, *Carmen de virginitate* [*Song of virginity*], is a foundational literary work of the early Middle Ages, studied, copied, and imitated for several hundred years.[9] The work amounts to a lengthy anthology of male and female virgin martyr stories written in Latin, challenging definitions of what counts as the content of a national, vernacular literary tradition in at least two ways: first, its language is not English, and second, its content is explicitly religious and didactic, if highly polished and self-consciously ornate. Aldhelm's *De virginitate* makes for difficult reading; its Latin is prolix to the extreme, and its graphic and often repetitive content makes unusually heavy demands of its readers. It even challenges our modern assumptions about how early medieval texts were read, since it is possible that it was read, like saints' lives and other spiritual anthologies, in sections. Those readers were women, at least in the first instance.

The story of Hild and Cædmon complicates modern assumptions about how early medieval poetry is the product of a single male author. So too the story of the nuns who commissioned Aldhelm's two virginity books shows how early medieval texts are collaborations with multiple patrons and readers determining their form, content, and reception. Aldhelm reports that the work is commissioned by Hildelith, abbess of Barking and her female religious colleagues, Justina, Cuthberg, Aldgyth, Scholastica, Hydburg, Beorngith, Eulalia, Thecla, and Osburg (perhaps Aldhelm's own relative). However unfamiliar to us now are the names on this impressively long list of female religious, who may well be associated with other double monasteries in Wessex as well, it is clear that it is their cultural capital as patrons which elicits Aldhelm's prose text so celebrated for its authoritative Latin style.[10] As wealthy, older women with established aristocratic networks, these women are in a position to commission Aldhelm to write two books that will enhance the prestige and learning of their monastery and related houses, providing them with a reputation for knowledge and learning that persists well after the seventh century. Furthermore, these female patrons also change the terms of theological debate in this period by their commission, as we have already suggested. Female virginity had previously been strictly limited to those whose bodies were intact: *De virginitate* expands this category to include widows as well as the formerly married and thereby accommodate the demographic of Barking Abbey and other early double monasteries.

Bede points out that his knowledge of Barking comes from a now lost history of the abbey, which was almost certainly written by the nuns. There are also letters and possible visionary texts associated with Hildelith. But to associate these women with a lost book, a couple of letters, and Hildelith's possible commissioning of a vision of the monk of Much Wenlock is a narrow measure of Barking's corporate cultural power in the seventh century.[11] The female network centred on the Barking nuns occasioned the writing of Aldhelm's *De virginitate*, their very existence determined in some measure its content, but most importantly their learning shaped Aldhelm's style and its much celebrated sophistication. And they did it twice. Not content with a prose *De virginitate*, they commissioned from Aldhelm a second poetic version, elaborate in its own terms, revealing the extent to which the literary tastes of these women were on the cutting edge for Latin literature of this period. Literary history in the twenty-first century must imagine early medieval nuns as creative agents in the production of learned literary texts in the seventh century.

Neither Whitby with its royal and elite religious connections nor Barking with its network of highly educated women are unique in the early Middle Ages. In the mid-eighth century, Wimborne Abbey in Wessex was so well known as a centre for Christian learning that the future Saint Boniface (remembered as the Apostle of the Germans because of his role in the conversion of that region) requested permission from the abbey for one of its nuns, the poet Leoba, to join him on his mission. The Latin correspondence of Boniface has given him an authorial stature parallel to Aldhelm's in modern literary histories of this period for Boniface corresponded extensively with the female religious of his generation. The letters provide much information about the lives of learned religious women like Leoba and their mission abroad, and the list of other Anglo-Saxon religious women who correspond with Boniface is another long one that includes Bucge, Eangyth, Eadburg, Ecgburg, Cyneburg, and Berhtgyth. Because the genre of the epistle has long been known as a cultural resource for the history of women writers, Leoba is slightly better known than either Hild or Hildelith, especially in histories of religious women.[12] She is, furthermore, one of the few early Anglo-Saxon women known to have occasioned the writing of a hagiography. There was possibly once a now-lost *Life* of Hild and perhaps one of the saintly Æthelthryth too, to judge from the information that Bede offers us, but Leoba's *Life* is the only one to survive.[13] This is put together by Rudolph of Fulda at the request of Hrabanus Maurus, 'probably the most learned man of his age', but it is dedicated to another woman, the nun Hadamout.[14]

Indeed, more than the other works we consider in this chapter, this *Life* is women-centred and women-identified, and it is composed from the words and memories of women. As a result, it tells us a great deal about literate and literary practices in female religious communities at home and abroad. Let us not forget too, however, that Leoba was a poet, and one whose life is in fact better documented than Cædmon's.

As was the case with Cædmon's 'Hymn' and Aldhelm's virginity texts, central to the *Life of Leoba* is how to interpret authorship. Rudolph's account in his prologue emphasizes how he compiled the *Life* from the written notes of 'other, venerable men', particularly the monk and priest, Mago.[15] Yet, by this same account, these men took their information from four of Leoba's nuns or 'disciples', Agatha, Thecla, Nana, and Eoloba. According to Rudolph, '[e]ach one copied them down according to his ability and left them as a memorial to posterity'. This sentence is usually taken to mean that the oral reports of women were turned into written records by men. However, the Latin reflexive plural pronoun 'sui' used in this description, usually translated as 'his', is ambiguous and complicates the division of textual labour into oral and female as opposed to written and male: who is writing down whose words?[16] Furthermore, the *Life* itself dramatically opens up more possibilities for imagining how women worked in their textual communities. Leoba's own status as 'single' author of the often-cited short Latin poem, written in a style often identified as Aldhelmian and sent to Boniface for his feedback, must be understood in this much broader context of communal literacy:[17]

Vale, vivens aevo longiore, vita feliciore, interpellans pro me.
Arbiter omnipotens, solus qui cuncta creavit,
In regno patris semper qui lumine fulget,
Qua iugiter flagrans sic regnat gloria Christi,
Inlesum servet semper te iure perenni.

[Farewell, and may you live long and happily, making intercession for me.
The omnipotent Ruler who alone created everything,
He who shines in splendour forever in His Father's kingdom,
The perpetual fire by which the glory of Christ reigns,
May preserve you forever in perennial right.]

Leoba's sonorous Latin is hard to capture in any modern English translation. It is often seen as a poor imitation of Aldhelm's style, much as Cædmon's 'Hymn' is sometimes read as a routine but not particularly exciting Old English poem. Notably, both poems include praise of the Christian Creator. We include Leoba's poem here to give it its place in literary history as one of the earliest poems to have been written by an Anglo-Saxon female poet and to prompt re-evaluations of her style.

Leoba is not, however, identified as a poet in Rudolph's *Life*. And we can offer only two of the many examples of female textual community at Bishofsheim (now Tauberbischofsheim, near Würzburg) in the *Life of Leoba* here. The first, a description of the nuns reading to Leoba, gets to the heart of cultural understandings of reading and reception in this period; the second, Leoba's prophetic dream, addresses women's relation to the genre of hagiography itself.

To start with Leoba's reading nuns. According to her *Life*, even when the abbess Leoba is asleep, she teaches and models a spiritual life based on learning for her pupil nuns. On one evocative occasion, her nuns try to catch her out by making deliberate mistakes as they read to her when they thought she was sleeping. She, however, caught them out.[18] Reading in this *Life* is not a solitary activity. Rather, it is a communal process of teaching and of learning and, as such, it is as much about relationships between women as it is about women and their books. The spiritual practice of reading builds female communal bonds (a process evident elsewhere in the *Life*). Worth noting in this context is Leoba's name. Formerly known as Leofgyth, Leoba is renamed after the Beloved of the Song of Songs, itself very popular throughout the Middle Ages. The story of the reading nuns in this *Life* is an early example of how the scriptural *topos* of the bridal song can be used to figure love and spiritual affection between women. Leoba's religious practice, her name suggests, combines loving and learning in the study of the sacred texts in female communities.

To turn now to Leoba's dream. Criticism about the female lives of saints often emphasizes the extent to which we need to read against the genre to get at the lives of the women it purports to celebrate. Indeed, even as Rudolph shapes the record of Leoba's life according to hagiographic convention, the narrative escapes him, its content breaking through the constraints of his form. Few dream visions are as viscerally evocative of the endless process of interpretation that attends the production and reception of saints' lives as the 'purple thread' which issues from Leoba's mouth, and which she then pulls out 'as if it were coming from her very bowels'.[19] The thread is without end and in her dream Leoba rolls it up into a ball, exhausted by her labour. The *Life* tells us that Leoba's dream is interpreted by an older nun as a prediction of how Leoba will go on to teach and instruct the divine mysteries, following as it were the thread without limit. The purple thread which comes from within Leoba is a powerful affective image of how the saint and her community are linked to the divine through the practice of communal exegesis, through reading and interpretation. In short, Leoba and her nuns take the ball and run with it.

We have explored three early medieval stories about women's participation in literary production to get away from the idea that the only story to be told about literature in this period is that of Cædmon and his dream. We conclude with some further suggestions about how to continue to re-evaluate the paradigms of orality and literacy, authorship and readership, Latin and English, poetry and prose that underpin so much conceptualization of literary history in this period. Reading across medieval literary history opens up many productive intersections and appositions. Leoba's eighth-century dream examined alongside Cædmon's in the seventh indicates that there are alternatives to literary history's privileging of the singular male author with his divinely inspired text. We might also explore the *Life of Leoba*, with its evidence for the processes of female literacy in affective communities, alongside the better-known ninth-century account of King Alfred competing with his brothers to win a book of English poetry from his mother, Osburh, if only he would learn to read.[20] There is not only one way to 'do' literature, these examples suggest. The chastising and punitive ways that the homilist Ælfric and his colleague Ælfric Bata characterize the disciplinary process of learning Latin by the 'pueri' ['young monks'] in the late Anglo-Saxon monastery offers yet another communal model of textual production, very different from those of the loving Leoba and her teasing nuns or Alfred and his mother.[21]

We can also read against conventional literary periods. The shaping of virginity as a spiritual practice *and* as genre of literature by the highly literate nuns of Barking Abbey and their wider religious community has a long trajectory. The twelfth-century *Life of Edward the Confessor* written by an anonymous nun at Barking is resourced by the similar trope of chaste marriage.[22] To put twelfth-century virginity literature against that of the earlier seventh century *associated with the same place* reminds us how women's writing in one generation can be a rich resource for women in later ones. So too the complexities of female patronage and their innovations in formulating genres and texts is vital to understanding cultural production in the eleventh century, as Catherine A. M. Clarke points out in this volume.

Women's participation in the creation of literary genres reminds us, finally, that their voices and agency may be found in other, unexpected ways and texts as well. The simple fact that most texts in this period are anonymous in terms of their authorship cuts across their classification as poetry or prose, Latin or English. This is less a problem than a possibility, however, because it enables the consideration of a whole range of forms and genres, from wills to charters, from riddles to sermons, from saints' lives to heroic poetry. Literary history usually gives us only two female-voiced, anonymously authored poems for this entire period: the virtually untranslatable *Wulf and Eadwacer* and *The Wife's Lament* (perhaps as much anthologized now as Cædmon's 'Hymn').[23] But what of the powerful voice of Margaret as she talks back to the devil in the Old English *Lives* of St Margaret, or that of Elene as she debates with the Jews in the poem of the same name, or Judith's rallying speech to her army in that poem, or all those mouthy women whose poise and Christian learning make life so difficult for their would-be spouses and tormentors in numerous Latin and English prose female saints' lives?

Or what about those visceral laments produced by women in *Beowulf*, not to mention the elaborate formal speeches of Queen Wealhtheow in the same poem?[24]

Women's writing in the early Anglo-Saxon period? Women? Writing? What, were they writing? Of course they were. We just need to read, listen, and write our literary histories differently.

Notes

1. See Clare A. Lees and Gillian R. Overing, *Double Agents: Women and Clerical Culture in Anglo-Saxon England* (Philadelphia: University of Pennsylvania Press, 2001; repr. with new preface, Cardiff: University of Wales Press, 2009), pp. 1–18.
2. A useful survey is R. D. Fulk, Christopher M. Cain, and Rachel S. Anderson, *A History of Old English Literature* (Oxford: Blackwell, 2002).
3. For introductions to these issues, see Phillip Pulsiano and Elaine Treharne (eds.), *A Companion to Anglo-Saxon Literature* (Oxford: Blackwell, 2001), pp. 325–99.
4. Bede, *Ecclesiastical History of the English People*, ed. and trans. B. Colgrave and R. A. B. Mynors (Oxford: Clarendon Press, 1969), book IV, chapter 24.
5. See, for example, Allen J. Frantzen and John Hines (eds.), *Cædmon's Hymn and Material Culture in the World of Bede* (Morganton: West Virginia University Press, 2007), which does not, however, address Hild's relation to Cædmon.
6. Lees and Overing, *Double Agents*, pp. 19–55.
7. Bede, *Ecclesiastical History*, book IV, chapters 6–10.
8. Aldhelm, *Prosa de virginitate: cum glosa Latina atque anglosaxonica*, ed. Scott Gwara, Corpus Christianorum Series Latina (Turnhout: Brepols, 2001), CXXIV (introductory materials) and CXXIVA (texts); *Aldhelm: The Prose Works*, trans. Michael Lapidge and Michael Herren (Woodbridge: Boydell and Brewer, 1979), pp. 59–132; and *Aldhelm: The Poetic Works*, trans. Michael Lapidge and James Rosier (Woodbridge: Boydell and Brewer, 1985), pp. 102–67.
9. See Stephanie Hollis, *Anglo-Saxon Women and the Church: Sharing a Common Fate* (Woodbridge: Boydell and Brewer, 1992), pp. 75–112 and Andy Orchard, *The Poetic Art of Aldhelm* (Cambridge: Cambridge University Press, 1994).
10. See Aldhelm, *Prosa de virginitate*, CXXIV, pp. 47–55.
11. Bede, *Ecclesiastical History*, book IV, chapter 10 and Jane Stevenson, 'Anglo-Latin Women Poets', in *Latin Learning and English Lore: Studies in Anglo-Saxon Literature for Michael Lapidge*, ed. Katherine O'Brien O'Keeffe and Andy Orchard (Toronto: University of Toronto Press, 2005), II, pp. 86–107.
12. See Christine E. Fell, 'Some Implications of the Boniface Correspondence', in *New Readings on Women in Old English Literature*, ed. Helen Damico and Alexandra Hennessey Olsen (Bloomington, IN: Indiana University Press, 1990), pp. 29–43; Hollis, *Anglo-Saxon Women and the Church*, pp. 271–300.
13. Bede, *Ecclesiastical History*, book IV, chapters 19–20, 23.
14. As Elizabeth Petroff puts it in *Medieval Women's Visionary Literature* (Oxford: Oxford University Press, 1986), p. 85.
15. *Anglo-Saxon Missionaries in Germany*, ed. and trans. C. H. Talbot (London: Sheed and Ward, 1954), pp. 205–26 (at p. 205).
16. Ibid.; for the Latin, with its reflexive pronoun, see *Vita Leobae Abbatissae Biscofesheimensis Auctore Rudolfo Fuldensi*, ed. G. Waitz, Monumenta Germaniae Historica SS 15.1 (Hanover: Impensis Bibliopolii Hahniani, 1887), pp. 118–31

(at p. 122): 'Ego enim gesta illius omnia non didici, sed pauca quae refero a viris venerabilibus ad meam noticiam pervenerunt, qui ea quattuor discipularum eius, Agathae vidilecet et Teclae, Nanae et Eoleobae, *fideli relatione comperta, singuli pro captu ingenii sui* sicut sibi tradita sunt litteris mandare et ad exemplum posteris relinquere studuerunt' (our emphasis).

17. Leoba's poem (trans. Ephraim Emerton, in *The Letters of Saint Boniface* [New York: Columbia University Press, 1940, repr. 2000], pp. 37–8) and letter, together with other examples of Boniface's correspondence with women, are available online: *Epistolae: Medieval Women's Letters*, http://epistolae.ccnmtl.columbia.edu/letter/374.html, accessed 8 December 2009.

18. *Anglo-Saxon Missionaries*, ed. and trans. Talbot, pp. 215–16.

19. Ibid., p. 212.

20. For Asser's *Life of Alfred*, see *Alfred the Great*, trans. Simon Keynes and Michael Lapidge (Harmondsworth: Penguin Classics, 1983), pp. 67–110.

21. *Anglo-Saxon Conversations: The Colloquies of Ælfric Bata*, ed. and trans. Scott Gwara and David W. Porter (Woodbridge: Boydell and Brewer, 1997) and *Ælfric's Colloquy*, ed. G. N. Garmonsway (London: Methuen, 1939). See also Irina A. Dumitrescu, 'The Grammar of Pain in Ælfric Bata's *Colloquies*', *Forum for Modern Language Studies*, 45.3 (2009), 239–53.

22. See Jocelyn Wogan-Browne, *Saints' Lives and Women's Literary Culture: Virginity and Its Authorizations* (Oxford: Oxford University Press, 2001), pp. 249–56.

23. Both of these poems are found in the tenth-century Exeter Book manuscript. See *The Exeter Book*, ed. George Phillip Krapp and Elliott van Kirk Dobbie, Anglo-Saxon Poetic Records, 3 (New York: Columbia University Press, 1933), pp. 179–80 (*Wulf and Eadwacer*) and pp. 210–11 (*The Wife's Lament*).

24. See *The Old English Lives of St Margaret*, ed. Mary Clayton and Hugh Magennis (Cambridge: Cambridge University Press, 1994); *Elene*, ed. P. O. E. Gradon, Exeter Medieval Texts and Studies (Exeter: University of Exeter Press, 1958, rev. edn. 1977); *Judith*, ed. Mark Griffith, Exeter Medieval Texts and Studies (Exeter: University of Exeter Press, 1997); *Ælfric's Lives of Saints*, ed. and trans. Walter. W. Skeat, Early English Text Society, o.s. 76, 82 and 94, 114 (London and Oxford: Trübner and Kegan Paul, Trench and Trübner, 1881, 1885 and 1890, 1900; repr. as 2 vols., London, Oxford University Press, 1966); and *Klaeber's Beowulf: Fourth Edition*, ed. R. D. Fulk, Robert E. Bjork, and John D. Niles with Helen Damico (Toronto: University of Toronto Press, 2008).

2
Literary Production Before and After the Conquest

Catherine A. M. Clarke

The role of women in literary culture from the late tenth to the mid-twelfth century forces us to reframe the parameters within which we conventionally situate texts and authors, and to interrogate the expectations we bring to literary studies. The dynamics of writing in this period challenge us to reconsider modern assumptions about authorship and agency, presenting models of female patronage, collaboration, and a range of complex transactions and collusions which facilitate and shape literary production. The evidence of the period *c.*980–1140 also urges us to question the very notion of 'Britishness' in relation to literature: the texts generated by these women resist national categorization in modern terms, instead linking the literary, linguistic, and political cultures of the British Isles, the European continent, and Scandinavia. New scholarship is focusing attention on women's roles within this complex historical context, and in particular on the ways in which female patrons used texts to negotiate and intervene in the rapidly changing cultural and political world on either side of the Norman Conquest.

Current research reveals the power and influence of women as literary patrons in this period, showing their direct participation in textual production and their use of literature as a tool for promoting specific political or religious agendas, or personal prestige more generally. Yet sources rarely record female patronage in explicit, direct terms: instead, evidence for female agency is inscribed in complex, coded ways, often at the 'edges' of texts in material such as dedicatory verses, prologues, and epistolary passages. Through close attention to this kind of textual material, we can begin to recover the contributions of women to literary culture in the period, and the ways in which these contributions are framed within rhetorical and generic conventions. However, the textual evidence for female literary patronage across the tenth to the twelfth centuries is fraught with complexity, contradiction, and compromise. The power of women as patrons is articulated within carefully circumscribed social and gendered roles (with a few exceptions, which generate dangerously subversive connotations for contemporary audiences). Women are able to commission, instigate, and attract literary production, but their own voices remain elided, displaced. As Gerald A. Bond comments in his study of authorship and identity in Romanesque France, these female patrons of 'bespoke' texts must ultimately remain 'bespoken', their own voices and agency mediated through (male) authorship.[1] This short chapter will look at a range of female patrons across this broad period, focusing in more detail on certain selective examples, and concentrating especially on the 'edges' of key texts in order to recover evidence for women's agency and involvement in literary production.

In the last quarter of the tenth century,[2] the Anglo-Saxon Chronicle, one of the most important documents of early English history and identity, was reworked in Latin by the Anglo-Saxon nobleman Æthelweard at the instigation of Abbess Matilda of Essen, Germany. The chronicler Æthelweard can be identified with the ealdormann Æthelweard, who appears in numerous sources as a powerful and influential figure during the reign of Æthelræd II (978–1016), and who also acted as literary patron to Ælfric of Eynsham.[3] Matilda of Essen, to whom the text is addressed, was the granddaughter of King Otto I and his first wife Queen Edith, herself daughter of Edward the Elder, king of England (899–924).[4] Æthelweard's dedicatory epistle at the beginning of the *Chronicon* indicates that the work was produced at the initiative of Matilda: in deeply affective language addressed to 'the most talented Matilda' he remarks that he has 'received the letter I desired from you', which apparently represents some form of commission, or at least the acceptance of a suggestion which he had previously advanced.[5] The dedication goes on to explain that both he and Matilda are descended from the Anglo-Saxon king Æthelwulf (839–58), emphasizing their family ties and the genealogical imperative which underpins this new version of the Anglo-Saxon Chronicle. Æthelweard calls attention to the text as the product of a culture of shared memory, family tradition, and oral history, commenting that in the subsequent text he will 'dwell in plain style upon our family in modern times and upon the re-affirmation of our relationship, so far as our memory provides proof, and as our parents taught us'.[6] For Matilda, the *Chronicon* commemorates her royal English ancestry and its associated prestige. Her active involvement in the production of the text is suggested in the dedication: Æthelweard appeals to her for assistance, commenting that 'it is your task to bring information to our ears'.[7]

Æthelweard's claim in the dedicatory epistle to write in 'plain style' is not borne out by the rest of the *Chronicon* text: indeed, successive scholars since the medieval period have critiqued the pretention, eccentricity, and inaccuracy of his Latin.[8] More recent studies have treated Æthelweard's language more sympathetically, suggesting its value as an example of rhetorical and metrical experiment, or its attempted synthesis of Old English poetic idioms with Latin literary language.[9] The use of Latin as the language of Æthelweard's *Chronicon* is certainly significant: it makes the Anglo-Saxon Chronicle accessible for Matilda, and effectively bridges linguistic and cultural difference to mobilize a version of history which promotes the importance and venerability of her English family. This iconic Anglo-Saxon text, rewritten in Latin for a German abbess, demonstrates women's networks of kinship and cultural contact which stretch across linguistic and national boundaries. Yet, as van Houts observes, this powerful royal nun and patron was still 'at the mercy of a man for her request to be answered'.[10]

The career of Emma, patron of the Latin prose *Encomium Emmae Reginae* (written *c.*1041–2), epitomizes the multilingual, cross-cultural, transnational experience of many high-status women in the decades around 1066.[11] Born into a noble family in Normandy, Emma became the second wife of the Anglo-Saxon king Æthelræd (1002–16), after his death marrying the Danish king of England Cnut (1017–35). Perhaps one of the best-known literary works instigated by a woman in this period, the *Encomium* shows Emma's ability to use text to skilfully negotiate the partisan politics and tensions of the English court in the mid-eleventh century. Once again, Latin presents an appropriate choice of literary language both for gathering the prestige and authority of classical rhetorical and mythological models into Emma's version of recent history and her role within it, and also for its capacity to reach across the linguistic and cultural divides – and associated factionalism – of the Anglo-Danish court.[12] Until recently, only one medieval manuscript of the *Encomium Emmae Reginae* (dating to the middle of the eleventh century) was known to exist.[13] However, in 2008, Sotheby's auctioned a newly discovered manuscript of the *Encomium*, apparently representing a slightly later version of the text, which will undoubtedly generate exciting new scholarship and interpretations over the coming years.[14] Traditionally, scholarship has attributed authorship of the *Encomium* to a monk of Saint-Bertin in Flanders, suggesting that the text was then brought to England for presentation to Emma.[15] Yet more recent studies have explored the possibility that the *Encomium* was produced in England from within the court of Harthacnut, Emma's son by Cnut, allowing the anonymous encomiast much more immediate engagement with its culture and politics, and with the aims and intentions of Emma herself.[16] Though the exact political purpose of the text remains unclear and subject to debate, the *Encomium* evidently presents an account of recent history which promotes Emma's interests (and those of her son, Harthacnut), justifying her actions, eliding problematic aspects of her career (such as her first marriage to King Æthelræd), and seeking to establish her legitimacy and power in the role of queen-mother.

The opening Prologue and Argument deal with Emma's role – and that of the encomiast – most explicitly. Here the encomiast reflects self-consciously on his literary project, on the implications of undertaking Emma's commission, and on the politics of balancing the demands of a patron with the pressures of memory and public opinion. He acknowledges the convention that history-writing should not 'deviate from the straight path of truth', yet recognizes the necessity of producing a text which supports Emma's political agendas. In a surprisingly explicit confrontation of the difficulties this entails, he comments that:

> Quoniam uero, quin scriptures sim, euadere me non posse uideo, unum horum quae proponam eligendum esse autumo, scilicet aut uariis iudiciis hominum subiacere, aut de his, quae mihi a te, domina regina, precept sunt, precipientem negligendo conticessere.

> [Since, indeed, I see that I cannot avoid writing, I aver that I must choose one of the alternatives which I am about to enunciate, that is either to submit to a variety of criticisms from men, or to be silent concerning the things enjoined upon me by you, Lady Queen, and to disregard you who enjoin me.][17]

Elizabeth Tyler has commented on the encomiast's 'keen interest in issues of complicity' here, and the ways in which his discussion deliberately complicates and erodes the binary opposition between categories of 'truth' and 'lies'.[18] In the Prologue, the encomiast insists that praise of Emma is at the centre of his work throughout, and that 'I nowhere deviate from her praises'.[19] He compares Emma to Octavian, whose praise, he asserts, is implicit throughout Virgil's *Æneid*, drawing on the prestige of classical precedent to bolster her authority. Yet this defining comparison also generates more troubling implications. Emma is figured here as a man, suggesting the potentially dangerous ways in which this ambitious, politically active woman escapes the usual categories of femininity and female agency shaped by conventional rhetorical tropes. With Emma as the text's Octavian, the role of her son, Harthacnut – current ruler of the Anglo-Danish Empire and perhaps a more obvious choice for comparison with a Roman emperor – is marginalized, even elided.[20] This recalls, perhaps, the frontispiece of the *Encomium* itself (in the British Library manuscript) in which Emma is depicted enthroned, crowned, and dominating the image, whilst her sons Harthacnut and Edward (later 'the Confessor') are literally sidelined, 'marginal, secondary, subservient'.[21] In the text as a whole, such multilayered, polyvalent use of classical allusion sits alongside literary features drawn from Old English and Scandinavian literary culture.[22] As does Emma herself, the *Encomium* engages with the diverse cultures, discourses, and traditions current in the multilingual court of mid-eleventh-century England in order to forge power, authority, and a voice that must be heard.

Just a few years later than the *Encomium Emmae Reginae*, with its composition spanning the Norman Conquest itself (1065–7),[23] the *Vita Ædwardi*, written for the wife and widow of King Edward the Confessor, Edith, similarly negotiates a context of political upheaval and uncertainty. Again, probably written by a monk from the Flemish monastery of Saint-Bertin, the *Vita Ædwardi* both commemorates the life of an Anglo-Saxon king and also, crucially, works to shape a new role and new legitimacy for Edith at this difficult time of transition in which her status has changed so radically.[24] The *Vita* again reflects the complexity of writing history and serving the needs of a patron, with the text's own form suggesting the difficulties of producing a single, coherent (and favourable) perspective on Edward's reign and Edith's role. Its prosimetrical structure, with alternating sections in verse and prose, allows the author to explore different idioms and discourses, together with the variety of (often conflicting) interpretations which they generate, and throughout the work the author debates with his muse, Clio, on the challenges of treating recent history and writing for an audience which includes Edith as the text's primary recipient.[25] For example, at the beginning of Book II, having closed Book I with the death of Edward, and now reflecting on the horrors of civil (and family) conflict and the deaths in battle of Earl Tostig, Harald Hardrada, Harold Godwineson and others, the author protests to Clio that he cannot find 'the appropriate words' to express such terrible events.[26] Allusions to Lucan and Statius cluster in this section of the text: as in the work as a whole they lend prestige and authority from the world of classical myth and history, whilst simultaneously inviting in disturbing associations with the dangerous, fragile political contexts of Caesar and Pompey, Troy or Thebes.[27] In fact, throughout the *Vita*, the text's project of celebrating and rehabilitating Edith is constantly in jeopardy. As Monika Otter has observed, for example, the problematic issue of Edith's childlessness, which is avoided in any direct narrative, becomes an insistent undercurrent throughout the work, emerging in repeated imagery of progeny, mothering, and reproduction.[28] Overtly, however, the *Vita Ædwardi* is emphatic in its praise of Edith and her family. In the opening verses, the author begs his muse to command him as she will, asserting that he is ready to write anything in praise of his 'lady', Edith, who watches closely over his enterprise.[29]

In addition to Edith, the audience of the *Vita Ædwardi* probably included the wider community of Wilton – an important Anglo-Saxon nunnery, home to many royal and noble women – where she ended her life.[30] Wilton itself plays a significant role in this period as a centre of female learning and a site of women's involvement in literary production. In particular, works written by the Flemish monk Goscelin of Saint-Bertin (died around 1099), who had strong associations with the Wilton community, are currently receiving renewed critical attention and can offer further insights into women's role in the collaborative production of texts in this period. These include the *Liber confortatorius*, an epistolary text written for the former Wilton nun, Eve, with advice and consolation now that she has entered the anchoritic life, and the Legend of Edith, which presents a hagiography of St Edith (*c.*963–84), daughter of King Edgar by his first wife Wulfthryth, who was herself (like her mother) educated at Wilton and became the community's patron after her death.[31] The Legend of Edith, in particular, reflects the possibilities – and limits – of women's agency and authority in the eleventh century. The Bodleian Library manuscript of the Legend begins with a prologue dedicating the work to Archbishop Lanfranc of Canterbury.[32] But the text goes on to reveal a more complex context of patronage and production. Goscelin explains that he produced the Legend at the request of Wilton's 'spiritual mothers of the present time', drawing on oral material from these noble, pious women 'whose high birth and religious lives are recognised as being equal in credibility to books'.[33] Once again, as in the earlier case of Matilda of Essen, we see the role of royal nuns as 'transmitters of information, as carriers of tradition',[34] who make a crucial contribution to the production of a written text. Yet Goscelin is compelled to defend the evidence gathered from these women and their participation in the creation of hagiography.

> Neque uero is sexus a testimonio ueritatis refellendus erit, qui Domini uerbum portauit, qui sua fide apostolorum incredulitatem arguit et angelica legatione dominica[m] resurectionem predicavit.[35]

> [Nor will their sex be a reason for detracting from the truth of their testimony – [that sex] which carried the word of the Lord; by which its faith convinced the incredulity of the Apostles and preached the Lord's Resurrection with an angel-borne message.][36]

The authority of the Wilton nuns is expressed through a physical, bodily metaphor and the figure of the Virgin Mary, who carried the true 'Word' in her womb. Goscelin's prologue acknowledges the active role played in the Legend of Edith by the Wilton women, whilst still suggesting the need to justify female authority. Yet Goscelin's 'Wilton' texts also underscore the vital contribution of women to textual production in this period and the wide extent of the cultural and literary networks within which these high-status women participated.

Into the early twelfth century, we find noble and royal women at the centre of networks of kin and court which reach across Britain and into northern continental Europe. The question of women's agency and influence in this context is complex: high-status women use literary patronage effectively to enable them to engage with – and formulate a place within – the emergent culture of courtliness, yet the influential new rhetoric of love, desire, and service simultaneously establishes a restrictive, limiting set of female roles (in both rhetorical and social terms). The lengthy Latin poem, 'Adelae Comitissae' ['To Countess Adela'] presented by Baudri of Bourgeuil to Adela of Blois, daughter of William the Conqueror (sometimes known as Adela of England), exemplifies some of these tensions and contradictions. In an extended ekphrasis of what is supposedly the elaborate decoration of

Adela's bedchamber, the poem offers an encyclopaedic collection of knowledge, from pagan and biblical mythology to medieval science and medicine – even, perhaps, a description of the scenes from her recent family history depicted in the Bayeux Tapestry.[37] In the opening 'envoy' to his poem, Baudri praises Adela's 'ear for verse' noting that

> Hec etiam nouit sua merces esse poetis
>   A probitate sua nemo redit uacuus.
> Rursus inest illi dictandi copia torrens
>   Et preferre sapit carmina carminibus.[38]

> [Also, she's well aware that the poet deserves his stipend;
>   Through her largesse, no poet must leave her court unpaid.
> She herself has a lively talent for writing poems,
>   And shows remarkable taste in judging the good from the bad.][39]

The poem brings together a latent eroticism (as Baudri enters and beholds his lady's private bedchamber) with deference to Adela as a powerful ruler – the figure of 'female lordship' explored by Kimberley LoPrete.[40] The opening verses of the Anglo-Norman *Voyage of St Brendan*, written by an unidentifiable 'Benedeit' for Henry I's first queen Edith-Matilda (or perhaps his second wife, Adeliza of Louvain – the manuscript dedications vary), address the text's recipient, a powerful figure of both 'law' and justice, and in the mannered language of courtesy, as she is greeted 'a thousand times and a thousand more'.[41] The emergent language of courtly love is also evident in the dedicatory opening lines of Philippe de Thaon's *Bestiaire*, addressed to Adeliza of Louvain, in which she is described as 'a jewel, who is a very handsome woman'.[42] Across these early twelfth-century works, the relation of author to patron is expressed in terms of submission to both authority and to erotic desire – the complex concept of 'dominism' as identified and coined by Gerald Bond.[43] Whilst a detailed investigation of these texts and their contexts is beyond the scope of this chapter, they show the continued involvement of female literary patrons in the multilingual, multicultural environment of northern Europe in the period after the Norman Conquest, and their role (however mediated and limited) in the formation of the idea of the court as a centre of learning, literature, and love.

From the late tenth to the early twelfth centuries – across decades of political and cultural transition – we see the ability of female literary patrons to engage with a multilingual culture which reaches across national boundaries, to select the appropriate literary language to communicate with their intended audience, to gather prestige and authority from a range of literary cultures and models, and to use texts to advance their own personal interests. Yet the examples discussed here achieve all this only through the mediation of male authors, who enable their participation in textual culture. Often inscribed at the edges of texts, women's agency is represented (and circumscribed) through established models and rhetorical tropes such as those of epistolary writing and its affective language, panegyric literature, the Bible and Christian theology, or the emergent discourse of courtly love and desire. Where the depiction of a woman breaks out of these conventional categories – such as the image of Queen Emma as Octavian – the power of a female patron can dangerously destabilize the text and its surrounding political context. The texts discussed here deliberately call attention to the complex series of transactions enacted between patrons and authors, whether in terms of the exchange of information, the provision of material rewards in payment for service, or the bartering of truth and fiction in the production of a politically driven, 'bespoke' text. Their 'bespoken' female patrons are complicit in this process of political, moral, and aesthetic bargaining, winning the capacity to make their mark in contemporary textual culture, but in exchange surrendering their own voices.

Notes

1. Gerald A. Bond, *The Loving Subject: Desire, Eloquence, and Power in Romanesque France* (Philadelphia: University of Pennsylvania Press, 1995), p. 157.
2. Elisabeth van Houts, 'Women and the Writing of History in the Early Middle Ages: The Case of Abbess Matilda of Essen and Æthelweard', *Early Medieval Europe*, 1 (1992), 53–68 (65–6).
3. A. Campbell (ed.), *The Chronicle of Æthelweard* (London: Thomas Nelson and Sons, 1962), pp. xii–xvi.
4. Van Houts, 'Women and the Writing of History', p. 62; Wojtek Jezierski, 'Æthelweardus redivivus', *Early Medieval Europe*, 13 (2005), 159–78 (160).
5. Campbell (ed.), *The Chronicle of Æthelweard*, p. 1.
6. Ibid., pp. 1–2.
7. Ibid., p. 2.
8. F. M. Stenton, *Anglo-Saxon England*, 3rd edn. (Oxford: Oxford University Press, 1971), p. 461; Kenneth Sisam, 'Anglo-Saxon Royal Genealogies', *Proceedings of the British Academy*, 39 (1953), 287–348 (320–1).
9. Michael W. Winterbottom, 'The Style of Æthelweard', *Medium Ævum*, 36 (1967), 109–18; D. R. Howlett, 'The Verse of Æthelweard's Chronicle', *Bulletin du Cange*, 58 (2000), 219–24; Angelika Lutz, 'Æthelweard's *Chronicon* and Old English Poetry', *Anglo-Saxon England*, 29 (2000), 177–214.
10. Van Houts, 'Women and the Writing of History', p. 68.
11. See Elizabeth M. Tyler, 'Crossing Conquests: Polyglot Royal Women and Literary Culture in Eleventh-Century England', in *Conceptualizing Mutlilingualism in England, 800–1250*, ed. Elizabeth M. Tyler (Turnhout: Brepols, forthcoming).
12. Elizabeth M. Tyler, 'Talking about History in Eleventh-Century England: The *Encomium Emmae Reginae* and the Court of Harthacnut', *Early Medieval Europe*, 13 (2005), 359–83 (esp. 368–70).
13. *Encomium Emmae Reginae*, ed. and trans. A. Campbell (London: Offices of the Royal Historical Society, 1949), repr. with supplementary introduction by Simon

Keynes (Cambridge: Cambridge University Press for the Royal Historical Society, 1998), p. xli.

14. See Timothy Bolton, 'A newly emergent mediaeval manuscript containing *Encomium Emmae reginae* with the only known complete text of the recension prepared for King Edward the Confessor', *Mediaeval Studies*, 19 (2009), 205–21.

15. *Encomium*, repr. Keynes, pp. xxxix–xli.

16. Pauline Stafford, *Queen Emma and Queen Edith: Queenship and Women's Power in Eleventh-Century England* (Oxford: Blackwell, 1997), pp. 28–40; *Encomium*, repr. Keynes, pp. xxxv–xxxvi, lxix; Andy Orchard, 'The Literary Background to the *Encomium Emmae Reginae*', *Journal of Medieval Latin*, 11 (2001), 156–83.

17. *Encomium*, ed. Campbell, pp. 4–5.

18. Elizabeth M. Tyler, 'Fictions of Family: The *Encomium Emmae Reginae* and Virgil's *Aeneid*', *Viator*, 36 (2005), 149–79 (152).

19. *Encomium*, ed. Campbell, p. 7.

20. Tyler, 'Talking about History', pp. 378–81.

21. Pauline Stafford, 'The Powers of the Queen in the Eleventh Century', in *Queens and Queenship in Medieval Europe*, ed. Anne Duggan (Woodbridge: Boydell Press, 1997), pp. 3–26 (p. 5).

22. Orchard, 'Literary Background'.

23. *The Life of King Edward who rests at Westminster, Attributed to a Monk of Saint-Bertin*, ed. and trans. Frank Barlow, 2nd edn. (Oxford: Oxford University Press, 1992), pp. xxix–xxxiii.

24. Monika Otter, 'Closed Doors: An Epithalamium for Queen Edith, Widow and Virgin', in *Constructions of Widowhood and Virginity in the Middle Ages*, ed. Cindy L. Carlson and Angela Jane Weisl (Basingstoke: Macmillan, 1999), pp. 63–94, esp. p. 64; Stafford, *Queen Emma and Queen Edith*, pp. 40–50.

25. Victoria B. Jordan, 'Chronology and Discourse in the *Vita Ædwardi Regis*', *Journal of Medieval Latin*, 8 (1998), 122–55; Elizabeth M. Tyler, 'The *Vita Ædwardi*: The Politics of Poetry at Wilton Abbey', *Anglo-Norman Studies*, 31 (2009), 135–56.

26. *The Life of King Edward*, ed. and trans. Barlow, pp. 84–5.

27. Tyler, 'The *Vita Ædwardi*', pp. 139–49.

28. Otter, 'An Epithalamium'.

29. *The Life of King Edward*, ed. and trans. Barlow pp. 4–5.

30. Tyler, 'The *Vita Ædwardi*', pp. 152–6.

31. Stephanie Hollis *et al.* (eds.), *Writing the Wilton Women: Goscelin's* Legend of Edith *and* Liber confortatorius (Turnhout: Brepols, 2004).

32. 'Goscelin's Legend of Edith', trans. Michael Wright and Kathleen Loncar in *Writing the Wilton Women*, ed. Hollis *et al.*, pp. 17–93 (p. 17).

33. Ibid., p. 24.

34. Van Houts, 'Women and the Writing of History', p. 54.

35. A. Wilmart, 'La Legende de Ste Edith', *Analecta Bollandiana*, 56 (1938), 5–101, 265–307 (37).

36. 'Goscelin's Legend of Edith', trans. Wright and Loncar, p. 24.

37. Monika Otter, 'Baudri of Bourgueil, "To Countess Adela"', *Journal of Medieval Latin*, 11 (2001), 60–141; Shirley Ann Brown and Michael W. Herren, 'The *Adelae Comitissae* of Baudri of Bourgueil and the Bayeux Tapestry', in *The Study of the Bayeux Tapestry*, ed. Richard Gameson (Woodbridge: Boydell Press, 1997), pp. 139–56.

38. *Adelæ Comitissæ*, ll. 38–42, in Baldricus Burgulianus, *Carmina*, ed. Karlheinz Hilbert (Heidelberg: Carl Winter Universitätsverlag, 1979), p. 150.

39. Otter, 'Baudri of Bourgeuil', p. 67.
40. Kimberley A. LoPrete, *Adela of Blois: Countess and Lord, c.1067–1137* (Dublin: Four Courts Press, 2007), p. 193.
41. Benedeit, *The Anglo-Norman Voyage of St Brendan*, ed. Ian Short and Brian Merrilees (Manchester: Manchester University Press, 1979), esp. p. 4 and p. 30, ll. 1–13.
42. Philippe de Thaon, *Bestiaire*, in *Popular Treatises on Science Written During the Middle Ages in Anglo-Saxon, Anglo-Norman and English*, ed. Thomas Wright (London: Historical Society of Science, 1841), available at http://bestiary.ca/etexts/wright1841/wright1841.htm.
43. Bond, *The Loving Subject*, p. 136.

3
The French of the English and Early British Women's Literary Culture

Catherine Batt

Anglo-Norman studies are crucial to reconstructing women's participation in Britain's literary culture because the language and literature owe so much to women's creative and practical endeavour, as patrons, teachers, audiences, and writers. Recent valuable work is rethinking Britain's multilingual culture, rewriting uncritical assumptions about historical breaks and cultural hostilities; female patronage, for example, effects significant affiliations and continuities between Anglo-Saxon and Norman cultures in the eleventh and twelfth centuries.[1] General readers have hardly been aware of women's writing in Anglo-Norman, let alone appreciated it, because Anglo-Norman itself can appear anomalous in traditional models of literary history, with, *inter alia*, their rigid and exclusive associations of language with national identity, and also because only recently have these texts been available in translation. But the work of these important, often trend-setting, poets, with their self-consciousness about their art, their sensitive handling of octosyllabic verse, and their acknowledgement of their reading communities, urges fresh awareness of female authorship's contribution to the participatory cultural dynamic of literature, in the later twelfth century and beyond.

Rachel Cusk observes, of a twenty-first-century woman surgeon's story, that a duty of 'female writing' is to chart 'the struggle to remain individual and hence moral'.[2] There are six major texts self-declaredly written by women in England in the later twelfth century (setting aside speculation over anonymous texts, and knowledge of lost female-authored work), and all convey a sense of moral integrity. Yet if one expects to conflate 'individual' values with the autobiographical, the corpus is perplexing, for it may represent the work of as few as two authors, or as many as four, so scant is the documentary evidence, and so little hard information do the internal signatures provide. Marie de France, the woman writer of this time whose name is most familiar to specialists and non-specialists alike, is now generally agreed to have composed a group of twelve romance *Lays* (c.1160–70); a collection of Aesopian *Fables*, written some time later, and *Saint Patrick's Purgatory* (c.1190), a reworking of a later twelfth-century Latin treatise by the English Cistercian Henry of Saltrey.[3] Some also identify her as author of the *Life of St Audrey*. However, the 'Marie' who authors this important translation (*c*.1200) of a post-Conquest Latin account of the life and miracles of St Etheldreda (in Anglo-Saxon, Aethelthryth), founder of Ely Abbey, has also been associated with the Benedictine convent of Chatteris. Alternatively, *Audrey* and the *Purgatory* may have a common author distinct from the author of the *Lays*.[4]

The *Life of St Audrey* is one of three female-authored saints' lives of a corpus of some seventy surviving Anglo-Norman examples of this enormously popular medieval genre. The saints' lives have until latterly been viewed diffidently by modern audiences, who perhaps expect to find in them only limited and repetitive narratives of saintly struggle and spiritual triumph with, in the case of female virgin martyrs, a sometimes inappropriate focus on physical torture. *Audrey* and the two productions from the Benedictine Abbey of Barking – a *Life of St Edward the Confessor* (*c*.1163–89), about the historical Edward, King of England (1043–66), by an anonymous nun, and a *Life of St Catherine* (*c*.1175–1200), about the legendary virgin martyr of Alexandria, by a Clemence of Barking (who may or may not have also written *Edward*) – demonstrate the sheer literary range this genre can encompass in these authors' capable hands, from sharp political and social insight to spiritual conviction, from theological disputation to sensitivity to human emotion.[5] Barking, originally an Anglo-Saxon foundation and double monastery for monks and nuns, was by the later twelfth century functioning as a seat of learning and as a particularly powerful religious and cultural centre for women, a nunnery with links to the royal court. If women were denied professional careers in places of higher learning and the Church, other than in single-sex institutions, the erudition and literary quality of the texts they produce demonstrate that those from elite groups, at least, had access – whether through religious foundations such as Barking, or via aristocratic household and court networks, or both – to instruction in the languages, literatures, and registers of both scholarly and courtly cultures, which included knowledge of Latin and continental and insular vernaculars. The women granted such an education certainly impart, in Cusk's terms, an urgent moral sense in their writing; in terms of 'individual' voice, however, their ambition is to make the female, historical, and conceptual, central to the integrity of the texts on which they work, and to prompt in their audiences the recognition of a shared moral responsibility.

For all her stout self-inscription as author, 'Marie de France' is arguably as much reconstructed as real.[6] The little evidence and (sometimes free) conjecture about her biography nevertheless place this highly educated woman from northern France in aristocratic and royal circles in England as a writer (the dedicatee 'noble king' of the *Lays* is probably Henry II, 1154–89), and perhaps later, given her evident learning and connections, in an English convent. A court poet, Denis Piramus, claiming moral prestige for his own writing, has made concrete both a 'Lady Marie' and the fondness and admiration she and her 'verses of lays' attract among the high-born, although he asserts that such lays are 'by no means true'.[7] Appreciated in her own time (although manuscript evidence gives the *Fables* broader medieval dissemination), the *Lays* are also the most immediately popular with modern readers – their delicate stories of heterosexual love compare with Jane Austen's self-declared painstaking miniaturist work.[8] Marie too, in her *Prologue*, declares her own scrupulous attention to detail in reworking the oral Celtic stories she now recrafts as lasting, written, art; but like Austen, she exercises a tough-minded rhetorical control. Her *Lays*, as is typical of a genre that seeks to trouble categories, offer both pleasure and intellectual challenge, setting up and interrogating narrative, moral, social, sexual, and gendered ways of ordering and interpreting the world, with particular focus on both material and conceptual borderlines, on what evades easy classification, interpretation, and judgement.

These brief narratives of love and desire fulfilled, frustrated, crossed, transformed, transcended, existing in contexts now supernatural, now realist, individually offer different (and not always internally coherent) emphases. In *Equitan*, an adulterous couple's trick to be rid of an inconvenient husband rebounds on them, drawing a stern narratorial moral. Others have a strong fantasy element. In *Yonec*, a young woman, married against her will, seemingly wishes into existence a lover-knight, who appears in bird-form, in a land where, she has been told, such 'adventures' were once commonplace. In *Guigemar*, a wounded androgynous hind directs the eponymous hero to the fulfilment of his sexual destiny. A lay might reflect on the art of writing itself, as when *The Wretched One/Chaitivel* asks who owns the narrative, and whose experience, male or female, should be privileged, in a tale of love frustrated by catastrophe. *Honeysuckle/Chevrefoil* offers a glimpse of Tristan, the most famous of medieval lovers, fashioning a love metaphor from nature as a message to his beloved. *The Nightingale/Laüstic* describes at length the commemoration of a love unconsummated. *The Two Lovers*, similarly, memorializes two deaths: that of a young man who has refused a strength-giving potion as greater tender of his love than obtaining his desired lover by such means, and that of his grief-stricken lady. Some tales are in dialogue one with another; *Milun*'s story of love lost and found, of paternity obscured and revealed, is similar to *Yonec*, but allows its characters altogether happier circumstances than does *Yonec*, with its dark accounts of vengeful killings. Some celebrate female resourcefulness and power. In *Le Fresne*, a woman's unthinking spitefulness is redeemed through her lost daughter's humility and her own remorse. In *Lanval*, the will of an otherworldly Lady who comes to claim the Arthurian knight Lanval eclipses his own volition. The heroine of *Eliduc*'s generosity towards her wayward husband's lover transforms the relations that obtain between all three of them, and redefines love itself.

The *Lays* offer no single, settled, perspectives on their subjects. In the form of her telling, Marie questions moral certainties. *Bisclavret* is particularly disturbing: a werewolf, betrayed by his terrified wife, nonetheless demonstrates such fealty to a king who hunts him that he is adopted at court. But at court also he attacks his now remarried wife, tearing her nose from her face. Under torture, the wife confesses her betrayal, and is exiled, her punishment recorded for ever on the faces of female descendants who are born without noses. Bisclavret, thanks to his sovereign, returns to his human form and social status. But does he remain lycanthropic? Does this primarily indict human judicial systems, or satirize patronage, or moralistic narrative itself? Is the werewolf an image of the ambiguous position of the female writer? Who is truly the alien? This strange tale asks one above all to ponder what is left out of the telling, and what this reveals of the reader. Marie has been compared to Angela Carter in her fearless treatment of heterosexual relations, but Alice Munro is perhaps the modern writer who shares her gift of looking aslant at material, of withholding information, or divulging it, in such a way as makes one perceive the world anew.

The only manuscript to contain Marie's twelve *Lays* and their Prologue is the thirteenth-century Reading Abbey-owned British Library Harley 978, which also preserves a copy of the *Fables*, and includes medical texts, satirical Latin verses, and drinking songs. This work of Marie is apparently primarily courtly; the *Fables* are dedicated to a 'Count William' (*Fables*, p. 257, vv. 9–12). Yet it takes its place in entertaining and instructing clerics, and participates in the games of male scholarly discourse. Marie's pre-emptive move against a man's appropriation of her work (*Fables*, pp. 257–8, vv. 1–22) robustly foregrounds female agency and claims to authority, gender, and authorship become important interpretative tools in these 103 moralizing stories. Whether rooted in reality or fantasy, in the human or animal world, the stories delight in satirical and political observation, a clash of perspectives, a sceptical attitude to human language and its capacity as forensic tool, and (as in the *Lays*) a teasing questioning of human epistemological and categorizing procedures. Antifeminist tropes – that 'women have an art more than the devil', for example (Fable 45) – emerge less as definitive than as part of a play with moral and linguistic relativism that demands continuing engagement and questioning, rather than passive acceptance. Fable 21's tale of a resourceful sow, for example, notes that lying is sometimes not only expedient but necessary for the greater good.

Marie's translation, *St Patrick's Purgatory* (*c.*1190), centres on an account of a physical journey to purgatory. Station Island on Lough Derg, County Donegal, identified to St Patrick as its entrance, was already a pilgrimage site. Marie's text seems to require an act of faith rather than the exercise of intellectual scepticism. One of several vernacular versions to popularize the idea of purgatory in the later twelfth century, Marie's text, recast for a secular audience (*St Patrick's Purgatory*, vv. 2297–2302), works as an act of piety, but also as an adventure story which lends credence, in this version, to the theology it seeks to promulgate.[9] The knight Owein, figuratively armed with 'faith, good hope, Justice and belief' (*St Patrick's Purgatory*, vv. 666–7), enters purgatory in expiation of his sins, and witnesses the horrors of hell – and risks experiencing them for himself – in a series of ever more exquisite and gruesome tortures visited on the bodies of sinful humanity, before he is rewarded with a vision of the Earthly Paradise and a return to his own world. The narrative raises questions about integrity and language. Owein, whose religious conviction is not in doubt, escapes time and again from his would-be tormentors by remembering to call on the name of Christ. There seems to be some comfort for the reader here, in the intimation that, as Church doctrine would counsel, one can bring about relief for departed souls in torment simply by offering up the appropriate form of prayer. Moreover, the devils seem transparently powerless. They espouse a self-defeating illogicality in threatening Owein's disobedience to them with those very torments that await the damned, and the temporary enjoyment of transitory delights they promise are clearly inferior to Heaven's eternal joys. Yet, a problematic concluding anecdote, told as a warning against the devil's wiles, contributes to the troubling of this vision. A devil who has failed to corrupt humanity is himself soundly beaten. The priest who was his intended target escapes his clutches by mutilating himself rather than give in to his impulse to have intercourse with a girl in his charge, and subsequently places her in a convent. We learn of this young woman only that she has agreed to the priest's sinful proposition. The abruptness of the narration raises characteristically complex questions of responsibility and morality that in turn prompt us to revisit the moral straightforwardness of Owein's vision, and its applicability to the human condition.[10]

Women's voices offer their audiences the opportunity to debate meaning and interpretation while acknowledging that gender matters, making it important to chart how women themselves might receive such literature. Questions of authorship apart, London, British Library, MS Additional 70513 provides valuable evidence of the *Life of St Audrey*'s place in religious women's spiritual experience. This significant collection of Anglo-Norman saints' lives contains the unique copy of *Audrey*, as well as copies of the Barking *Edward* and *Catherine*. It was donated to Campsey nunnery, Norfolk, probably in the early fourteenth century, to be read at meal-times. These lives are well suited to a recreational but still sober milieu. Entertaining, humorous, erudite, intellectually probing, and dazzlingly literary, they rework human social relationships to spiritual purpose.

The *Life of St Audrey* witnesses to the long-lived vitality of this saint's cult. Æthelthryth (d. 679), daughter of King Anna of the East Angles, had two chaste marriages, to a minor prince, Tondberht, and to Ecgfrith of Northumbria, before, as a religious, she founded Ely (*c.*672). Marie's story initially belongs to a recognizable hagiographic narrative type, that of the resolute virgin who forsakes men to vow herself to Christ, 'the Husband Who can never die' (*Life of St Audrey*, v. 1166). At the same time, *Audrey* has a keen eye for concrete realities. The poem emphasizes how the saint uses land dowered to her to further her spiritual ambitions. She exercises a shrewd control of material resources that would have been of interest to high-status, once-married, medieval women, for whom she historically provides a practical model for a religious career.[11] Marie's account is also pleasingly inclusive, for Audrey combines in her practical spirituality the traditionally discrete virtuous models offered to women by the active busy housewife Martha and the contemplative Mary, the conditions for whose untroubled meditation on spiritual matters it is usually Martha's lot to provide (*Life of St Audrey*, vv. 1229–49).

In Ely's history, traumatic rupture owes more to Danish violence than to Norman conquest; sacked in 870, it was refounded as a male institution in 970. Audrey's own miracle-working body (as in the poem) provides continuity when Ely is materially destroyed, and in this stout defender of the foundation's rights the monks of Ely had a powerful figurehead for their cause.[12] Marie's presentation is more personalized. Half of *Audrey*'s 4,625 lines concern post-mortem miracles and visions. In death a vigilant custodian of Ely's interests and a jealous promoter of her own cult, Audrey proves a miracle-working friend to believers. She also proves an implacable enemy to those who cross her, from the desecrating Dane (*Life of St Audrey*, vv. 2429–42) and the cheating Norman (*Life of St Audrey*, vv. 3005–26) to those negligent in honouring her, whom she threatens with sudden 'cruel death' (*Life of St Audrey*, vv. 2835–40). Audrey's sometimes remarkably aggressive visitations offer powerfully satisfying vengeance fantasies. These stories of believers and non-believers also contribute to a cumulative memorialization that is the poem itself, a text Marie authorizes as Audrey's votary, having presented her poem initially as a 'good work' written to 'good purpose' (*Life of St Audrey*, v. 1). 'One is indeed foolish who forgets herself', notes Marie pragmatically, and she is careful to ensure she is 'remembered' (*Life of St Audrey*, vv. 4623–5) for her literary commemoration of 'glorious...Saint Audrey' (*Life of St Audrey*, v. 4618).

The *Life of St Edward the Confessor*, translated by a nun of Barking, is similarly spiritually and politically aware. The canonization (1161) of Edward, a king of both Saxon and Norman lineage, was itself politically driven. As Wogan-Browne points out, it was probably astute of Barking to align itself, via translation, with the political continuity that Aelred of Rievaulx's 1163 Latin *Life* of Edward traced for the line of Henry II, its dedicatee. It is significant also that one manuscript seamlessly assimilates the nun's translation at the appropriate point in a chronicle, Wace's *Brut*.[13] History is both moralized (bad things happen to bad people) and allegorized. Edward's early exile is compared to spiritual exile, and his resistance of the Danes (themselves 'devils') offered as a figure of how 'we' must fight sin (*Life of*

St Edward the Confessor, vv. 749–82). But the nun's central concern is with how Edward safeguards his chastity within the 'weak vessel' (*Life of St Edward the Confessor*, v. 1107) of his body. This chastity is described as '*fin amur*' or exquisite love, in which Edith, his queen, gladly shares (*Life of St Edward the Confessor*, vv. 1343–86). Chastity becomes a political force, as well as the spiritual connection between Edward, Edith, and God. It is the origin of Edward's miraculous powers of healing, whether of his individual subjects or of his own country, which prospers in his care, and of his gift of prophecy.

In the surviving fragment of her prologue, the nun says she knows only a 'false French of England' (*Life of St Edward the Confessor*, v. 7), a phrase that modern scholars have turned against both her ability and Anglo-Norman itself. She asks for those who have learnt their French 'elsewhere' to emend her work accordingly. With these words, however, the writer is also locating herself in a particular cultural milieu at least as much as she modestly recognizes her limitations. Her perfectly grammatical exposition of a supposed linguistic and literary incompetence offers a competitive riposte to male scholarly snobbery.[14] In her epilogue, the nun names only the community of Barking, where she is a 'servant' of Christ (*Life of St Edward the Confessor*, vv. 5304–7). She shows the humility appropriate to a hagiographer, while her prayer that we may one day join the blessed in Heaven also registers a pious wish that the 'presumption' (*Life of St Edward the Confessor*, v. 5319) of translating Edward's life might be rewarded with spiritual translation.

Clemence of Barking's *Life of St Catherine*, the first extant insular vernacular account of this popular virgin saint, was itself evidently popular, anthologized with other saints' lives in England and abroad, and its lines borrowed for preaching purposes.[15] If there are theological and stylistic parallels with the earlier *Edward*, Clemence sounds more like Marie de France in her self-authorizing introduction, eager to use her intellectual gifts morally (*Life of St Catherine*, vv. 1–10). Of the three lives, this is perhaps the most sustainedly 'poetic', while also theologically probing. Saint Catherine defeats fifty philosophers appointed by the Emperor Maxentius to turn her from Christianity. When Catherine converts them instead, and refuses Maxentius's overtures to her, she is imprisoned, but Christ visits and sustains her, and she converts both the Emperor's wife and his captain, Porphiry. A torture machine devised for her is miraculously destroyed, the Emperor's wife and Porphiry killed, and Catherine is finally decapitated, her body translated to Mount Sinai.

Clemence's great achievement is to draw her courtly female religious audience in, not only (as *Edward* does) by giving a spiritual dimension to the language of *fin amur* or secular love, but by sustaining the spiritual force of that register, suggesting that only in relation to love of Christ, the perfect lover, can such language find its perfection. 'I love him so much that I cannot be parted from him; for I love him alone, and him alone do I desire' (*Life of St Catherine*, vv. 1365–6) explains Catherine, while the Emperor's abuse of love language, as when he asks his wife how they can live without one another even as he prepares her death (*Life of St Catherine*, vv. 2175–6), exposes him as pathologically self-deluded. At the same time, Clemence herself incorporates the finer details of current theological debate and proves herself more than a match for the saint's Latin hagiographer. She draws, for example, on Anselm of Canterbury's (d. 1109) writings on Christ's power and volition in becoming man and dying for humankind, in fine, punning poetry that conveys complex theology through French wordplay on being and time (*fust* [was], and *fruit* [fruit]) to represent Christ as the fruit of the cross that fully restores what Adam lost through the forbidden fruit of the tree in Paradise (*Life of St Catherine*, vv. 977–90).[16]

These female poets worked within a multidisciplinary and multilingual culture that gave them the means and the space to innovate with skill and versatility. Women used the medium of Anglo-Norman, as writers and patrons, to contribute to and shape mainstream culture, both clerical and secular, and they continued to do so throughout the medieval period, especially with regard to lay devotional literature, as later chapters demonstrate.

Notes

1. Elizabeth M. Tyler, 'From Old English to Old French', in *Language and Culture in Medieval Britain: The French of England, c.1100–c.1500*, ed. Jocelyn Wogan-Browne *et al.* (York: York Medieval Press, 2009), pp. 164–78. This volume is an excellent guide to current trends in Anglo-Norman studies.

2. Rachel Cusk, publisher's review for Gabriel Weston, *Direct Red: A Surgeon's Story* (London: Vintage, 2010), inside cover.

3. Marie de France, *Lais*, ed. Alfred Ewert (Oxford: Blackwell, 1944); *The Lais of Marie de France*, trans. Glyn S. Burgess and Keith Busby, 2nd edn. (Harmondsworth: Penguin, 1999); Marie de France, *Fables*, ed. and trans. Harriet Spiegel (Toronto: University of Toronto Press, 1994); *Saint Patrick's Purgatory: A Poem by Marie de France*, trans. Michael J. Curley (Binghamton: NY: Medieval and Renaissance Texts and Studies, 1993). All in-text references to these texts are to these editions.

4. Virginia Blanton, *Signs of Devotion: The Cult of St. Aethelthryth in Medieval England, 695–1615* (University Park, PA: Pennsylvania State University Press, 2007); June Hall McCash, '*La vie seinte Audree*: A Fourth Text by Marie de France?', *Speculum*, 77.3 (2002), 744–77; William MacBain, 'Anglo-Norman Women Hagiographers', in *Anglo-Norman Anniversary Essays*, ed. Ian Short (London: Anglo-Norman Text Society, 1993), pp. 235–50. All in-text references to the text are to *The Life of Saint Audrey: A Text by Marie de France*, trans. and ed. June Hall McCash and Judith Clark Barban (Jefferson, NC, and London: McFarland, 2006).

5. Nun of Barking, *La vie d'Edouard le confesseur: poème anglo-normand du XIIe siècle*, ed. Östen Södergård (Uppsala: Almqvist and Wiksells, 1948); *The Life of St. Catherine by Clemence of Barking*, ed. William MacBain, Anglo-Norman Texts 18 (Oxford: Blackwell, 1964). All in-text references to these texts are to these editions. See also *The Life of St Catherine*, in *Virgin Lives and Holy Deaths: Two Exemplary Biographies for Anglo-Norman Women*, trans. Jocelyn Wogan-Browne and

Glyn S. Burgess (London: Everyman, 1996); on common authorship of *Edward* and *Catherine*, see the relevant contributions to Jennifer Brown and Donna Bussell (eds.), *Barking Abbey: Authorship and Authority* (Woodbridge: Boydell and Brewer, forthcoming 2011).

6. See Jennifer Summit, 'Women and Authorship', in *The Cambridge Companion to Medieval Women's Writing*, ed. Carolyn Dinshaw and David Wallace (Cambridge: Cambridge University Press, 2003), pp. 91–108 (p. 95).

7. *La Vie Seint Edmund le rei*, ed. Hilding Kjellman (Göteborg: Wettergren and Kerber, 1935), vv. 35–48.

8. *Jane Austen's Letters*, ed. Deirdre Le Faye (Oxford: Oxford University Press, 1995), p. 323.

9. *St. Patrick's Purgatory*, trans. Curley, pp. 22–6.

10. See also Roberta L. Krueger, 'Marie de France', in *Cambridge Companion*, ed. Dinshaw and Wallace, pp. 172–83 (p. 181).

11. Jocelyn Wogan-Browne, 'Rerouting the Dower: The Anglo-Norman Life of St. Audrey by Marie (of Chatteris?)', in *Power of the Weak: Studies on Medieval Women*, ed. Jennifer Carpenter and Sally-Beth MacLean (Urbana: University of Illinois Press, 1995), pp. 27–56 (pp. 41–3); Blanton, *Signs of Devotion*, pp. 173–228.

12. Blanton, *Signs of Devotion*, pp. 132–71.

13. Jocelyn Wogan-Browne, *Saints' Lives and Women's Literary Culture, c.1150–1300: Virginity and its Authorizations* (Oxford: Oxford University Press, 2001), pp. 250–1, 249–50.

14. Delbert Russell, ' "Sun num n'i vult dire a ore": Identity Matters at Barking Abbey', in *Barking Abbey*, ed. Brown and Bussell. My thanks to Professor Russell for so generously sharing his work with me pre-publication.

15. *St. Catherine*, ed. MacBain, pp. xv–xx; Wogan-Browne, *Saints' Lives*, pp. 243–4.

16. Wogan-Browne, *Saints' Lives*, pp. 227–45.

4
Women Writers in Wales

Jane Cartwright

In a ground-breaking article on Welsh women's poetry published in *Y Traethodydd* in 1986, Kathryn Curtis, Marged Haycock, Elin ap Hywel, and Ceridwen Lloyd-Morgan highlighted the importance of uncovering poetry composed by women before 1800 in an attempt to counterbalance the gender-biased view of Wales's past and called for further research on Welsh women writers.[1] Anthologies of Welsh poetry published in the twentieth century frequently gave the impression that the renowned hymn-writer Ann Griffiths (1776–1805) was the first Welsh woman whose verse had survived.[2] Yet Ann herself knew otherwise. At her home in Dolwar Fach, in the parish of Llanfihangel-yng-Ngwynfa, a manuscript preserved some of the work of the fifteenth-century Welsh poet Gwerful Mechain. Since Gwerful's poetry was still recounted orally in the area up until the nineteenth century and she was also reputedly buried in the churchyard at Llanfihangel-yng-Ngwynfa, it is highly likely that Ann Griffiths was familiar with at least some of Gwerful's work.[3] Other named female poets writing in Welsh during the period 1430–1555 include Gwerful Fychan (b. *c.*1430), Gwenllïan ferch Rhirid Flaidd (*fl. c.*1460), Alis ferch Gruffudd ab Ieuan ap Llywelyn Fychan (b. *c.*1500), Catrin ferch Gruffudd ap Hywel (*fl. c.*1500–55) and Elsbeth Fychan (*fl. c.*1530).

The pioneering article by Curtis *et al.* marked the beginning of a new interest in medieval Welsh women's poetry and several valuable studies have appeared since then (in Welsh and English), many by some of the original contributors.[4] In 1993, Ceridwen Lloyd-Morgan noted in her important contribution to Carol M. Meale's edition of *Women and Literature in Britain, 1150–1500*: 'the poetry itself is almost entirely unpublished, there are no proper editions of women's poetry earlier than the works of the eighteenth-century hymnist Ann Griffiths, and only in the last few years have a few examples of criticism appeared'.[5] Fortunately, the twenty-first century has seen the publication of reliable editions of Welsh women's medieval poetry including Nerys Ann Howells's edition of the poetry of Gwerful Mechain[6] and Cathryn Charnell-White's invaluable anthology of

Welsh women's poetry *Beirdd Ceridwen: Blodeugerdd Barddas o Ganu Menywod hyd tua 1800.*[7] This chapter aims to highlight some of the major milestones in the study of women's writing in Wales, provide an up-to-date survey of the subject, and discuss a selection of the poems produced in the period 1430–1555. Although women are frequently referred to, described, and eulogized in Welsh poetry throughout the medieval period, there would appear to be no extant poetry by women prior to *c.*1430. In the late Middle Ages and the early modern period there was a flurry of literary activity by women in Wales. Since it is often difficult to date poems precisely, I have avoided strictly imposing an artificial cut-off date of 1500 in this chapter and the present study will also include female poets writing in the first half of the sixteenth century whose work spanned the period before, during, and after the Reformation.

Accurately establishing authorship is one of the first problems encountered in any study which involves discussing the work of a particular medieval or early modern poet. Given that relatively few poems have survived by each of the female authors and these circulated orally for many years before being recorded in writing, it is extremely difficult to establish authenticity and use stylistic features to determine which particular poems belong to a particular named individual. Poems attributed in the manuscripts to Gwerful Fychan are also attributed to Gwerful Mechain; one *englyn* (short poem) attributed to Gwerful Mechain which chastises the poet's father for marrying a much younger woman, occurs in a slightly different version attributed to Alis ferch Gruffudd ab Ieuan. Cathryn Charnell-White suggests that the *englyn* may refer to Alis's father's second marriage to Alis ferch John Owen and Ceridwen Lloyd-Morgan proposes that the poem, which is attributed to five different poets in all, became a popular traditional verse upon which each poet put her own slightly different stamp.[8]

Other *englynion* attributed to Alis's sister Catrin ferch Gruffudd ab Ieuan are also attributed to Catrin ferch Gruffudd ap Hywel of Llanddeilionen and Charnell-White argues convincingly that they are most likely the work of Catrin ferch Gruffudd ap Hywel who was married to Robert ap Rhys, a Catholic priest. Unofficial marriages to Catholic clergy were common in Wales at this time. Their son became the parson of Llanddeiniolen and the intensely spiritual nature of Catrin's poetry is devoutly Catholic. In one poem she prays and weeps in her bed at night, visualizing Christ's suffering at the Crucifixion; confessing her sins, she prepares for death.[9] The anguish expressed in the poem perhaps suggests that she was ill at the time of the poem's composition or that she anticipated death with both fear and relief. In another series of *englynion* she writes on a similar theme, but is openly critical of religious reforms at the Protestant Reformation, lamenting the fact that 'No mass is to be had by any priest':

> Y côr a'r allor a ddrylliwyd – ar gam
>   Ac ymaith y taflwyd,
>   A'r Lading a erlidiwyd
>   O gôr a llan y Gŵr llwyd.[10]

[The choir and altar have been destroyed – wrongly
And cast aside,
The Latin language has been persecuted
[and ousted] from the choir and church of the holy Man.]

The poetry is a rare testament to a Welsh woman's personal reaction to the assault on her religion and it is interesting to note that Latin is her chosen language of worship rather than Welsh, although Welsh is naturally the language she chooses for the literary expression of her religious beliefs. Latin, of course, symbolizes her allegiance to Catholicism. Charnell-White argues that, since Catrin ferch Gruffudd ab Ieuan and her family turned their back on Catholicism, it is unlikely that this Catrin (Alis's sister) is the author of the devotional poetry.

The same poems are not only attributed to poets with similar names, but also different poets from within the same family. A light-hearted poem to two 'smelly wanderers' from Anglesey who would quarrel when intoxicated is attributed most frequently to Alis ferch Gruffudd ab Ieuan, although one manuscript attributes this to her sister Gwen. The poet calls upon the Virgin Mary to assist her in handcuffing the two drunks together, as she persuades them to make peace with each other. In another poem the 'three hinds from Denbighshire' (presumably Alis and her two sisters Catrin and Gwen) offer advice to potential lovers.[11]

Welsh women's poetry is often interesting for the light it sheds on a variety of different relationships that 'real' women experienced (with lovers, husbands, siblings, and parents, as well as fellow poets). Alis described her ideal husband in two *englynion* which record the conflict which must frequently have arisen when a girl's father wished her to marry someone she considered to be repulsive:

> Hardd fedrus, gampus pes caid, a dewr
>   I daro o bai raid,
>   Mab o oedran cadarnblaid
>   A gwr o gorff gorau gaid.
>
> Fy nhad a dd'wede im hyn mai gorau
>   Im garu dyn gwrthun
>   A'r galon sydd yn gofyn
>   Gwas glân hardd ysgafn ei hun.

[Handsome, able, excellent, if possible – and
Brave to strike a blow if need be,
A young man of robust age
And a man with the best possible body.

My father would tell me this – that I should
Best love an abhorrent man,
And my heart desires
A handsome young man who sleeps lightly.][12]

And in another *englyn* she expresses sadness and disappointment when her partner leaves her for Gwen o'r Dalar. Reconciliation with her brother, Morgan Fychan, is the subject of Elsbeth Fychan's lengthy poem written *c.*1530: troubled by their quarrel, she seeks Christ's help to make amends and compares herself to the penitent Mary Magdalene as she offers to wash her brother's feet and dry them with her hair.

Clyw dy chwaer a'r feddwl du[wiol]
A chalon bur edifeiriol;
Yr hon âi i'r Purdan drosod,
Yn dymuno cael dy gymod.[13]

[Listen to your sister with holy mind
And a pure repentant heart;
She who would go to purgatory for you,
wishes to make amends.]

Of the thirty-two poems attributed to Gwerful Mechain in various manuscripts, Nerys Ann Howells accepts thirteen poems into the 'canon', rejects fourteen, and concedes that a further five poems are likely to have been composed by Gwerful.[14] Not surprisingly none of the poems survive in Gwerful's hand and the earliest manuscript which preserves her work (London, British Library, Add MS 14967) belongs to the first quarter of the sixteenth century. This difficulty in establishing authorship is not unique to the work of female poets and there is still some debate regarding the canon of Dafydd ap Gwilym, one of Wales's most prolific and well-known poets.[15] Gwerful Mechain's 'Cywydd y gont' [Cywydd to the cunt] is attributed to Dafydd ap Gwilym in some manuscripts.

Helen Fulton has criticized the tendency to collect together all of the 'authentic' work of one 'genuine' author, as though by the very act of naming the poet we lend more authority to the text. Successful marketing demands that a poet is named and there are, no doubt, other poems by women lurking amongst the many 'anonymous' poems, as well as those of uncertain authorship. Fulton warns against the pitfalls involved in creating a biography for a poet based on the details found in his/her poetry since creadigaethau yw'r testun a'r awdur fel ei gilydd...n[i]d oes modd ail-rithrio'r beirdd mewn unrhyw ffordd sy'n hanesyddol arwyddocaol, dim ond eu hadeiladu ar sail tystiolaeth y cerddi a briodolir iddynt dro ar ôl tro.[16]

[the text and author are both creations...it is not possible to bring the poet back to life in any way which is historically significant: one can only build them up on the basis of the evidence found in the poetry which is attributed to them time and time again.]

This problem is particularly acute when attempting to build up a biography of Welsh women writers on the basis of the incomplete and fragmentary evidence which survives and perhaps one can only acknowledge from the outset that the picture produced will inevitably be imperfect.

One example of how a poem taken literally can create a rather mislead-ing picture of the poet's life is 'Gwerful wyf o gwr y lan' [I'm Gwerful from the riverbank], a *cywydd* (an important metrical form in Welsh poetry) attributed to Gwerful Mechain in which the poet is a landlady of a tavern called the Ferry and the purpose of her poem is to request a harp from a local man called Ifan ap Dafydd. As tempting as it is to imagine the jubi-lant Gwerful entertaining the guests at her packed public house and singing her poetry to the accompaniment of the harp, Howells rejects this *cywydd* from the Gwerful Mechain canon and Enid Roberts suggests that the poem should be attributed to Gwerful ferch Gutun who lived in Tal-y-sarn and was composing poetry at least a century later than Gwerful Mechain.[17] Stu-dents studying medieval poetry who discover the poem in an anthology attributed to Gwerful Mechain and read how it is likely that Gwerful in this poem is taking on board the *persona* of a landlady, may be forgiven for being confused.

Gwerful Fychan of Caer-gai (b. *c*.1430), the daughter of Ieuan Fychan and Mallt ferch Llywelyn, came from the same area as Gwerful Mechain (Maldwyn). She was married to the poet Tudur Penllyn and no doubt moved in the same literary circles as her husband, possibly learning the craft of strict-metre poetry from him. Charnell-White tentatively attributes five poems to Gwerful Fychan including two which appear in *Gwaith Gwerful Mechain* but are ascribed 'uncertain authorship'. In one poem (a series of two *englynion*), she describes struggling home through the snow, surrounded by the freezing cold, mountainous Welsh landscape:

> [...] Eira gwyn ar fryn fry – a'm dallodd,
> A'm dillad yn gwlychu;
> O! Dduw gwyn, nid oedd genny'
> Obaith y down byth i dŷ![18]

[White snow on the hill above blinded me
And my clothes were soaking wet
Oh dear God I thought I had no
hope of ever reaching a house.]

Two other poems attributed to her refer to horses: in one *englyn* she seeks
hay for an old horse and in a *cywydd* to a splendid stallion she describes the
lithe, strong movements of the horse as he gallops and jumps the river. The
latter poem is problematic as, at some point, it appears to have become
conflated with a *cywydd* by Tudur Aled requesting a horse from Dafydd ab
Owain, abbot of the Cistercian Abbey of Aberconwy: twelve lines from Tudur
Aled's poem appear to have become inserted into Gwerful's in eighteenth-
century copies.[19] Gwerful Fychan and Tudur Penllyn had two children, both
of whom were poets – Ieuan ap Tudur Penllyn and Gwenllïan ferch Rhirid
Flaidd.

For several years Gwenllïan was thought to be the earliest recorded Welsh
female poet (*fl. c.*1180–1200), for confusingly Gwenllïan's *nom de plume* associates her with the head of her ancestral line Rhirid Flaidd rather than
her father Tudur Penllyn. Dafydd Johnston identified Gwenllïan in the
genealogies and demonstrated that the style of her one surviving *englyn*
is far more in keeping with the style of the Poets of the Gentry than the
Poets of the Princes. Thus there has been a significant shift in the dating of Gwenllïan's unique *englyn*: she is now thought to have been active
*c.*1460 and was therefore a contemporary of Gwerful Mechain. Her tongue-
in-cheek four-line response to a male poet from Anglesey (possibly Gruffudd
ap Dafydd ap Gronw) who accused her of fleeing poverty in Penllyn and
coming to Anglesey in search of bread is somewhat similar to the attitude
displayed in some of Gwerful Mechain's feisty debate poems:

> Nid er da bara'n y byd – o'r diwedd
> Y deuai ferch Ririd
> At y gwas bras o Brysaeddfed;
> Adnebydd dywydd dafad.[20]

> [Not for any bread at all
> did the daughter of Rhirid at last come
> to the uncouth youth from Prysaeddfed;
> She feels a sheep's swelling.]

The poem has been understood as a riposte in which Gwenllïan confronts
Gruffudd with the fact that she's pregnant and that he is the father. Whilst
this is perhaps the most likely interpretation, the final line in the *englyn* is
rather opaque and other interpretations are also possible. One does not necessarily have to assume that Gwenllïan is comparing herself to the sheep

of course. By referring to herself in the third person and highlighting the importance of her family line, her primary concern seems to be to raise her own status and depict herself in a position of power. An alternative meaning for the final line could be that she 'recognizes when the pregnant sheep's udder is swollen with milk' and the punch line could be that she has not come to beg for crumbs from Gruffudd's table, but intends to take him for far more.[21] A more radical rereading of the final line, splitting the difficult word 'dywydd' into two – 'Adnebydd dy wŷdd' [She knows your lineage] – implies that Gwenllïan is insulting the male poet directly, casting doubt on the status of his family line.[22] Contrary to what he has suggested in his *englyn* (that Gwenllïan is poor), she emphasizes that she is of superior status. Gwenllïan's father wrote praise poetry to the household at Prysaeddfed and Dafydd Johnston suggests that Gwenllïan may have visited with her father.[23] She would almost certainly have been familiar with other poets attracted to the house.

Gwerful Mechain refers to advice that she is given by an older woman called Gwenllïan (possibly Gwenllïan ferch Rhirid Flaidd) in her *cywydd* to jealous wives. Gwerful, the daughter of Hywel Fychan of Llanfechain, was familiar with a number of Welsh poets and moved in the same literary circles as Dafydd Llwyd o Fathafarn, Llywelyn ap Gutun, Ieuan Dyfi, and Guto'r Glyn.[24] She is the only Welsh female poet by whom a substantial corpus of medieval poetry has survived and it is entirely appropriate that her work has been included in the Poets of the Gentry series rather than published in isolation, for her poetry makes an important contribution to the Welsh bardic tradition and the study of fifteenth-century Welsh culture. As noted by Katie Gramich and Catherine Brennan:

> Gwerful Mechain's poetry belongs centrally to the Welsh bardic tradition: it is clearly not part of a feminine sub-culture nor of a separate female tradition; on the contrary, Mechain engages in poetic dialogues with her male contemporaries, using the same forms, metre, tropes, and vocabulary as they. Certainly, she often adopts a female point of view, and takes them to task for the arrogance and exclusiveness of their male stances, but she attacks them not from the position of marginality or outsiderness but rather as a full participant in the tradition.[25]

A number of Gwerful's poems were written in response to poems by other poets. In an extremely skilful *cywydd* to the poet Ieuan Dyfi she responds to one of his poems in which he provides a vitriolic character assassination of his lover Anni Goch and criticizes the whole of womankind. Ieuan composed five poems in all to Anni and, when their relationship turned sour, he complained bitterly in a poem to Anni that he was the innocent party naming a whole host of other men who had suffered at the hands of women. Gwerful Mechain responded by defending Anni and naming various virtuous women in her *cywydd* to Ieuan.[26] The list of heroines and admirable females includes women from the Bible, the Apocrypha, classical and native Welsh texts and demonstrates the breadth of Gwerful's knowledge and learning. A number of the women praised are associated with male wrongdoers such as Judas Iscariot or Pontius Pilate and, at one point in the *cywydd*, Gwerful makes the point that 'No girl, adulterer [...] has ever raped a man.' This is particularly poignant because Llinos B. Smith has uncovered references in the records of the Hereford Consistory Court which reveal that Anni alleged that Ieuan Dyfi had raped her.[27] Her husband, John Lippard, was accused of selling her to Ieuan, but lest we imagine that Anni was entirely the innocent party, the court records also reveal that she admitted committing adultery twice and was also accused of attempting to kill her husband.

Gwerful's religious poetry was perhaps her most popular and widely cir-culated work. Her *cywydd* 'Dioddefaint Crist' [Christ's suffering] is extant in sixty-eight manuscripts which contain a large number of variant readings, no doubt due to the fact that the poem circulated orally for many years.[28] The poem focuses on Christ's Passion and his Resurrection and ends with a plea that God, the Holy Trinity, will pardon the poet from purgatory and grant everlasting grace.

The strong sexual nature of the *ymryson*, bardic debate, between Gwerful Mechain and Dafydd Llwyd o Fathafarn certainly gives the impression that the two poets were lovers; yet their sexual banter and boasting does not have to be taken literally and the poems are more humorous than they are erotic. Gwerful was married to John ap Llywelyn Fychan and they had a daughter called Mawd (possibly named after Gwerful's sister). It is often queried whether Gwerful composed her erotic poetry before her marriage to John, presumably because it would have been unseemly for a married woman to recite poetry of a sexual nature to other male poets. Yet if the pri-mary purpose of the poetry was entertainment, it is not beyond the realms of possibility that Gwerful continued to entertain in this manner after her marriage, especially considering the self-confidence she displays in her liter-ary work and it is difficult to imagine that her strong sense of humour either waned or was tamed over time.

Nevertheless, in one *englyn*, which was supposedly written to her husband, she refers to an abusive domestic relationship and fantasizes about wreaking violent revenge on him for beating her:

> Dager drwy goler dy galon – ar osgo
> I asgwrn dy ddwyfron;
> Dy lin a dyr, dy law'n don,
> A'th gleddau i'th goluddion.[29]

> [[Stab] a dagger through your ribs to your heart – on a slant
> to your breast bone;
> May your knee[s] break, your hand[s] wither,
> and your sword [thrust] into your intestines.]

Only the title provided in the postscript, 'Gwerrvul Mechain yw gwr am ei churo' [Gwerful Mechain to her husband for beating her], suggests that the poem was composed in the context of domestic abuse, since in the poem itself the author is the perpetrator of violence rather than the victim. However, the postscript explanation appears in various guises in all of the manuscripts. Howells suggests that the poem may not necessarily refer to Gwerful's own relationship with her husband and that it could be seen as a kind of cathartic therapy written on behalf of all women who have suffered physical abuse.[30]

In Gwerful Mechain's 'Cywydd y gont' [Cywydd to the cunt] she berates male poets for praising every part of the female body, except the genitalia, in their courtly love poetry. The poem is as much a humorous rebuke which parodies poems in the courtly love genre, as it is a celebration of the female body. In an extended metaphor drawing on imagery from clothing and the natural world which usually feature in courtly love poetry in quite a different context, Gwerful describes the 'warm quim':

> Sawden awdl, sidan ydiw,
> sêm fach, len ar gont wen wiw,
> lleiniau mewn man ymannerch,
> y llwyn sur, llawn yw o serch,
> fforest falch iawn, ddawn ddifreg,
> ffris ffraill, ffwrwr dwygaill deg,
> breisglwyn merch, drud annerch dro,
> berth addwyn, Duw'n borth iddo.

> [Sultan of an ode, it is silk,
> little seam, curtain on a fine bright cunt,
> flaps in a place of greeting,
> the sour grove, it is full of love,
> very proud forest, faultless gift,
> tender frieze, fur of a fine pair of testicles,
> a girl's thick grove, circle of precious greeting,
> lovely bush, God save it.][31]

Rather than coyly arrange a tryst in the forest, in this poem Gwerful Mechain's metaphorical 'very proud forest' becomes the true location for love in a frank and confident expression of female sexuality.

The erotic nature of some of Gwerful's poetry no doubt explains why Leslie Harries decided to omit her poetry from a collection of Middle Welsh verse he published in 1953. Harries included early editions of Gwerful's poetry in his MA thesis in 1933, but when it came to publishing the work he made the excuse that there was not enough room in the collection for her poetry as well.[32] Harries, much-maligned for comparing Gwerful Mechain to a prostitute, was quite simply a product of his era. He was no doubt well aware of the fact that a 1950s Welsh audience was perhaps not ready to read Gwerful's overtly sexual and often bawdy poetry. Yet Harries obviously had enough foresight to include Gwerful in his academic thesis. Since the late 1980s scholars have been at pains to emphasize that Gwerful's erotic poetry forms only one aspect of her work; yet it could also be argued that to a twenty-first-century audience this is perhaps her most refreshing and intriguing poetry. Now that her work has been edited (along with the work of other Welsh female poets), we realize that women in Wales were not in fact totally excluded from the mysteries of strict-metre poetry; bardic training was passed on from one family member to another; and women not only sponsored, heard, and enjoyed strict-metre poetry, but also took part in bardic debates, composed poetry on a wide variety of different themes, and, on occasions, played an active role in the literary circles of their day.

Roughly three hundred years before Ann Griffiths composed her hymns orally, female poets were expressing a variety of emotions in complex Welsh verse. They shed light on religious beliefs, familial and marital relationships, and a variety of experiences in fifteenth- and sixteenth-century Wales. Violence, vengeance, reconciliation, love, sex, humour, and hatred are all expressed in the poetry – often with a high level of wit and intelligence providing viewpoints which strike us as surprisingly modern.[33]

Notes

1. Kathryn Curtis, Marged Haycock, Elin ap Hywel, and Ceridwen Lloyd-Morgan, 'Beirdd Benywaidd yng Nghymru cyn 1800', *Y Traethodydd*, 141 (1986), 12–27 (12).
2. *The Oxford Book of Welsh Verse*, ed. Thomas Parry (Oxford: Oxford University Press, 1962); *Welsh Verse*, trans. Tony Conran (Bridgend: Seren, 1967); *Cywyddau Cymru*, ed. Arthur Hughes, 3rd edn. (Bangor: Jarvis a Foster, 1926).
3. Aberystwyth, National Library of Wales, Cwrtmawr MS 1491 (Llyfr Dolwar Fach); E. Wyn James, 'Ann Griffiths: Y Cefndir Barddol', *Llên Cymru*, 23 (2000), 147–70 (168).
4. For example, Marged Haycock, 'Merched Drwg a Merched Da: Ieuan Dyfi v. Gwerful Mechain', *Ysgrifau Beirniadol*, 16 (1990), 97–110; Ceridwen Lloyd-Morgan, '"Gwerful, ferch ragorol fain": Golwg Newydd ar Gwerful Mechain', *Ysgrifau Beirniadol*, 16 (1990), 84–96; Ceridwen Lloyd-Morgan, 'Oral Composition and Written Transmission: Welsh Women's Poetry from the Middle Ages and Beyond', *Trivium*, 26 (1991), 89–102.
5. Ceridwen Lloyd-Morgan, 'Women and their Poetry in Medieval Wales', in *Women and Literature in Britain, 1150–1500*, ed. Carol M. Meale (Cambridge: Cambridge University Press, 1993), pp. 183–201 (p. 183).
6. *Gwaith Gwerful Mechain ac Eraill*, ed. Nerys Ann Howells (Aberystwyth: Canolfan Uwchefrydiau Cymreig a Cheltaidd Prifysgol Cymru, 2001).
7. *Beirdd Ceridwen: Blodeugerdd Barddas o Ganu Menywod hyd tua 1800*, ed. Cathryn A. Charnell-White (Llandybïe: Cyhoeddiadau Barddas, 2005). See also *Welsh*

Women's Poetry, 1460–2001: An Anthology, ed. Katie Gramich and Catherine Brennan (Llandybïe: Honno, 2003), which includes English translations by Katie Gramich, and *Early Modern Poets (1520–1700): An Anthology*, ed. Jane Stevenson and Peter Davidson (Oxford: Oxford University Press, 2001), which includes the work of Alis ferch Gruffudd ab Ieuan and Catrin ferch Gruffudd ab Ieuan/Catrin ferch Gruffudd ap Hywel. Translations of the Welsh poems are my own unless otherwise stated. The translations provide a sense of the meaning of the original poems, but the complicated system of sound chiming, internal rhyme, and alliteration of the *cynghanedd* found in Welsh strict-metre poetry is unfortunately completely lost.

8. *Beirdd Ceridwen*, ed. Charnell-White, pp. 366–8.
9. Ibid., p. 368. C. Charnell-White, 'Barddoniaeth Ddefosiynol Catrin Ferch Gruffudd ap Hywel', *Dwned*, 7 (2001), 93–120. See also Nia Powell, 'Women and Strict-Metre Poetry in Wales', in *Women and Gender in Early Modern Wales*, ed. Michael Roberts and Simone Clarke (Cardiff: University of Wales Press, 2000), pp. 129–58 (pp. 135–6).
10. *Beirdd Ceridwen*, ed. Charnell-White, p. 91.
11. Ibid., pp. 75–7, 82–4, 364–8.
12. Powell, 'Women and Strict-Metre Poetry', p. 137.
13. *Beirdd Ceridwen*, ed. Charnell-White, p. 98.
14. *Gwaith Gwerful*, ed. Howells, pp. 26–31.
15. See the note on authorship by Dafydd Johnston, *Dafydd ap Gwilym.net* [online]. Swansea University (http:www.dafyddapgwilym.net, accessed 15 March 2010); Ann Parry Owen, '"Englynion bardd i'w wallt": Cerdd Arall gan Ddafydd ap Gwilym?', *Dwned*, 13 (2007), 47–75.
16. Helen Fulton, 'Awdurdod ac Awduriaeth: Golygu'r Cywyddwyr', in *Cyfoeth y Testun: Ysgrifau ar Lenyddiaeth Gymraeg yr Oesoedd Canol*, ed. Iestyn Daniel, Marged Haycock, Dafydd Johnston, and Jenny Rowland (Caerdydd: Gwasg Prifysgol Cymru, 2003), pp. 50–76 (p. 72).
17. Enid Pierce Roberts, *Dafydd Llwyd o Fathafarn*, Darlith Lenyddol Eisteddfod Genedlaethol Cymru, Maldwyn a'i Chyffiniau (1981), p. 12.
18. *Beirdd Ceridwen*, ed. Charnell-White, p. 46.
19. *Detholiad o Gywyddau Gofyn a Diolch*, ed. Bleddyn O. Huws (Caernarfon: Cyhoeddiadau Barddas, 1998), pp. 66–8; Dafydd Johnston, 'Gwenllïan Ferch Rhirid Flaidd', *Dwned*, 3 (1997), 27–32 (32).
20. Johnston, 'Gwenllïan', 27.
21. According to *Geiriadur Prifysgol Cymru* 1154 one meaning of 'dywydd' is the quantity of milk in a cow's udder which is about to calf.
22. Although this improves the internal rhyme and does away with the difficulty that 'dywydd' is not mutated after the concise verb 'Adnebydd' (present indicative of the third person singular 'adnabod'), the 'f' now remains unanswered in the *cynghanedd sain*, perhaps indicative of an amateur poet.
23. Johnston, 'Gwenllïan', p. 30.
24. *Gwaith Gwerful*, ed. Howells, pp. 4–16.
25. *Welsh Women's Poetry*, ed. Gramich and Brennan, pp. xvii–xviii.
26. For a detailed analysis of the poem see Haycock, 'Merched Drwg'.
27. Llinos B. Smith, 'Olrhain Anni Goch', *Llên Cymru*, 19 (1993), 107–26.
28. *Gwaith Gwerful*, ed. Howells, pp. 25, 49–62, 125–9.
29. Ibid., p. 115.
30. Ibid., p. 169.

31. *Canu Maswedd yr Oesoedd Canol Medieval Welsh Erotic Poetry*, ed. and trans. Dafydd Johnston (Caerdydd: Tafol, 1991), pp. 42–3.
32. Leslie Harries, 'Barddoniaeth Huw Cae Llwyd, Ieuan ap Huw Cae Llwyd, Ieuan Dyfi a Gwerful Mechain' (unpublished Master's thesis, University of Wales, Swansea, 1933); *Gwaith Huw Cae Llwyd ac Eraill*, ed. Leslie Harries (Caerdydd: Gwasg Prifysgol Cymru, 1953).
33. I would like to thank Cathryn Charnell-White, Dafydd Johnston, and Ann Parry Owen for discussing various aspects of this chapter with me and suggesting improvements. Any errors which remain are entirely my responsibility.

5
Medieval Antifeminism

Anke Bernau

The pervasive misogyny encountered in medieval writings, especially those that proliferated from the twelfth century onwards, had its roots in much older literary, philosophical, and religious traditions.[1] Drawing on the works of authors such as Aristotle (384–322 BCE), Ovid (43 BCE–18 CE), Tertullian (c.160–c.225), or St Jerome (c.342–420), we can see medieval authors making use of a diverse legacy that stretches far back into the past, emerging from both Judaic law and early Greek culture.[2] Despite their range of approaches, themes, and purposes, their different emphases and generic specificities, these sources tended to agree on the inferiority – physical, intellectual, and moral – of women. As Marbod of Rennes (c.1035–1123) sums it up: 'Woman the unhappy source, evil root, and corrupt offshoot, who brings to birth every sort of outrage throughout the world.'[3]

This ongoing discourse must be taken into account when thinking about medieval women's literary culture. Hearing and reading accounts of 'women's nature' undoubtedly would have coloured the ways in which medieval women thought about themselves, their social relations, and how they experienced and engaged with contemporary culture. As patrons, audiences, writers, or even just as members of a community, medieval women could not hope to avoid or ignore such representations; whether they accepted and perpetuated, or resisted and critiqued them, interaction on some level was inevitable.

Early Christianity inherited the older traditions outlined above and added to them its own ideas concerning, in particular, human sexuality. The writings of the early Church Fathers – such as Tertullian, Ambrose, Jerome, and Augustine – addressed the role and nature of humanity through a consideration of the nature of human sexuality, which was also a consideration of human salvation: this was not surprising since, after all, the Scriptures begin with an account of the Fall, whose main protagonists are a man, a woman, and Satan. The Fall of humanity is a narration not just of disobedience, but of pride, desire for knowledge, seduction, rebellion against authority, and punishment.

The disobedience of Adam and Eve to God – of the lower creation to the higher Creator – is, after the Fall, paralleled in their humanity: their bodies no longer obey the higher part of their nature, reason. Augustine believed that, before the Fall, human reason exerted full control over the body, yet rebellion and pride, in leading to disobedience and the Fall, then came to manifest themselves more fully. This does not only show itself in sickness, ageing, and, ultimately, in death, but also in unruly bodily desires that cannot be quelled easily by reason or will: the male erection is the most visible evidence for this. As Augustine writes: 'Sometimes the [sexual] impulse is an unwanted intruder, sometimes it abandons the eager lover, and desire cools off in the body while it is still at boiling point in the mind.'[4] Thus the consequences of the Fall were not only mortality and mutability, but also the capitulation of reason to fleshly desire. In the Church Fathers' interpretations of this original drama we can find a consolidation of the gender differences outlined by earlier, non-Christian writers; the dualism they promoted continues to echo throughout Western culture in the nearly two millennia of Christianity that have followed, up until this day.

The division of the world into binary oppositions structures much Western thought before and after the advent of Christianity. Some of the main oppositions are, for instance, 'man' and 'woman'; 'strong' and 'weak'; 'soul' and 'body'; 'spiritual' and 'carnal'; or 'active' and 'passive'. These pairs are not self-contained, and the two terms that make up each one are not equal. Thus, 'man' is valued more highly than 'woman', just as 'soul' is valued more highly than 'body'. The pairs frequently speak to one another, with each 'higher' term suggesting a correlation with the other higher terms: 'man' is associated with strength, soul, spirit, and activity, whereas 'woman' is associated with weakness, body, carnality, and passivity. If we consider 'man' and 'woman' within this conceptual context, we can see how either one is interwoven with a range of other, associated qualities that are believed to reveal something about their respective ontology and character as well as worth.

According to Joyce E. Salisbury, the Church Fathers' dualistic world-view meant that they distinguished between 'that which was carnal (sexual) and that which was not (spiritual)'.[5] Each individual Christian had to choose which mode of life she would follow, whether to live spiritually or carnally. Christ and the saints were models as to how one might live a holy, spiritual life, yet this was a difficult path for normal humans to follow, since all humans were tainted by original sin. For some of the early Fathers, such as St Jerome, the difference between human nature before the Fall (prelapsarian) and human nature after the Fall (postlapsarian) was expressed through sexual difference: prelapsarian humanity was virginal; postlapsarian humanity was sexual. Thus, sexuality could become the very sign of fallen nature; this was compounded by the idea that original sin was passed on from parents to their children – children which had been generated by sexual activity.

While original sin affects all humans, there were also differences between the two constituent parts of humanity. Man was perceived to be more closely aligned with the spiritual, since he was made in God's image. Woman, who was made from Adam's rib, was more fully associated with the material world, and hence with carnality. Because of this, women were thought to be more in thrall to their senses and, through them, to sexual desire. The different natures of men and women required that the 'proper' – that is, the 'natural' – power relationship between them was maintained. Just as man owed obedience to God, woman owed obedience to man (as well as God). This view is evident in the following example of late-medieval marriage vows, which stipulate that a man will vow to 'have and to hold' his wife 'for better, for worse, for richer, for poorer, in sickness, and in health, till death do us part', while the equivalent vow for women is worded in the same manner except for the additional phrase stating that she will be 'cheerful and obedient, in bed and at board'.[6]

For women, the consequences of such an outlook were expressed most starkly in the hierarchical ordering of women according to their sexual status (which was believed to reflect also their spiritual status): thus, the thirteenth-century treatise on female virginity, *Holy Maidenhood*, tells its audience that there are three lawful conditions of womanhood – virginity, widowhood, and marriage – but they are not equal.[7] Virginity is the most perfect (and difficult!), while marriage comes only third, and this ranking also entails differing rewards in the afterlife. Any condition outside of these three sanctioned roles is not even mentioned. The high value early and medieval Christianity placed on virginity makes it unsurprising that much misogynous literature takes marriage as its subject. This is given added impetus after the Gregorian Reform of the mid-eleventh century aggressively promoted clerical celibacy.[8]

The openness that was said to characterize women's bodies, making them penetrable as well as causing them to exude bodily liquids such as menstrual blood and breast milk, was also thought to characterize their senses more generally. Thus, for instance, they were frequently associated with gossip, which was understood as an inability to control their speech. Woman's natural openness in turn explained why she was more fickle and open to influence – this was proven by the fact that Satan chose to approach Eve in the Garden of Eden, rather than Adam. Yet the Fall also showed that man was particularly susceptible to the persuasions and charms of woman, and the warnings to men about the dangers of listening to women show that this was a source of anxiety to Christian writers. Frequently repeated tropes are: that women are sexually voracious, lacking in moral virtue, emotionally fickle, irrational, and physically weaker than men.

As stated above, just as the ancient sources of medieval misogyny were varied, medieval misogyny also expressed itself in a range of discourses. This was not least because of the importance that medieval culture attached to the *auctoritas* [authority] provided by the past.[9] In relation to medieval ideas about natural philosophy, for instance, we can see the ongoing influence of such thinkers as Galen and Aristotle, throughout and even beyond the Middle Ages,[10] and, as we have seen, the authority of the early Church Fathers was also of immense importance. As Bernard of Chartres is alleged to have said in the twelfth century, contemporary (medieval) thinkers were like dwarves standing on the shoulders of giants. And medieval writers could easily find earlier authorities to confirm or draw on for the negative representations of women and of female 'nature' – regardless of whether they were writing conduct literature, anti-marriage satires, treatises on virginity or marriage, drama, or the comic and bawdy stories known as *fabliaux*.[11] Many of these genres thus drew on the same sources, resulting in a process of reiteration and mutual confirmation which must have brought with it a consolidation of their 'truth value', even as it also generated rebuttals and critiques.

Conduct literature is a good example of this: as Diane Bornstein notes, it is a particularly interesting source for understandings of gender, since such texts 'reveal a great deal about the roles women were expected to play in the Middle Ages, the restrictions they were supposed to observe, and the responsibilities they had to fulfil'.[12] Here, parents are frequently defined as people who do not just replicate themselves biologically through their offspring, but also morally and socially. All three of these categories bring with them expectations about 'proper' gender behaviour, which also intersects with expectations of social class. The values that a 'good' mother passes on to her daughter are defined as those which ensure that the daughter grows up *to be* her mother; this does not mean anything as vague as becoming a woman – it means becoming a certain kind of woman.

Anti-marriage writing, another long-lived and popular genre, could be either religious or secular, and included serious texts written by clergymen or monks warning men against women in general and wives in particular. They partake of the same characteristics that Kathleen Forni identifies as typical of misogynous literature – a use of 'proverbial lore and pastiche', which they draw on in order to warn 'readers of the atavistic deceptiveness, fickleness, and treachery of women'.[13] One common theme is that, while an unmarried maiden may *appear* meek and obedient, she will soon reveal her 'true' nature once she is married. As one poem, incorrectly attributed by the antiquarian John Stow (*c*.1525–1605) to Geoffrey Chaucer, warns its audience:

> Whan maydons ar weddyd and householdys have take,
> All theyre humylyté ys exylyd awey,
> And the cruell hertes begynneth to awake;
> They do all the besy cure that they can or may,
> To wex theyr housholdes maisters, the soth forto sey;
> Wherfore, ye yong men, I rede yow forthy,
> Beware alwey, the blynde eteth many a fly.[14]

Perhaps the most famous Middle English example that comments on this tradition is Geoffrey Chaucer's 'Wife of Bath's Prologue', which includes a veritable *tour de force* of misogynous truisms about the nature of women, particularly of wives. When the Wife recalls the 'Book of Wicked Wives' that her husband Jankyn used to read nightly, we can see a role-call of the most influential misogynous authors, as well as the resentment their textual authority causes in the Wife, who can only respond to the power of the book by tearing its pages:

> He hadde a booke that gladly, nyght and day,
> For his desport he wolde rede alway;
> He cleped it Valerie and Theofraste,
> At which book he lough alwey ful faste.
> And eek ther was somtyme a clerk at Rome,
> A cardinal, that highte Seinte Jerome,
> That made a book agayn Jovinian;
> In which book eek ther was Tertulan,
> Crisippus, Trotula, and Helowys,
> That was abbesse nat fer fro Parys,
> And eek the Parables of Salomon,
> Ovides Art, and bookes many on,
> And alle thise were bounden in o volume.[15]

As Alcuin Blamires remarks, 'antifeminist discourse proves to be such a "small world"', in which '[o]ld friends (or enemies) keep turning up over and over again'.[16] The very existence of Jankyn's book underlines the sheer ubiquity of material that presented women negatively. The ensuing fight between Jankyn and the Wife suggests that domestic strife could ensue as a result of such texts, though the Prologue is famously resistant to any straightforward interpretation of it as either misogynous or critical of misogyny.

Apart from anti-marriage literature, there was also a wide range of literary discourses that took as its subject matter amorous relations between men and women more generally. Forni notes that the different genres dealing with such topics 'rang[e] from the serious to the satirical ... the sentimental to the sophisticated' and 'includ[e] the panegyric, valentine, amorous complaint, lovers' dialogue, and sacred parody'.[17] One of these is a medieval literary genre that generated what appears to be a highly idealized representation of women (or at least of aristocratic women): romance.[18] In the romance tradition, which developed from the twelfth century onwards, the object of male desire is the courtly lady: beautiful, often married, and socially superior to the would-be lover-knight. Representations of the courtly lady might present her in hyperbolic terms of praise, but she is also often what threatens to unravel the order on which a patriarchal social order is based. As feminist critics have pointed out, the elevation of the courtly lady to a position of seeming power is a fantasy rather than a reflection of reality; from this crit-ical perspective, the lady in romance is often little more than a plot device which allows the knight to develop his identity and his masculinity more fully.[19]

While the medieval paragon of womanhood, the Virgin Mary, was offered as a positive counterpart to Eve, she also proved an impossible model to emulate – praised so highly precisely because she was perceived to be exceptional.[20] The polarized pair of Mary and Eve acted as a model for characterizations of women more generally, as either superlative (beauti-ful, virtuous) or as reviled (ugly, duplicitous). Yet the opposing categories of 'good' and 'bad' women, or of 'virgin' and 'whore', are never stable; a woman is never able to escape an insidious logic, which can always turn against her. Indeed, there is evidence to suggest that even Mary was not free from the suspicion with which all women were viewed. Provocative and challenging in her denial of all polar opposites which usually shaped conceptions of female sexuality and gender identity, Mary could not be understood in relation to any one of the several categories according to which medieval society classified women. It is therefore not surprising that some late-medieval drama chooses Mary's singular, virginal pregnancy as material for comic – perhaps anxious? – commentary. In one of the Marian pageants in the fifteenth-century N-Town manuscript, for instance, we see Joseph's dismay and disbelief when he returns home from a trip, only to find his much younger bride visibly pregnant. Because she embodies a condition that is utterly unique, Mary is judged by the standards applied to 'normal' women and is unjustly accused of sexual misconduct by him and her com-munity. While some of the humour of this situation arises from the fact that the audience realizes Joseph's error, it is also the case that Joseph's suspicions are understood to be entirely reasonable. The implication is that if this were any other woman, she would indeed be lying and Joseph's fears would be justified.[21]

Nonetheless, literary use of misogynist tropes ends up being much more indeterminate and nuanced than such ubiquity initially suggests. In the 'Wife of Bath's Prologue', for instance, we see the same sources being used to argue strikingly different perspectives: is the voice of the Wife to be read as participating in misogynous discourses, or as challenging them by showing how easily they can be manipulated to suit a range of positions? Persuasive arguments have been made for either reading.

Even those texts that we would consider as belonging to scientific, med-ical, historical, or legal discourses frequently drew on the same sources as more self-consciously literary ones in order to explain gender differences. Yet the 'literariness' of many misogynous texts is an important aspect of their creation, dissemination, and influence throughout the Middle Ages and beyond. As numerous scholars have pointed out, their purpose was not nec-essarily or even primarily a promotion of sincerely held misogynous beliefs;

often writers engaged in an established literary tradition in order to display their own rhetorical skills. Thus we see numerous writers composing both misogynous and praise literature: famous late-medieval English examples include Chaucer and John Lydgate. Blamires argues that '[t]here can be little doubt that the intelligentsia did regard the rhetorical formulae of misogyny as a game', and drew on them in order to 'exercise their own, and their readers', dialectical skills'.[22] The display of such rhetorical control and virtuosity of course also heightens the contrast between masculine authoritative linguistic skill on the one hand, and the stereotypical incontinence of speech and body it ascribes to women on the other.[23] Acknowledging this skill is not to diminish or underestimate the implications of such representations, for they provided a framework within which 'womanhood' was defined and thus made legible, both intra- and extra-textually. For bodies, too, were 'read', especially within a Christian culture that believed that outer appearance could either reflect or hide the person's true 'inner' nature. The formative relationship between texts and bodies, and the means for interpreting the latter that the former provided, are evident in the persistence of some of the misogynous discourses that have survived, if not unchanged, throughout the centuries in Western culture.

Bodies – especially female bodies – were thought of and used as positive and negative *exemplary* models in texts: as suggested above, then, rhetoric and bodies were intimately connected in a number of ways. One of the clearest instances of this is to be found in the depictions of virtuous or sinful women in medieval sermon stories. As Joan Young Gregg remarks, this was one of the most popular and widespread forms of narrative in the late Middle Ages, and it most frequently depicts women as 'vain and corrupt, vulnerable to damnation by their nature and a threat to the salvation of the male' through their main characteristics of 'pride, disobedience, and carnality'.[24] This is an important point to take into account, for sermon stories were not only ubiquitous, but also partook of the authority invested in the role of the preacher. Carolyn Dinshaw and David Wallace point out that '[t]he pulpit was (indeed perhaps still is) the most potent signifier of masculine authority over women; for it is the point of delivery, in a society of restricted literacy, of forms of common knowledge scripted by men'.[25]

Sermons reached an increasingly wide audience from the thirteenth century onwards, especially in urban areas; by the late fourteenth century, this was also true of more rural districts.[26] In addition, because they were spoken, access to them was not dependent on the listener being able to read. The sermon form was flexible, and drew on allegorical, scriptural, satirical, dramatic, folkloric, and mythical elements in order to make its message more appealing.[27] Because they were meant to be comprehensible and accessible to a diverse audience, late-medieval sermons were written in the vernacular, and often used imagery that was familiar to those it addressed; sermons also included many moral stories that vividly illustrated a particular point – these were called *exempla*. One of the most famous medieval collections of sermons was Jacques de Vitry's (*c*.1170–1250) Latin *Sermones Vulgares*; the many *exempla* it contained 'were later extracted to form one of the period's anthologies of ready-to-use preachers' stories', translated into a variety of European vernaculars, including English.[28] One typical example warns men about the hypocrisy and deceit of women:

> Do not believe her, because 'the iniquity of a man is better than a well-meaning woman'. When the time comes she will spread her wings, since if an opportunity discloses itself she'll fly off and quit. In this respect woman can be called a virtuoso artist, as they say; because she has one skill – that is, one way of deceiving – more than the devil.[29]

Does all of this suggest that it was a question of mainly male authors replicating *ad nauseam* an established misogynous repertoire for mostly male audiences? What roles did women play in medieval textual culture? Other chapters in this volume take up such questions more extensively. Nonetheless, while it is important to acknowledge both the pervasiveness and the longevity of misogynous ideas and writings in Western culture, from before the Middle Ages up until today, on its own this is not enough. As Rita Felski among others has pointed out, 'complaining about the sexism of the western canon is not an especially sophisticated or fruitful idea'.[30] Instead, we need to think about how texts – particularly also literary texts – demand from readers (in their own and in later contexts) a recognition of the many complex interactions between reader and text. For Felski this means acknowledging that readers always bring along their own 'assumptions, biases, or prejudices', while texts are 'saturate[d]' with 'ideas, symbols, and myths of gender'.[31]

Recent scholarship has highlighted the importance of understanding terms such as 'authorship' and 'reader' in relation to a medieval context, especially also when considering questions of gender. Diane Watt notes that we need 'more enabling and elastic definitions of authorship' when we speak of medieval textual production, in order to be able to consider the large number of 'pseudonymous, anonymous and collaborative texts', as well as 'translations and compilations', and to take into account questions of patronage, circulation, and audience.[32] As women were involved in such processes, the production and reception of misogynous writing cannot be viewed in terms of a simple opposition between men and women. Dinshaw and Wallace remind us that '[i]t is naïve . . . to try to separate authentic female voices from masculine textual operations' even as literary productions 'continue to hold interpretive possibilities for female readers once men depart the scene'.[33] Approaching medieval misogynous texts thus raises a host of fundamental questions about how we can enter into a dialogue with them, and also how medieval women (and men) might have responded to the ideas they espoused.

The misogynous views outlined in this chapter did not go unopposed: both male and female writers in the Middle Ages challenged and refuted these stereotypes, accusing those who perpetrated them of ignorance, prejudice, and malice. Sometimes the 'defence' of women was even mounted by a writer who had elsewhere attacked them – thus Marbod of Rennes writes that: 'Of all the good things which are seen to have been bestowed through God's gift to the advantage of humanity, we consider nothing to be more beautiful or better than a good woman.'[34] In the thirteenth-century English debate poem, *The Thrush and the Nightingale*, the Nightingale responds indignantly to the Thrush's assertion that there is nothing to praise about women since they are 'fickle; at heart they are liars', who may seem 'radiant and fair' to look at but are 'cheats underneath'. The Nightingale calls the Thrush 'loathsome', arguing heatedly that one could '[t]ake a line of ladies and count them with care: / Not one in a thousand is evil, I'd swear'.[35] Blamires notes that there is a strong medieval tradition of such 'defences' of women. Despite the critique one could make of the validity of such a defence (especially as the womanly virtues singled out for praise, such as meekness or obedience, might not be considered straightforwardly commendable by today's standards), or the assumptions underpinning it, Blamires argues that it is important to acknowledge it as a counterpoint to misogynous writings. Writing belonging to the 'praise of women' category responds directly to misogynous commonplaces:

> [I]t questions the motives and morality of misogynists, who seem to forget that women brought them to life and that life without women would be difficult; it denounces antagonistic generalization; it asserts that God showed signs of special favour to women at creation and subsequently; it revises the culpability of Eve; it witnesses women's powerful interventions throughout history (from the Virgin Mary and scriptural heroines to Amazons and modern notables); and it argues that women's moral capacities expose the relative tawdriness of men's.[36]

And while such opposition did not amount to a movement for change, or articulate a political position, it, too, offered models and tropes which reflected as well as shaped the ways in which women were viewed (by men but presumably also by themselves) and written about.

As this chapter has shown, it is depressingly easy to find misogynous tropes in a very wide range of medieval writings and discourses. Yet it is important to remember that merely identifying them does not tell us how they were read, or by whom, or how we should read them today. The power, and serious consequences, of antifeminism are undeniable, both in medieval and in post-medieval cultures; nonetheless, medieval instances also reveal how such views were not only replicated and accepted, but also manipulated, mocked, undermined, and critiqued in their own time.

Notes

1. See Alcuin Blamires, *The Case for Women in Medieval Culture* (Oxford: Clarendon Press, 1997), p. 9.
2. Alcuin Blamires, 'Introduction', in *Woman Defamed and Woman Defended: An Anthology of Medieval Texts*, ed. Alcuin Blamires, with Karen Pratt and C. W. Marx (Oxford: Clarendon Press, 1992), pp. 1–15 (p. 2).
3. Marbod of Rennes, 'De Meretrice', in *Woman Defamed*, ed. Blamires, pp. 100–3 (p. 100).
4. Joyce E. Salisbury, *Church Fathers, Independent Virgins* (London: Verso, 1991), p. 43.
5. Ibid., p. 12.
6. Cited in *Love, Sex, and Marriage in the Middle Ages: A Sourcebook*, ed. Conor McCarthy (London: Routledge, 2004), p. 83.
7. *Holy Maidenhood*, in *Anchoritic Spirituality: Ancrene Wisse and Associated Works*, ed. and trans. Anne Savage and Nicholas Watson, with a preface by Benedicta Ward (New York: Paulist Press, 1991), pp. 223–43.
8. See Dyan Elliott, *Fallen Bodies: Pollution, Sexuality, and Demonology in the Middle Ages* (Philadelphia: University of Pennsylvania Press, 1999); and Anke Bernau, *Virgins: A Cultural History* (London: Granta, 2007).
9. Carolyn Dinshaw and David Wallace, 'Introduction', in *The Cambridge Companion to Medieval Women's Writing*, ed. Carolyn Dinshaw and David Wallace (Cambridge: Cambridge University Press, 2003), pp. 1–10 (p. 2).
10. See Joan Cadden, *Meanings of Sex Difference in the Middle Ages: Medicine, Science, and Culture* (Cambridge: Cambridge University Press, 1993).
11. See Simon Gaunt, *Gender and Genre in Medieval French Literature* (Cambridge: Cambridge University Press, 1995).
12. Diane Bornstein, *The Lady in the Tower: Medieval Courtesy Literature for Women* (Hamden, CT: Archon Books, 1983), p. 13. See also Kathleen M. Ashley and Robert L. A. Clark (eds.), *Medieval Conduct* (Minneapolis: University of Minnesota Press, 2001). See Myra Seaman's chapter in this volume for more on conduct literature.
13. Kathleen Forni, 'The Antifeminist Tradition: Introduction', originally published in *The Chaucerian Apocrypha: A Selection*, ed. Kathleen Forni (Kalamazoo, MI: Medieval Institute Publications for TEAMS, 2005). Available at TEAMS online (http://www.lib.rochester.edu/camelot/teams/forantint.htm).
14. 'Of Theyre Nature', ll. 8–14. Available at TEAMS online (http://www.lib.rochester.edu/camelot/teams/forantint.htm).
15. Geoffrey Chaucer, 'The Wife of Bath's Prologue', in *The Riverside Chaucer*, ed. Larry D. Benson (Oxford: Oxford University Press, 3rd edn. 1991), pp. 105–16 (p. 114, ll. 669–81).
16. Blamires, 'Introduction', p. 7.
17. Kathleen Forni, 'Literature of Courtly Love: Introduction', originally published in *Chaucerian Apocrypha*, ed. Forni. Available at TEAMS online (http://www.lib.rochester.edu/camelot/teams/forantint.htm).
18. See Helen Cooper, *The English Romance in Time: Transforming Motifs from Geoffrey of Monmouth to the Death of Shakespeare* (Oxford: Oxford University Press, 2004); and Roberta L. Krueger (ed.), *The Cambridge Companion to Medieval Romance* (Cambridge: Cambridge University Press, 2000). For more on romance, see Corinne Saunders's chapter in this volume.
19. Ruth Mazo Karras, *From Boys to Men: Formations of Masculinity in Late Medieval Europe* (Philadelphia, PA: University of Pennsylvania Press, 2002), p. 25.

20. See Miri Rubin, *Emotion and Devotion: The Meaning of Mary in Medieval Religious Cultures* (Budapest: Central European University Press, 2009).
21. *The N-Town Play*, ed. Stephen Spector, 2 vols., EETS, s.s. 11, 12 (Oxford: Oxford University Press, 1991). All of the plays are in Volume I.
22. Blamires, 'Introduction', p. 12.
23. See Anke Bernau, 'Bodies of Knowledge', *Florilegium*, 25 (2008), 75–91 (81).
24. Joan Young Gregg, *Devils, Women, and Jews: Reflections of the Other in Medieval Sermon Stories* (Albany: State University of New York Press, 1997), p. 19.
25. Dinshaw and Wallace, 'Introduction', p. 6.
26. See John Shinners (ed.), *Medieval Popular Religion, 1000–1500: A Reader* (Peterborough, Ontario: Broadview Press, 2007), pp. 28–9.
27. See G. R. Owst, *Literature and Pulpit in Medieval England: A Neglected Chapter in the History of English Letters and of the English People* (Cambridge: Cambridge University Press, 1933).
28. See *Woman Defamed*, ed. Blamires, p. 144.
29. Jacques de Vitry, from *Sermones Vulgares*, in *Woman Defamed*, ed. Blamires, pp. 144–7 (pp. 146–7). For a translation of the complete collection, see: *The Exempla or Illustrative Stories from the Sermones Vulgares of Jacques de Vitry*, ed. Thomas Frederick Crane (London: David Nutt, 1890). Available online (http://www.archive.org/stream/theexempla00vitruoft#page/n9/mode/2up).
30. Rita Felski, *Literature after Feminism* (Chicago: University of Chicago Press, 2003), p. 3.
31. Ibid., pp. 9, 12.
32. Diane Watt, *Medieval Women's Writing: Works by and for Women in England, 1100–1500* (Cambridge: Polity Press, 2007), pp. 4, 5.
33. Dinshaw and Wallace, 'Introduction', pp. 5, 7.
34. Marbod of Rennes, from 'De Matrona', in *Woman Defamed*, ed. Blamires, pp. 228–32 (p. 228).
35. 'The Thrush and the Nightingale', in *Woman Defamed*, ed. Blamires, pp. 224–8 (p. 225, ll. 38, 39, 40; 50, 51–2).
36. Blamires, *Case for Women*, p. 9.

Part II
Bodies, Behaviours, and Texts

6
Romance

Corinne Saunders

The connection between women and romance is intimate but also shifting. Post-medieval romance has often been viewed as a characteristically feminine genre, written and read by women, and engaging with both conventional female stereotypes and women's desires for fulfilment and escape. In the medieval period, however, though these characteristics were present, most romance writers were male, and romances were directed to and read by both men and women. Medieval romance is a fluid notion: the term *romanz* originally signalled the use of the vernacular, and hence entertainment rather than instruction, and the genre developed only gradually over the medieval period. Medieval romances treat an extraordinarily diverse range of material – classical, historical, legendary – and span both popular and courtly culture. Yet despite their variety they are linked by the motifs or 'memes', as Helen Cooper has termed them, that echo through the genre: love and chivalry, exile and return, quest and adventure, name and identity, pagan and Christian.[1] Romances require heroes and heroines, figures distinguished from the everyday by their ideal quality, and offset by similarly extreme, negative figures; typically they oppose a social, usually conservative, ideal of order with the threat of various kinds of disorder. The focus is not the nation represented or protected by the hero so much as the individuals and the ideals they defend. The pursuit of love, the special realm of the individual, is the particular, though by no means the only, subject of romance, and this is often combined with the pursuit of chivalry. Romances frequently open on to an exotic or aggrandized world, whether that of faery or of Charlemagne's France. They can also, however, allow for incisive social comment, for the exploration of gender and relationships, and for engagement with the deep structures of human existence. The interweaving of fantastic and mimetic elements in romance renders it a flexible, creative genre with the potential to probe individual experience and to explore anxieties and desires. While romance plays on familiar, disempowered female stereotypes of the damsel in distress and the lady as desired love object, it also presents strikingly active figures – the wooing woman, the mother, the healer, the queen, the enchantress. Vulnerability and strength combine in romance women to powerful effect, and romance narratives offer imaginative spaces that both reflect on and transform the female predicament.

Recent scholarship has demonstrated enduring links between women and romance, particularly French Arthurian romance, in medieval England and France. Carol M. Meale observes that romances 'form the second largest generic grouping amongst women's books in the Middle Ages as a whole': as Melissa Furrow remarks, this is particularly striking given the predominance of the spiritual in medieval culture.[2] Meale instances a series of fourteenth- and fifteenth-century examples of women known to have owned the romances of Lancelot and Tristan; Chaucer's *Nun's Priest's Tale* refers ironically to 'the book of Launcelot de Lake, / That wommen holde in ful greet reverence' (ll. 3212–13).[3] As Furrow emphasizes, however, to distinguish a characteristic female reading of romance is impossible, for the stances of women readers, like those of men, are likely to have been as various as those of romances themselves, echoing the dialogue and debate surrounding women in the medieval period. Internal evidence implies that romances were read aloud in courtly circles and aristocratic households to mixed audiences, as well as by individual male and female readers; there may also have been groups of female readers, as suggested by the depiction in Chaucer's *Troilus* of Criseyde and her women listening to a maiden read the tale of the siege of Thebes (II, ll. 80–109).

Perhaps it is not coincidental that of the two twelfth-century secular writers whose names survive and who were largely responsible for shaping the genre of courtly romance, one was a woman, Marie de France (also discussed in this volume by Catherine Batt).[4] Denis Piramus, introducing his didactic poem on the life of King Edmund, comments on the frivolous enjoyment of Marie's work by men, but emphasizes too the pleasure taken by women in the *lais*, 'De joie les oient e de gré, / Qu'il sunt sulum lir volenté' [they listen to them joyfully and willingly / for they are just what they desire].[5] If the identity of Marie is enigmatic, her work is, as Diane Watt remarks, 'unambiguously literary' and intertextual: it is courtly, engaged with clerical culture, and highly intellectual, drawing on French, Latin, English, and Celtic sources, and employing sophisticated poetic conventions.[6] Marie's self-naming, 'de France', reflects her choice to write in French, the 'feminine vernacular', for the English court of (probably) Henry II (1154–89), and perhaps also gestures to the taste of Henry's queen, Eleanor of Aquitaine, a celebrated patron of the arts. Chrétien de Troyes's romance *Le Chevalier de la Charrete*, the first to narrate the love of Lancelot and Guinevere, is presented as written in direct response to the request of Eleanor of Aquitaine's daughter, Marie de Champagne.

Marie's twelve *lais* relate stories told by the Bretons, 'aventure[s]' from long ago, set in a never-never world of courtly romance, its landscape sometimes explicitly Arthurian, sometimes marked only by the occasional place name or precise custom.[7] Their brief, cryptic quality allows for a focus on intense

moments of emotion and wonder, and a crucial part is played by the supernatural. Yet despite their folk- or fairy-tale quality, the narratives engage
acutely with the predicament of women in a world of social constraints.
Their female characters span a wide range of types, from damsels in distress,
especially *malmariées*, to the powerful faery lady of *Lanval*, who bears her
lover away to Avalon. While the supernatural repeatedly intervenes to shape
their destinies, these women are also bold lovers, whose passions can move
them to extreme actions. Thus the *malmariées* of *Guigemar* and *Yonec* eventually escape their imprisonment by jealous old husbands, the lady of *Lanval*
seeks out her beloved from afar, and the lady of *Milun* preserves the life of her
illegitimate child. Many of the *lais* emphasize the pains of illicit love in the
context of arranged marriages; *Laüstic* and *Chevrefoil* preserve the memory
of tragically separated lovers. Love lacking in *mesure* can also have evil consequences: the lady of *Equitan* plots the murder of her husband, causing her
own death as well as that of her lover, the king; and the failure of the lady of
Chaitivel to choose between her four lovers leads to their deaths. Love, the
motivating force of the *lais*, opens up spheres of possibility: as well as lovers,
women figure as mothers, avenged in *Yonec* and *Milun* by their sons, and as
healers, caring for the wounded hero in *Guigemar*. Most remarkable of all
Marie's women is the protagonist of the last *lai*, the wife of Eliduc, who, on
seeing the gem-like beauty of her husband's unconscious beloved, is moved
despite her grief to restore the lady to life, and to reunite the lovers, adopting
the religious life:

> 'Jo sui sa spuse vereiment,
> Mut ai pur lui mun quor dolent;
> [...]
> Que vive estes grant joie en ai;
> Ensemble od mei vus en merrai
> E a vostre ami vus rendrai.
> Del tut le voil quite clamer,
> E si ferai mun chef veler.'

(ll. 1093–1102)

[Truly, I am his wife and my heart grieves for him. [...] I am overjoyed
that you are alive and shall take you with me and return you to your
beloved. I shall set him free completely and take the veil.]

(125)

The fluid, timeless mode of these noble stories of the past allows Marie
to realize the transformative power of love and generosity, which in these
narratives repeatedly counters fallible humanity and the imprisoning circumstances of arranged marriage and religious mores.

As Marie's writing suggests, romance is a collaborative genre, engaging with story matters of the past and dependent on shared ideals and expectations of behaviour. English romances, mainly dating from the late thirteenth century onwards, employ what have become deeply familiar, archaic literary conventions, but continue to reshape these to create meaningful narratives of both courtly and more 'popular' kinds. With some notable exceptions (such as the works of Chaucer and the *Gawain*-poet) Middle English is less engaged than French romance with the acute realization of emotion or the probing of individual psychology, and more with the depiction of character through the accruing of action. The powerful agency of romance women is demonstrated through their roles as lovers, healers, and enchantresses, while romance also continues to engage with the constraints on women. English narratives, like Marie's, image both the wishes and fears surrounding the female body.

Although love in romance is always an invasive, irresistible force, for both men and women, Middle English sustains the emphasis of Anglo-Norman romance on women as bold and proactive in their pursuit of love.[8] One of the earliest extant romances, *King Horn* (c.1225), exemplifies the 'wooing woman' in the princess Rymenhild.[9] Her passion for Horn is described frankly – 'Heo [she] lovede so Horn child / That negh heo gan wexe wild' [she became nearly mad] (ll. 251–2) – and she is startlingly direct, inviting him into her bedchamber and proposing marriage.[10] The appositely named lady 'Le Fere' (The Proud One) in *Ipomedon* sets a series of impossible tasks for her knight, and demands 'respyte' (l. 1797) before choosing a lord in marriage.[11] The memorable protagonist of *Sir Beves of Hamtoun*, Josian, is startlingly assertive: 'Ichauede þe leuer to me lemman [I would rather have you as lover], / Þe bodi in þe scherte [shirt] naked, / Þan al þe gold, þat Crist haþ maked' (ll. 1106–8).[12] Her offer to convert to Christianity proves, in the context of this Crusading narrative, the purity of her desire. Josian not only woos her chosen beloved, but also defends her chastity through a sequence of threats of enforced marriage, most remarkably, when, in a narrative sequence recalling the story of Judith and Holofernes, she encourages her newly-wed husband earl Miles's revelry, and then strangles and hangs him (in the Anglo-Norman and later English versions, by means of a slip-ring in her own girdle, emblem of her chastity). Nowhere is female agency more compellingly depicted than in Chaucer's *Troilus and Criseyde*, through Criseyde's extraordinary interior monologues on her freedom of choice to love, and the constraints on independence that marriage may bring.

But as *Troilus and Criseyde* so vividly recalls, romance also engages repeatedly with the tradition of the exchange of women, usually (as in *Beves*) for the purpose of marriage. Chaucer's *Man of Law's Tale* expresses with memorable pathos the predicament of its heroine, Custance, sent across the sea to marry the Sultan:

Allas, what wonder is it thogh she wepte,
That shal be sent to strange nacioun
Fro freendes [friends] that so tendrely hire kepte,
And to be bounden under subjeccioun
Of oon, she knoweth nat his condicioun?

(ll. 267–71)

The following lines seem to offer a narratorial comment: ' "Wommen are born to thraldom and penance, / And to been under mannes governance" ' (ll. 286–7). This tale combines the motif of enforced marriage with another popular story matter, that of the calumniated lady, often a queen, falsely accused and given up to the mercy of providence. The woman's need for a protector is memorably conveyed in *Ywain and Gawain* (an adaptation of Chretien's *Le Chevalier au Lion*). After Ywain kills the lady Alundyne's husband, her companion Lunete clearly articulates her vulnerability:

'If twa knyghtes be in the felde
On twa stedes, with spere and shelde,
And the tane [the one] the tother may sla [kill]:
Whether [who] es the better of tha?'
Sho said, 'He that has the bataile [victory].'

[...] The lady thoght than, al the nyght,
How that sho had na knyght,
Forto seke hir land thorghout,
To kepe Arthur and hys rowt [company].

(ll. 999–1003; 1021–4)[13]

Lunete advocates marriage to the very knight who has killed her lady's husband. This narrative intimates the impossibility of female independence within a chivalric society where might is equated with right, and there is no recourse against the man who wins the woman in battle.

In the Constance story and its analogues, providence intervenes to defend the innocent woman, exiled on land or sea. Chaucer's *Wife of Bath's Tale*, in its defence of female sovereignty, responds more radically to the recurrent subtext of force in romance narratives. In the Wife's radical reworking of Arthurian romance, the knight whose rape of a maiden begins the tale becomes the bound husband, his partner not an unwilling virgin but a loathly old hag, and his actions not those of sexual desire and force but constraint and flight:

> Greet was the wo the knyght hadde in his thoght,
> Whan he was with his wyf abedde ybroght;
> He walweth [tossed] and he turneth to and fro.
> His olde wyf lay smylynge everemo...
>
> (ll. 1083–6)

The old hag's answer to the riddle, that women most desire 'sovereynetee / As wel over hir housbond as hir love' (ll. 1038–9), is enacted in the marriage, and the knight's subsequent granting of 'maistrie' to his wife, though the tale concludes ambiguously with the wife's promise of obedience to her husband. Chaucer, as so often, leaves his audience uncertain, both exploiting and questioning the stereotypes and ideals of his time.

The old hag's disquisition on *gentillesse* draws on clerical traditions of rational argument, refuting in its very form the antifeminist texts instanced by the Wife in her prologue, which emphasize female irrationality. Though such moral didacticism most recalls Boethius's Lady Philosophy or Langland's Holy Church, romances do depict women as learned, not only in courtly arts, but also in the traditional seven liberal arts, most particularly medicine. Felice in *Guy of Warwick* has been taught the seven arts by the monks of Toulouse, while in *Sir Beves of Hamtoun* (c.1300), Josian is distinguished by her learning, especially her sophisticated medical knowledge:

> While ʒhe was in Ermonie,
> Boþe fysik and sirgirie
> ʒhe hadde lerned of meisters grete
> Of Boloyne þe gras [the great] and of Tulete [Toledo],
> Þat ʒe knew erbes mani & fale [numerous],
> To make boþe boute & bale [healing and harm].
>
> (ll. 3671–6)

Partonope of Blois contains a comparable description of the arts of the lady Melior, also a great enchantress. Though rare, the female physician is not a romance invention: records survive of female medical practitioners across Europe, and the medical school at Salerno was associated with the legendary female healer Trotula, said to have practised there in the twelfth century.[14] Josian is imagined as having access to an ancient, especially Arabic tradition of learned medicine, and verisimilitude is heightened by the naming of the great centres of medical learning, Bologna and Toledo. Her medical skills allow her to heal Beves with 'an oyniment' (l. 715) and 'riche baþes' (l. 732) that soon make him 'boþe hol and sonde' (l. 734). Later, she acts as her own midwife at the birth of her twins. Her herbal knowledge produces marvellous effects: when she is seized by the giant Ascopart, the herb she plucks transforms her appearance to that of a leper, causing 'A foule mesel on to se' (l. 3688), and dramatically repelling the enemy king who pursues her. Most remarkable is her use of a ring containing a stone 'of swiche vertu' (l. 1470) that it preserves her chastity when she is married against her will to the same king. This romance plays on the idea of medicine as natural magic, which includes knowledge of the virtues of plants and stones. Such beneficent magic is opposed to the potentially demonic magical arts of the Saracens, and characterizes Josian as wise woman and healer.

In other works, magic is explicitly supernatural, connected with the otherworld of faery that is so prominent a romance *topos*. The otherworld can be highly menacing to women, most memorably in *Sir Orfeo*, where the queen Heurodis, sleeping under an 'ympe-tree' (l. 46) or grafted tree in her orchard at noon, a place and time associated with faery, wakes to reveal that she has been bidden to accompany the King of Faery to his world.[15] Heurodis's actions write on her body the force of the command:

> Ac as sone as she gan awake,
> She crid and lothly bere [cry] gan make;
> She froted [tore at] hir honden and hir feet,
> And crached hir visage – it bled wete.
> Hir riche robe hie al to-rett [rent]
> And was reveysed [driven] out of hir wit.

> (ll. 53–8)

Despite the guard of a thousand armed knights, the King of Faery's summons is fulfilled: Heurodis is spirited away to the sinister world of the un-dead. In its violence, made explicit in Heurodis's madness, self-mutilation, and deathly appearance, this 'taking' is analogous to the faery and demonic rapes of *Sir Degarré* and *Sir Gowther*. Desire for the female body, possession, and violent death intersect in this most unsettling of romances.

On the whole, however, magic empowers romance women, and there are comparatively few male counterparts for romance's many enchantresses, named and unnamed. The faery lady is a powerful romance type, both fearful and fascinating, her magic usually concerned with the feminine domain of love and desire. She may be either the faery mistress or the witch. Marie's *Lanval* offers a paradigm for the faery mistress motif in its narrative of Lanval's encounter with an unnamed otherworldly lady who has sought him from afar, her love expressed both in the wealth she showers upon him and in the open gift of her body. As is typical of this narrative pattern, however, wish-fulfilment is also dependent on a magical condition set by the lady. The Middle English *Sir Launfal*, which identifies the lady as Tryamour, daughter of the King of Faery, heightens her forcefulness: her condemnation of the Arthurian court is violently enacted in her final gesture of blinding Guinevere. The combination of love and force, faery and witch, is captured in the romance of *Melusine*, with its part-serpent, part-woman protagonist. *Sir Gawain and the Green Knight* memorably presents both the erotic and menacing faces of the enchantress in its portrayal of Bertilak's lady, Gawain's seductress, and her companion, the loathly old woman, mysteriously swathed and veiled, who proves to be Morgan le Fay.

Malory's *Morte Darthur* makes clear both the powerful agency afforded women by magic and the unease surrounding this in a world where witchcraft was seen as posing a genuine threat to society. In the *Morte* (and in the French Arthurian prose romances that are Malory's source), Morgan le Fay plays a key role as the half-sister and powerful rival of Arthur: 'the false sorseres and wycche moste that is now lyvyng' (VIII.34, 430).[16] Malory emphasizes the dangers of occult learning: Morgan 'was put to scole in a nonnery, and ther she lerned so moche that she was a grete clerke of nygro-mancye [black magic]' (I.2, 10). The threat of such arts to the homosocial bonds of the Round Table is still more apparent in Malory's depiction of the enchantress Hellawes, whose macabre ambition is to possess the body of her beloved Launcelot dead if she cannot have it alive: 'Than wolde I have bawmed [embalmed] hit and sered [wrapped it in waxed cloth] hit [...] and dayly I sholde have clypped [embraced] the and kyssed the, dispyte of quene Gwenyvere' (VI.15, 281). Here the term 'nigromancy', usually denoting dark, potentially destructive magical arts, takes on the modern sense of necro-mancy, and desire, sex, and death interweave menacingly as enchantment replaces physical force. Yet Malory is not wholly negative concerning female magic. Morgan's counterpart and opponent is the enchantress Nenyve, an ambiguous figure who confines Merlin, but who is also the practitioner of benign magical arts. Nenyve is a damsel of the Lady of the Lake, who offers Arthur the gift of Excalibur, and she appears at crucial moments across the narrative, usually to endorse Arthur's rule and defend right: 'ever she ded grete goodnes unto kynge Arthure and to all his knyghtes thorow her sorsery and enchauntementes' (XVIII.8, 1059). Perhaps most striking is Malory's depiction at the end of the book of the black-hooded ladies who bear the wounded Arthur by barge to Avilon, and who include both Morgan and Nenyve. Practitioners of white and black magic are brought together in this haunting image of women as healers and mourners who oversee the great king's departure. Malory's grand Arthurian history gestures to medieval per-ceptions of both the empowering and the dangerous possibilities of learned magic. These women, who escape the constraints of the courtly world, care for, desire, and pursue the bodies of the knights who move across the romance landscape; at their most negative, they become demonic forces, but they retain too the potential to guide, protect, and heal.

If romance is a collaborative project, it is also a conversation concern-ing women. Female bodies are catalysts within the narrative structures of romance, the objects of both human and otherworldly desire. They also experience and pursue their own desires, for love, power, and knowledge, to both good and evil ends. Their agency can be wish-fulfilling and transformative, but also threatening, predatory, and violent. Their arts as healers are learned, and they make medical practice their own; they can also stray into more negative magical practices that transform and threaten male bodies. In widely differing ways across romance texts, they profoundly influence those they encounter, their bodies and behaviours playing shaping roles in the enactment of destiny and the realization of the self. For medieval writers and audiences, these imaginative fictions had the potential to open up questions and anxieties concerning fundamental aspects of female existence, in particular the intertwined topics of love and freedom, and to probe in fluid, creative, and sometimes controversial ways the issues of oppression, empowerment, and agency.

Notes

1. Helen Cooper, *The English Romance in Time: Transforming Motifs from Geoffrey of Monmouth to the Death of Shakespeare* (Oxford: Oxford University Press, 2004), p. 3.
2. Carol Meale, '...alle the bokes that I haue of latyn, englisch, and frensch: Laywomen and their books in Late Medieval England', in *Women and Literature in Britain, 1150–1500*, ed. Carol Meale (Cambridge: Cambridge University Press, 1993), pp. 128–58 (p. 139); see also Julia Boffey, 'Women Authors and Women's Literacy in Fourteenth- and Fifteenth-Century England', in *Women and Literature in Britain*, ed. Meale, pp. 159–82; and Melissa Furrow, *Expectations of Romance: The Reception of a Genre in Medieval England* (Cambridge: D. S. Brewer, 2009), pp. 5–6.
3. *The Riverside Chaucer*, ed. Larry D. Benson (1987; Boston: Houghton Mifflin, 1991).
4. See also Diane Watt, *Medieval Women's Writing: Works by and for Women in England, 1100–1500* (Cambridge: Polity Press, 2007), pp. 39–62.
5. *La Vie Seint Edmund le Rei: poème anglonormand du xiie siècle*, ed. Hilding Kjellman (Göteborg: Elanders, 1935), vv. 46–8; for the modern English translation, see *The Lais of Marie de France*, ed. and trans. Glyn Burgess and Keith Busby (Harmondsworth: Penguin, 1999), 'Introduction', p. 11.
6. Watt, *Medieval Women's Writing*, pp. 39 and 40.
7. *Guigemar*, in Marie de France, *Lais*, ed. Alfred Ewert (Oxford: Blackwell, 1944, repr. 1978), l. 24; trans. Burgess, p. 43.
8. See further Cooper, *English Romance in Time*, p. 230.
9. See Judith Weiss, 'The Wooing Woman in Anglo-Norman Romance', in *Romance in Medieval England*, ed. Maldwyn Mills, Jennifer Fellows, and Carol M. Meale (Cambridge: D. S. Brewer, 1991), pp. 149–61.
10. *King Horn*, in *Of Love and Chivalry: An Anthology of Middle English Romance*, ed. Jennifer Fellows (London: Dent, 1993).
11. *Ipomadon*, ed. Rhiannon Purdie, EETS o.s. 316 (Oxford: Oxford University Press, 2001).
12. *The Romance of Sir Beues of Hamtoun*, ed. Eugen Kölbing, EETS e.s. 46, 48, 65 (London, 1885, 1886, 1894).
13. *Ywain and Gawain*, in *Ywain and Gawain, Sir Percyvell of Gales, the Anturs of Arther*, ed. Maldwyn Mills (London: Dent, 1992).

14. See Nancy G. Siraisi, *Medieval and Early Renaissance Medicine: An Introduction to Knowledge and Practice* (Chicago: University of Chicago Press, 1990), p. 27; and Monica H. Green, 'Women's Medical Practice and Medical Care in Medieval Europe', *Signs*, 14 (1989), 434–73.
15. *Sir Orfeo*, in *Middle English Verse Romances*, ed. Donald B. Sands (Exeter: Exeter University Press, 1966, repr. 1986).
16. *The Works of Sir Thomas Malory*, ed. Eugène Vinaver, rev. P. J. C. Field, 3rd edn., 3 vols. (Oxford: Clarendon Press, 1990).

7
Saints' Lives

Shari Horner

Conventional images of medieval women readers depict them as quietly passive, sitting alone or in a motionless group, reading a psalter or Book of Hours. These images do not seem to correspond with representations of women seen in one of the most popular medieval genres, the saint's life, in which the young female subject is shown actively fighting dragons, debating energetically with scholars, or enduring extensive and varied physical torture, from being stretched on a spiked wheel to having her skin flayed off while still alive. It is hard to imagine these active, aggressive female saints pausing to ruminate quietly on Scripture. What, then, might be the connections between the subjects of medieval virgin martyr narratives, so full of talk and action, and the subjects of medieval scenes of reading, which often emphasize passivity and stillness? How might we usefully connect the female hagiographic subject with the reading practices of medieval women?[1] How do saints' lives figure scenes of reading, writing, or textual production? This essay will argue that Middle English virgin martyr narratives are in fact deeply infused with scenes of literacy, including reading, writing, textuality, and textual production. The texts within these texts are the bodies of the virgins themselves, both written upon and read by writers and readers within and outside of the narratives. Saints' bodies, I will argue, especially in scenes of torture, function as both texts being written and texts to be read – as literal and visible artefacts that contain deeply spiritual messages. Reading and writing the saint's body thus provides medieval women readers and writers with the kind of literate textual strategies that will benefit them in their own literary endeavours. In their intense focus on the body, saints' lives enact a wide range of textual practices.

Today, when books are cheap, plentiful, disposable, or even virtual, it is easy to forget that the physical book itself comprised a substantial part of the reading process. Hagiographical texts carried a particular kind of physical meaning, since, as Mary Beth Long has argued, 'people tended to think of them as holy objects' – that is, as significant both in their own materiality and for the messages contained therein.[2] The bodies of the saints within the texts are analogous to the physical artefacts of the texts themselves: although readers are seeking spiritual messages, it is impossible to overlook or, more precisely, not to look at the literal bodies that transmit those messages.

In a recent study, Catherine Sanok has convincingly shown the extent of women's textual participation in hagiographic traditions; as readers or patrons of saints' lives, women participated fully in the production and reception of these texts.[3] Women themselves were more typically consumers rather than producers of these texts, and direct representations of either writing or reading are infrequent. Nonetheless, scenes of writing and textual production are actually quite common, but with a twist: the public display of violence means that the body itself functions as a kind of text, not just to be seen or watched, but read and interpreted. Acts of torture produce signs on the body – scraped, torn, mutilated flesh, marked by instruments such as rakes, rods, or swords. The saint herself often invites or suggests the torture; she writes her own story and provides reading lessons, and in both cases the text that she produces and interprets is her own body. Virgin martyr narratives precisely illustrate this hermeneutic principle; while readers or viewers, both inside and outside of the narrative, can be tempted to focus solely on the saint's naked body, they risk their spiritual welfare in doing so. Reading beyond the letter of the text produces new spiritual messages – produces, in a sense, new texts.[4] In saints' lives, torture scenes create a kind of writing on the body (using sharp instruments, producing flowing blood), and, as a text, the saint's body can be read and interpreted not for itself, but for the spiritual truth it contains.

Within the saints' lives of the Katherine Group, a collection of texts from about 1200 evidently read by the female anchoritic audience of the *Ancrene Wisse*,[5] the emphasis is on the active defence of virginity among the three virgin martyrs, Saints Margaret, Katherine, and Juliana. In all three lives, scenes of looking or witnessing figure prominently, as the bodies of the virgins are subjected to public nudity and torture. The *Life of St Margaret* exemplifies the contrast between literal sight and spiritual insight. When the saint rejects the torturer's advances, he responds by graphic threats of violence, but the saint's subsequent prayer suggests her awareness of the impact of the visual spectacle on the torturers and bystanders – even as she affirms the spiritual message: 'If my body is torn apart, my soul will be at peace among the righteous; through sorrow and bodily pain, souls are saved' (p. 53).[6] As she prays to maintain her virginity, however, her literal body is being pierced and lacerated, literally opened up so horrifically that the gathered bystanders *can't* look – they hide their faces, unable to bear the gruesome sight of the saint's bleeding body. Olibrius insists upon the visual spectacle in the apparent belief that opening up and gruesomely exposing Margaret's body will counteract her prayer (p. 57). In the *Life of St Juliana*, too, the pain of torture is made explicitly visual: when Eleusius commands his men to dismember Juliana on an iron-spiked wheel, the graphic descriptions of the saint's mangled body are the object of the spectators' (and by extension, the readers') gaze: 'Those who stood about could *see* the greatest grief' (Winstead, p. 22; my emphasis).

At the beginning of the *Life of St Katherine*, the saint draws the sign of the cross on her body, teeth, and tongue (p. 263), thereby imbuing her body with spiritual power through a textual act, and subsequently amazing the emperor with her bold eloquence (perhaps the effect of tracing the cross over her tongue). St Margaret, too, writes the sign of the cross on her body, an act that destroys the dragon that swallowed her (p. 61). These scenes both require and deny the value of visible proof, and the bodies of both saints become, via this act of writing, the means to their salvation. Once St Margaret has written the sign of the cross on the text of her body, that text has become powerful enough to destroy the dragon and she emerges from the dragon's belly without a mark. When Olibrius prepares to resume torturing the saint, a crowd gathers 'to see the suffering' (p. 75). As the torturers burn her flesh with lighted candles, she recites the prayer of David: 'High Saviour God, with the healing fire of the Holy Ghost, comfort of mankind, kindle my heart, and let the fire of your love burn in my loins' (p. 75), thus aligning her literally burning body with a sacred text and transforming the literal flames into spiritual meaning.

Just before her death, Margaret anticipates the material transformation of her body into the written text of her *Life*, praying that whoever writes or reads about her life will have their sins forgiven (p. 79). Here, Margaret, in effect commissioning the text of her own life, envisions the full range of possibilities for female participation in textual culture – as writer, as patron, as book-owner, as reader, or as listener – and she indicates the spiritual power of the text she expects her body to become. The textualization of the saint's body is evoked twice more in this *Life*: first, when God assures Margaret of the spiritual power her written *Life* will possess after death, and finally, when the narrator, Teochimus, informs readers that after he witnessed first-hand her imprisonment and passion, he 'had her whole life set down in a book [and] sent it out widely throughout the world' (pp. 81, 83). Thus the thirteenth-century *Life of St Margaret*, like the saint herself, envisions its own textual production, as the saint's textualized body, exhibiting bloody and symbolic signs for all viewers to interpret. In all three lives from the Katherine Group, in fact, the message is the same: the saint's preservation of her bodily integrity brings about the increasingly violent physical torture that ruptures her literal body, even as that body functions as a spiritual text to be read and interpreted by viewers both inside and outside of each narrative. The saint herself, as exemplified by St Margaret, performs what we might call a kind of corporeal autography, in which that spiritual meaning is written onto the saint's body by the saint herself.

Such corporeal autography takes on a particular urgency in the late thirteenth-century *South English Legendary*, as its texts direct attention to the graphic display of saintly bodies even as they *deflect* attention away from those bodies as immaterial.[7] Shorter and less sophisticated than the lives of the Katherine Group, the virgin martyr narratives found in the *South English Legendary* are no less concerned with graphically describing the violence enacted on female saints by their male persecutors; in fact the brevity of the lives within the *South English Legendary* makes those scenes seem more prominent. The lives of Saints Agatha and Lucy exemplify the short, action-filled narratives found within this collection, illustrating the paradoxical assertion that within virgin martyr narratives, the saint's body both does and does not matter.

In the *South English Legendary*, St Agatha's breasts are the particular object of gruesome torture. In a vivid description that includes instruments of torture that may well have been easily visualized by a thirteenth-century lay audience, Quintianus 'had hooks and willow twists bound to [Agatha's] breasts and torturers twisted them off' (Winstead, p. 30). Yet unlike other virgin martyrs, Agatha addresses this specific form of torture in her rebuke to Quintianus: 'Aren't your sins great enough? Why do you hurt the very part you suckled on your own mother?' (p. 30). Agatha situates her individual, literal body into a more universalizing historical frame, joining her body to the collective bodies of all women, and signalling to Quintianus (and to her readers) that literal bodies may well contain more than surface meaning. The rapidity with which God's apostle, who appears in Agatha's jail cell, heals her wounds confirms the body's relative unimportance; in spite of the graphic descriptions of her mutilated breasts, we learn simply that 'as soon as he rubbed her wounds, they were healed' (p. 30).

In the *South English Legendary*'s *Life of St Lucy*, too, the saint's body itself signifies its own insignificance. When Lucy distributes her wealth among the poor and is brought before a judge to explain, she includes her own body as part of the transaction: 'now I'm ready to give up my body, sir judge, yielding each limb to [Christ's] service' (p. 33). But whereas Lucy uses a literal image ('each limb') to describe a spiritual condition, the judge interprets her words only literally: 'Now I see!' said the judge, '[...] Now that you have no more to spend, you say you'll spend your body. You talk like a whore' (p. 33). Yet Lucy maintains her distinction between her literal flesh and her spiritual meaning by turning to the Augustinian principle that states that no virgin can be stripped of her virginity without her consent: 'If you defile my body against my will, my virginity is all the purer and my reward all the greater' (p. 33). Lucy's subsequent miraculous resistance to all attempts to move her into the brothel displays the young woman's strength in the face of the supposedly powerful (but ultimately weak) non-Christian authorities. Neither men, ropes, nor even oxen can make her move, and Lucy herself glosses her own meaning by citing the biblical authority of David (p. 34). Her reference to the psalter is her means of interpreting, for the audiences within and outside the text, the incomprehensible power of her own body. The end of Lucy's life (and *Life*) confirms the paradoxical nature of a body that both does and does not matter, reminding viewers to focus instead on the meanings contained therein. The judge's final command is to have Lucy stabbed in the throat 'intending to quench her speech and her holy life with a single blow' (p. 34). Yet even this fails: Lucy speaks better than before, even with a stab wound in her throat, so that, lest the message be lost on readers, the word triumphs fully over the letter of the flesh.

Like the *South English Legendary*, Osbern Bokenham's fifteenth-century *Legend of Holy Women* had a primarily lay audience.[8] Overall, Bokenham's lives feature less graphic violence than earlier texts, and, as Karen Winstead has shown, they tend to focus more on theological or moral questions, and pay more attention to the saint's emotions and interactions with her interlocutors.[9] Nonetheless, Bokenham's lives preserve the intense attention to visuality and spectacle seen in earlier lives. Saints Dorothy and Cecelia, for example, both request that God send visual proof of his power to confirm the saint's belief. In the *Life of St Dorothy*, the emphasis on vision and blindness is established early, when the non-believers convert to Christianity after Dorothy's miraculous resistance to torture. And when her physical appearance actually improves after a forced nine-day fast, her torturer is 'blinded by this miracle' (Delany, p. 96). As the tortures intensify, Dorothy's miraculous imperviousness persists: 'not a spot or wound appeared on her' (p. 97). As always, the torturer's astonishment stems from the fact that the saint's body transcends the purely literal. Desperate, Fabricius's final act is to order Dorothy's disfigurement; she is beaten 'until [...] there was no face left' (p. 97) and imprisoned. The next day her face is miraculously restored and Fabricius has her beheaded, as though, having failed to mutilate her face, his last resort is simply to remove it altogether. In a miracle after her death, Dorothy converts a textual authority, the judge's scribe, thereby confirming that participants in literal, textual culture know how to read the signs of her body, even if the pagan torturers do not.

Bokenham's 'Prologue' to the *Life of Saint Cecelia*, too, is concerned with issues of blindness and sight. In his etymological analysis of the saint's name, derived from Jacobus de Voragine's *Legenda Aurea* (or *Golden Legend*), Bokenham explains that Cecelia 'was both way and guide to the blind':

> Voragine says that she is also 'lacking blindness' by the great brightness of wisdom that she had outstandingly, as people can see who read her legend earnestly... [J]ust as the people physically ['materyally'] see the sun and moon and the seven stars in heaven, so in Cecelia they may spiritually perceive the distinct brightness of distinct virtues.
>
> (p. 142)

The distinction that Bokenham draws here between seeing 'materyally'[10] and perceiving 'spiritually' is the lesson readers learn when reading her *Life*.

Somewhat unusually, Cecelia is married to Valerian, a non-Christian, who demands visual proof before he will convert. Cecelia leads him to an old man carrying 'a text written with letters of gold' (p. 145), and Valerian, upon reading, swears his belief in God. The text itself has produced a belief which is sustained even when the text is no longer in front of him. For Valerian's brother Tibertius visual proof is likewise necessary to effect belief, with examples ranging from flowers that can be smelled but not seen, to Cecelia's use of literalistic examples such as snow, hail, and ice to explain the threefold nature of God (p. 146). Cecelia's examples provide the first step in achieving spiritual understanding; just as the text with golden letters provided a physical artefact that led to Valerian's spiritual belief, so too the visual evidence demanded by both men leads to their spiritual understanding. She confirms this point, finally, by providing her torturer Almachius with the same reading lesson with which Bokenham began the Prologue: although Almachius insists on the power of his stone idols, Cecelia argues the reverse: that belief in the power of literal objects through seeing is, in fact, spiritual blindness, and that only by rejecting the literalism of visual objects can true Christian believers gain spiritual insight (p. 154).

Nowhere does the opposition between sight and belief come more sharply into play than in William Paris's late fourteenth-century *Life of St Christine*. The narrative begins by focusing intensely on Christine's physical beauty in anticipation of the impending gruesome torture scenes. When the saint smashes her father's statues of false gods, he orders her beaten and tortured in ways that far exceed the mild descriptions of torture seen in Bokenham:

> Urban then commanded that her clear white flesh be scraped from her bones with sharp hooked nails. He ordered all her limbs broken, one by one [...] When Christine saw her flesh, she took a slice and threw it right at Urban's eye; if he hadn't ducked, she would have hit him. Then the witty maiden said to her supposed father, 'Have a morsel, tyrant! Go ahead! After all, it's the flesh you produced.'
>
> (Winstead, p. 65)

The horrors of the torture scene are both intensified and mitigated by Christine's own brand of dark humour, as she does her father one better: not only does she endure the physical torture without pain, but she treats her own flesh so dismissively that she thinks nothing of picking it up and throwing it, almost playfully (but grotesquely) at her father, as her words serve to associate him – and not herself – with the flesh.

Julian, furious when Christine continues to pray in spite of the torture, orders that her tongue be cut out: 'it's hurting me'. The irony of his statement is immediately apparent:

When her tongue lay at her feet, that lovely maiden spoke as well as if it had never been cut out. Everyone saw and heard her. She picked her tongue up and threw it at Julian's eye; from then on, he couldn't see from that side. She smiled a little when she hit him [...] He looked aside with his one eye and said to the tongue, 'While you were in her big fat mouth, you hurt me with your words. Your blow has hurt me even more by taking out my eye!'

(p. 68)

Of course, the fact that losing her tongue does not impede Christine's ability to speak proves decisively that her flesh does not matter. Although Julian addresses the tongue directly, it is Christine who responds. Thus the spiritual word destroys Julian's literal sight and readers are reminded that while the literal body may not ultimately matter to the saint herself (Christine's cavalier treatment of chunks of her own flesh makes this abundantly clear), its existence is essential for readers hoping to understand the spiritual truths that texts such as this convey.

Within medieval virgin martyr narratives, certain plot details are always present: the young female saint resists horrific forms of physical torture, thus overpowering the demands of her non-Christian persecutors, and converting many bystanders to Christianity in the process. Beyond the basic plot details, however, the function of this structure is hermeneutic: virgin martyr narratives use the intense visual focus on the saint's body to instruct readers in how to read. The literal images of the saint's tortured body are necessary to transmit the spiritual messages of Christianity *embodied* by the saint. Throughout these lives, the saint and her viewers/readers both inside and outside the text read and interpret the various meanings of the displayed body. Saints' lives, in other words, teach key lessons about reading and textual interpretation. In texts that purport not to be about the body at all, the saint's body *is* the text, written upon, read, and interpreted by all readers seeking spiritual meaning.

Notes

1. If we have relatively few texts known to have been authored by women in the period spanning 700–1500, we have even fewer saints' lives by women authors. There are numerous instances, however, where women were named as patrons or readers of such lives. See Diane Watt, *Medieval Women's Writing: Works by and for Women in England, 1100–1500* (Cambridge: Polity Press, 2007), pp. 63–90; Jennifer Summit, 'Women and Authorship', in *The Cambridge Companion to Medieval Women's Writing*, ed. Carolyn Dinshaw and David Wallace (Cambridge: Cambridge University Press, 2003), pp. 91–108; and Jocelyn Wogan-Browne, *Saints' Lives and Women's Literary Culture, ca. 1150–1300: Virginity and its Authorizations* (Oxford: Oxford University Press, 2001) for the best treatments of this point. See also Wogan-Browne, 'Saints' Lives and the Female Reader', *Forum*

for Modern Language Studies, 27 (1991), 314–32, for a discussion of how female readers might have responded to virgin martyr narratives.

2. Mary Beth Long, 'Corpora and Manuscripts, Authors and Audiences', in *A Companion to Middle English Hagiography*, ed. Sarah Salih (Cambridge: D. S. Brewer, 2006), pp. 47–69 (p. 49).

3. Catherine Sanok, *Her Life Historical: Exemplarity and Female Saints' Lives in Late Medieval England* (Philadelphia: University of Pennsylvania Press, 2007), p. ix; see also Watt, *Medieval Women's Writing*, and Summit, 'Women and Authorship'.

4. See my discussion of how this Augustinian hermeneutic plays out in the Old English *Life of St Juliana*: 'Spiritual Truth and Sexual Violence: The Old English *Juliana*, Anglo-Saxon Nuns, and the Discourse of Female Monastic Enclosure', *Signs: Journal of Women in Culture and Society*, 19 (1994), 658–75.

5. In addition to the anchoritic readers, these lives are believed to have been read by a diverse group of both lay and religious readers: see Bella Millet, 'The Audience of the Saints' Lives of the Katherine Group', *Reading Medieval Studies*, 16 (1990), 127–55; and Eric J. Dobson, *The Origins of Ancrene Wisse* (Oxford: Clarendon Press, 1976).

6. All quotations from the lives examined in this essay will be taken from Modern English translations for purposes of accessibility and consistency. References to the *Life* of Saint Margaret are taken from *Medieval English Prose for Women from the Katherine Group and Ancrene Wisse*, ed. Bella Millet and Jocelyn Wogan-Browne (Oxford: Clarendon Press, 1990). References to the *Life of Saint Juliana* are from *Chaste Passions: Medieval English Virgin Martyr Narratives*, ed. and trans. Karen A. Winstead (Ithaca and London: Cornell University Press, 2000). References to the *Life of Saint Katherine* are from *Anchoritic Spirituality: Ancrene Wisse and Associated Works*, ed. Anne Savage and Nicholas Watson (New York: Paulist Press, 1991). Page numbers are given parenthetically in the main text.

7. *The South English Legendary*, ed. Charlotte D'Evelyn and Anna J. Mill, EETS o.s. 235, 236 (London: Oxford University Press, 1956); and *The Early South English Legendary or Lives of Saints*, ed. Carl Horstmann, EETS o.s. 87 (London: N. Truebner and Co., 1887). Again, all parenthetical page references are to Winstead's translations in *Chaste Passions*.

8. All references will be to the modern English translation, *A Legend of Holy Women: A Translation of Osbern Bokenham's Legends of Holy Women*, trans. Sheila Delany (Notre Dame, IN: Notre Dame University Press, 1992), with page numbers cited parenthetically in the main text. For the Middle English text see Osbern Bokenham, *Legendys of Hooly Wummen*, ed. Mary S. Serjeantson, EETS o.s. 206 (London: Oxford University Press, 1938; repr. New York: Kraus Reprint Co., 1971).

9. Karen A. Winstead, *Virgin Martyrs: Legends of Sainthood in Late Medieval England* (Ithaca and London: Cornell University Press, 1997).

10. Bokenham, *Legendys*, p. 202.

8
Devotional Literature

Michelle M. Sauer

To some degree, talking about medieval devotional literature almost seems redundant, since most works, even with a secular function, contained a spiritually didactic message. Some of the more obvious types of such works include hagiographies, Books of Hours, visionary texts, and even early forms of drama. The less discussed devotional genre encompasses prose treatises and prayers, many of which were composed for women, both nuns and laywomen, and a number adapted from monastic works. No matter what source material or audience, however, medieval devotional treatises for women constructed an image of woman and an accompanying gender identity for their readers. Not content with guiding a woman into a holy life, these works also sought to govern her body as well as her soul.

The treatises that reflect an identifiable female audience span the high-to-late Middle Ages (thirteenth–fifteenth centuries). Some of the more important ones include: fourteenth-century works such as *The Abbey of the Holy Ghost*, *The Doctrine of the Heart*, *Gratia Dei* [*Glory of God*], and *The Poor Caitif*; late fourteenth- or early fifteenth-century pieces such as *The Ladder of Four Rungs*, *The Chastising of God's Children*, and *The Seven Points of True Love and Everlasting Wisdom*; and fifteenth-century works like *The Tretyse of Loue* (1493), *Speculum devotorum*, *Disce mori* [*Learn to Die*], *Contemplations on the Dread and Love of God*, *The Mirror of Our Lady*, *Formula noviciorum*, and *The Devout Treatise of the Tree and Twelve Fruits of the Holy Ghost*, alongside various texts of the Passion,[1] and the body of anchoritic literature including *Holy Maidenhood*, *Custody of the Soul*, *Ancrene Wisse*, and the prayers of the Wooing Group,[2] which date back to the thirteenth century. Many of these works also experienced overlap between lay and religious consumption. *The Abbey of the Holy Ghost*, for instance, was written for lay people, but encourages the reader to imagine herself as a member of an order. Anchoritic texts written for women recluses also reflected both lay and religious perspective, since anchoresses were neither required nor expected to profess vows before entering the cell. Anchoritic literature in particular proved enduringly popular and increasingly relevant through the Middle Ages, and much of later devotional literature, particularly that directed towards women, grew out of that tradition.[3] Thus, I will be looking here at various devotional materials alongside the anchoritic texts of the Wooing Group and *Ancrene Wisse*. These texts were available in the English vernacular, a strong indication of female and possibly lay piety. They tend to direct the reader to imagine not only her soul, but also Christ's image, her reactions to him, and the various bodily gestures associated with these imaginings, often in connection with the Passion. In each of these texts, the performance of religion becomes tantamount to the devotional fulfilment of the reading. These are, in essence, directed performances that inscribe upon the reader the role of *sponsa Christi* (spouse of Christ), a status achieved through her body, but imprinted on her soul.

The anchoritic texts, the earliest of the devotional works to be examined, established a devotional tradition based on performance that carried through to later devotional treatises. *Ancrene Wisse* especially relies on human posture and gesture to assist in creating a prayerful environment. This fits with medieval devotion, as demonstrated in studies of the *Nine Ways of Prayer of St Dominic* (*c*.1260–88), in which the 'ways of prayer' include overt gestures and postures such as kneeling, lying prostrate, sitting, and standing. Posture is a staple of devotion, and gesture is a way of expressing such devotion. As Jean-Claude Schmitt explains: 'Gesture is the movement and figuration of the body's limbs with an *aim*.'[4] Both the *Nine Ways of Prayer of St Dominic* and the works of Hugh of St Victor were crucial in developing the idea that gestures indicate the state of the inner soul on the outside body, and thus must be governed and disciplined. The prologue of *Nine Ways* demonstrates awareness of its role in starting a new tradition, as 'according to the author, priests and theologians agreed to underline the interaction of the movements of the body and the soul'.[5] The combination allows the body to contribute to the soul's development by experiencing ecstasy and/or rapture, and leading the soul into bliss. For Dominic, the gestures he uses to pray outside of mass and when he is alone with Christ, whom he views as immediately and truly present, are essential to salvation.

It is this last that especially links Dominic's rituals to the anchoritic ones. Alone in her cell attached to a church, the anchoress was always in the presence of Christ, through the crucifix in her cell and the squint overlooking the tabernacle. She could see mass through the squint, generally located beyond the rood screen, in a way that most medieval people could not, providing a sense of the personal to her relationship with Christ. The gestures she used, and the bodily postures she assumed, took on ritualized aspects, especially as codified by the author of *Ancrene Wisse*. For instance:

> When you first get up, *cross yourself* and say [...] keep saying this prayer until you are fully dressed. Keep this prayer much in use and often in your mouth whenever you can, *sitting or standing* [...] *prostrate yourself*

there with these salutations [...] (So you shall also do when the priest holds up the host at mass, an before the 'I confess' when you are to take communion.) After this, *fall to your knees* before the crucifix [...] and with these words *beat your breast* [...] and *cross yourself* with each of these salutations; and with these words [...] *beat your breast, make a cross* on the earth with your thumb, and *kiss it*. Then turn to the image of our Lady and *kneel* [...] *bow or kneel* to the other images, and to your relics [...] say our Lady's Matins [...] *bowing* somewhat downward [...] *make a cross* with the thumb on your mouth [...] and *fall to the earth* if it is a workday [...] or *bow down* if it is a holy day.[6]

By insisting on this course of events, the *Ancrene Wisse* author ritualizes the movements and prayers contained in the opening of Book 1, which is primarily concerned with external actions, bodily conduct, and daily living in the anchorhold. The most frequently used gesture is the sign of the cross. On four occasions, the anchoress is directed to cross herself or make a cross – and once to follow this cross with a kiss. The emphasis on the cross reminds the anchoress she is Christ's devoted spouse; that she crosses herself while kneeling in front of a crucifix also connects her to the crucifixion itself, enveloping her in the scene, and kissing the cross reminds her both of Christ's sacrifice and of her role as his bride. Penitential gestures are the second most common, with instructions to fall prostrate twice and to beat her breast twice. Both are part of the penitential rite. As Mary Clemente Davlin points out, the 'posture known in some religious orders as the *venia* or pardon posture, is also an ancient part of Christian ritual, used in some places and times by penitents before confession'.[7] The anchoritic life, while not one of extreme asceticism and penance, was nevertheless organized around penitence, as indeed much of medieval religious devotion was, since humanity was seen as fundamentally sinful, thus necessitating God's constant intercession and forgiveness. Kneeling and bowing are almost interchangeable in this opening section of *Ancrene Wisse*, both indicating respect and humility, and both certainly part of the liturgy, and therefore part of the medieval women's repertoire of devotional postures. *Ancrene Wisse* thus represents stylized ritual postures and gestures that create a liturgical environment in the anchoress's cell, but in doing so, the reliance upon bodily movements perhaps invites a fear of too much emphasis on the physical body, and not enough connection with the spiritual imagination. The anchoritic prayers of the Wooing Group establish a sense of imaginative performance and combine gestures and meditation into something like 'performative viewing'.[8] By this I mean the combination of action, reaction, prayer, and meditation into an imaginative performance that is at some level directed by the author of the text. For instance, in the Wooing Group prayers, the anchoress is repeatedly invited to gaze at Christ's face and body, to imagine his beauty and soft skin, to touch, hold, and caress him. In places, she begs Christ to look at her in return: 'Beloved Lord, Jesus Christ, look towards me.'[9] This encourages the anchoress to imagine herself connected to the scene, almost as a part of it. Even more, in *þe Wohunge of Oure Laured* [*The Wooing of Our Lord*], the titular piece of the group, the anchoress is incorporated into the scenes unfolding around her. In particular, she is deliberately invited to participate in the Crucifixion, an action that combines the increased devotional focus on the Incarnation and Passion with the performative aspects of imaginative viewing. As directed by the author of the prayer, the anchoress consciously identifies with Christ through concentration on the Crucifixion until she is wholly absorbed into the scene:

> May my body hang with your body nailed upon the cross, enclosed transversely within four walls! And I will hang with you, nevermore to come off my cross until I die [...] Ah, Jesus, so sweet it is to hang with you![10]

In this way, the anchoress's body becomes both a spectator's body and a participant's body. Jill Stevenson notes, 'spectators generate meaning for themselves through the actors' bodies, and through their own bodily presence [at the event]'.[11] Though speaking about medieval mystery plays, Stevenson makes an excellent point – the anchoress in *The Wooing* does indeed garner meaning from Christ's presence both on the cross (e.g. on her crucifix) and in her imagination. Her performance of the Crucifixion assists her in creating devotional understanding; in fact, bodily participation becomes crucial for the pious experience. *The Wooing* author closes the prayer with the following exhortation:

> Pray for me my dear sister. This have I written for you, inasmuch as words often enchant the heart, to think on our Lord, and therefore, when you are at ease, talk to Jesus and say these words, and envision that he hangs beside you, bloody upon the cross.[12]

Here the author acknowledges the power of guided imagination, and demands bodily performance. The anchoress is expected to pray, especially for the author, and to imagine the crucified Christ – but more than that, she is expected to participate in the Crucifixion, so that he may hang bloody (and bodily) next to her.

A similar process occurs in the meditative life of Christ, *Speculum devotorum*, a fifteenth-century text compiled by a Carthusian monk for a Brigittine nun at Syon Abbey.[13] The prologue positions this work as one of imaginative performance as it discusses the benefits of meditating on the Passion. The reader will be expected to identify with the scene unfolding before her, Christ's final moments. Like the anchoress in *The Wooing*, the nun of the *Speculum* does not simply watch the scene; rather, she is incorporated into it. However, here she identifies with Mary instead of supplanting her.

The author 'makes even more explicit the identification between Mary and a Syon nun' in describing the risen Christ's first appearance to his mother, but the 'imitation of Mary's behaviour is, however, most strongly advocated when she is a mourner at the Crucifixion'.[14] Mary's reactions are described, and the reader is encouraged to share in them. Her emotional responses are guided by Christ's sufferings, paralleling the intensification of events and the increasing physicality of the descriptions. When, for instance, Christ is nailed on the cross, Mary echoes this not only through her emotional devastation, but also in physical gestures, especially weeping and falling prostrate with grief. As Rebecca Selman points out, 'Through her physical responses, Mary thus demonstrates her ability to read and interpret Christ's suffering body.'[15] The author directs the reader to imagine herself as part of this scene: 'you must think to yourself in your imagination as though you were present with them [Mary and St John] and one of them'.[16] At various points she is directed to mourn alongside Mary and John, to weep with them, and to share their pain. On Christ's journey to Calvary, she is enjoined to 'imagine also what service you might have done for our lady'.[17] In becoming part of the scene, the reader actively performs her role as *sponsa Christi*, assuming her rightful place at Christ's side. As Katherine Zieman notes, the understanding of certain texts was 'grounded in the body' through a visceral relationship; thus, 'meaning is perceived in the body, not in the mind'.[18] In this instance, the body becomes an agent of devotional viewing and experience. Both modern phenomenology and medieval practice see the body as a liminal space between self and world, or as a mediator between soul and heaven. How the body is used, what acts it performs, can determine the extent of salvation.

Somewhere between proscribed ritual, such as that found in *Ancrene Wisse*, and performative imagination, such as the crucifixion scenes in *Speculum devotorum* and *The Wooing of Our Lord*, we find an observational performance such as that found in *The Abbey of the Holy Ghost*, a late fourteenth-century English version of a spiritual guide for laywomen originally written in French. Although one English version attempts to broaden the audience with its opening – 'my dear brothers and sisters', which directly echoes the anchoritic tradition – it is clear that the text is truly meant just for women, as the other extant versions demonstrate.[19] Julia Boffey points out: 'The text of the Abbey in MS Stowe 39 opens with an unusual gender-specific address to "My dere systres" (fol. [1.sup.r]) and is followed on folios 8v–9r by a large illustration that depicts nuns at work in the abbey.'[20] If we presume, then, that *The Abbey* is a primarily female-oriented text, we can also assume the directive within is more specifically coded for women. The saints invoked (e.g. Mary Magdalene), the objects depicted (e.g. precious jewels), and the main functionaries (e.g. an abbess) all invoke a female audience as well. Although more descriptive and less directly performative, *The Abbey* uses previously established sensory images. Most specifically, there are continual references to the 'burning love' that contact with the Saviour invokes, which is clearly meant as a physical reaction as well as a spiritual one. This burning love is frequently coupled with longing and physical proximity. For instance, the reader is to 'yearn with arms of love, and then sweetly to kiss [Christ]',[21] and after a feast, the knowledge of their Saviour 'enflames them with the bliss of love so that they can taste and feel how sweet he is, how good he is, and how lovable he is'.[22] To welcome them in, Christ opens his hands, stretching them out in love.[23]

The reader is not wholly incorporated into the action; instead, she hovers on the edge, not quite a participant, but able to bodily perceive and understand the actions within the text. *The Ladder of Four Rungs* exhibits similar performance moderation. The name alone implies some sort of bodily activity – in order to achieve union with God in heaven, the reader must 'climb' the ladder. *The Ladder of Four Rungs* is a late fourteenth-century translation of the twelfth-century *Scala Claustralium* and, as noted by many scholars, has been rearranged to appeal to its audience, presumably nuns and laywomen. It explains each of the rungs in terms of physical and spiritual activity: first is 'besy lokyng', or careful reading of Holy Scripture, next is meditation, the 'studious inner searching with the mind', followed by prayer, the 'devout longing of the heart', and ending with contemplation, a 'rising of the heart that tastes of sweetness'.[24] Each rung of perfection is accompanied by a bodily action. Each step can only be achieved through the carefully controlled body and the senses. Perfection is unlocked through proper performance. The reader is also reminded that she is God's 'lover in contemplation', and when so reminded, is invited to kiss him and taste the sweetness. Thus fleshly desire is overcome, as the body is used to enhance, rather than damage, the soul.

Many of these middling performances concentrate on two aspects – preparing the soul for union with God and reminding the reader that she is a bride of Christ. For instance, another Syon text, *The Mirror of Our Lady*, also encourages identification with Mary and reminds the nuns that they are the brides of Christ without incorporative performance. In this work, the author merely informs the readers, whom he addresses as sisters, to lift up their eyes and gaze upon Mary. Here the reader is invited to imagine, but is not wholly integrated into the tableau. The body is still a necessary function of the imagination here – her soul has eyes and must actively look in order to achieve her desire – but she can remain physically outside the frame of the action.

Late devotional treatises often included a section on meditation. While not precisely evoking the sense of imaginative performance previously discussed, these passages indicate the importance of governing the reader's perceptions and inner thoughts as well as her outer bodily actions. Indeed, physical movement was often coupled with meditation even in perfunctory treatments. For instance, in *Learn to Die*, the main function is to instruct

'Dame Alice', either a female religious or a devout laywoman, in matters of sin, penance, and the Creed, accompanied by a Form of Living; yet there is also a push for meditation on what the Creed means, how the commandments aid spiritual perfection, and how penance prepares the soul. Complicating the matter slightly is the failure of most of the text to eradicate the masculine pronouns taken from the source materials (e.g. opening the treatise with a reference to Dame Alice, using masculine pronouns, and then returning to 'my sister' in the last part, the Form of Living). The unstable gender identity is alleviated by the emphasis on guiding the body properly. Though distinctly less directed than other incorporative performances, nonetheless, the instructions to 'meditate and contemplate' insist that the body not be forgotten, and suggest appropriate prayerful motions. In order to fully produce the desired devotional effect, the reader's body and soul must work together. *Learn to Die* is, in part, drawn from *The Chastising of God's Children*, which, in turn, is based on portions of *Ancrene Wisse*. Interestingly, *The Chastising* contains an even less overt meditation sequence, and none of *Ancrene Wisse*'s prayerful gestures, bridging the two with a focus on love and desire gained through movement into God's presence. As noted in the text, 'the play of love is joy and sorrow [...] we perceive by his absence what matter we have to love him [...] the joy of his presence causes sorrow in his absence [...] I have rehearsed here, briefly, what manner of sorrow we have in his absence.'[25] The author goes on to detail how joy comes after the sorrow, but all is either gained or lost by the almost bodily movement of the soul into God's presence or away from it. The reader is not, however, invited into the scene linguistically. Instead, she is directed to read the text and then put the principles into action.

Although different from the devotional treatises in question, early English drama supports the importance of performance as a necessary part of devotion. The clearest example of this is Katherine Sutton, abbess of Barking (d. 1376), who redacted and adapted existing liturgical drama into unique presentations of the Easter observances. Sutton's alterations are centred on gendered performances. For instance, in the *Depositio crucis* [*Internment of the Cross*], the corpus was removed from the crucifix and washed in water and wine before burial. This act is directly reflective of the feminine, as it was the female role to prepare bodies for burial by bathing and anointing them. The addition of wine recalls not only the side wound, but also the forthcoming Resurrection and Eucharist. The act of washing, however, incorporates the women into the scene and into the aftermath of the Passion in a manner similar to many of the prose treatises discussed above. In Stevenson's terms, the spectators and participants are merged.

Sutton and her nuns also became literal performers. As abbess, she assumed the role of patriarch locked in limbo awaiting the Harrowing of Hell. Later, three nuns filled the roles of the three Marys, while the abbess approached them with white veils. Finally, the abbess 'ends the dramatic office: the priests wait for her signal to depart after the *Te deum'*.[26] The women do not simply act as the Marys, but also they become the Marys like the reader of *Speculum devotorum* does. However, the abbess retains personal identity and authority throughout. Scholars speculate that Sutton created these performances primarily for the edification of the faltering laity. If so, she then also directed their returning spirituality, with a focus on female performance.

The medieval female reader of devotional texts was a gendered reader, for she came to understand her gendered subjectivity through her reading, and a performative reader, for she accessed many of these texts through her body and its actions. Many of these texts ask their readers to strive to uphold certain standards of behaviour; others give guidelines of behaviour that will result in perfection. As a whole, these texts produced and/or maintained the ideologies of gender, personal devotion, and physical action, especially by establishing a direct connection with the audience. Direct addresses such as 'my sister', and linguistic constructions such as the historical present give the author more control over the actions and imaginations of the reader, causing her to perform in a proscribed manner, presumably for her own good. Even when the text had been adapted from a male text, or failed to change the pronouns despite a female audience, the reader was expected to perform as a 'proper' pious woman and bride of Christ.

Notes

1. Especially *De Perfectione vitae ad sorores*, a thirteenth-century text by Bonaventure. See Thomas H. Bestul, *Texts of the Passion: Latin Devotional Literature and Medieval Society* (Philadelphia: University of Pennsylvania Press, 1996).
2. See n. 8 below for texts included in this group.
3. See Hope Emily Allen, 'Some Fourteenth Century Borrowings from "Ancren Riwle"', *The Modern Language Review*, 18.1 (1923), 1–8.
4. Jean-Claude Schmitt, 'Between Text and Image: The Prayer Gestures of Saint Dominic', *History and Anthropology*, 1 (1984), 127–62 (127).
5. Ibid., p. 130.
6. *Ancrene Wisse* in *Anchoritic Spirituality: Ancrene Wisse and Associated Works*, ed. Anne Savage and Nicholas Watson (New York: Paulist Press, 1991), pp. 53–5; my emphases.
7. Mary Clemente Davlin, 'Devotional Postures in *Piers Plowman* B, with an Appendix on Divine Postures', *The Chaucer Review*, 42.2 (2007), 161–79 (164).
8. From 'A Song of Love Pertaining to Our Lord', ll. 76–7, in *Þe Wohunge of Ure Laured*, ed. W. Meredith Thompson, EETS o.s. 241 (Oxford: Oxford University Press, 1958). Also includes: *On Uriesun of Ure Lourerde*; *On Wel Swuðe God Ureisun of God Almihti*; *On Lofsong of Ure Louerde*; *On Lofsong of Ure Lefdi*; *þe Oreisun of Seinte Marie*. All translations are my own.
9. Ibid.
10. Ibid., ll. 590–3. Again the translations are my own.
11. Jill Stevenson, 'The Material Bodies of Medieval Religious Performance in England', *Material Religion*, 2.2 (2006), 204–32 (213).

12. *Wohunge*, ll. 645–56.
13. See *The Speculum Devotorum of an Anonymous Carthusian of Sheen, Edited from the Manuscripts Cambridge University Library Gg. I. 6 and Foyle, with an Introduction and a Glossary*, ed. J. Hogg, 2 vols. (Salzburg: Analecta Cartusiana, 1973–4).
14. Rebecca Selman, 'Spirituality and Sex Change: *Horologium sapientiae* and *Speculum devotorum*', in *Writing Religious Women: Female Spiritual and Textual Practices in Late Medieval England*, ed. Denis Renevey and Christiania Whitehead (Cardiff: University of Wales Press, 2000), pp. 63–79 (pp. 67, 68).
15. Ibid., p. 69.
16. *Speculum devotorum*, p. 261, ll. 11–13.
17. Ibid., p. 263, l. 18.
18. Katherine Zieman, 'Reading, Singing, and Understanding: Constructions of the Literacy of Women Religious in Late Medieval England', in *Learning and Literacy in Medieval England and Abroad*, ed. Sarah Rees Jones (Turnhout: Brepols, 2003), pp. 97–120 (pp. 101, 103).
19. Citations from *The Abbey of the Holy Ghost* are taken from *Religious Pieces in Prose and Verse: Ed. from Robert Thornton's Ms. (Cir. 1440) in the Lincoln Cathedral Library*, ed. George Gresley Perry (London: Trübner, 1914), p. 51. My translations.
20. Julia Boffey, 'The Charter of the Abbey of the Holy Ghost and its Role in Manuscript Anthologies', *Yearbook of English Studies*, 33 (2003), 120–30 (120).
21. *Abbey of the Holy Ghost*, p. 56, l. 6.
22. Ibid., p. 59, ll. 22–4.
23. Ibid., p. 60, l. 36.
24. See George R. Keiser, ' "Noght how long man lifs; bot how wele": The Laity and the Ladder of Perfection', in *De Cella in Seculum: Religious and Secular Life and Devotion in Late Medieval England*, ed. Michael G. Sargent (Cambridge: Cambridge University Press, 1989), pp. 145–59. My translations.
25. *The Chastising of God's Children and the Treatise of Perfection of the Sons of God*, ed. J. Bazier and E. Colledge (Oxford: Oxford University Press, 1957), pp. 264–5.
26. Nancy Cotton, 'Katherine of Sutton: The First English Woman Playwright', *Educational Theater Journal*, 30.4 (1978), 475–81 (479). See also Clifford Davidson, *Festivals and Plays in Medieval Britain* (Aldershot: Ashgate, 2007).

9
Marian Literature

Sue Niebrzydowski

Devotion to Mary was central to medieval spirituality. Mary was worshipped in a variety of guises including virginal Mother of God, Queen of Heaven, and Intercessor. The details of her life were familiar from the Nativity Gospels of Matthew and Luke, the apocryphal stories that grew up around her childhood and the manner of her death, and the popular collection of saints' lives, the *Legenda Aurea* (*Golden Legend*).[1] By the later Middle Ages numerous Marian feasts were celebrated: her Purification (2 February), the Annunciation (25 March), the Assumption (15 August), Nativity (8 September), her Presentation at the Temple (21 November), and her Immaculate Conception by St Anne (8 December). The Mother of God was venerated in public homilies and the liturgy, and privately praised in the Offices of the Virgin in Books of Hours. Marian sites of pilgrimage in England were many and held in high regard, most notably Our Lady of Walsingham in Norfolk. They were visited frequently by women or benefited from their donations. In 1443 Margaret Paston wrote to her husband, John, that she sought Mary's aid in curing him of an ongoing illness by promising to go on pilgrimage to Walsingham.[2]

Many critics have suggested that real women faced a dilemma in seeing Mary as a role model, a view summarized by Priscilla Martin:

> The Madonna seems to have everything. But this image has significant omissions and ambiguities. She is all powerful but lacks power in her own right: it is deputed to her by the Father and the Son. She lacks adult sexuality, except as the chaste object of sublimated devotion. She is *unfailingly* loving, gentle, compassionate and long-suffering. Does that not make her essentially different from all women and encourage the labelling of them as destructive Eves rather than redemptive Maries?[3]

Mary is powerful but only at the command of others (her Son and God) and Mary's experience of conception and childbirth renders her, as was often emphasized by male writers, absolutely 'alone of all her sex'.[4] Men viewed

Mary's chastity, obedience, and silence at the Annunciation as a role model for 'ideal' female behaviour. Mary was employed in this fashion in the exhortation of Adam Marsh, Franciscan Oxford lecturer, to Eleanor de Montfort (wife of Simon and sister of Henry III) that she curb her temper and submit herself to 'the most placid grace of the most pious Virgin Mary'.[5]

Medieval women were surrounded by constant reminders of the unique manner of the conception and birth of Christ, and of Mary's assumption, as commemorated in the fabric of the parish churches in which they marked their own cradle-to-grave experiences of marriage, childbirth, widowhood, and death. Yet in spite of the differences between themselves and the Mother of God, women owned Marian works. Married women, such as Dame Elizabeth Wyndsore, Anne Andrew, and Jane Fitzlewis, possessed copies of John Lydgate's *Life of Our Lady* (1421–2),[6] a work that emphasizes Mary's virginal life. Women also produced new texts or reinterpreted others to recognize connections between their lives and that of the Virgin, even as male authors emphasized the differences.

At some point in the 1420s Dame Eleanor Hull made a translation of the Anglo-Norman work, the *Meditations Upon the Seven Days of the Week*,[7] and her work as a translator is explored in detail in Alexandra Barratt's essay included in this volume. The *Meditations* contains, among other things, contemplations on the 'Name of Mary' and on the days of the week, Saturday's being the five joys of the Virgin; the Annunciation, Nativity, Resurrection, Ascension, and Assumption. 'Never in alle here lyfe at o tyme she spak nere sang so myche' describes how the Virgin Mary was moved to compose the *Magnificat* at Christ's conception (Luke 1:46), to translate, if you will, the word made flesh into the flesh made word. Mary was a poet and as such, a model for other women writers or indeed translators of spiritual works.

The fact of Eleanor's translation raises questions concerning medieval women's textual relationship to the Virgin Mary. How did women position themselves in an already long-established male textual tradition of Marian devotion? What forms did women's texts take and what do they reveal about the ways in which medieval women related to such a hugely powerful female icon? Did women's responses to Mary depend upon the stage in her life-cycle she as a woman had reached, or, put another way, was there a particular 'Mary' for different stages in a woman's life?

This essay seeks out testimony of the relevance of the Virgin Mary to the lives of ordinary women in works in a variety of genres: those written or dictated by women, and performances of texts that they watched or in which they participated. Sisterhood with the Virgin was not simply the perception of those who became brides of Christ. Nor do women's words merely reaffirm the unbridgeable gap between medieval womanhood and the Mother of God identified by so many male writers. Female-associated Marian texts demonstrate that women perceived Mary as a malleable symbol, aspects of whose marriage, childbirth, and motherhood were sufficiently similar to their own to inspire a variety of textual practices. The Marian texts associated with secular women in particular were frequently an act of *translatio* – of translation in the sense of interpretation and appropriation – that reveals the significance of the Mother of God to her earthly sisters.

Eleanor Hull's translation of the *Meditations* demonstrates one woman's textual appropriation of the Mother of God. Carolyne Larrington has suggested that 'the act of translation allowed a self-effacement on the part of the writer: she became a mediator rather than an "auctor" or originator'.[8] Eleanor's work reveals something more independent: women adapting male-authored texts to reflect female views and responses to the Virgin Mary. Barratt identifies Eleanor's role as more akin to 'auctor' than translator:

> The translator, by eliminating the first two parts of this tripartite structure, has created a resonance that was not evident in her original, for now the two meditations on the Names of Jesus and Mary are presented side by side.[9]

Barratt demonstrates how Eleanor modified the original opening passage of the *Meditations* through omitting the meditation on the crucified Christ flanked by St John and the Virgin Mary, and a second on the graces received by St John, to focus on the third meditation on the 'Name of Mary'. In an act of 'editing' that places the focus on the power of Mary's name, Eleanor raised Mary's profile. No longer merely a witness with St John at the Crucifixion as in the Anglo-Norman original, Mary is a universal mediator on whose name all Christians should call in their hour of need in the manner in which they had traditionally called upon the 'Name of Christ': 'Ther is not on of us, lytelle nere grete, old nere yong, yf he bethenke wele in himself, but that he hath fulle oft found comfort in the mercy of our swete Lady, blessyd Seynte Marye.'[10] Eleanor perceived Mary's intercession equal to that of Christ and equally available to all, including secular women such as herself, as is emphasized in the closing Latin prayer not derived from the Anglo-Norman original, '*Dulce nomen domini nostri Jesu Christi et nomen gloriose verginis Marie sint benedicta in secula Amen. Deo gracias*'[11] [In the sweet name of our lord Jesu Christ and in the name of the glorious Virgin Mary may they be blessed for ever Amen. Thanks be to God].

Mary held exemplary significance for young women.[12] Her obedience towards her parents was portrayed on the medieval stage in pageants devoted to her childhood in the Temple.[13] Visual portrayals of Mary as a young girl demonstrated also the importance of teaching young girls to read. From the late thirteenth century in England, images of Mary's mother, St Anne, and Mary viewing a book became popular in church glass, wall painting, sculpture, ecclesiastical embroidery, and in Books of Hours, a literary genre that was particularly popular with women.[14] For the non-literate, these images were intended to stress to mothers the importance of teaching their children to pray.[15] Examination of the texts that appear in the book that Mary or St Anne holds suggests that it is also *literacy* that is being taught.[16] This is done either with an 'a.b.c.' or a book upon which is written Psalm 50:17, *'Domine labia mea aperies'* [Lord open thou my lips], the first line of the office in honour of the Virgin in the primer, and a text that is apposite

> because first reading books were often primers, Books of Hours, and psalters […] Mary learns to read, then, by beginning, as anyone learning to read from the primer would, with an office in honour of the Virgin. (The text is also wittily appropriate for someone learning to read aloud.)[17]

Mary is shown being taught to read by her mother and learning to do so through Marian worship.

Evidence of aristocratic women's recognition of Mary as exemplary reading model for young girls and of her mother, St Anne, as instructor in (devotional) literacy can be found within Books of Hours of female ownership. Worthy of note is Anne of Burgundy's portrait in *The Bedford Hours*.[18] The book dating from the 1420s was made to celebrate the marriage of Mary of Bohun's son, John of Lancaster, to Anne on 13 May 1423. Anne's portrait appears on folio 275v, where she is depicted in the central image with her patron saint and namesake, St Anne, who is teaching Mary to read from a book complete with it resplendent green velvet book bag. The Christ child standing beside his mother blesses the Duchess of Burgundy who kneels before the Holy Family. The text on the Virgin's book is only just visible but that of Anne of Burgundy's begins with a large red letter 'D' and again reads *'Domine labia mea aperies'* [Lord, open my lips]. Thus in her own book created to celebrate her marriage, Anne of Burgundy sees herself as part of a female-led reading community in which mothers teach their daughters to read – a salutary lesson for a new bride who would hope to continue the Lancastrian dynasty. We have no evidence that the book was used to instruct girls but on Christmas Eve 1430, Anne gave it to her nine-year-old nephew, Henry VI, one assumes for his delight and education.[19]

Mary also 'spoke' to brides and mothers. Discussion of Mary's marriage appears in written texts and visual representations in England from the thirteenth century onwards. By the later Middle Ages, Mary was presented as having participated in a recognizably contemporary wedding ceremony. In the plastic arts and in drama, Mary and Joseph are often shown 'handfasting' – the moment in the wedding ceremony after which the couple have given their consent and the priest transfers the woman into the legal power of her husband.

Male-authored texts mention Mary's marriage in order to define and illustrate wifely obedience. This is seen in *The Book of the Knight of La-Tour Landry* (1371 and translated into English in the fifteenth century),[20] a conduct book written by Geoffrey La Tour Landry for his three daughters of marriageable age in the absence of their deceased mother's guidance (and discussed by Seaman in her contribution). In the chapter 'Of the Virgin Mary' (ch. 109), the Knight tells his daughters that 'the holy / mayden honoured and was obeissaunt vnto her husbonde Ioseph, wherein the scripture praisithe her highly' (p. 147). He continues to explain that Mary's humility towards Joseph should be emulated, 'here / is good ensaumple vnto all women to loue this vertu of / humilite, that is to saie, to be humble vnto God and vnto / the worlde, and for a wedded woman to be obedient and humble vnto her husbonde' (p. 147). The Knight portrays Mary as the archetypal obedient wife, articulating without making overt that Mary, despite being Joseph's superior in terms of God's salvific schema, still owed her husband obedience. This was, after all, what women promised in the marriage ceremony.

Some wives clearly associated their own marital status and duty with that of the Mother of God. The moment of Mary's handfasting is included on folio 32 of *The Bedford Hours*, created, as we have seen, for the celebration of John of Lancaster's marriage to Anne of Burgundy. It is placed in the final miniature of the Annunciation page. Many women bequeathed to statues of Mary the symbol of their wifehood – their wedding ring – as did, for example, Agnes Petygrewe of Publowe in the diocese of Bath and Wells who in 1499 left to 'the B. M. de le Peler [Pillar] of the said church of Publow [All Saints] my weding ring' and Anne Barrett of Bury St Edmunds who bequeathed to Our Lady of Walsingham her 'corrall bedys of thrys fifty [her rosary], and my maryeng ryng' in 1504.[21] Rather than taking the similarity in their marital status as an exhortation to obedience, however, women's texts choose to celebrate Mary's parturition and motherhood of Christ. Although Mary's somatic experience of childbirth was unique (she remained, after all, virgin post-partum), women were able to appropriate those aspects of Mary's pregnancy and childbirth with which they might empathize.

Women watching medieval Nativity plays could sympathize with the physical effects of Mary's pregnancy common to all women: 'Nowe hasse shee gotten her, as I see / a great bellye.'[22] Women recognized the efficacy of Marian texts in protecting a mother in labour. In the *Knowing of Woman's Kind in Childing*, a late-medieval gynaecological treatise written for a female audience, midwives were encouraged to use a strip of parchment on which was written either the Virgin Mary's name and that of St Margaret (the patron saint of childbirth), or 'in a longe scrow all þe psalme of Magnificat anima mea & gyrde hit a-boute here', either to the woman's thigh or around her middle as an aid during labour.[23] In the mid-fourteenth century, Ellen de Rouclif of York owned just such 'a piece of writing' which she sent to her friend, Anabilla Pynder, after Ellen had successfully given birth to her son,

John.[24] Women's wills testify also to the importance of birthing belts sancti-
fied by contact with the Girdle of Our Lady or containing a thread from this
relic. Eufemia Langton bequeathed to her daughter, Margaret Meyryng, wife
of Sir John Langton of Farnley, near Leeds, a silver-gilt cross, an Agnes Dei,
and *zonam Beatae Mariae Virginis* [a belt of the Blessed Virgin Mary] in her
will dated 26 August 1463.[25]

Margery Kempe (*c.*1373–post 1439) has left us testimony in her *Boke*[26]
of her personal devotion to the Mother of Christ. Her work is examined
in detail by Diane Watt elsewhere in this volume but the particularity of
Margery's Marian devotion is worthy of comment here. Having given birth
to fourteen children, Margery recognizes with Mary (and also with St Anne)
a shared experience of motherhood. Margery perceives herself gathering the
accoutrements for a lying-in: spiced wine, strips of linen for swaddling bands
for the baby, and linen for Mary's childbed: 'Also sche beggyd owyr Lady fayr
whyte clothys & kerchys for to swathyn in hir Sone whan he wer born, and
whan Ihesu was born, sche ordeyned beddyng for owyr Lady to lyg in wyth
hir blyssed Sone.'[27] Margery clearly assumes that Mary, like all mothers, will
have needed such items for her own comfort and that of her newborn son.

Mary's motherhood is also the focus of Dame Eleanor Percy's *Prayer*.[28]
The *Oratio Elinore Percie Ducissa Buckammie*, a macaronic verse prayer, has
survived on the recto and verso of the final page of the Book of Hours,
now BL, Arundel MS 318, f. 152. It is believed to have been written out
by Anne Arundel, Eleanor's sister.[29] The daughter of Henry Percy, Duke
of Northumberland, in 1500 Eleanor married Edward Stafford, Duke of
Buckingham and bore him a son and three daughters. Her prayer begins
as follows:

> Gawde, Vergine and mother beinge
> To Criste Jhesu, bothe God and Kinge,
> By the blessed eyare [ear] him consevinge.
> > *Gabriellis nuncio* [by Gabriel's message]
>
> Gawde, Vergine off all humylytie,
> Showinge to us thy sonnes humanitie
> Whan he without paine borne was of thee
> > *In pudoris lilio* [in the lily of chastity][30]

Eleanor, herself a mother of four, praises Mary's motherhood and although
she recognizes the difference in their experience of childbirth (Mary's is pain-
less) may have shared a similar pride in 'showinge' off her own newborn to
an appreciative audience.

Women celebrated Mary's success in mothering through another kind
of text: that of performance. Every year in Beverley in Yorkshire, a female
member of the Guild of St Mary played the starring role in the Candlemas

Procession of the Guild of St Mary which was led by 'one of the gild [...] clad in comely fashion as a queen, like to the glorious Virgin Mary, having what may seem a son in her arms'.[31]

This same appropriation of Mary's motherhood happened periodically in every parish church, when a new mother would come to be churched after the birth of her child. Margery Kempe describes how she ritually connected herself with Mary at the churchings of the women of her parish.[32] Churchings might take place before the altar in the Lady Chapel as was the case in Ranworth Church in Norfolk, where new mothers placed their candle of thanksgiving for a safe delivery before the comforting gaze of the Virgin Mary and St Anne.[33] In these performances it is the similarity between their own successful motherhood and that of the Virgin that women celebrate, not the difference that so many male writers were keen to stress.

Mary's continued chastity, both pre- and post-partum, and her life of service in the Temple, clearly functioned as a role model for those women who chose to become brides of Christ. 'Lives of the Virgin Mary' are known to have belonged to nuns. Dame Pernelle Wrattisley, who lived at the Dominican Priory of the Blessed Virgin Mary and St Margaret at Dartford, owned a copy of Lydgate's *Life of Our Lady*.[34] It is possible that Dame Pernelle read this work alone or out loud to a gathering of her sisters.

Holy women composed their own praises of Mary. The 'Hymn to the Virgin' is ascribed to 'an holy Ankaresse of Maunsffeld' by John Shirley (d. 1456), compiler of Oxford Bodley MS Ashmole 59 in which the lyric is recorded.[35] Comprising five eight-line stanzas, each verse, and many lines within each stanza, begins with the salutation 'Heyle' in replication of Gabriel's greeting to Mary at the Annunciation. The composer employs many epithets in praise of Mary's virginity, such as 'mayde and moder in virgynitee' (l. 256), and reiterates this in Mary's description as 'closet of clennesse' (l. 268), 'chaste lylye' (l. 269), 'mayde makelesse' (l. 271), and 'floure of virtue which that may not fade' (l. 286). These are familiar from many Marian lyrics and one wonders to which texts the anchoress of Mansfield had access, either before or during her enclosure. As one might expect from an author who has chosen a life of chastity, all of Mary's special qualities stem from her inviolate virginity: Empress of Heaven, recipient of pain-free childbirth, and bodily assumption after her death. Like Eleanor Hull, this anchoress is most devoted to Mary as intercessor, 'mediatryce, and meene for mankynde. / Heyle , salve to seeke, us sinners send succour' (ll. 291–3).

Women were associated in many ways with a variety of Marian texts throughout the Middle Ages. The somatically distant yet ever-present figure of Mary could only be assimilated straightforwardly into the textual lives of a few, those who had chosen a life of virginity. Those who chose to live as wives and mothers successfully made connections between their lives and that of the Mother of God – as recorded in their wills, life-writing, poetry, and prayers – by interpreting and appropriating Mary's successful childbirth and motherhood. We should not doubt that the women, observed by Thomas More adoring an image of the Virgin, did indeed imagine that she smiled at them.[36]

Notes

1. Chris Maunder, 'Mary in the New Testament and Apocrypha', in *Mary: The Complete Resource*, ed. Sarah Jane Boss (Oxford: Oxford University Press, 2007), pp. 11–49. *Jacobus de Voragine: The Golden Legend. Readings on the Saints*, ed. and trans. W. Granger Ryan, 2 vols. (Princeton, NJ: Princeton University Press, 1993), vol. II.

2. *The Paston Letters*, ed. John Warrington (London: Dent, 1924; revised edition, 1978), p. 5.

3. Priscilla Martin, *Chaucer's Women: Nuns, Wives and Amazons* (London: Macmillan Press, 1990, repr. 1996), p. 19.

4. This quotation, taken from a translation of the fifth century *Paschalis Carminis* by Caelius Sedulius (Book II, lines 68–9), '*Nec primam similem visa es nec habere sequentem: Sola sine exemplo placuisti femina Christo*', is used by Marina Warner as the title for her study, *Alone of All Her Sex: The Myth and Cult of the Virgin Mary* (London: Picador, 2nd edn. 1985).

5. F. Gies and J. Gies, *Women in the Middle Ages: The Lives of Real Women in a Vibrant Age of Transition* (New York: Harper & Row, 1978), p. 134.

6. Carol Meale, '"...alle the bokes that I haue of laytn, englische, and frensch": Laywomen and their Books in Late Medieval England', in *Women and Literature in Britain, 1150-1500*, ed. Carol Meale (Cambridge: Cambridge University Press, 1993, repr. 1996), pp. 128–58 (p. 152, n. 44). For Lydgate's poem see *A Critical Edition of John Lydgate's Life of Our Lady*, ed. J. A. Lauritis *et al.* (Pittsburgh: Duquesne University Press, 1961).

7. Alexandra Barratt (ed.), *Women's Writing in Middle English* (London: Longman, 1992), pp. 219–31.

8. Carolyne Larrington, *Women and Writing in Medieval Europe: A Sourcebook* (London: Routledge, 1995), p. 226.

9. Alexandra Barratt, 'Dame Eleanor Hull: The Translator at Work', *Medium Aevum*, 72.2 (2003), 277–97, available at http://lion.chadwyck.co.uk.

10. Barratt, *Women's Writing*, p. 227.

11. Barratt, 'Dame Eleanor Hull'.

12. Kim M. Phillips, *Medieval Maidens: Young Women and Gender in England, 1270–1540* (Manchester: Manchester University Press, 2003), pp. 73–4 and 78.

13. *The N-Town Play: Cotton Vespasian D. 8*, ed. S. Spector, 2 vols., EETS s.s. 11 and 12 (Oxford: Oxford University Press, 1991), pp. 68–71.

14. Peter Coss, *The Lady in Medieval England, 1000–1500* (Stroud: Sutton Publishing Limited, 1998), p. 169.

15. Richard Marks, *Image and Devotion in Late Medieval England* (Stroud: Sutton Publishing Limited, 2004), p. 149.

16. Wendy Scase, 'St Anne and the Education of the Virgin: Literary and Artistic Traditions and their Implications', in *England in the Fourteenth Century: Proceedings of the1991 Harlaxton Symposium*, ed. Nicholas Rogers (Stamford: Paul Watkins Publishing, 1993), pp. 81–96 (p. 92).

17. Ibid., p. 93.
18. Janet Backhouse, *The Bedford Hours* (London: The British Library, 1990), p. 58.
19. Ibid., p. 59.
20. *The Book of the Knight of La Tour-Landry*, ed. T. Wright, EETS o.s. 33 (London: Kegan Paul, Trench, Trübner & Co., 1868, revised edition, 1906).
21. *Somerset Medieval Wills (Second Series) 1501–1530 with some Somerset Wills preserved at Lambeth*, ed. F. W. Weaver, Somerset Record Society, vol. 19 (London: Printed for Subscribers Only, 1903), p. 2. Also *Wills and Inventories from the Registers of the Commissary of Bury St Edmunds and the Archdeacon of Sudbury*, ed. Samuel Tymms, Camden Society Series I, no. 49 (London: J. B. Nicholls and Son, 1850), p. 95.
22. *The Chester Mystery Cycle*, ed. R. M. Lumiansky and D. Mills, vol. I, EETS s.s. 3 (London: Oxford University Press, 1974), pp. 130–1.
23. *The Knowing of Woman's Kind in Childing: A Middle English Version of Material Derived from the Trotula and Other Sources*, ed. Alexandra Barratt (Turnhout: Brepols, 2001), ll. 369–74.
24. P. J. P. Goldberg, *Women in England, c.1275–1515* (Manchester: Manchester University Press, 1995), p. 74.
25. E. Waterton, *Pietas Mariana Britannica: A History of English Devotion to the Most Blessed Virgin Mary Mother of God* (London: St Joseph's Catholic Library, 1879), p. 91.
26. *The Book of Margery Kempe*, ed. Sanford Brown Meech and Hope Emily Allen, EETS o.s. 212 (London: Oxford University Press, 1940). All quotations are taken from this edition.
27. Ibid., p. 19.
28. Barratt, *Women's Writing*, pp. 279–81.
29. Ibid., p. 279.
30. Ibid., p. 280.
31. A. H. Nelson, *The Medieval English Stage: Corpus Christi Pageants and Plays* (Chicago: University of Chicago Press, 1974), p. 88.
32. *Book of Margery Kempe*, p. 198.
33. Eamon Duffy, 'Holy Maydens, Holy Wyfes: The Cult of Women Saints in Fifteenth and Sixteenth Century England', *Studies in Church History*, 27 (1990), 175–96 (p. 196).
34. Meale, ' "…alle the bokes that I haue" ', p. 152, n. 44.
35. Barratt, *Women's Writing*, pp. 277–8.
36. Marks, *Image and Devotion*, p. 21.

10
Late-Medieval Conduct Literature

Myra J. Seaman

In 2009 Doofus's and Darling's *Manners for the Modern Man: A Handy Guide for Today's Ambiguous Etiquette Situations* appeared. This parodic manual presents forty-nine familiar scenarios, each consisting of two contrasting 'comic book' panels with instructive captions.[1] On the left, Doofus demonstrates 'what not to do', while on the right, Darling's behaviour offers a corrective. Doofus channel-surfs, checks his BlackBerry incessantly, spreads rumours, drinks excessively, drives aggressively, and objectifies women; Darling places the needs of his friends, relations, and dates before his own. A barely concealed foundation to the contrasts is Doofus's crass materialism and Darling's quietly confident wealth. Doofus's selfish greed and lack of self-control betray his worst fault: impecuniousness. Darling, in contrast, exudes fiscal ease. Manners, for 'the Modern Man', depend upon his being able to afford them.

If concerns with manners seem an occasion for humour in our post-etiquette twenty-first century, in contrast the fifteenth century in England might be described as 'The Century of Conduct' in that it witnessed an eruption in the making and reading of conduct literature.[2] A flourishing book trade stimulated by the relative affordability of paper and the promotion of lay-piety education by Archbishop Thoresby's reforms made conduct books newly available even to artisans and peasants with the means to buy them.[3] Booksellers targeted those who, in the words of Claire Sponsler, 'had a vested interest in both commercial activity and self-enhancement',[4] especially members of the merchant classes.[5] Such enhancement was possible through the commodification of manners in conduct texts appropriated from courtly and clerical domains, which promised merchant consumers an improved social status to match an enhanced economic status.[6] When engaged by this readership, conduct texts, despite their seemingly rigid and conservative aims, fostered social mobility, allowing owner-readers to distinguish themselves from the non-elite through their claim to certain virtues associated with the aristocracy. Rather than being read simply as 'a structure, system, or code', conduct has recently been theorized 'as social practice, […] an activity, event, or performance'[7] with conduct texts 'work[ing] ideologically to make bodily control something the rational subject wants, […] to create categories and hierarchies based on the marketing of acquirable traits such as manners'.[8] Seen this way, conduct literature was not restricting so much as enabling. It was at this time, after all, in most cases 'acquired by bourgeois readers as guides to upward mobility'.[9] Instead of demanding extreme denial of one's urges, governance was the means to producing the desired self and acquiring the desired social positioning,[10] promoting an active social acquisition previously unavailable.[11] Studying this transformation and the strategies that it effected, points to new fifteenth-century attitudes towards and methods for social negotiation.

The shift in conduct literature's orientation from aristocratic to bourgeois audiences is accompanied by a shift in its gender orientation. For aristocratic families the man – who inherited the wealth and status of his father and his father before him – affirmed and maintained the family's honour, so their conduct texts encouraged the development of 'masculine gentility and codes of courtesy'.[12] For merchant families in fifteenth-century England, the desired change to the family's social status – to match their accumulated wealth – was achieved through the marriage of the family's daughters to those who could offer, through their own family name, the desired social capital. Conduct texts directed towards bourgeois women thus focused on strategies for increasing their social value, since they embodied the family's potential for social self-improvement. As a result, while in aristocratic contexts men were encouraged to control themselves in order to be in the position to control others, in non-aristocratic contexts women were encouraged towards 'regulation of the self and of the household', both working together to ensure family honour.[13] For those families seeking to improve their status and then maintain it, honour depended upon 'thrift'[14] – a word used recurrently in these texts to mean 'the condition of thriving or prospering' but also increasingly in the sense of 'the means of thriving; industry, labour; profitable occupation'.[15] One needed to be educated to consume sufficiently but moderately, so as to maintain the goods and the improved status they made available.[16] This improvement, and that following the preservation of the status as indicated by the family's wealth, was possible through the daughters of the aspirant family, who were aided in this undertaking by conduct literature.

A small number of conduct texts were directed specifically at women in late-medieval England: *Thewis [Customs] of Gud Women*, *The Good Wyfe Wold a Pylgremage*, *The Good Wife Taught Her Daughter*, and Caxton's English translation of the French *Book of the Knight of La-Tour Landry*. All of these survive in copies from the last half of the fifteenth century, and they all model a type of good womanhood defined by her literal and figurative relation to the household. Indeed, they emphasize the pragmatic and generally leave the symbolic to be supplied by the ideologically attuned reader. *Thewis of Gud Women*, a poem of just over 300 lines, presents the instruction of a good wife whose aim is to show that even a poor woman can be made valuable with proper behaviour; the treatise thus focuses especially on the way young girls should be raised to develop that potential social worth.[17] The text's main lesson is not, as might be anticipated, religious or even moral, but practical: the audience is discouraged from behaviour that 'oft [...] makis a foul endynge' (l. 176)[18] and encouraged to behave in ways that 'eftir cum to gret valoure' (l. 227). They should avoid what will harm them socially, and pursue what will help their reputations (advice given also to young men in other conduct texts). The text notably includes the following instruction:

> And eftir nwne, one the halyday,
> Owthir pray or play at honest play,
> To reid bukis or lere wefinge,
> Be occupeid euir in sum thinge.
>
> (ll. 167–70)

Reading is encouraged for the purpose of self-improvement, specifically the development of good housewifery. *The Good Wyfe Wold a Pylgremage* is a short poem (84 lines) that takes the form of advice from mother (a particular 'Gud Woman') to daughter, with the mother's emphasis on practical advice that will help her daughter, during the mother's trip to the Holy Land, 'to gowerne well this hous' (l. 3)[19] and keep herself from shame, concerns frequently expressed in terms of the marketplace: the daughter is discouraged from appearing to be merchandise for sale (she should be careful how she dresses herself, for example, or 'thus men wyll tell, "The corsser hathe his palfrey dy[gh]t all reydy for to sell"' [l. 24]). Yet even as she ought not to represent herself as merchandise for sale, she is encouraged to consider herself and her value in precisely those terms. The key metaphor of the text is thus 'He [th]at spendyth mor [th]en he gettythe, a beggerrys lyfe he schall lede' (l. 76): the daughter must be sure to accumulate more than she needs, to prevent that situation from becoming her own. A good woman is a good housewife who, in turn, is a good fiscal manager. Another mother-to-daughter advice text is *The Good Wife Taught Her Daughter*, a 200-line poem more overtly religious in orientation than the preceding two, yet sharing with them the central metaphor of exchange. Indeed, here the treatment of others' goods determines spiritual well-being ('Borowyd thing muste nedys go home, / If that thou wyll to heven gone' [ll. 191–2]),[20] with the daughter herself a 'borowyd thing' that will in the case of her right conduct be returned to its proper 'home', 'heven'. The daughter is to beware of the market's ability to commodify what it ought not:

> Ne go thou not to no merket
> To sell thi thryft; bewer of itte.
> Ne go thou noght to the taverne,
> Thy godnes for to selle therinne.

> (ll. 63–6)

Instead, and very literally, she ought to protect her goodness and prosperity by staying home: 'Houswyfey wyll thou gon / On werkedeys in thine awne wone' (ll. 111–12). The daughter is further warned about the instability of her prosperity, which it is her duty to secure.[21] As with the other two poems, the ultimate goal is to 'Be thow, doughter, a houswyfe gode' (l. 123) – with full awareness that the success of the family depends upon the guidance and wisdom of the housewife.

Unusual among conduct texts directed at late-medieval English-speaking women is *The Book of the Knight of La-Tour Landry*,[22] in that it is a translation into Middle English from the original French. A number of other features distinguish it from the three short advice poems for women discussed above: its length (144 chapters, each as long as the complete text of *Good Wyfe Wold a Pylgremage*); its authority (the advice comes from a father to his daughters, rather than from a mother); its having a named author (the others, like much conduct literature, are anonymous); and its form (the advice comes not through proverbial sayings and warnings but through brief exemplary narratives modelling behaviour to imitate and to avoid). The text thus seems generically anomalous, despite promoting the same ideological investment. However, as a collection of individual tales presented in ways that encourage an audience to make thematic connections among them, it is representative of late-medieval English bourgeois reading habits, for if the fifteenth century might be called 'The Century of Conduct', it might also be termed 'The Century of the Anthology'.[23] The *Book of the Knight of La-Tour Landry* combines these two 'trends', as both conduct text and anthology of connected narratives. The manuscript anthologies in which Middle English conduct texts such as *The Good Wife Taught Her Daughter* and *The Gode Wyfe Wold a Pylgremage* reside present them alongside an array of devotional and secular texts such as romances, saint's lives, didactic tales, prayers, proverbs, and Scripture narratives. Traditionally, literary history has read a manuscript's contents individually, and primarily in terms of diachronic and generic influence – a romance in relation to other romances, and in terms of earlier manuscript appearances of the given romance, for instance; more recently, such texts have been read in terms of the synchronous influence exerted and experienced by the cohabitants of a given volume, regardless of genre or genealogy. By considering them together within the context of fifteenth-century audiences' reading environments, those texts traditionally excluded from the 'conduct' category (romances and devotional texts, for example) can be seen to share ideological purposes with those conduct texts that are their manuscript neighbours within these anthologies.

Similarly, our sense of the audiences implied by these texts can be usefully complicated by performing such a reading, in that conduct texts ostensibly for young men or for girls or women share audiences with romances and devotional texts that, as Saunders and Sauer argue in their contributions to this volume, would point towards an adult and often female audience. As Diane Watt has explained, '[W]riting cannot be understood in isolation from its intended and/or actual readership or audience', with our understanding aided by 'exploring the ways authors and readers/audience work together to produce meaning'.[24] The ways texts 'work together' help us to generate meaning as well, in the process finding readers and audiences that we might otherwise not perceive when investigating texts in textual isolation. Read side by side, the romances and devotional items are seen to be modelling the same virtuous behaviour prescribed by the conduct texts, while the didactic narratives of disobedient women that also appear in these anthologies demonstrate the unwanted results of failing to pursue the virtues advocated by the conduct texts. Such an influence of conduct literature on texts traditionally considered denizens of very different generic territory has been demonstrated by Kathleen Ashley in the context of late-medieval drama, where, she claims, '[t]he ideology of the conduct book inscribed upon the cycle form transformed the religious drama and gave it new social functions in the late Middle Ages'.[25] The same influence can be observed in the household books in which conduct texts appeared, such that the romances no longer serve primarily the social functions of the aristocracy to whom they were addressed centuries earlier, and the devotional texts present a religious sensibility deeply infused with an attention to the earthly and social ramifications of a salvific economy. The bourgeois women in the audience of such anthologies contribute to the nature of this redirection, and by '[e]xtending our definition of women's writing further', following Watt's development of Carol M. Meale's model, 'to include writing that is produced for and read by women', we can develop 'a more subtle understanding of women's engagement with medieval literary culture'.[26]

Oxford, Bodleian Library, MS Ashmole 61,[27] produced in Leicestershire in the late fifteenth century, is a household anthology of forty-one items that in a number of its features points towards a female audience. We know nothing about the volume's ownership prior to its becoming part of the collection of Elias Ashmole in the seventeenth century, though it contains two notes in sixteenth- or seventeenth-century hands that suggest an Oxfordshire location,[28] and another note intriguingly says 'Delivered d [sic] dame Elizabeth', indicating a possible female owner. Virtually all of the anthology's items are in verse, half of them narratives and the other half lyrics and didactic pieces; they are largely anonymous and include saints' lives (of St Margaret and of St Eustace), exempla (such as *The Jealous Wife, The Tale of an Incestuous*

Daughter, The Adulterous Falmouth Squire, and *The Knight Who Forgave His Father's Slayer*), romances (*Sir Isumbras, Lybeaus Desconus, Sir Orfeo*, and others), passion narratives, devotional verse (such as a Marian lament), prayers (some specifically suited to morning and to night), and comic tales (including an allegorical debate and two drinking competitions). The single scribe of this anthology, who identifies himself by signing 'Amen quod Rat[h]e' at the end of half of the manuscript's items, seems particularly invested in redeploying conduct literature. His versions of extant poems are idiosyncratic enough to suggest that he regularly made at times extensive changes to his sources, and he includes a unique text, *Dame Curtasy*, which is perhaps original to him; further, he situates the items in the collection such that poems not traditionally identified as conduct literature serve a purpose complementary to that of the explicit conduct texts. In this case, women readers are active contributors to that appropriation, with the central good encouraged in these exemplary and prescriptive poems being the success of the household, achieved and maintained in large part through women's thrift and social wisdom. Just as the seemingly miscellaneous narratives in the *Book of the Knight of La-Tour Landry* work as conduct literature because of the larger purpose to which their anthologizer puts them collectively, the non-conduct items in Ashmole 61, when read with the conduct texts prominent in the manuscript, behave as conduct literature as much as they do romances or saints' lives, for instance, with – as in *The Book of the Knight of La-Tour Landry* – a distinct focus on women.

The anthology's concern with public behaviour and reputation is furthered by a distinctly public orientation in its encouragement both of oral reading and of social (rather than private or strictly religious) virtues. A female audience is particularly well served by a collection suited to group reading occasions, and such a community of readers is suggested by the contents of this anthology, especially in the ways they intersect with one another. The romances emphasize strong wives who help their knight-husbands overcome adversity and ultimately preserve the family in the face of extreme threats; the exemplary narratives in almost every case demonstrate the challenges bourgeois women face integrating their public and private selves; the devotional texts invite women's spiritual investment through associations with female saints and mothers. Together, the items in this anthology appeal to the concerns of a female audience in relation to matters that are fundamentally economic. The rewards for social and religious virtuous living are consistent and very much in the present.

Ashmole 61 contains two unique items that, in being exclusive to this collection, point towards a special interest on the part of its scribe: they offer women positions of authority concerning important household issues of thrift and honour, both of them rooted in economic prudence. *Dame Curtasy* provides instruction typical of conduct texts addressed to young men, but in this case the speaker is Dame Curtasy herself, taking on the same role as the Good Wife in *Good Wife Taught Her Daughter* (which precedes it in the manuscript) but passing on social wisdom that is not gendered specifically feminine. Its main focus is etiquette at table and the avoidance of swearing or lying, slandering or flattering, those behaviours that allow for a young man's success in the household of a social superior. *Dame Curtasy's* lessons, like those elsewhere in the collection, encourage 'a combination of bourgeois industriousness with aristocratic elegance'.[29] Similarly, though with an emphasis on industriousness over elegance, *The Carpenter's Tools* also depends upon a woman to deliver its lessons on appropriate, profitable behaviour. In this case, however, the lessons come not in the form of a conduct text but as an allegorical debate about the vices and future prospects of a carpenter, engaged in by his personified tools, focusing on his lack of thrift that results from his excessive drinking. Some of them come to his defence and claim he is worthy to be a sheriff or knight (ll. 105–6, 162), but such aspiration is rejected by others, with one for instance insisting, 'A carpenter to be a knyght? / That were ever ageyn ryght' (ll. 167–8). The poem ultimately depends upon the Carpenter's Wife to proclaim what is socially just, and she does so based on her marriage to him, which she presents in terms of bondage:

> I ame to hym bounde so faste
> That off my halter I may not caste.
> Therfor the preste that bounde me prentys,
> He shall treuly have my curse.
>
> (ll. 267–70)

The Wife is herself apprentice (like the tools) to an improper master, and she reads her marriage as a bargain for her husband but not for her. In her acquired wisdom, she reveals the same danger warned of by the conduct texts for bourgeois English women: selling oneself too cheaply, and binding oneself unprofitably. Both Dame Curtasy and the Carpenter's Wife model a social wisdom and understanding of duty that Ashmole 61 shows to be the purview of women, even in contexts traditionally considered the domain of men.

Duty is a central virtue in conduct literature for the non-nobility, with an orientation towards service. *The Carpenter's Tools* encourages 'treuly that ye do your labore, / For that wyll be to youre honour' (ll. 275–6). Other texts in the collection focus on the duties associated with service to God, and especially those duties performed by women. The duties and sacrifices of mothers in particular are addressed by the anthology's *Lamentacion Beati Mariae* [Lament of Mary], which uses the 'maternal bond [to achieve] its rhetorical power', as Shuffelton points out,[30] uncommon in a Passion lyric or even among medieval lyrics generally. Mary holds a special position in the anthology, as in *The Jealous Wife* where the husband's utter devotion to her (including regular services throughout the night) raises his wife's suspicion, leading her to kill her children and herself; yet his devotion also allows the wife's soul to be saved from condemnation to hell after her death. The family therefore benefits from the husband's religious duty, which is itself rightly attuned to the spiritual model offered by the woman exalted above all women, affirming women's authority in matters of social and religious behaviour.

Religious dutifulness is shown to generate social success in exemplary tales that also tend to focus on the experiences of women, with family relationships vital to the outcome,[31] as in the exemplary narratives *Incestuous Daughter* and *Knight Who Forgave his Father's Slayer*. Among the forty-one items in the collection, seven reassure with reunited families.[32] This reunion almost always depends upon a reunion of the family with its property, a plot development central to four of the romances (*Sir Isumbras, Sir Cleges, The Earl of Tolous, Lybeaus Desconus*) and one saint's life (*St Eustace*). One romance, *Sir Cleges*, resolves profitably for the family only because of the wise intervention of the hero's wife, Dame Clarys. When her husband misinterprets the central symbol of the narrative – reading in the miracle of the unseasonable fruit a bad omen – she correctly sees it as a sign of future good. Previously, she had pulled him out of his mourning when it led the family to descend into poverty. She sees their way through the material challenges with her dutiful thrift, keeping the family's honour sound, a woman who models the instruction for becoming the 'good housewife' provided by the conduct texts.

Many texts in Ashmole 61, including narratives and devotional pieces, encourage women readers towards the thrift and family honour promoted in conduct texts for bourgeois women readers. Vital to the manners they promote – which is to say the behaviour coded to allow one's membership in elite society – is the means to express it, as with Doofus and Darling with whom I began this essay. Success depends, for a twenty-first-century middle-class young man or a fifteenth-century upwardly mobile young woman and her family, upon the ability to translate economic prosperity into social advancement. Ashmole 61 and the women who are its audience thus illustrate Watt's claim that

> the blurring of the distinction between women-authored and women-oriented texts that I trace could be extended to other medieval texts, from conduct books to romances, and to a broader range of devotional material produced for and read by women, including manuscripts and miscellanies known to have been owned by women.[33]

While the fifteenth-century owners of this anthology remain unnamed, the woman-oriented texts – the conduct books, romances, and devotional material – and particularly the way they work together to encourage a particular version of active and influential bourgeois womanhood allow us further insight into the collaborative writing women were engaged in, sometimes almost too quietly for us to hear until we learn how to listen.

Notes

1. David Hoffman, *Doofus and Darling's Manners for the Modern Man: A Handy Guide for Today's Ambiguous Etiquette Situations* (New York: Black Dog and Leventhal Publishers, 2009).
2. Mark Addison Amos, ' "For Manners Make Man": Bourdieu, de Certeau, and the Common Appropriation of Noble Manners in the *Book of Courtesy*', in *Medieval Conduct*, ed. Kathleen Ashley and Robert L. A. Clark (Minneapolis: University of Minnesota Press, 2001), pp. 23–48 (pp. 24–5).
3. Kim M. Phillips, *Medieval Maidens: Young Women and Gender in England, 1270-1540* (Manchester: Manchester University Press, 2003), p. 65.
4. Claire Sponsler, *Drama and Resistance: Bodies, Goods, and Theatricality in Late Medieval England* (Minneapolis: University of Minnesota Press, 1997), p. 54.
5. Kathleen Ashley, 'The *Miroir des bonnes femmes*: Not for Women Only?', in *Medieval Conduct*, ed. Ashley and Clark, pp. 86–105 (p. 88).
6. Claire Sponsler, 'Eating Lessons: Lydgate's "Dietary" and Consumer Conduct', in *Medieval Conduct*, ed. Ashley and Clark, pp. 1–22 (p. 5).
7. Sponsler, *Drama and Resistance*, p. 50.
8. Ibid., p. 57.
9. Ashley, 'The *Miroir des bonnes femmes*', p. 101.
10. Sponsler, *Drama and Resistance*, pp. 53, 68.
11. Robert L. A. Clark, 'Constructing the Female Subject in Late Medieval Devotion', in *Medieval Conduct*, ed. Ashley and Clark, pp. 160–82 (p. 160).
12. Ashley, 'The *Miroir des bonnes femmes*', pp. 97 and 102.
13. Sarah Salih, 'At Home, Out of the House', in *The Cambridge Companion to Medieval Women's Writing*, ed. Carolyn Dinshaw and David Wallace (Cambridge: Cambridge University Press, 2003), pp. 124–40 (p. 134).
14. *Codex Ashmole 61: A Compilation of Popular Middle English Verse*, ed. George Shuffelton, TEAMS: Middle English Text Series: Kalamazoo, MI: Medieval Institute Publications, 2008, p. 427.
15. 'Thrift'. Def. 1a, 1b. *The Oxford English Dictionary*. 2nd edn. 1989 (http:// dictionary.oed.com.nuncio.cofc.edu) [accessed 1 June 2010].
16. Sponsler, 'Eating Lessons', pp. 7–8.
17. Diane Bornstein, *The Lady in the Tower: Medieval Courtesy Literature for Women* (Hamden, CT: Archon Books, 1983), p. 136.
18. Quotations from *Thewis* are taken from Tauno F. Mustanoja's edition in *The Good Wife Taught Her Daughter, The Good Wyfe Wold a Pylgremage, The Thewis of Gud Women* (Helsinki: Suomalaisen Kirjallisuuden Scu, 1948); I use the copy from Cambridge University Library MS Kk.1.5, which appears here in parallel-text form with the copy from St John's College, Cambridge, MS G.23.
19. *The Good Wyfe Wold a Pylgremage*, ed. Mustanoja.
20. Quotations from *Good Wife* are taken from *Codex Ashmole 61*, ed. Shuffelton.
21. Felicity Riddy, 'Mother Knows Best: Reading Social Change in a Courtesy Text', *Speculum*, 71 (1996), 66–86 (69).

22. Geoffroy La Tour Landry, *The Book of the Knight of La Tour-Landry*, ed. Thomas Wright, rev. edn., EETS o.s. 33 (London: Kegan Paul, Trench, Trübner & Co., 1906).

23. Here I push a bit at Seth Lerer's description of English medieval literary culture as exhibiting an 'anthologistic impulse', in 'Medieval English Literature and the Idea of the Anthology', *PMLA*, 118 (2003), 1251–67 (1253).

24. Diane Watt, *Medieval Women's Writing: Works by and for Women in England, 1100–1500* (Cambridge: Polity Press, 2007), p. 2.

25. Kathleen M. Ashley, 'Medieval Courtesy Literature', in *The Ideology of Conduct: Essays on Literature and the History of Sexuality*, ed. Nancy Armstrong and Leonard Tennenhouse (New York: Methuen and Co., 1987), pp. 25–38 (p. 26).

26. Watt, *Medieval Women's Writing*, p. 5; Carol M. Meale, *Women and Literature in Britain, 1150–1500* (Cambridge: Cambridge University Press, 1996).

27. Edinburgh, National Library of Scotland, MS Advocates 19.3.1 works similarly.

28. *Codex Ashmole 61*, ed. Shuffelton, p. 3.

29. Ibid., p. 445.

30. Ibid., pp. 11 and 526.

31. Ibid., p. 11.

32. Ibid.

33. Watt, *Medieval Women's Writing*, p. 2.

Part III
Literacies and Literary Cultures

11
Women and their Manuscripts

Carol M. Meale

'Item to Alianore Stratton my doughter 1. ffedirbed and oon transon . and 1 pair fustians and a booke cou*e*ryd with red veluet the whiche was my mod-ers [...]'. So decreed Alianore Nicholson of East Dereham in mid-Norfolk on the 'ixth day of Novembyr', 1487.[1] Thus is encapsulated the rewards and the frustrations of working with last wills and testaments for evidence of women's book ownership, the primary source for such evidence aside from the comparatively rare examples of women's names occurring within extant codices. At one and the same time such references act as signifiers of the manuscript as an object of value and of attachment, and yet we can often remain ignorant of their content, whether secular or religious. In the case of Alianore we might perhaps infer that the book was a personal service book, such as a primer, but of Alianore herself we know no more than that she was a 'wydowe'; that, in the absence of the naming of any other children, her daughter may have been her sole survivor; and that she was probably a mem-ber of the guild of St Withburga in her home town, since she bequeathed it four shillings.[2]

Given, though, that the testament offers potentially unparalleled insight into the lives, families, friendships, and book ownership of medieval women, this essay will concentrate on the testament as evidence, and so some assess-ment of the strengths and pitfalls involved in using the material is in order. To begin with, Norman Tanner has noted that only 'a small proportion' of the inhabitants of Norwich, one of the most important cities in England throughout the Middle Ages, are represented by the city's wills, of which a large number (1,804) survives.[3] Then women in general, unless they were given permission by their husbands to make a will, were only free to do so once they were widowed, so the age-group of book-owners derived from this source is, inevitably, skewed in favour of older women.[4] As to the num-bers of women's wills, in Norwich, for example, Tanner has estimated that among lay testators 'men exceeded women by slightly more than three to one' in the period 1370 to 1532, whereas in London, where overall statistics are not yet available, due to the large number of church courts in which it was possible to enrol wills, and the thousands which survive (approximately 15,000), in the one extant register from the archdeaconry court, covering the years 1393 to 1415, only 17 per cent were made by women.[5] In terms of class, a majority of wills were made by members of the middle classes (gentry and mercantile) and above, as might be expected. This, at least, is the finding of Anne Dutton, from her survey of published wills from the country as a whole, which is supplemented by examination of York diocesan wills, both printed and unprinted, and the work of Norman Tanner.[6] Yet in York itself, however, as Jeremy Goldberg has demonstrated, 'a substantial number of artisans and their wives' are represented in the 2,300 wills of laypeople registered between 1321 and 1500, although not many actually owned books.[7] While not focused on women, the study concludes that a 'significant proportion of books', particularly primers, were bequeathed either by, or to, them, although no precise statistics are given.[8]

These figures or estimates, then, provide some of the parameters for the study of women's book ownership as it stands at present, and the importance of this continuing statistical work, leading to what have been termed by Richard Smith 'collective biographies', should not be ignored.[9] At the same time, as he also points out, this approach runs the risk of 'simplification' which then suppresses 'particularity'.[10] It is therefore the intention in the remainder of this essay to seek out the particular, by looking at individual women's wills in East Anglia for the evidence they can provide as to reading matter and how it figured within women's lives, in as much as these may be recovered.[11] This regional emphasis is adopted primarily because East Anglia has such rich resources in regard to the evidence of literacy (it can be no coincidence that both Julian of Norwich and Margery Kempe hailed from this area); but in addition, there is a wide body of scholarly work on the area which may be used to sketch in the detail of how women's lives were lived.

The publication by Colin Richmond of excerpts from the will of Thomasin Gra, daughter of London mercer Thomas Fauconer and wife to Sir John Gra (d. 1459), is a case in point. Fauconer, a Norfolk man by birth (he grew up in Honing) was an alderman of London and Mayor in 1414–15.[12] The marriage of his younger daughter, Thomasin, was not financially propitious. Her husband, son of a merchant and mayor of York was, although a soldier and of gentle status, impoverished, and constantly engaged in lawsuits over land.[13] Nevertheless, Thomasin's will, made on 30 January 1475 and proved exactly three months later, mentions a choice selection of books.[14] To a female friend she left a primer with 'ymagerie'; to Thomas Fitzwilliam, another primer, together with 'an englisshe booke with the xij monythes of the yere therin specified. Also another boke wherin is conteyned the appocalipse in Frenssh'.[15] To Thomas Wase (or Wace), gentleman of Norwich, she left 'a litill prymmer'.[16] Most interestingly of all, to John Castor of the Exchequer she bequeathed 'an englisshe booke wherin is conteyned the victorious dedes of Kyng Richard Cure de Lyon' and 'a booke of the lives of Seint

Fraunceys and Seint Cecille in Englisshe'. The latter two works could perhaps be excerpts from the verse *South English Legendary*, or the prose *Gilte Legende* of 1438, of which fourteen manuscripts remain, or even fragments of Osbern Bokenham's lost *Legendary*, whilst the romance is certainly the early fourteenth-century work of that name.[17] This might be seen as an unusual book for a woman to have owned, long as it is on chivalric valour and (historically accurately in this case) short on the role of women within chivalry; but Thomasin's ownership of it should caution against any easy assumptions as to women's tastes in reading matter.

Equally intriguing is the question of where she could have obtained these books. Inheritance or the second-hand market should not be ruled out: there are not, for example, any apocalypses in French made in England in the fifteenth century surviving, as opposed to the thirteenth and fourteenth.[18] *Richard Coeur de Lion*, on the other hand, was still being copied during the fifteenth century, as six of its ten manuscripts testify.[19] As for the primers, they could have been heirlooms, or English, French, or Flemish productions. London, with its busy trade in old and new books may be the obvious candidate for the supply of any of these volumes, and that the Gras spent time in London after their marriage is clear from the fact that Sir John was buried in the church of St Margaret's, Westminster, where Thomasin also expressed a wish to be interred, next to him. Provincial production should not, however, be ruled out: East Anglia in particular is rich in evidence of such production, even if the situation prevailing in Norwich itself is still (puzzlingly) unclear, although there must have been a book trade of sorts in the city to support the needs of the cathedral and other beneficed clergy.[20] Even leaving out of account organized production, though, there remains the possibility of individual commissions from a scribe whose full-time profession was not necessarily that of copying books.

Despite Thomasin Gra's ownership of a copy of *Richard Coeur de Lion*, the number of women known to have bequeathed romances in Middle English remains small, although this is not to say that there is not hard evidence to support the notion that they did read texts in the genre.[21] In wills, however, French romances figure more strongly, and Elizabeth Wolferstone in her testament of 9 January 1417 fits with this profile.[22] She appears to have been domiciled at the Augustinian nunnery of Campsea Ash in Suffolk: she requested burial in the church of 'Campesse' before the altar of the Holy Trinity, and bequeathed money to the nunnery and some of its inhabitants. This could mean that she was a vowess, although there can be no certainty on the point. She makes bequests to a number of churches in the region, including Wolferstone itself, and she is meticulous in her detailing of what of her personal belongings are to go to whom. It is to her granddaughter, Anne, that she leaves '1 . librum de ffranco de sege de troye & de Godfride de Bolneye [*sic*]'. The double interests revealed by her piety and reading tastes recall those of her more famous younger contemporary, Joan Beaufort, countess of

Westmorland, especially in the latter's choice of *Le Viage de Godfrey Boylion*, which she lent to her half-nephew, Henry V.[23] Once again, this example should act as a reminder that books should not be classified exclusively by what is thought to be appropriate to the gender of the owner/reader. Clear examples of this lack of bias occur where a manuscript is bequeathed from a man to a woman or vice versa. In 1389, for example, Sir Bartholomew Bacon of Erwarton, south-east of Ipswich, left a book called 'Romaunce' to his wife for her lifetime, and although the description may simply refer to the text being in French rather than constituting a romance as we understand the term, it does emphasize the fact that we should not ignore cross-gender interests.[24]

This is a point worth bearing in mind when considering the great desiderata of present and future studies of women and their manuscripts: firstly that of establishing reading networks; and, secondly, that of placing women's book ownership within the contexts of their lives and contemporary society, so that we may begin to understand more fully their cultural import. Valuable work has been and is being carried out on these issues, notably by Felicity Riddy, Julia Boffey, Mary Erler, and others, and in the context of this essay the will of Beatrix (or Beatrice) Balle, dated 30 January 1458, proved 18 March 1466, the original of which was stamped with her own seal, provides a richly textured picture of a late-medieval female book-owner.[25] Listed as a widow and assessed at the value of £4 in 1451, she was the late wife of Thomas Balle, citizen and spicer of Norwich, who had been one of two treasurers of the city in 1432, and sheriff in 1434, whose will (not proved) is dated 1446.[26] One of her executors was John Gilbert, whom she describes as alderman, but who was a former mayor.[27] She requested burial in the church of St Peter Mancroft, next to her husband. To 'Joha*ne* filie mee' she left '1 libru*m* vite *sancte* margarete' (probably the *Life* of St Margaret of Antioch),[28] and to the same daughter, later given her surname of Schelton, she also left her primer, covered with 'cloth of Gold'. The rest of her goods appear to have been of equally good quality, including a maser which she left to her daughter Isabelle, along with coral beads and a crucifix in precious metals; bed coverings including a 'testyr cum rosis'; and several gowns. To the altar of the cathedral she left a ring with a ruby. She left sums of money to Joanna, or Joan, and her other children (three daughters) and the many Scheltons named, presumably Joanna's family. She also bequeathed, to 'D*omi*ne margarete purdaunce', a ring with a sapphire. Such a gift to a younger woman from an older one implies close and valued friendship, and given that Margaret Purdaunce (d. 1481) is known to have been a serious and devout book collector, this evidence of a close association between the two women is of significance.[29] They had other acquaintances in common. Purdaunce was left a cloth painted with an image of Christ by the Norwich hermit, Richard Ferneys in 1464, and Balle left 6s 8d to 'Ric*ardus* hermite', who may have been the same man.[30] Ferneys was at the centre of a devout circle embracing laywomen and hermits, anchorites and anchoresses, and Beatrice Balle left gifts to other hermits and anchoresses.[31] To 'Do*mi*ne Juliane lampett', anchoress at the nearby Carrow nunnery, she bequeathed 3s 4d and the same sum to the apparently otherwise unknown anchoress 'de Conesfford' in Norwich itself, 'Agnete kyte'; and to a hermit named Thomas, who may have been resident at Berstreet Gate, 8d.[32]

Like Margaret Purdaunce, Beatrice remembered female religious houses in Norfolk and north Suffolk, and individual women – sometimes only identified by their office – within them. Her bequests included the houses of Flixton, Carrow, Bruisyard, and Thetford, whilst to the prioress of Carrow she left 2s; to Domina Elizabeth Mortimer, nun of Bruisyard, 3s 4d; to the prioress of Thetford 20d; to the sometime prioress of Blackborough, 3s 4d and to sister Elizabeth there, 2s. Within Norwich itself she left 4d each to the sisters of Normans hospital, and to Cecily Mortimer (presumably a relative of Elizabeth) of the said hospital, 3s 4d. To the paupers of St Giles she left 2d and to the sisters there, 4d. The only male religious she remembers are the Friars Mendicant, to whom she left 10s. Aside from this she left what may be regarded as bequests typical of a woman of her status at this time, namely to the upkeep of local churches (St John Maddermarket and St Laurence); to the College of St Mary in the Fields; and to the prisoners in the Guildhall and the Castle. Altogether, it is a testament in which women predominate in a circle of shared piety and apparent friendship.

Women's engagement with devotion and learning extended, however, beyond the act of possession of books, and to conclude some account will be given as to the commitment of two women to scholarship within a monastic milieu. In 1458, Margaret Wetherby, late wife of Thomas, mayor of Norwich in 1427 and 1432 and MP in 1429 and 1431, made her testament.[33] Thomas had had a turbulent career in the city, opposing the names of two men put forward by the Common Council (one of them Margaret Purdaunce's husband) for election as his successor. This event, in 1433, precipitated a civic crisis which lasted for over five years and involved the unpopular William de la Pole, then earl of Suffolk, and the Crown. Margaret's attitude to all of this is, perhaps not surprisingly, unknown, but she requested burial alongside Thomas in the Augustinian priory of Norwich, though she had been living, with her husband, until his death, in a house within the precincts of Carrow Priory.[34] She paid 1s for this privilege. One of the Wetherby daughters, Alice, was a nun in the house: her mother bequeathed her ten marks. One of her co-residents in the precinct was Christian Veyle, who occupied a tenement at an annual rent of 6s 8d. She was a member of the circle including Margaret Purdaunce and Richard Ferneys and, presumably, Beatrice Balle.[35] This is a spare document, principally concerned with charitable bequests, and reflects none of the material richness of Beatrice Ball's will, but for the last but one clause. Here, Margaret leaves the extraordinarily large sum of 100 marks (£66 13s 4d) for the building of a new library for the Augustinian friary on condition that in the window-glass and on each one of the desks intended for the books, the names of her and her husband should be inscribed. (The spiritual reward for this was to be the yearly celebration of their souls and the soul of John Wakeryng, late bishop of Norwich, by one friar.)[36] This extravagant memorial is, to my knowledge, unparalleled, especially in the respect for learning which underpins it, but it is clearly designed with the prospect of relief from purgatorial suffering in mind – a sentiment common in the late Middle Ages.

Around the same time, in 1459, another widow, Alice Foster, whose husband had been a hosier, left to the repair of the library of the Dominicans the much lesser sum of 13s 4d: one mark.[37] I have been unable to find any trace of Alice Foster's will, but she evidently did not belong to the civic elite, unlike Margaret Wetherby and Beatrice Balle. This does not, however, make her final contribution to the cause of scholarship and its dissemination amongst the populace any the less moving, or significant.[38]

This latter discussion highlights what remains a problem for scholars working in the area of women's book ownership, namely that for women lower down the social scale evidence of both their reading habits and their intellectual and/or devotional aspirations as well as of their lives is too often occluded by the passage of time. Nonetheless, there is evidence to be recovered, as the examples of Alice Foster and Alianore Nicholson demonstrate, and while we may never be able to reconstruct some of the large events and minutiae of detail which characterize Beatrice Balle's life, all of the women considered here may justifiably be said to have shared in a like-minded community composed of those who respected books and learning.

Notes

1. London, The National Archives, Public Record Office, Probate Record 11/18, fols. 177v–178r. I am indebted to Sebastian Sutcliffe for informing me of this will and that of Elizabeth Wolferstone, below.
2. Withburga was a daughter of the seventh-century king Anna of the East Angles who founded a Benedictine nunnery in East Dereham: Francis Blomefield, *An Essay Towards a Topographical History of the County of Norfolk*, 11 vols. (London: Bulmer, 1805–10), X, p. 217.
3. Norman P. Tanner, *The Church in Late Mediaeval Norwich, 1370–1532*, Studies and Texts 66 (Toronto: Pontifical Institute of Mediaeval Studies, 1984), pp. 113–15.
4. Caroline M. Barron, 'The Widow's World in Late Medieval London', in *Medieval London Widows, 1300–1500*, ed. Caroline M. Barron and Anne F. Sutton (London and Rio Grande: Hambledon, 1974), pp. xiii–xxxiv.
5. Tanner, *The Church in Late Mediaeval Norwich*, pp. 115, 113 and n.2; Barron, 'The Widow's World', p. xvi.
6. Anne M. Dutton, 'Passing the Book: Testamentary Transmission of Religious Literature to and by Women in England, 1350–1500', in *Women, The Book and The Godly*, ed. Lesley Smith and Jane H. M. Taylor (Cambridge: D. S. Brewer, 1995), pp. 41–54 (pp. 43–7).

7. P. J. P. Goldberg, 'Lay Book Ownership in Later Medieval York: The Evidence of Wills', *The Library*, 6th ser., 16 (1994), 181–9 (182 and Table, 183). A difference in methodology between Tanner and Goldberg in calculating the numbers of wills extant is that the former includes ecclesiastics. See *The Church in Late Mediaeval Norwich*, p. 114, n.7.

8. Goldberg, 'Lay Book Ownership', p. 189.

9. Richard Smith, 'Introduction' to Eileen Power, *Medieval People* (London: Methuen, 1986), p. xvi, quoted by Barron, 'The Widow's World', p. xv.

10. Smith, 'Introduction', p. xix.

11. *Medieval London Widows*, ed. Barron and Sutton, possibly remains the most influential book-length study of the lives of a socially diverse selection of medieval women.

12. Sylvia L. Thrupp, *The Merchant Class of Medieval London, 1300–1500* (Ann Arbor: University of Michigan Press, 1948, repr. 1977), pp. 339–40; Anne F. Sutton, *The Mercery of London: Trade, Goods and People, 1130–1578* (Aldershot: Ashgate, 2005), pp. 138, 146, 160, 220, 555, 556, 565.

13. Colin Richmond, *John Hopton: A Fifteenth-Century Suffolk Gentleman* (Cambridge: Cambridge University Press, 1981), pp. 16–20.

14. Colin Richmond, *The Paston Family in the Fifteenth Century: Endings* (Manchester: Manchester University Press, 2000), p. 125, n.152. Her will is Oxford, Magdalen College, Multon Hall 47.

15. On the seeming popularity of apocalypses amongst women see Carol M. Meale ' "…alle the bokes that I haue of latyn, englisch, and frensch": Laywomen and their Books in Late Medieval England', in *Women and Literature in Britain, 1150–1500*, ed. Carol M. Meale, 2nd edn. (Cambridge: Cambridge University Press, 1996), pp. 128–58 (pp. 151–2, n.40).

16. On Wase, who was also a beneficiary of Lady Isabel Morley's will, see Roger Virgoe, 'A Norwich Taxation List of 1451', *Norfolk Archaeology*, 40 (1988), 145–54 (p. 149) and Carol M. Meale, 'The World and the Soul: The Will of Lady Isabel Morley (d. 1467)', in *Recording Medieval Lives*, Harlaxton Medieval Studies 17, ed. Julia Boffey and Virginia Davis (Donington: Shaun Tyas, 2009), pp. 189–203 (pp. 192 n.14, 198, 201).

17. Julia Boffey and A. S. G. Edwards, *A New Index of Middle English Verse* (London: The British Library, 2005), nos. 2899 and 3494; 2873; 1979; *Gilte Legende*, ed. Richard Hamer, 2 vols., EETS o.s. 327, 328 (Oxford: Oxford University Press, 2006, 2007), II, pp. 652–60, 854–62; 729–44. Osbern Bokenham, the Augustinian friar of Clare Priory wrote a life of St Cecilia, but his account of St Francis has only recently come to light: see *Index*, no. 589 and Simon Horobin, 'A Manuscript Found in the Library of Abbotsford House and the Lost Legendary of Osbern Bokenham, *Regional Manuscripts, 1200–1700, English Manuscript Studies, 1100–1700*, 14, ed. A. S. G. Edwards (London: The British Library, 2008), pp. 130–62. Chaucer's Second Nun's Tale also tells Cecilia's story, but the possibility of this being the work in question seems remote, since it is specifically paired with the life of St Francis. The texts are highly unlikely to have been from the Scottish *Legendary*.

18. Kathleen L. Scott, *Later Gothic Manuscripts, 1390–1490*, 2 vols., A Survey of Manuscripts Illuminated in the British Isles (London: Harvey Miller, 1996). On the second-hand book trade see Kate Harris, 'Patrons, Buyers and Owners: the Evidence for Ownership and the Role of Book Owners in Book Production and the Book Trade', in *Book Production and Publishing in Britain, 1375–1475*,

ed. Jeremy Griffiths and Derek Pearsall (Cambridge: Cambridge University Press, 1989), pp. 163–99 (pp. 172–7).

19. Gisela Guddat-Figge, *Catalogue of Manuscripts Containing Middle English Romances* (München: Wilhelm Fink, 1976), pp. 83, 161, 205, 216, 263.

20. Richard Beadle, 'Prolegomena to a Literary Geography of Later Medieval Norfolk', in *Regionalism in Late Medieval Manuscripts and Texts*, ed. Felicity Riddy (Cambridge: D. S. Brewer, 1991), pp. 99–108; Kathleen L. Scott, 'Lydgate's Lives of Saints Edmund and Fremund: a Newly-Located Manuscript in Arundel Castle', *Viator*, 13 (1982), 335–66 and *Dated and Datable English Manuscript Borders, c.1395–1499* (London: The British Library for The Bibliographical Society, 2002), pp. 84–7.

21. Carol M. Meale, ' "Gode men / Wiues maydnes and alle men": Romance and Its Audiences', in *Readings in Medieval English Romance*, ed. Carol M. Meale (Cambridge: D. S. Brewer, 1994), pp. 209–25 (pp. 221–5).

22. Norwich, Norfolk Record Office, Norwich Consistory Court (hereafter NRO, NCC) Register Hirning, fols. 42v–44v. For other French romances see Meale, ' "... alle the bokes that I haue" ', pp. 134, 136, 139–42.

23. Anthony Tuck, 'Beaufort, Joan, countess of Westmorland (?1379–1440)', *Oxford Dictionary of National Biography* at http://www.oxforddnb.com/view/article/53026 [accessed 6 May 2010]; Meale, ' "... alle the bokes that I haue" ', pp. 140–1, 142, 144–5, 157 n.92.

24. Henry Harrod, 'Extracts from Early Wills in the Norwich Registers', *Norfolk Archaeology*, 4 (1855), 317–39 (320–1). The will is listed here as Diocesan Register Harsyk, fol. 148r, but I could find no trace of it in the Norfolk Record Office and Bacon's name does not appear in NROCAT, the Norfolk Record Office online catalogue.

25. See Felicity Riddy, ' "Women talking about the things of God": a Late-Medieval Sub-Culture', in *Women and Literature in Britain*, ed. Meale, pp. 104–27 on the interchange of books between laywomen and religious; Julia Boffey, 'Some London Women Readers and a Text of *The Three Kings of Cologne*', *The Ricardian*, 10 (1996), 387–96 and Carol M. Meale and Julia Boffey, 'Gentlewomen's Reading', in *The Cambridge History of the Book in Britain*, vol. III: *1400–1557*, ed. Lotte Hellinga and J. B. Trapp (Cambridge: Cambridge University Press, 1999), pp. 526–40 on networks; Mary C. Erler, *Women, Reading, and Piety in Late Medieval England* (Cambridge: Cambridge University Press, 2002); and Carol M. Meale, 'Wives, Mothers and Daughters: Lineage, Books and the Will of Isabel Lyston of Norwich (1490)', in *Much Heaving and Shoving: Essays for Colin Richmond*, ed. Margaret Aston and Rosemary Horrox (Lavenham: Lavenham Press, 2005), pp. 95–108. Beatrice Balle's will is NRO, NCC Register Brosyard, fols. 273v–274v.

26. Virgoe, 'A Norwich Taxation List of 1451', p. 149; *The Records of the City of Norwich*, 2 vols., compiled and ed. Rev. William Hudson and John Cottingham Tingey (Norwich and London: Jarrold, 1906), II, pp. 389–90; Blomefield, *An Essay*, III, p. 165. Thomas Balle's will is NRO, NCC Register Wylbey, fols. 78r–v.

27. Tanner, *The Church in Late Mediaeval Norwich*, pp. 128, 131.

28. See Boffey and Edwards, *A New Index of Middle English Verse*, nos. 203, 4114, 439 (Lydgate), 2651 (Bokenham), 2672 and 2987 (*South English Legendary*) for lives of St Margaret. Again, it is unlikely that the text was from the Scottish *Legendary*.

29. Erler, *Women, Reading, and Piety*, pp. 68–84.

30. Ibid., p. 71. For a list of hermits and anchorites in the city see Tanner, *The Church in Late Medieval Norwich*, pp. 198–203.

31. On Ferneys see Tanner, *The Church in Late Mediaeval Norwich*, pp. 60–3, 202, and pp. 233–4 for his testament; also Erler, *Women, Reading, and Piety*, pp. 72, 75, 79–83.

32. Beatrice's husband also remembered this hermit in his will: see n.26 above and Tanner, *The Church in Late Mediaeval Norwich*, p. 201 and n.38.

33. NRO, NCC Register Brosyard, fols. 83r–84r. Thomas's will, dated 12 November 1444 and proved 30 July 1445, is NRO, NCC Register Wylbey, fols. 30r–32r. On Thomas see Basil Cozens-Hardy and Ernest A. Kent, *The Mayors of Norwich 1403 to 1835* (Norwich: Jarrold, 1938), pp. 20–2 and Blomefield, *An Essay*, III, pp. 143–9.

34. *Calendar of Patent Rolls, 4, Henry VI, 1441–46* (London: HMSO, 1908), p. 366; Lilian J. Redstone, 'Three Carrow Account Rolls', *Norfolk Archaeology*, 29 (1946), 41–88 (43). Thomas had described himself in his will as 'Armiger' of 'Carhowe'.

35. Redstone, 'Three Carrow Account Rolls', p. 43; Erler, *Women, Reading, and Piety*, pp. 72, 82; Tanner, *The Church in Late Mediaeval Norwich*, p. 233.

36. NRO, NCC Register Brosyard, fols. 83v–84r; Dawson Turner (ed.), *Kirkpatrick's History of the Religious Orders etc. of Norwich* (London: Edwards and Hughes; Norwich: Stevenson and Matchett, 1845), pp. 140–1.

37. Turner (ed.), *Kirkpatrick's History*, p. 31.

38. I am grateful to the archivists of the Norfolk Record Office for their assistance in trying to locate Alice's will. Her name does not appear in NROCAT.

12
Women and Reading

Lara Farina

One of the most recognized scenes in all of medieval literature is of a woman attacking a book: with a nod and a wink, Chaucer's Wife of Bath proudly recalls how she ripped the pages right out of her husband's compendium of 'wicked women' and survived the beating that followed.[1] Yet the antipathy between women and books shown in this portion of the Wife's monologue belies a much more complex history of female readership in the Middle Ages, one that even the Wife, were she playing straight with her audience, would have to acknowledge. Medieval women readers were generally neither passive recipients of 'clerkish' tracts nor resentful book-burning illiterates estranged from textual culture. Rather, women readers were often intimately involved in determining the content and impact of even the most doctrinaire of texts. As patrons of textual production, performers of acts of reading, and agents shaping the reception and distribution of books and other written texts, women readers had a cooperative role in shaping the textual culture of the Middle Ages.

When earlier feminist critics drew attention to the exclusion of women from the canon of English literature, their first impulse was usually to correct the omission by giving attention to neglected female authors of the past. This recovery of women's writing has profoundly reshaped our idea of literary traditions and is, indeed, part of the rationale for this very literary history. However, the author-centred focus has always frustrated medievalists and posed problems for the inclusion of medieval texts in surveys of women's writing. A vast amount of medieval writing is not attributed to any author; we know almost nothing, for example, about the authors of even some 'masterpieces' like *Gawain and the Green Knight* or the plays of the Corpus Christi celebrations. Although a woman-friendly revision of the canon might helpfully point out that there is little evidence for ruling out female authorship of these works, criticism cannot proceed in the same way as it does with texts that are the self-claimed works of later women writers. Further, the example of the Corpus Christi plays points to the probable collaborative nature of the authorship behind some medieval literature. Oral traditions, borrowings from liturgical services, performative adaptations, and groupthink (the plays were performed by guilds) undoubtedly all contributed to the play scripts we now see recorded in manuscripts. In short, authorship itself was a very different kind of thing in the Middle Ages.

Given the paucity of definitively named authors and the complexity of textual production, it makes sense to look towards those other shaping influencers of written works, their readers. Sociological studies of reading, like Janice Radway's highly influential *Reading the Romance*, have shown that, even when the relationship between writers and readers is distant or seemingly non-existent, readers, simply by choosing what to read, how often, with whom, and under what circumstances, can exert a powerful influence on what gets written, distributed, and read. Radway's study, which followed a group of female readers of popular romance in the 1980s, also provocatively suggested that readers' collective interpretation of a text can radically alter its social meaning, both in terms of textual content and as concerns the uses of books. Some standard features of popular romance, for example, were regarded as unimportant by Radway's readers, while using romance reading as a way to legitimize time apart from a spouse or partner was crucial.[2] Studying readership, then, not only fills in some of the gaps of literary history but also gets at the all-important question of the relation between literature and life.

Unlike Radway, medievalists do not have live readers to interview; thus, some ideas about the meaning of medieval women's reading will always remain speculative. And the material evidence for it is often ambiguous, partial, and difficult to come by. Wills, for example, are a major source of information about book ownership, but most records of women's bequests are in the wills of widows. Married women and young women, whose property reverted either to their husbands or parents, are seriously underrepresented by this data. Religious reading is more often mentioned than secular reading, simply because it was regarded as more worthy, and devotional books (often costly and ornamental) were more likely to be recorded as family heirlooms. Literary portraits of women readers are often idealized or rhetorically inflected. Yet, despite such obfuscating factors, enough information can be gained from these sources (together with that in letters, manuscript marginalia, and textual collections intended for women) that a thriving field of scholarship is answering the following questions: Which women read? What did they read? How and under what conditions did they read?

To understand which women were reading in medieval Britain, we need first to clarify what we mean by 'reading'. We tend to understand that a 'literate' person is one who can read and write, but the distinction is hardly so simple in the Middle Ages. First, the medieval term *litteratus* usually referred to someone who could read and write in Latin, and very often designated someone whose profession depended on this ability. Reading and writing in the vernacular did not necessarily grant one this professional or semi-professional status of literate, despite there being a great deal of overlap in the contents of Latinate and vernacular textual traditions. Second, the ability to understand a written text was not necessarily accompanied by the ability to write. In an age when writing materials were costly and manuscripts labour-intensive, writing was a specialized skill often undertaken by professional scribes. This fact undermines one potential source of evidence for women's reading: signatures in manuscripts. Not every female reader or book-owner could write her name in her books, even if she could understand them easily. For example, Margaret Hungerford, a fifteenth-century noble-woman who owned several books and could read both English and French, could barely write in a 'large, sprawling hand'.[3] Third, medieval readers' methods of understanding written texts were not limited to private, silent reading. Reading was often a group activity, and the experience of reading that of being read to. A reader quite often would have learned a text word-by-word by hearing it recited aloud (particularly in the case of prayers and other liturgical texts) before ever seeing it on the page. Is seeing a written work with prior knowledge of what it says 'reading'? An interesting test case is medieval women's use of textual amulets for childbirth. These were strips of parchment written upon with prayers and charms to be used by midwives. The parchment was placed on the pregnant woman's body as the texts were recited, probably from memory.[4] Is this ritual use of texts reading? Certainly the amulets' contents and purpose were well understood by their users, even if the written words were the loosest of prompts.

If we do take such an expansive view of reading, future scholarship may broaden a reading population that is otherwise heavily weighted towards the aristocratic. Before the fifteenth century, when the use of faster cursive hands, paper, and printing made books more affordable, reading materials were luxury items, often extravagant ones. The most popular type of book in medieval Britain (at least as far as we can judge by extant manuscripts) was also one of the most expensive: the Book of Hours, a variable collection of liturgical texts for the household devotions of the laity. As treasured possessions of affluent households, these 'Primers' were made to last; they were written in careful hands, lavishly illustrated, and often bound in bejewelled covers.[5] Our sense of the reading population of the Middle Ages is thus determined not only by the fact that only the wealthy could afford such labour-intensive items, but also by (potentially misleading) rates of textual survival. As major investments, expensive books would be carefully preserved. Amulets, small rolls, and other ephemera, which might be more affordable and thus more popular, are less likely to have stayed intact (some amulets were even intended to be eaten after reading).[6]

The expense of books generally also meant that they were more likely to be owned by institutions than individuals, particularly in the earlier periods. Not surprisingly then, a major source of evidence about women's reading is the tracing of extant manuscripts to women's religious houses. While we lack catalogues of nuns' libraries, and therefore cannot know the true number of books they possessed, the surviving manuscripts indicate that, even among women's houses, where reading was a necessary activity, book ownership required substantial wealth. The largest and most impressive collections are those of unusually affluent houses, such as the royally founded abbeys of Barking and Syon.[7] Early portraits of women readers also usually depict well-born nuns, as is the case with the representation of Queen Edith of Wessex in the *Life of Edward the Confessor* written at Barking in the twelfth century.[8] The Barking text represents the queen as pious and bookish from the start and explains her childlessness as the result of the royal couple's mutual vow of chastity, thereby making her subsequent religious career at Wilton Abbey (to which the historical Edith gave generously) seem spiritually related to her marriage to King Edward. The influence of lineage is a motif in the work, one not surprising for the aristocratic milieu of Barking, although it has been argued that Edith's piety is depicted as improving the family stock.[9]

As one might expect from an archive heavily dependent on the textual possessions of monastic houses, most medieval women's reading appears to have been devotional in nature. The majority of texts at convents were liturgical (prayers, psalms, offices, litanies, calendars, etc.); also prevalent are other devotional works (lives of saints, lives of the church fathers, and vernacular guides to meditation, such as *The Pricke of Conscience*, Walter Hilton's *Scale of Perfection*, and Nicholas Love's *Mirror of the Blessed Life of Jesus Christ*). The remnant of nuns' reading is rounded out by some theological treatises in Latin and the occasional secular work, like the compilation of Lydgate's *Siege of Thebes* and Hoccleve's *De regimine principum* owned by Amesbury Priory (a manuscript probably donated by Elizabeth de Burgh, a fourteenth-century Duchess of Clarence).[10] But pious reading was not limited to nuns, and many of the works owned by convents were read by other women as well. The 'semi-religious', so termed not because they were lukewarm believers but because they pursued non-monastic religious careers, were another notable population of women readers. This category includes anchoresses and vowesses, who dedicated themselves to chastity, prayer, and asceticism but did not join a community of nuns.

Anchoresses are particularly interesting for the history of British women's reading. This form of devotion required women to take a vow of lifelong enclosure. While they were generally not hermits, in the sense that they were more often located in towns than in uncultivated land, anchoresses' often solitary enclosure and removal from monastic oversight placed them in a spatially and institutionally distinctive reading environment. Responsible for organizing their own devotional regimen, they requested reading material to assist with their meditation. Goscelin of St Bertin wrote the *Liber confortatorius* c.1082 for Eve of Wilton, a literate (i.e. Latin-reading) nun who later became a recluse. An illuminated psalter was made c.1123 for the twelfth-century laywoman-turned-recluse Christina of Markyate. Soon after, the Cistercian Aelred of Rievaulx wrote *De institutione inclusarum* for his anchoress sister, acknowledging that 'for many years now, my sister, you have been asking me for a rule to guide you in the life you have embraced for the sake of Christ'.[11] In the thirteenth century, the *Ancrene Wisse*, a much longer, vernacular advisory guide for anchoresses, was produced at the behest of three sisters; it was copied repeatedly soon after, translated into French and Latin, and survives in various forms in an impressive number of manuscripts.[12]

While not restricted in movement as anchoresses were, vowesses (usually widows pledging themselves to a life of chastity) also numbered among the reading semi-religious. The will of one fifteenth-century vowess, Margery de Nerford of London, provides a rare glimpse of a private library owned by a woman. Supported by pious and bookish friends and family during her lifetime, she left, at her death, a book on the Virgin Mary (in French) to the Franciscan nuns at Denny, a glossed two-volume psalter to her executor, a breviary and other books to her chaplain, a book to Joan Cobham (wife of executed heretic Sir John Oldcastle), and the choice of the rest of her books to an anchoress near Bishopsgate.[13] Her will thus offers tantalizing suggestions of book circulation between religious, semi-religious, and the laity – even the heterodox laity.

Laywomen, for whom prayer was a regular practice but not a career, could possess a wider range of literature, provided they could afford to do so. Noting Chaucer's reference to women who idolize 'the book of Lancelot de Lake', Carol Meale has suggested that women owners of romance texts were indeed particularly partial to those featuring the heroes Lancelot and Tristram.[14] Other secular works that were likely to have been owned by laywomen include writing by Lydgate, Hoccleve, Gower, and Christine de Pizan. And although Chaucer is often associated with a masculine audience, much attention has been given recently to the fifteenth/sixteenth-century Findern manuscript, which contains selections from his work, together with excerpts from Gower, Clanvowe, Hoccleve, and Roos. The compilation was likely to have been produced according to the directions and desires of a female readership: the presence of several women's names in the manuscript suggests that it was circulated among women of the Derbyshire gentry.[15]

Yet like their religious and semi-religious contemporaries, laywomen, too, gravitated towards devotional reading. Books of Hours were, from the start, predominately associated with laywomen's piety. The earliest surviving example, the *de Brailes Hours*, was made in 1240 for a female patron portrayed in the manuscript's illustrations. Further, Books of Hours usually centre on the 'Little Office of the Virgin', and most often include texts about the Virgin Mary and/or her mother, St Anne. While Marian devotion was not the exclusive domain of women, it did feature strongly in their spirituality, and prayers to St Anne alongside those to Christ and Mary would have recalled late-medieval images of the *trinubium* (Anne, Mary, and the Christ Child), associated with matrilineal affiliation and women's family roles.[16] Books of Hours, psalters, and breviaries are the most common books mentioned in laywomen's wills, though mention is also made of devotional treatises in the vernacular, from the affective but pragmatic *Ancrene Riwle* to the mystical works of Richard Rolle and Walter Hilton to the fire-and-brimstone harangue of *The Prick of Conscience*. Authorial/scribal acknowledgement of female patrons yields further evidence of women's interest in a variety of devotional texts: many of the patrons for Lydgate's religious poetry were women, and the saints' lives that are collected in Osbern Bokenham's *Legendys of Hooly Wummen* were in part written at the request of various laywomen readers in East Anglia.

In short, the reading of affluent laywomen was not too different from that of their professed contemporaries. The compendious Vernon Manuscript is a good example of the overlap. A nearly fifty-pound tome containing a veritable library of devotional texts (primarily in English but with some French and Latin), the manuscript could have been produced either for a convent or the women of a wealthy lay household, if we are to judge from content alone. But the presence of the Bohun family arms on the manuscript suggests, however ambiguously, a connection with the laity.[17] Scholarship has, in fact, increasingly tended to emphasize that the boundaries between enclosed religious (nuns and anchoresses) and the laity were quite permeable. Nuns tended to be from the same social class as their noble benefactors, and medieval patterns of book patronage and circulation were often familial. For example, the fourteenth-century Duchess of Gloucester, Eleanor de Bohun, whose will mentions fourteen books, left seven of them to her daughter Isabel, a nun at the London house of minoresses who later became its abbess. Books themselves were thus ways of preserving ties between religious and their lay relatives and friends. As Mary Erler has argued, 'in the act of reading, as at so many other times, women made connections among themselves, sometimes despite a degree of official discouragement'.[18]

However piecemeal the evidence for women's reading may be, one fact about it is indisputable: women readers had a major impact on the development of vernacular literature in Britain, on writing, that is, in English, Anglo-Norman French, and/or the Celtic languages.[19] An intriguing example of women's multilingual patronage is Queen Matilda's commissioning, in the early twelfth century, of a French translation of *The Voyage of St Brendan*. *The Voyage* features an Irish saint, and yet it is more like a romance than a hagiographic *vita* (it is a tale of marvellous adventures in octosyllabic couplets); consequently, the work has been called an early predecessor of the twelfth- and thirteenth-century flowering of French romance. Thus Matilda, who had a reputation for being a liberal patron of 'sweet-singing clerks', seems to have had a taste for literary experiments, including the blending of Latin devotional material and vernacular language forms.[20] She also commissioned works in Latin, including a *vita* of her sainted mother, Margaret of Scotland.[21] So Matilda's taste for vernacular literature was not the result of an estrangement from Latin textual traditions, and her education at Wilton Abbey would make it likely that she was a competent reader of Latin. But like her mother Margaret, Matilda seems to have been interested in melding Anglo-Norman, Celtic, and Latin culture, possibly for political reasons, and her literary directives resulted in new intersections between pious reading and the life and language of her court.

The desire to blend devotional material with appealing elements from vernacular genres may well have been behind the later production of the 'AB' texts, a collection of influential thirteenth-century works in English. These include the guide for anchoresses *Ancrene Wisse*; the lives of the virgin martyr saints Catherine of Alexandria and Margaret of Antioch; the anti-marital tract *Hali Meiðhed*; the allegory *Sawles Ward*; and the ecstatic prayers of the 'Wooing Group'. Romance elements are particularly noteworthy in this collection. Christ is portrayed as the reader's chivalric suitor in the *Ancrene Wisse* and in the Wooing Group prayers, while the saints Catherine and Margaret are themselves like the heroes of romance, idealized aristocratic paragons who do spiritual battle with their heathen enemies. Again, rather than take the vernacular language of these works as evidence of the limited literacy of their initial readers, we might understand it as resulting from those readers' desire to expand and reshape the material to be used for pious meditation and prayer. Such a reworking of meditative texts and techniques had already been undertaken in the writings of eleventh- and twelfth-century 'affective' theologians such as Bernard of Clairvaux, Hugh of St Victor, and Anselm of Canterbury. The AB texts suggest that female patrons/readers saw great potential in the combination of this new style of affective devotion (*devotio moderna*) and vernacular reading. The envoi of the *Ancrene Wisse* even contains some indication that its writer may have had to be goaded by the 'three sisters' into producing such a work, since he or she states, 'God knows I would rather set out for Rome than start it over again!'

The AB texts set a precedent for the types of devotional texts that would become the most popular literature in medieval Britain. Hagiographic narratives, particularly lives of virgin martyrs, would continue to be well known and much requested, as Bokenham's *Legendys of Hooly Wummen* attests. The prayers of the Wooing Group prefigure the mystical works of Rolle and Hilton, whose writings in English were also composed at the request of women readers. And the *Ancrene Wisse*, which anticipates so much later medieval 'literature of counsel', itself continued to be read and copied for a diverse range of readers – men and women, monastic and lay. Modern readers may find the tone and content of some of this work to be restrictive, even lamentable; virginity, humility, and enclosure are much emphasized, and the advisory works often contain misogynistic harangues on the faults of womankind. Yet their popularity among women suggests that their original readers saw them as advancing their interests, both spiritually and socially. Works such as the *Life of Christina of Markyate*, which was composed with possible input from Christina herself, help explain some of the literature's appeal. In it, the young Christina recites the *Life* of St Cecilia when resisting her parents' attempts to give her in marriage against her will.[22] Fortified by her knowledge of Cecilia's commitment to God, Christina aggressively pursues a religious career of her own, becoming, in turn, a model of self-determination for the readers of her *vita*.

To conclude, women played important roles as patrons, collectors, donors, and planners of books, all actions that enable written texts to materialize in a culture, to come into being, that is, in the social life of individuals and communities. Women readers influenced the kinds of writing produced in medieval Britain, its circulation between religious and the laity, and its authorization as a source of instruction and inspiration. While it is often impossible to know precisely how much of a given work's content can be attributed to a female patron or reader, the evidence for the overall impact of female audiences should allow us to re-appraise their role in medieval literary history.

Notes

1. Geoffrey Chaucer, 'The Wife of Bath's Prologue', in *The Riverside Chaucer*, 3rd edn., ed. Larry D. Benson (Boston: Houghton Mifflin, 1991), ll. 666–812.
2. Janice A. Radway, *Reading the Romance: Women, Patriarchy, and Popular Literature* (Chapel Hill, NC and London: University of North Carolina Press, 1991), pp. 58–62.
3. M. A. Hicks, 'The Piety of Margaret, Lady Hungerford (d. 1478)', *Journal of Ecclesiastical History*, 38 (1987), 19–38 (at 23).
4. See Don C. Skemer, *Binding Words: Textual Amulets in the Middle Ages* (University Park, PA: Pennsylvania State University Press, 2006), pp. 235–78.
5. See Eamon Duffy, *Marking the Hours: English People and Their Prayers, 1240–1570* (New Haven, CT: Yale University Press, 2006).
6. Skemer, *Binding Words*, p. 237.
7. David N. Bell, *What Nuns Read: Books and Libraries in Medieval English Nunneries* (Kalamazoo, MI: Cistercian Publications, 1995), p. 11.
8. *La vie d'Eduoard le confesseur, poème anglo-normand du XIIe siècle*, ed. Ö. Södergaard (Uppsala: Almqvist and Wiksell, 1948).
9. Jocelyn Wogan-Browne, 'Women and Anglo-Norman Hagiography', in *Women and Literature in Britain, 1150–1500*, 2nd edn., ed. Carol Meale (Cambridge: Cambridge University Press, 1996), pp. 61–85 (at p. 69). See also Jocelyn Wogan-Browne, *Saints' Lives and Women's Literary Culture, c. 1150–1300: Virginity and its Authorizations* (Oxford: Oxford University Press, 2001).
10. See Bell, *What Nuns Read*, for a complete list of manuscripts and books attributed to nuns' houses.
11. Aelred of Rievaulx, *Treatises and Pastoral Prayer* (Kalamazoo, MI: Cistercian Publications, 1995), p. 43.

12. See Yoko Wada (ed.), *A Companion to Ancrene Wisse* (Cambridge: D. S. Brewer, 2003), especially A. S. G. Edwards, 'The Middle English Manuscripts and Early Readers of *Ancrene Wisse*', pp. 103–12.

13. Mary C. Erler, *Women, Reading, and Piety in Late Medieval England* (Cambridge: Cambridge University Press, 2002), pp. 48–67.

14. Carol M. Meale, ' "...alle the bokes that I haue of latyn, englisch, and frensch": Laywomen and their Books in Late Medieval England', in *Women and Literature in Britain*, ed. Meale, pp. 128–58. The reference is from the 'Nun's Priest's Tale'.

15. Sarah McNamer has proposed that some of the manuscript's lyrics were written by Margery Hungerford, Anne Schyrley, and Frances Kruker. See her chapter 'Lyrics and Romances', in *The Cambridge Companion to Medieval Women's Writing*, ed. Carolyn Dinshaw and David Wallace (Cambridge: Cambridge University Press, 2003), pp. 195–209. Other recent work on the manuscript includes: Ashby Kinch, ' "To thenke what was in hir wille": A Female Reading Context for the Findern Anthology', *Neophilologus*, 91.4 (2007), 729–44; and Kara A. Doyle, 'Thisbe Out of Context: Chaucer's Female Readers and the Findern Manuscript', *Chaucer Review*, 40.3 (2006), 231–61.

16. For examples, see *Women's Books of Hours in Medieval England: Selected Texts*, trans. Charity Scott-Stokes (Cambridge: D. S. Brewer, 2006). On St Anne, see Kathleen Ashley and Pamela Sheingorn (eds.), *Interpreting Cultural Symbols: Saint Anne in Late Medieval Society* (Athens, GA and London: University of Georgia Press, 1990) and Sheingorn, ' "The Wise Mother": The Image of St. Anne Teaching the Virgin Mary', in *Gendering the Master Narrative: Women and Power in the Middle Ages*, ed. Mary C. Erler and Mayanne Kowaleski (Ithaca: Cornell University Press, 2003), pp. 105–34.

17. See Derek A. Pearsall (ed.), *Studies in the Vernon Manuscript* (Woodbridge: Boydell and Brewer, 1990).

18. Erler, *Women, Reading, and Piety*, p. 5.

19. There has been less work on women's reading in medieval Wales and Ireland, but see Jane Cartwright, *Feminine Sanctity and Spirituality in Medieval Wales* (Cardiff: University of Wales Press, 2008).

20. June Hall McCash, 'Cultural Patronage: An Overview', in *The Cultural Patronage of Medieval Women*, ed. McCash (Athens, GA: University of Georgia Press, 1996), pp. 1–49 (p. 20). See also Lois L. Huneycutt, ' "Proclaiming Her Dignity Abroad": The Literary and Artistic Network of Matilda of Scotland, Queen of England, 1100–1118', in *The Cultural Patronage*, ed. McCash, pp. 155–74.

21. On Margaret of Scotland's patronage, see Richard Gameson, 'The Gospels of Margaret of Scotland and the Literacy of an Eleventh-Century Queen', in *Women and the Book: Assessing the Visual Evidence*, ed. Jane H. M. Taylor and Lesley Smith (London and Toronto: The British Library and University of Toronto Press, 1997), pp. 148–71.

22. See *The Life of Christina of Markyate: A Twelfth Century Recluse*, ed. and trans. C. H. Talbot (Toronto: University of Toronto Press, 2001), p. 51.

13

Women and Networks of Literary Production

Elizabeth Robertson

The period from 1066 to 1500 in medieval Britain is surprisingly rich in women's literature, especially texts written about, for, and by women pursuing a rigorous form of the contemplative life either as solitaries or anchoresses, that is, female recluses who chose to be shut into a room or rooms usually attached to a church in order to devote their lives solely to the contemplation of God. One means of identifying the place of the literature associated with these extraordinary women in literary history is through a study of the material objects most closely linked to them, the manuscripts that, either directly or indirectly, record their voices. A consideration of the manuscripts associated with three prominent pieces of women's literature – the twelfth-century Latin *Vita* of Christina of Markyate, the thirteenth-century Middle English religious prose guide to the contemplative life known as the *Ancrene Wisse* [*Guide for Anchoresses*], and the late fourteenth-century writings of Julian of Norwich – shows us that the production of writing by, about, and for these women in the Middle Ages, in spite of the apparent solitariness of their spiritual enterprise, required networks of support. These networks included those persons who encouraged and materially enabled the contemplative in her choice of life, the authors who wrote for and about them, the scribes who wrote down the words they said, and the monks, friars, secular canons, and antiquarians who preserved and transmitted their literature.

As one of the earliest accounts of an English woman's experience of the religious life, the twelfth-century *Vita* of Christina of Markyate occupies an important place in a history of English women's literature. Told to a monk of St Albans, Christina's *Life* recounts the extraordinary obstacles Christina overcame in order to pursue a contemplative life. While critics often turn to her as an example of the 'triumph of the individual' over society and celebrate her endurance as a solitary contemplative, Christina in her life both in and out of a hermitage, and indeed in and out of secular life, was very rarely alone.[1] As a member of a family from the Anglo-Saxon nobility who successfully merged with the new Norman nobility, Christina throughout her life was well connected with both secular and religious servants, advisers, confessors, and supporters, almost all male. As Henrietta Leyser points out, the *Vita* tells us of over twenty men and 'a network of highly influential hermits' who played significant roles in her pursuit of a contemplative life.[2] Until recently, critics have underestimated the complexity of the social and religious web within which Christina moved, including the full extent of the multilingual world she inhabited, for as a member of an old Anglo-Saxon family newly allied with the Norman nobility, Christina might well have spoken Anglo-Saxon and Norman French, and undoubtedly knew some Latin.

Not only does the history within the *Vita* reveal a male support network active in Christina's lifetime, but also the manuscript that has come down to us tells us that her *Life* was produced, transmitted, and preserved by yet another religious male network. Christina's *Vita* survives as the last text in volume two of a collection of saints' lives, London, British Library, MS Cotton Tiberius E1, titled the *Sanctilogium Angliae*. Dated palaeographically to the fourteenth century and compiled by a secular priest associated with St Albans, John of Tynemouth, the collection includes a large variety of insular English saints from St Edmund to St Walburga.[3] These liturgically arranged lives are followed by four additional lives of English saints, and at the end by a hastily copied version of Christina's *Life* that breaks off abruptly.[4] Codicological evidence suggests that a folio has been lost, but it is unlikely that the original version was ever finished. Preserved initially in Sir Robert Cotton's seventeenth-century collection before being passed on to the British Museum, the manuscript was damaged in the 1731 fire at Ashburnham house that destroyed so many items of Sir Robert's collection. We are lucky that this woman's semi-autobiography survived at all.

As a witness to fourteenth-century concerns, the manuscript reveals the compiler's interest in formulating a specifically *English* history of sanctity. A marginal inscription tells us that contemporaries thought of this collection as designed for the edification of male readers. The inscription says that Thomas de la Mare, abbot of St Albans (elected Abbot of St Albans in 1349) sent his copy of the *Sanctilogium Angliae* to sixteen monks of Redbourne in order to provide virtuous examples for their instruction.[5] Although this revealing inscription did not survive the Cotton fire, it comes down to us because, in 1637, Friar Augustine Baker, someone whose name appears surprisingly often in accounts of women's literary history, copied it, thus allowing us a glimpse of the fourteenth-century function of Christina's *Life*.

That Christina never actually officially became a saint might make us wonder why her *Life* is included in a collection of saints' lives. It is probable that her *Life* was originally written to support a canonization process that was never completed. By the time the compiler put the collection together, however, she may have come to be known as a saint. The seventeenth-century Cottonian cataloguer, Thomas Smith, who may have simply recorded a fourteenth-century header, designates her *Vita* as that of 'Saint Theodora', without comment. It is probable that she had come to be known as a saint by the fourteenth century and perhaps even earlier. The fourteenth-century compiler may simply have included her in his collection as yet another example of insular sanctity.

There may also have been specifically local reasons for the compiler's choice to include her *Life* in his collection, that is, he may have chosen to include Christina's *Vita* because of her association with her two protectors, Roger the Hermit, beloved by the monks of St Albans and buried in their abbey, and her later friend and supporter, the abbot of St Albans, Geoffrey. Two summaries of her *Life* also survive, one an early Nicholas Roscarrock's seventeenth-century digest apparently based on the Tiberius manuscript before it was damaged in the Cotton fire, and a second, an interpolated abbreviated *Life* in the *Gesta Abbatum* of St Albans.[6] That both the digest and the abbreviated *Life* highlight the virtues of Roger suggests that Christina's *Life* was understood as a text that cast positive light not on her but rather on St Albans. Closely associated with St Albans, John of Tynemouth may at the last moment have added Christina's *Life* to his compilation not just as an exemplum of English sanctity, but more narrowly as a story illuminating the holiness of St Albans. Christina's virtues are tertiary, at best, then, to the compiler's overriding interests first in St Albans and second in the history of English sanctity.

What we can reconstruct about the production of the original twelfth-century *Vita* upon which the fourteenth-century extant version is based reinforces the idea that the story was originally written not because it recounts the exceptional exploits of a female solitary, but because of the remarkable efforts of yet another literary network – this one contemporary to Christina – made up of an abbot, an author, scribes, and readers, most of whom are likely to have been monks, guided by their own self-interest. Evidence suggests that a monk of St Albans wrote the original version of the story at the instigation of the abbot and close friend of Christina, Geoffrey of St Albans, probably as part of a scheme to canonize her in order to enhance not her, but rather Geoffrey's reputation. At the same time, Geoffrey also encouraged the production of the lavish St Albans Psalter, a work adapted to highlight Christina's importance to the abbey of St Albans and at some point presented to Christina.[7] We know the author of the *Vita* was a monk because he refers to 'nostrum monasterium' ['our monastery'], to Roger as 'noster monachus' ['our monk'], and describes Christina's vow 'in hoc monasterio' ['in this monastery']. That the monk/author reproduces Christina's words themselves suggests that Christina was closely involved in the *Vita's* production. Paulette L'Hermite Leclercq suggests that Christina's family, several of whom were professed religious with her, may have participated in the production of the *Life*. Her *Vita* is, then, from the beginning a collaborative production of Christina, the monk who wrote her story, the powerful abbot who befriended her, Geoffrey of St Albans, and possibly the religious among her own family, and comes to be preserved and transmitted by networks of monks, secular clergy, and antiquarians.

Any history of medieval English women's literature after the Conquest must contain a discussion of the early thirteenth-century rule for anchoresses called the *Ancrene Wisse*, a work that emerges from an unusually close-knit post-Conquest West Midlands literary and religious network. Although the original work is now lost, traces of the history of its production remain in the author's statement that he wrote the work at the request of three biologically related devout upper-class sisters who wished to have a guide to their chosen life. Given the rigours of solitary anchoritic contemplation the author describes, it is easy to overlook that the original anchoresses were themselves hardly alone: even the sparse information provided about them in one manuscript, London, British Library, Cotton Nero A xiv, tells of a substantial community made up of three anchoresses living together, servants, a local lord who provides for them materially, and an adviser intimately involved with them.

Closely related in dialect and theme to one manuscript of the *Ancrene Wisse*, Cambridge, Corpus Christi College, MS 402, are works found in another manuscript, Oxford, Bodleian Library, MS 34, called the Katherine Group, which includes three saints' lives (of Katherine, Margaret, and Juliana) a tract on virginity, *Hali Meidenhad* [*Holy Virginity*], and a homily on the soul, 'Sawles Warde' ['The Guardianship of the Soul'], clearly created to meet the needs of female anchoritic audiences. J. R. R. Tolkien was one of the first to notice that the similarities between these works suggest that the remote area in which they were likely to have been produced – the Welsh Marches of Herefordshire – was a vibrant literary centre, one whose impetus to produce religious literature in English came, as critics argue, from the combined pressure of the Fourth Lateran Council decree of 1215 that every individual confess yearly and the particular needs of women readers, especially anchoresses.[8]

While Bodley 34 is a unique manuscript and seems not to have proliferated as a collection, the *Ancrene Wisse* is an unusually flexible text, what Ian Doyle has called a 'dynamic' work, one quickly adapted from addressing the needs of the three biological sisters to those of larger groups of nuns, then of communities of men and women, and later of broader lay spiritual audiences; these audiences variously required texts in English, Latin, or French.[9] The extant manuscripts of the text point not only to scribes and authors, but also to librarians, antiquarians, and religious reformers as crucial to the preservation and transmission of the original text.[10]

What we can surmise about the creation of the original text and its quick reproduction reinforces Tolkien's idea that a distinctive literary network was in place in thirteenth-century Herefordshire, indeed one describable as a collaborative community of authors, scribes, and readers, at first female and later male and female. While one might not wish to go as far as Anne Savage in calling the original text a *deliberately* collaborative product of the three female anchoresses and the author, the original three anchoresses certainly provide the impetus for its creation and their needs and those of later readers influence its astonishingly rapid proliferation.[11] Within a few decades of the creation of the original, the work is adapted quickly to address the needs of a community of women that has already grown, as Cambridge, Corpus Christi College, MS 402, a manuscript close in date to the original tells us, to 'twenty nuthe or mare' ['twenty now or more'].

The extant contemporary manuscripts also suggest that the author, scribes, and readers of the *Ancrene Wisse* were unusually closely involved in the reproduction and adaptation of the work. The Cleopatra manuscript (London, British Library, MS Cotton Cleopatra C.vi) reveals the complexity of the literary and religious network in place in the West Midlands for it is written not only by one scribe but by three, all of whom, as Bella Millet suggests, performed editorial as well as scribal roles.[12] Whether authorial or scribal, additions and corrections are added, in Millett's view, not to preserve or return to an originary text, but rather to aid the work's reception by growing, increasingly varied groups of readers; as Millett puts it, the history of the manuscripts suggests 'the continuing adjustment of a work of practical instruction to the needs and understanding of its users'.[13] Furthermore the 'multi-layered and sometimes multi-stranded process of revision' suggests that the author and the scribes influenced each other.[14] That the multiplying versions also show signs of cross-collation reinforces the notion that those in the community who produced versions of the *Ancrene Wisse* were closely interconnected. While the *Ancrene Wisse* was proliferating, other writers from the same geographical area produced other kinds of religious texts, saints' lives, tracts on virginity, prayers, and sermons (such as those found in MS Bodley 34 and the prayers and lyrical meditations in praise of God known as the 'Wooing Group'), specifically for, and perhaps in some cases by, the same or similar female audiences. The West Midlands deserves special attention in women's literary history, then, as the location in which significant literary activity for and perhaps by women took place.

Our third example of women's writing embedded in a literary and religious network is Julian of Norwich's account of her visions in a shorter and a longer version. As one of the few extant autobiographical accounts of a woman's spiritual visions in English, Julian's revelations are crucial to any literary history of women's writing in English.[15] Julian's work, as a material object, teases us with its simultaneous evanescence and durability: the original account has long since vanished, and we know of it primarily through the few seventeenth-century copies that remain. Despite the scarcity of manuscripts, her work has become one of the best loved and most widely read Catholic guides to meditation, one that now even has a vibrant life on the internet.

Julian's visions elicit praise for her individuality, and her reconstructed cell testifies to the powerful imaginary her solitariness produces to this day. Yet, we fail to appreciate Julian fully if we do not acknowledge the various networks that supported her and produced and preserved her work. Even the account of her initial vision paints a picture of a woman in community. At the point of death, her mother, her priest, and a small child who holds a cross before her eyes surround her. Whether or not the mother is a spiritual mother, perhaps her abbess, or a biological mother, the priest, one of her order or a parish priest, and the child, one of the parish or her biological child, it is clear that at thirty and a half years old, Julian is already firmly placed within an orthodox Christian community. How and when Julian became an anchoress is unknown, but the history of anchoritism as a practice tells us that anchoresses were most often well established in a community, often approved of by a local bishop, and guided by male clerical figures, at least by a confessor. As Salih and Baker write, Julian 'was part of a network of lay and clerical enthusiasts for affective piety, and she would certainly have had clerical advisors, confessors, teachers, and scribes'.[16] The placement of Julian's cell at the centre of town reminds us of the dangers the *Ancrene Wisse* warns against that an anchoress is easily enticed outwards by those seeking her advice or just her ear. Margery Kempe's visit to Julian in 1413 in which she sought approval for her own visions further suggests Julian's authority in a community and her status as a person with reputation.

The account itself is both the product and the survivor of literary and religious networks at times difficult to discern. Julian's narrative survives in two versions, a short account, which describes her initial vision, and a longer more reflective account including a report of later clarifying visions. We do not know how these versions came to be written down. Unlike Margery Kempe's autobiography where we learn of her difficult relationship with several scribes, Julian's account does not tell us about her relationship to a scribe. Did she dictate her initial visions or did she write them down herself? How would she have learned to write and when? Her longer version, which may show her concern to minimize any possible Lollard associations her account might trigger, suggests that she had a guide helping her revise her initial account to remove any possible taint of heresy from it. These later versions of her revelations may have resulted from conversations with an adviser or confessor or perhaps, more radically, were the product of a confessor.

Like Christina's *Life*, and the *Ancrene Wisse*, both the short and long versions of Julian's work are preserved primarily because of predominantly male religious and antiquarian networks. The Short Text of Julian's visions survives in a single fifteenth-century manuscript, London, British Library, MS Additional 37790, a collection of vernacular mystical works including works by the medieval mystics Richard Rolle, Jan van Rusbroec, and Marguerite Porete. Believed to have been a product of a Carthusian monastery and designed specifically for male monastic contemplation, it descends from an exemplar probably composed sometime after 1373, the date Julian gives of her visions, and probably before the date of her later clarifying visions.[17] Also known as the Amherst Manuscript after its last owner, it was acquired by the British Museum in 1910.

The longer version, beginning with a preface stating that Julian was still alive in 1413, includes two later understandings of her vision from 1388 and 1393, and thus was probably composed sometime between those events and her death around 1416. It, too, survives due to the work of those involved in religious communities. Excerpts from this longer version appear in the early fifteenth-century London, Westminster Cathedral Treasury, Manuscript 4, a manuscript that also includes selections from other popular spiritual writers. That such texts together make a manuscript suitable for monastic contemplation suggests male religious networks were instrumental in preserving Julian's long version as well as the short one. We owe the survival of the fullest long versions, however, to the work of seventeenth-century nuns of Cambrai whose copies, Paris, MS Bibliothèque Nationale, fonds anglais 40 and London, British Library, MS Sloane 2499, are the earliest surviving full copies of the complete Long Text.[18] One of them, the Sloane Manuscript, is associated with a particular woman writer since it is written in a hand resembling that of Anne Clementine Cary, a Paris Benedictine nun who died in 1671.[19]

While women are crucial to the reproduction of Julian's work, it was undoubtedly a male religious figure that put Julian's account into their hands. In 1629, after previously working in the library of Cotton, Augustine Baker, a friar who, as mentioned earlier, indirectly provided support of various kinds for female contemplatives, arrived in Cambrai in 1624, wrote to Cotton and asked him to send a collection of religious works suitable for nuns including works by contemplatives such as Walter Hilton and Richard Rolle of Hampole: 'such bookes as you please, either manuscript or printed being in English, conteining contemplation Saints lives or other devotions. Hampoles workes are proper for them. I wishe I had Hiltons Scala perfecitonis in latein; it woulde helpe the understandinge of the English, and some of them understaned latien.'[20] We do not know if Julian's manuscript was among these books, but it seems likely that her work went first to the Cotton library and then to Cambrai.

Salih and Baker conclude that the Cambrai Benedictine nuns made their copies of the Long Version in or near 1650 either at Cambrai or in Paris. We can assume that Cambrai had acquired a manuscript well before then because in the 1630s Dame Margaret Gascoigne of Cambrai quoted from several chapters of Julian's work. Augustine Baker, who comes into our story of the preservation and transmission of women's literature yet again, reports in a treatise he compiled at Margaret's death in 1637 her mention of 'an olde manuscript booke of her Revelations'.[21] Julian's account is also preserved at this time in Serenus Cressy's first print version probably based on the Paris manuscript. This print version in turn influenced the manuscript extracts in MS St Joseph's College, Upholland, also in a woman's hand although compiled by Augustine Baker. In the next century, another modernized manuscript version, Sloane 3705, was also made at Cambrai (London, British Library, MS Sloane 3705). The convent of Cambrai, a woman's community, is thus crucial in the survival of Julian's manuscript. However, it is important to note the important role men play in this preservation, for it was most probably a man – either Augustine Baker himself or one in his position – who asked that Julian's manuscript be sent to the nuns; and it is a male printer who preserves the manuscript in an influential print version. This extraordinary early example of women's writing survives primarily because of the writing of women – their handwriting – but the network that preserves it is also governed by powerful male religious figures.

A cursory look at the manuscripts that remain associated with female recluses, manuscripts that contain work either by them, about them, or at their request, reveals the seemingly solitary recluse to have been a person deeply embedded in a predominantly male religious network and their literature to have been produced, transmitted, and preserved because of the powerful concerns of that network. Early women's literature both comes into being because of networks of male advisers, authors, and scribes and is preserved and transmitted most often because of monastic reading needs, usually of monks but sometimes of nuns. Despite these mediations, medieval English women's literary voices nonetheless speak loud and clear.

Notes

1. R. W. Hanning, *The Individual in Twelfth-Century Romance* (New Haven: Yale University Press, 1977), p. 50; Rachel M. Koopmans, 'The Conclusion of Markyate's *Vita*', *Journal of Ecclesiastical History*, 51.4 (2000), 663.
2. Henrietta Leyser, 'Christina of Markyate: The Introduction', in *Christina of Markyate: A Twelfth-Century Holy Woman*, ed. Samuel Fanous and Henrietta Leyser (Abingdon: Routledge, 2005), p. 4.
3. Paulette L'Hermite-Leclercq and Anne-Marie Gras (eds.), *Vie de Christina de Markyate* (Paris: CNRS Editions, 2007), pp. 9–28.
4. See Koopmans, 'The Conclusion', pp. 696–7.
5. Cited in *The Life of Christina: A Twelfth Century Recluse*, ed. and trans. C. H. Talbot (Oxford: Oxford University Press, 1959; repr. Medieval Academy of America, 1998; Toronto: University of Toronto Press, 2001), pp. 1–2.
6. See Koopmans, 'The Conclusion', pp. 666, 672.
7. See Jane Geddes, *The St. Albans Psalter: A Book for Christina of Markyate* (London: The British Library, 2005) and Diane Watt's discussion of the relationship between the Psalter and Christina in chapter 1 of *Medieval Women's Writing: Works by and for Women in England, 1100–1500* (Cambridge: Polity Press, 2007).
8. J. R. R. Tolkien, '*Ancrene Wisse* and *Hali Meithhad*', *Essays and Studies*, 14 (1929), 104–26.

9. Cited in *Ancrene Wisse: A Corrected Edition of the Text in Cambridge, Corpus Christi College, MS 402 with Variants from other Manuscripts*, ed. Bella Millet, EETS O.S. 325 and O.S. 326 (Oxford: Oxford University Press, 2005), I, p. xxxvii. For further discussion of the readers of the *Ancrene Wisse* see Elizabeth Robertson, ' "This Living Hand": Thirteenth-Century Female Literacy, Materialist Immanence and the Reader of the *Ancrene Wisse*', *Speculum*, 78 (2000), 1–36.

10. See A. S. G. Edwards, 'The Middle English Manuscripts and Early Readers of *Ancrene Wisse*', in *A Companion to Ancrene Wisse*, ed. Yoko Wada (Cambridge: D. S. Brewer, 2003), pp. 109–10.

11. Anne Savage, 'The Communal Authorship of *Ancrene Wisse*', in *A Companion to Ancrene Wisse*, ed. Wada, pp. 45–57.

12. See *Ancrene Wisse*, ed. Millett, pp. xxxvii–lxi, and especially lv.

13. Ibid., p. lv.

14. Ibid., p. lx.

15. Sarah Salih and Denise Baker, 'Introduction', in *Julian of Norwich's Legacy: Medieval Mysticism and Post-Medieval Reception*, ed. Salih and Baker (New York: Palgrave Macmillan, 2009), p. 1.

16. Ibid., p. 6.

17. Ibid., p. 3.

18. Ibid., p. 5.

19. Alexander Barratt, 'Julian of Norwich and Her Children Today: Editions, Translations and Versions of Her Revelations', in *Julian of Norwich's Legacy*, ed. Salih and Baker, p. 14.

20. Salih and Baker, 'Introduction', p. 5.

21. Ibid.

14
Anonymous Texts

Liz Herbert McAvoy

The politics concerning the anonymity of medieval texts have become increasingly important to the project of medieval feminist scholarship in its attempts to recover – at least as much as is possible – the traces of female subjectivity within a culture where both subjectivity and creativity were deemed definitively male. Indeed, medieval literary theory, revolving around the idea of the author – *auctor* – as embodiment of *auctoritas* – the God-given authority to define, name, categorize, and represent – was fully in step with a grand narrative in which Adam, the first man, named not only the beasts of the field but the first woman too: 'And Adam said: This now is bone of my bones, and flesh of my flesh; she shall be called woman, because she was taken out of man' (Genesis 2:23). In effect, Eve could not be the writer, for she was the written upon. Like her medieval daughters, she became the product of a naming process which transformed her from blank parchment into written text, a script, moreover, frequently imbued with an entrenched and naturalized misogyny. The origin of writing as male, however, has been echoed in recent years by Jacques Derrida who, in *Of Grammatology*, identified the marking of the soil by the male-driven plough as itself an act of 'writing' which 'opens nature to culture' via the act of cultivation. For Derrida, 'writing is born with agriculture', and this physical act of spatial demarcation ('writing in furrows') links the land and its ownership with the authoritative (male) body.[1] Thus is revealed the logocentric project so fundamental to the Book of Genesis, which produced and perpetuated the notion of the medieval *auctor*: Adam, after all, was created by God because 'there was not a man to till the earth' (Genesis 2:5). Considering such conditions of authorship, we might join with Jane Chance in asking 'if ... misogynistic perceptions of gender difference were generally accepted by the patriarchal culture of the Middle Ages, what happened when women wrote (or at least articulated texts)?'.[2] Of course, the essays in this present volume all go some length towards answering this question, confirming too another premise of Chance's that 'when women did write ... they either consciously wrote *against* that misogynistic tradition, adapted it to their own feminized resistance, or ignored it and initiated new forms'.[3] As Diane Watt has also asserted, medieval women writers were not necessarily as alienated from patriarchal culture as is sometimes imagined and adopted a range of strategies which allowed for their own literary inclusion.[4]

The main issue at stake here, however, is that by far the greater proportion of the female authors receiving our attention are themselves *named* authors and, as such, make it easier for us to speak about their writing as 'women's writing'. It is therefore worth reiterating that, as exceptional women who certainly lay outside the norms for medieval women and their access to literary creativity, they are hardly paradigmatic. Moreover, the entire category of 'women's writing' has been queried in recent times by commentators such as Hélène Cixous, who claims of female authorship:

> [women] do someone else's – man's – writing, and in their innocence sustain it and give it voice, and end up producing writing that's in effect masculine. Great care must be taken in working on feminine writing not to get trapped by names: to be signed with a woman's name doesn't necessarily make a piece of writing feminine. It could quite well be masculine writing.[5]

Here, Cixous is preoccupied with the issue of women's ventriloquism in their use of the only language available to them which, like Derrida's conception of writing, is both male and masculine. Within their own attempts at creativity, therefore, women can only ever be 'decapitated', unless, of course, they make recourse to an alternative language arising from the specifics of their *own* bodily experiences.[6] Thus, we may add a further category to the possible strategies available to the medieval woman author (or the man who wished to speak through her): she could draw upon and develop an experiential language of the body (in Cixous' terms 'the flesh of language') which results in a 'tactility' and an 'outpouring' which 'crosses limits'.[7] Read within this framework, the issue of anonymous texts in the Middle Ages becomes problematized in a way which may prove fruitful for extending what we understand about the relation of women to literary expression and production.

In her appraisal of the anonymous medieval text, Laurie Finke takes the broadest view of what constitutes the 'woman writer', suggesting also that authorship *per se* has been theoretically perceived as a male concept, and the 'tests of authenticity' imposed upon a likely female-authored text are still much more rigorous than for its male-authored equivalent.[8] Thus, what she terms 'the hidden transcript' of medieval women's writing has frequently been overlooked or 'talked away'.[9] One case in point here is the way in which the greater body of Anglo-Saxon lyric poetry has long been attributed to male authorship, in spite of the fact that at least two poems from the important *Exeter Book* are written convincingly from a woman's perspective. Both

The Wife's Lament and *Wulf and Eadwacer* bear the hallmarks of a woman recording her own experience from a first-person perspective, articulating a specifically female treatment of those traditional Anglo-Saxon poetics concerning the mind-numbing issues of loss, longing, separation, and isolation which dominate many of the secular works of the period. These two poems leave us in no doubt of a female perspective, however, from their concerted use of feminine pronouns and adjectival forms which identify the speaker, at least, as a woman in each case. This, of course, does not necessarily attest to female authorship for, as Finke also notes, 'literary cross-dressing is too easy' for us to make assumptions about authorship purely on the basis of the subject-position adopted by the poetic voice.[10] This may, indeed, be true, but this should not preclude us from considering these two poems as a form of women's writing, even if originally composed by men. This would also concur with the demands of some feminist critical perspectives to focus on the gender of the text rather than the sex of the author.[11]

The two poems are widely acknowledged to be the most complex of the Anglo-Saxon lyrical corpus because of their riddle-like approach to the conundrum of human alienation. Indeed, unlike the male elegies alongside which they tend to be grouped, they retain a sense of double alienation: that of the exiled human, common to all the elegies, and that of the betrayed woman, which is gender specific. Thus, the exiled woman is doubly disadvantaged, rendering gender a pressing and central concern within these two poems, something which is not foregrounded in those elegies containing a male speaker. The speaker of *The Wife's Lament*,[12] for example, bemoans how 'Very often here the departure of my lord / cruelly laid hold of me' (ll. 32–3), and 'My cruel lord commanded me to be taken here' (l. 15). Similarly, in *Wulf and Eadwacer*, the female speaker recalls 'I pursued in my hopes the far journeys of Wulf / when it was rainy weather, and I sat, sorrowful' (ll. 9–10). This contrasts dramatically with the sentiments of the exiled speaker in, for example, *The Husband's Message*, which is both more linear and a less internalized lament for a lost wife (and a poem which, it has been suggested, should be paired with *The Wife's Lament* as a male perspective on the separation of the same partnership). For Elaine Treharne, the voice of the exile in *The Husband's Message* is an optimistic one, suggesting a man who does not wholly relinquish himself to the buffeting of fate.[13] In *The Wife's Lament* and *Wulf and Eadwacer*, however, the logic of a linear thought-process is entirely cast aside in favour of an almost stoic abandonment of self to solitude and lovelessness.

These poems also have no discernible beginning and no end: they begin *in media res* and resist both definition and the constraints of logic and closure, in fact adhering closely to Cixous' definition of the specifically feminine text which 'goes on and on' and which 'at a certain moment...comes to an end but the writing continues and for the reader this means a thrust into the void'.[14] In both poems we are left with a voice speaking into the void where the reader is invited to follow and thus take up a similarly female subject-position. This is perhaps one reason why within traditional Anglo-Saxon scholarship there has been a concerted attempt to bring these poems into line with the rest of the elegiac corpus by means of emendations and/or masculinizing allegorical readings.[15] The point I wish to make here, however, is that these poems, articulated from a convincingly female perspective, whether male- or female-authored, form an important part of women's literary history in that they offer up the possibility of articulating a specifically female response to the world, its joys and cruelties, giving access to the poetics embedded in such experience. In fact, they offer the possibility of a female subjectivity which is not dependent upon male definition for its construction but which takes the form of what Cixous terms 'a kind of disengagement... [a] metaphorical form of wandering, excess, risk of the unreckonable' because 'femininity is written outside anticipation: it really is the text of the unforeseeable'.[16] Read in this light, it is hardly surprising that each poem categorizes itself explicitly as *giedd*, a riddle, a form which defies traditional logic and ways of seeing, asking for – sometimes *demanding* – an alternative viewpoint from which to make sense of its unpredictable narrator-subject.

The female narrator as subject also makes its presence felt in an anonymous lyrical text from the thirteenth century written initially for an audience of anchoritic women: *þe Wohunge of Ure Lauerd*, extant in one single copy in London, British Library MS Cotton Titus D. xviii, fols. 127–33.[17] This text is closely associated with the male-authored *Ancrene Wisse* and other texts within the so-called 'Katherine Group'; indeed, some recent editors consider it was likely written by the same author as *Ancrene Wisse* to instruct his anchoritic audience in the intricacies of meditative Christic devotion.[18] This runs counter to the opinion of Eugen Einenkel, however, who was one of the first commentators to consider the poem as female-authored,[19] an opinion taken up by W. Meredith Thompson in 1958 who cast the author as 'a gifted woman writer'.[20] The argument has therefore followed the same trajectory as for the Anglo-Saxon poems examined earlier, but there is no doubt that *Wohunge* is saturated with the type of affective devotion which required the adoption of a female – and feminine – subject-position. In this poem, the speaking 'I' is clearly that of the female operating within a heterosexual matrix in her approach to Christ: 'If I will love any man for beauty, I will love you'; 'I want to choose a lover for his possessions'; '[you] made me lady over all the created things you shaped on earth' (p. 248). Whilst such a devotional approach to Christ is also arguably Bernadine and thus gender-inclusive on the level of practice, discursively the poet is undoubtedly female and feminine in the adopted subject-position. She is also clearly anchoritic in her passionate avowal to Christ which invokes the metaphors of anchorhold as womb, tomb, and bridal bed: 'You have brought me from the world to the bower of your birth, locked me in a chamber', from where she moves inexorably on to a moment of mystical union which is freighted with the erotic within that enclosed space: 'My body will hang with your body, nailed on the cross, fastened, transfixed between four walls', a merging which ultimately produces the ecstatic 'Ah Jesus, sweet Jesus, my love, my beloved, my life, my dearest love' (p. 265). Here, the identities of the woman and Christ merge so that their bodies and the meanings attached to them are utterly indistinguishable. In turn, this renders this poetic moment indisputably one of mystical union, fully in keeping with that frequently recounted in medieval mystical women's writing, particularly of continental provenance, and an experience which, in more recent times, Luce Irigaray has identified as 'the only place in the history of the West in which woman speaks and acts so publicly'.[21] For Irigaray, however, this speaking 'woman' can be genetically a man, but one who has 'given up his knowledge in order to attend to woman's madnesses', a man who 'can no longer find himself as "subject" any more'.[22] The necessary subject-position for the mystical encounter is, after all, one of relinquishment, absence, non-being. It was thus only a small step, not of distance but of degree, for women to become paradigmatic within this type of intense devotional activity. Once again, we find a text promoting a female subject-position but this time one which is offered as model for affective spirituality and, whilst no gender stereotyping is subverted, or even significantly disrupted, it does offer – or ventriloquize – a female voice which acknowledges the advantages of a female perspective on matters divine.

Such an important testimony to the value of a female perspective offers a moment of illumination within medieval women's literary history and, I would argue, certainly paves a clear pathway for the writing of women whose names *were* attached to their texts in the later Middle Ages (in England, Julian of Norwich and Margery Kempe, for example) and some whose names were not. Indeed, the fifteenth century bore witness to a burgeoning of the 'female-voiced' lyric, some of which were certainly of likely female authorship. Whilst again some critics have read these poems as a gesture of imitation by a male poet wishing to project his own desires onto the female voice within the poem,[23] and others have called for extreme caution when considering any of these poems to have been female-authored,[24] Sarah McNamer has suggested that these lyrics resound far more with the inner world of women living in the English provinces than they do with the artifice of male-authored poems and their obsession with *fin amour*.[25] Meanwhile, Alexandra Barratt has identified the prevalence of a stoic resignation to pain and loss within those lyrics directly attributable to named female authors, in direct contrast to an unmanageable despair which, so she claims, characterizes male attempts to ventriloquize the female voice.[26] This is also supported by Anne L. Klinck, whose analysis of a range of anonymous lyrics has led her to observe: 'it is [those poems] known to be authored by women which are the most self-assertive, as they confidently turn the love-complaint of the forsaken woman into a decidedly energetic and active proposition'.[27]

Also self-assertive in its female authorship is the anonymous late-medieval *Feitis and Passion of Oure Lord*,[28] composed by a nun, possibly of Syon Abbey, for one of her sisters at some stage in the fifteenth century. The text takes the form of a series of prayer-mediations focusing particularly on Christ's Passion and death. Unexpectedly, however, the prayers are not laid down to be read in any logical, linear way but in snatches according to the amount of time available to the reader: 'And sustir bindith not yow self to seye al ouir the preieres euery day, but seye summe on oon day and & summe on a nothir day, as ye haue leyser' (fol. 97). This type of instruction, of course, is highly reminiscent of the *Wohunge*, where concerted devotional practices, which have at their core an experiential bodily affect, frequently lie outside the laws of orderliness and logic and hold the key to the perceived 'femininity' of such texts. Again, this is something with which the author of the *Feitis*, living enclosed among female readers, appears to be fully conversant in her suggestion that, given time and practice, her words will become a text written in and on the bodies of her audience as they learn them, literally, by heart: 'I wolde ye couden the sentence wit outyn þe book, for and ye so coude, ye schulden fele mochil more comfort & vnyon in god to seye it so inforth than for to seie it be scripture' [i.e. to read it aloud] (fol. 98). Within this devotional practice, the body as 'knowing' entity is privileged over reason and intellect; the words on the page become transferred to the intrinsic 'selfhood' represented by that body. In this and those other anonymous texts examined here, therefore, we witness some of the ways in which a female perspective on matters emotional, devotional, or divine, whether scripted by men or by women, helped to open up the way for the rather more self-consciously female-authored texts which began to make their presence felt as the Middle Ages drew to a close, many of which are examined elsewhere in the present volume.

Two such texts remain to be examined, ones which have, perhaps, generated the most controversy regarding authorship to date. *The Floure and the Leafe* and *The Assembly of Ladies*[29] are poems which appear to have been erroneously attributed to Chaucer soon after their composition in the fifteenth century.[30] Adhering to the popular dream-vision genre, these poems are nevertheless disruptive because in both cases the dreamer-narrator is a woman, an innovation which both challenges and destabilizes traditional politics and poetics attached to the dreamer's gaze. This in itself has induced some critics to attribute them to female authorship (and, in the case of Skeat, the *same* female author).[31] Derek Pearsall, meanwhile, has been more cautious, although still locating both poems firmly within what he terms 'the interminable feminist controversy of the fifteenth century'.[32] Others have preferred to examine the poems in terms of genre, rather than authorship, deeming the sex of the author of little importance.[33] However, as Finke has asserted, in view of the fact that the objectifying gaze within this genre is almost always male, the femaleness of the author, overtly foregrounded as it is in both poems, would certainly have had an effect on a reader's response.[34] I would assert, however, that the importance of both poems to the history of women's writing is not the fact that they may or may not have been penned by women, nor that they offer a scenario which is subject to an objectifying female gaze (although both may indeed be the case) but that they self-consciously present at their conclusion a representation of a female self who is also a writer and who has a valid, authoritative voice. In *The Floure and the Leafe*, at the fading of the vision, the dreamer heads home with both alacrity and trepidation to record her experiences for others:

> And put all that I had seen in writing
> Under support of them that lust it rede.
> O little booke, thou art so unconning,
> How darst thou put thyself in prees for drede?

> (ll. 589–92)

In *The Assembly of Ladies*, the transition to writing is even more urgent, suggesting the need to record a verifiable 'female' vision before it fades into obscurity and anonymity along with so many acts of female creativity:

> 'Wher am I now?' thought I, 'al this is goon,'
> Al amased; and up I gan to looke.
> With that anon I went and made this booke,
> Thus simply reherseyng the substaunce
> Because it shuld nat out of remembraunce.

> (ll. 739–43)

Thus, I would fully concur with Simone Celine Marshall who recognizes in these conclusions an impetus which 'clearly elevates for the reader the notion of women's participation in literature', rendering authorial anonymity 'a deliberate act in order to elevate the issue of female participation'.[35] In this sense, the self-presentation of the authors of these poems and those other works which I have examined, in their anonymity and their production of a *mise en scène* in which the woman is seen to be the recorder of her own unmediated experience, adhere closely to the Foucauldian notion of the 'author-function' which is to 'characterize the existence, circulation, and operation of certain discourses within society'.[36] If, as Foucault asserts, authorship is discourse bound, then authorship, like discourse, can also become subject to strategic appropriation by the readers of the text.

The concept of the anonymous 'female' author, therefore, should be reappraised as a revelatory mechanism which ultimately has the capacity to lay down the foundations for what necessarily remains a still-developing history of women's participation in literary production, one which allows her to identify, name, and categorize her own experience.

Notes

1. Jacques Derrida, *Of Grammatology*, trans. G. C. Spivak (Baltimore: Johns Hopkins University Press, 1981), p. 287.
2. Jane Chance, *Gender and Text in the Middle Ages* (Gainesville: University Press of Florida, 1996), p. 5.
3. Ibid., p. 9.
4. Diane Watt, *Medieval Women's Writing: Works by and for Women in England, 1100–1500* (Cambridge: Polity Press, 2007), pp. 1–18.
5. Hélène Cixous, 'Castration or Decapitation', in *Authorship from Plato to the Postmodern*, ed. Seán Burke (Edinburgh: Edinburgh University Press, 2000, repr. 2003), pp. 162–77 (p. 173).
6. Ibid., p. 174.
7. Ibid., pp. 175–6.
8. Laurie A. Finke, *Women's Writing in English: Medieval England* (Harlow: Longman, 1999), p. 8.
9. Ibid., p. 85.
10. Ibid., p. 81.
11. See, for example, Marilynn Desmond, 'The Voice of Exile: Feminist Literary History and the Anonymous Anglo-Saxon Elegy', *Critical Enquiry*, 16.3 (1990), 527–90.
12. The edition used for the three poems cited here is Elaine Treharne (ed.), *Old and Middle English: An Anthology* (Oxford: Blackwell, 2000), and cited by line number parenthetically in the main text. Treharne's comment is on p. 80.
13. See, for example, Treharne's comments in *Old and Middle English*, p. 80.
14. Cixous, 'Castration', p. 174.
15. See Finke, *Women's Writing*, p. 88.
16. Cixous, 'Castration', p. 175.
17. All in-text references to this poem are from *Anchoritic Spirituality: Ancrene Wisse and Associated Works* (New York: Paulist Press, 1991), ed. and trans. Anne Savage and Nicholas Watson, pp. 245–58.
18. See, for example, the introduction to this text by Savage and Watson in *Anchoritic Spirituality*, p. 245.
19. Eugen Einenkel, 'Eine englische schriftstellerin aus dem anfange des 12. Jahrhunderts', *Anglia*, 5 (1882), 265–82.
20. *þe Wohunge of Ure Lauerd*, ed. W. Meredith Thompson, EETS o.s. 241 (London: Oxford University Press, 1958), p. xxii.
21. Luce Irigaray, 'La Mystérique', in *Speculum of the Other Woman* (Ithaca: Cornell University Press, 1974), pp. 191–202 (p. 191).
22. Ibid., p. 192.
23. See, for example, Kemp Malone, 'Two English *Frauenlieder*', *Comparative Literature*, 1.4 (1962), 106–17 (117).

24. See Susan Shibanoff, 'Medieval *Frauenlieder*: Anonymous was a Man', *Tulsa Studies in Women's Literature*, 2.2 (1982), 189–200.
25. Sarah McNamer, 'Female Authors, Provincial Settings: The Re-versing of Courtly Love in the Findern Manuscript', *Viator*, 22 (1991), 279–310.
26. Alexandra Barratt has edited a selection of such lyrics in *Women's Writing in Middle English* (London: Longman, 1992; 2nd edn., London: Pearson, 2010), here at p. 262.
27. Anne J. Klinck, 'Poetic Markers of Gender in Medieval "Women's Song"', *Neophilologus*, 87.1 (2003), 339–59 (354).
28. In-text references are from Oxford, Bodleian Library MS Holkham Misc. 41 and cited by folio number. There has been some debate surrounding the title of this work, primarily because of the damage to the manuscript at the point where the author names it. The debated word has been read variously as *feitis* [deeds], or *festis* [commemorative holy days], and either would seem to fit the textual content. Alexandra Barratt, who has edited extracts from this text, reads it as the former (for which see her essay in this volume), although Jo Koster Tarvers argues against this reading in 'Gender, Text, Critic: The Case of Holkham Misc. 41', *Medieval Perspectives*, 14 (1999), 229–41 (234–5). To revisit this debate is beyond the scope of this chapter but my own reading prefers *feitis* over *festis*.
29. All in-text references to these poems are to *The Floure and the Leafe; The Assembly of Ladies; The Isle of Ladies*, ed. Derek Pearsall (Kalamazoo: Medieval Institute Publications, 1990).
30. Finke, *Women's Writing*, p. 94.
31. W. W. Skeat, 'The Authoress', *Modern Language Quarterly*, 3 (1990), 111–12.
32. *Floure and the Leafe*, ed. Pearsall, p. 20.
33. See, for example, Julia Boffey, 'Women Authors and Women's Literacy in Fourteenth- and Fifteenth-Century England', in *Women and Literature in Britain, 1150–1500*, ed. Carol Meale (Cambridge: Cambridge University Press, 1993).
34. Finke, *Women's Writing*, p. 98.
35. Simone Celine Marshall, *The Female Voice in* The Assembly of Ladies (Cambridge: Cambridge Scholars Publishing, 2008), pp. 5, 25.
36. Michel Foucault, 'What is an Author?' in *Authorship from Plato to the Postmodern*, ed. Burke, pp. 232–62 (p. 235).

15
Women Translators

Alexandra Barratt

Dame Eleanor Hull (*c*.1394–1460) and Lady Margaret Beaufort (1443–1509) are the two women translators working between 1350 and 1500 known to us by name and whose existence is well documented. A third, Dame Juliana Berners (*fl*.1460), is a more shadowy figure. Dame Eleanor produced at least two surviving English translations from French or Anglo-Norman originals: *The Seven Psalms*, a commentary on the penitential psalms,[1] and *Orisons and Meditations*, a collection of prayers and meditations.[2] The first was 'a daring book for girls' and its choice is almost as surprising as the translator's existence: medieval scriptural exegesis is not a genre one immediately associates with women. Christopher de Hamel, however, notes the existence of a Peter Comestor (now British Library, MS Royal MSS, Royal 7 F III), copied in 1191–2 for the Benedictine nunnery of Elstow, Bedfordshire, at the command of its abbess; he goes on to comment that 'in the fifteenth century, it seems to have been quite common for nuns to be given books by their chaplains'.[3] The anonymous nun, a contemporary of Dame Eleanor's, who wrote *The Faits and the Passion of Our Lord Jesu Christ*, might well have benefited from this practice: she shows a surprising familiarity with the Glossa Ordinaria in one passage.[4]

Dame Eleanor surely translated *The Seven Psalms* first and foremost for her personal use, from a French (or Anglo-Norman) original. Richard Fox, a literate layman and 'procurator' or steward of St Albans Abbey, who compiled and partially transcribed Cambridge University Library, MS Kk. 1. 6, the unique manuscript, declares that the text was 'transelated out of Frensche in-to Englesche' (fol. 147). There is no reason to doubt this, and the internal evidence points in the same direction. But that French commentary incorporated the Latin text of the psalms, verse by verse, and by translating the whole thing into English Dame Eleanor was doing something not only unusual but maybe even dangerous.

In 1409, when she was still a girl, Archbishop Thomas Arundel had issued the Constitutions of Oxford, 'one of the most draconian pieces of censorship in English history', of which Article 7 'forbids anybody to make any written translation of a text of Scripture into English or even to own a copy, without diocesan permission, of any such translation made since Wycliffe's time'; apparently the wording was designed to 'include even single verses translated in written form'.[5] But the Constitutions did not forbid scriptural translation into Anglo-Norman or French as opposed to English, so there would be no problem in possessing the exemplar of her translation. Nor were the Constitutions primarily aimed at the gentry, which would have provided Dame Eleanor with some protection. And she, or her confessor, might well have applied to her bishop for the requisite permission: she was that sort of a girl. Indeed, she first appears in the records in 1413 as a young married woman ('damsel, noblewoman') requesting papal permission for a portable altar and, two years later, the right to choose her own confessor.[6] In 1421 and 1423 she purchased plenary indulgences for herself,[7] so she was no Lollard.

We know that Dame Eleanor owned a Vulgate and a Latin psalter, as she bequeathed them in her 1458 will to her spiritual adviser Roger Huswyf. Ownership of such books by layfolk was not unprecedented, although by the fifteenth century the more user-friendly Book of Hours had largely replaced the psalter on their prayer desks. Maybe back in 1407 her confessor had pressed them into her hands, saying, 'Well, if you really want to understand the Psalms, you'll just have to learn Latin.' But even if Dame Eleanor learnt to construe the literal sense of the Latin words she could often have found their import baffling. Perhaps when she asked her confessor for further guidance he offered her the French commentary, to use alongside her Latin psalter. It would be hard to use on its own: the verses quoted from the psalms are so extensively commentated and widely separated that a reader is often hard-pressed to hang on to the thread of the psalmist's, or the commentator's, thoughts.

French commentaries on the Psalms, as distinct from translations, are in fact quite uncommon: Dean and Boulton list only one, originally written in continental French in the twelfth century, although most of the extant copies are Anglo-Norman.[8] Unfortunately it is not Eleanor's source, which continues to elude us. Richard Rolle's English commentary on the Psalms, of which at least eighteen manuscripts survive, was surely known to her confessor. But as a number of copies had Lollard interpolations, he may have preferred a French commentary to protect his penitent's orthodoxy, or her reputation. But maybe (to speculate even further) Dame Eleanor found that, however good her language skills, the very effort required to decipher a manuscript written in French or Anglo-Norman on a complex theological subject was distracting her from the overall sense of the commentary. Making a translation would focus her mind, and once made it could be used again and again to understand and pray the psalms. Possibly her first venture into the field, the result was not for others, or for public circulation.

Dame Eleanor continued to be interested in biblical commentary. She and Roger Huswyf presented four enormous volumes of Nicholas of Lyra to St Albans Abbey in 1456 or 1457, with the proviso that the copy was to be for Huswyf's use during his life. This must have cost a small fortune (it probably took the scribe, Stephen Dodesham, five years' solid work to complete the manuscripts) and presumably was funded by Dame Eleanor, even if the original idea was Huswyf's or, more likely, Abbot John Whethamstede's. Huswyf himself later donated a copy of another scriptural commentary, Alexander Nequam on the Song of Songs, to the monks of Syon Abbey, of which he was a 'frater laicus' or associate.[9]

Dame Eleanor's other known translation, *Orisons and Meditations*, which survives in University of Illinois MS 80 as well as in CUL Kk. 1. 6, was probably made after the psalter commentary. Unlike the latter, it is exactly the sort of devotional text one would expect a devout woman to read and perhaps translate. The prologue describes it as 'party takyn of Seynt Austyn, party of Seynt Ancelm, party of Seynt Barnard, and party of oþer wrytyngis' (fol. 148r). The text does indeed use material widely thought in the Middle Ages to be Augustinian, together with extracts from authentic writings by St Bernard and part of St Anselm's letter to the Countess Mathilda of Tuscany that prefaced his own meditations. Such sources place it squarely in the tradition of medieval affective piety.

One of the four known versions of Dame Eleanor's partial source, the Anglo-Norman *Oreysons et Meditacions*, seems written for a female audience. In British Library, MS Arundel 288, where the translation reads, 'þo þat redyn this sholde not set ther ententis for-to rede hem [the prayers] all ouer at onys', we find specifically female pronouns: 'Ne ne deyt pas mettre entents, *cele* qe ces oroysons dit, *kele* chescune parlise tut outre'. Arundel 288 cannot be the manuscript actually used by Dame Eleanor for her translation as it contains only the prologue and a short extract,[10] but possibly her exemplar was also adapted for a woman, and this influenced her choice of this particular text.

Each of the surviving manuscripts of this Anglo-Norman text[11] presents a different selection from the hypothetical original. It is therefore difficult to draw any firm conclusions from apparent omissions in the translation. Specifically, Dame Eleanor appears to have omitted a long section on the Five Wounds, but we should not conclude that she shunned Passion devotion: she would have been an unusual devout women if she had. Rather, if she was already planning to supplement her translation of *Oreysons et Meditacions* with a much longer set of meditations linked to the days of the week – the source of which remains undiscovered but which bears all the marks of translation from French – she would already have known that the Meditation for Friday was devoted to the Passion, rendering an extended consideration of the Five Wounds superfluous.

The most surprising element in this otherwise rather predictable text is an interest in astronomy. The Meditation for Sunday, devoted to the joys of Heaven, approaches its subject rather literally by considering the planets, the firmament, and the empyreal heaven where God dwells. To this end it gives detailed figures, expressed in roman numerals, for each of the planets as to volume (in terms of the volume of the earth), and distance in miles to Earth (in terms of the Earth's diameter). A less conscientious translator would surely have excised such an indigestible hunk of (mis)information. In fact, the Illinois version of the text omits it altogether, and its scribe may well have felt that the sudden intrusion of astronomy into such an intensely devotional setting struck a discordant note. But Dame Eleanor seems to have faithfully transmitted her source, for even though the roman numerals have clearly been much garbled in transmission, there is method in their madness. They recognizably derive from the Arab astronomer Al-Farghâni or Alfraganus, whose elementary textbook on astronomy was widely used throughout the Middle Ages. The Meditation for Thursday cites him by name: 'And the erthe is VI M and VC myle þyk, as seyth Affragan' (fol. 161). Al-Farghâni does indeed establish to his satisfaction that the Earth's diameter is 6,500 miles, and all his subsequent calculations of volume and distance are done in terms of products of half this figure, that is, of the Earth's radius. Dame Eleanor's original seems to have used a Latin translation, of which there were two, one by John of Seville in 1137 and the other by Gerard of Cremona before 1175, or a lost French translation.[12]

The Seven Psalms and *Orisons and Meditations* would make a solid, and varied, list of outputs for any translator. But Dame Eleanor may have also translated a third text from Anglo-Norman, *The Twenty-one Passions of Our Lord*, found in CUL MS Kk. 1. 6, fols. 180–92. Richard Fox does not claim that this is her work, but he may simply have had no room to do so as this text finishes right at the bottom of a page. It clearly derives from, or rather elaborates, an Anglo-Norman text found only in BL MS Arundel 288, fols. 91vb–97.[13] More significant, however, is a recent suggestion that Dame Eleanor might be the Sinful Wretch who bravely undertook the *Gilte Legende* (*GiL*),[14] the first English translation of the *Légende Dorée* (*LD*), in its turn a French translation of the vast thirteenth-century collection of saints' lives made by Jacobus de Voragine, the *Legenda Aurea*.

Richard Hamer, one of the editors of the *GiL*, believes that his translator could well have been a woman: he observes a tendency to insert extra references to women into the text and to employ euphemism and self-censorship when writing about sex and other bodily functions. Further, the Sinful Wretch added an exceptionally long and detailed life of Sts Alban and Amphibalus, which suggests a very close connection with St Alban's Abbey. The *GiL* was completed by the Sinful Wretch in 1438, according to Oxford, Bodley MS Douce 372, and Dame Eleanor Hull is the only woman translator known to be active at the time. She was also a member of the confraternity of St Albans, gave the abbot and convent generous gifts, and often resided at Sopwell, a priory of Benedictine nuns dependent on St Albans.

Dr Hamer hypothesizes that Dame Eleanor might have translated the *GiL's* unique version of the St Katherine legend around 1420, when Henry V married Catherine de Valois: Dame Eleanor was lady-in-waiting to Henry IV's widow, Queen Joan, and could well have been in France for the wedding; she also had a particular devotion to the saint, as evidenced in her will. The Sinful Wretch added other texts to the basic *LD* collection, in particular the Lives of Sts John the Baptist, Alban and Amphibalus, Malchus, and the Conception of Our Lady. It is easy to think of reasons for Dame Eleanor's choice of such texts. Both her father and her husband were called John; St Jerome's romance of Malchus the Captive Monk and his chaste marriage could have resonated with her personal circumstances; the life of St Alban honoured an institution with which she had a longstanding symbiotic relationship; both the *Orisons and Meditations* and *The Twenty-one Passions*, which intersperses its Passion meditations with meditations on the Compassion or co-suffering of the Virgin, evidence intense Marian devotion. Furthermore, the Meditation for Wednesday in the *Orisons and Meditations*, devoted to the lives of saints, mentions in particular the Baptist, the Virgin Mary, and virgin saints in general as models (fols. 157v–161r). This theory is still being explored. Further progress would probably require the use of stylistic tests, which are difficult to devise, given our fragmentary knowledge of Dame Eleanor's originals.

Lady Margaret Beaufort is much better known, and better documented,[15] than Dame Eleanor, but the parallels between them are striking. Both women were heiresses, married off as girls, who quickly bore sons, the fathers dying while their wives were young: Dame Eleanor enjoyed the luxury of remaining a widow while the Lady Margaret contracted two further marriages, entirely for political reasons. Both were literate in English and French, had close connections with male as well as female religious houses (Dame Eleanor with St Albans and Sopwell, Lady Margaret with the Carthusians and Syon Abbey), and enjoyed the guidance of male spiritual advisers (Roger Huswyf and John Fisher). Such parallels, however, are not so much coincidences as the preconditions that allowed women to function as translators in the fifteenth century: independence, education, limited family responsibilities, disposable time as well as disposable income, and access to the kinds of material and intangible resources normally under male clerical control.

Their *oeuvres* are also similar: both worked from French, not Latin, exemplars, and both had their authorship publicly acknowledged – Dame Eleanor's by Richard Fox's statements in CUL MS Kk. 1. 6, and Lady Margaret's in the incipits to her two published texts. Both probably made other translations: as we have seen, Dame Eleanor may well have translated *The Twenty-one Passions of Our Lord* and the *GiL*, while John Fisher asserted that Lady Margaret owned many books in English and French and that 'for her exercyse & for the prouffyte of other she dyde translate dyuers maters of deuocyon out of Frensshe into Englysshe'.[16] Both may have collaborated with male clerics, Dame Eleanor with Roger Huswyf perhaps to translate the *GiL* Lives with Latin originals, Lady Margaret with Dr William Atkinson, who translated at her request the first three books of *De Imitatione Christi*.

It has long been known that Lady Margaret translated Book IV of *De Imitatione Christi*, concerned with the devout reception of the Blessed Sacrament, and the *Speculum Animae Peccatricis*, a disquisition in the *contemptus mundi* mode on human unworthiness, once attributed to Denis the Carthusian but now to another Carthusian, Jacobus Gruytroede of Liège. Both texts were first printed during the translator's lifetime, in 1503 and 1506 respectively. Only recently, however, have they been studied in detail by Brenda Hosington, who has succeeded in identifying the French versions from which the translator worked and can therefore write authoritatively about Lady's Margaret's qualities as a translator.[17] It is interesting that Professor Hosington picks out for comment strategies of 'explicitation' (a concern for clarity that leads to the translator glossing her text); 'personalization' (making the text more personal and inclusive); the use of doublets for intensification; and a certain shrinking from excessively harsh and negative language. Similar strategies can be demonstrated in Dame Eleanor's translations. Before the cry of 'essentialism' is raised, we should perhaps consider that both Dame Eleanor and Lady Margaret were conditioned by their class as well as by their gender. They were not only women, but female members of the upper class, of whom certain norms of decorum were expected.

Finally, the more crepuscular figure of Dame Juliana Berners may be contrasted with our two well-documented translators.[18] We do not know who she was or even whether she really existed. But we do know that the St Albans Schoolmaster-Printer attributed *The Boke of Hunting*, published in 1486, to 'Dam Julyans Barnes',[19] that this was repeated by Wynken de Worde ten years later, that Cambridge MS Magdalene College Pepys 1047 attached her name to a different text, a list of collective nouns,[20] and that a sixteenth-century bibliographer further identified her as Lady Juliana Berners, sister of Richard Lord Berners and prioress of Sopwell, the very priory where Dame Eleanor had lived from time to time. *The Boke of Hunting* is in large part a verse translation of the brief Anglo-Norman prose text *La Vénerie de Twiti*, composed around 1328 by King Edward II's huntsman, of which there are also two Middle English prose translations:[21] Dame Juliana, then, would be the first woman to translate into English verse. She may have chosen verse for its mnemonic potential, for the purpose of the resulting text seems primarily educational rather than scientific. The poem is full of entertaining information and misinformation about game animals, their correct designation, their reproductive and eliminatory habits, and how they should be butchered. It is ironic that such a text should be attributed to a nun (even if mistakenly), while the credit for translating substantial theological and devotional texts goes to two laywomen.[22]

The only factor shared by all three translators is that they worked from French or Anglo-Norman, and we should perhaps consider this a little further. Lady Margaret's originals were written in continental French, a language of which she would have had, as a great lady, a thorough knowledge. The *GiL* was also translated from continental French, but Dame Eleanor's other originals were probably Anglo-Norman. She could have gained a good knowledge of contemporary continental French both at home and later at court as lady-in-waiting to Queen Joan, who was born in Normandy, brought up in Navarre, married the duke of Brittany and lived with him there for twelve years before marrying Henry IV. But Dame Eleanor's knowledge of Anglo-Norman – and thirteenth-century Anglo-Norman in the case of the *Orisons* and *Twenty-one Passions* – is less expected. Dame Juliana Berners also apparently translated early fourteenth-century Anglo-Norman. In the later Middle Ages such knowledge was associated with women's religious houses. It was not only Chaucer's Prioress who spoke French 'after the scole of Stratford atte Bowe': shortly before the dissolution of the monasteries, it was noted that the Augustinian canonesses of Lacock Abbey had texts 'written in the frenche tonge which they understand well ... albeit that it ... is moche like the frenche that the common law is writen in'.[23] The comparison with Law French is suggestive, for Dame Eleanor came from a family which had strong legal as well as court connections. Her maternal grandfather, Sir John Hylle of Exeter, was Justice of the King's Bench from 1389 to *c.*1408; her uncle Robert Hylle, although not a lawyer, had a 'tidy, legal mind' and wrote some of the documents that he preserved in his cartulary in Anglo-Norman;[24] one of the executors of her will was Sir John Fortescue, Chief Justice of England and legal theorist; and her lifelong companion and adviser, Roger Huswyf, had been a successful common lawyer before being ordained priest.

We should not underrate the linguistic skills of medieval women. Modern scholars are eager to find proof that they knew Latin – *any* Latin – for Latin is evidence of academic and therefore 'male' learning.[25] Knowledge of French can all too easily be dismissed as a mere accomplishment, something 'picked up' in the course of life at court. On the contrary: knowledge of Anglo-Norman was a learnt, and learned, skill. But we must never forget that, above all, a medieval translator needed an excellent command of the appropriate written version of her own mother tongue if she was to be successful in her demanding task.

Notes

1. *The Seven Psalms: A Commentary on the Penitential Psalms translated from French into English by Dame Eleanor Hull*, ed. Alexandra Barratt, EETS o.s. 307 (Oxford: Oxford University Press, 1995).

2. Sheila H. Conard, 'Dame Eleanor Hull's *Meditacyons vpon the VII days of the woke*: The First Edition of the Middle English Translation in Cambridge University Library MS. Kk. i.6' (unpublished doctoral dissertation, University of Dayton, 1995).

3. C. F. R. de Hamel, *Glossed Books of the Bible and the Origins of the Paris Booktrade* (Woodbridge: D. S. Brewer, 1984), pp. 56–7.

4. Alexandra Barratt (ed.), *Women's Writing in Middle English*, 2nd edn. (London: Pearson, 2010), p. 219.

5. Nicholas Watson, 'Censorship and Cultural Change in Late-Medieval England: Vernacular Theology, the Oxford Translation Debate, and Arundel's Constitutions of 1409', *Speculum*, 70 (1995), 822–64 (826, 829).

6. *Calendar of entries in the Papal Registers relating to Great Britain and Ireland: Papal Letters VI, AD 1404–1415*, prepared by J. A. Twemlow (London: HMSO, 1904), pp. 346, 362.

7. *Calendar of entries in the Papal Registers relating to Great Britain and Ireland: Papal Letters VII, AD 1417–1431*, prepared by J. A. Twemlow (London: HMSO, 1906), pp. 308, 327.

8. Ruth J. Dean with the collaboration of Maureen B. M. Boulton, *Anglo-Norman Literature: A Guide to Texts and Manuscripts*, Anglo-Norman Text Society, Occasional Publications Series 3 (London: Anglo-Norman Text Society, 1999), no. 451–2, pp. 245–6.

9. *Syon Abbey*, ed. Vincent Gillespie, with *The Libraries of the Carthusians*, ed. A. I. Doyle, Corpus of British Medieval Library Catalogues 9 (London: British Library in association with the British Academy, 2001), pp. 136, 581–2.

10. See further Alexandra Barratt, 'Dame Eleanor Hull: The Translator at Work', *Medium Aevum*, 72 (2003), 277–96 (279).

11. Dean and Boulton, *Anglo-Norman Literature: A Guide to Texts and Manuscripts*, no. 942, pp. 473–4.

12. See Francis J. Carmody, 'Leopold of Austria, "Li compilacions de le science des estoilles", Books I–III edited from MS French 613 of the Bibliothèque Nationale, with Notes and Glossary', *University of California Publications in Modern Philology*, 33.2 (1947), p. 37.

13. Not listed in Dean and Boulton.

14. *Gilte Legende Volume I*, ed. Richard Hamer with the assistance of Vida Russell, EETS o.s. 327 (Oxford: Oxford University Press, 2006) and *Gilte Legende Volume II*, ed. Richard Hamer with the assistance of Vida Russell, EETS o.s. 328 (Oxford: Oxford University Press, 2007).

15. See Michael K. Jones and Malcolm G. Underwood, *The King's Mother: Lady Margaret Beaufort, Countess of Richmond and Derby* (Cambridge: Cambridge University Press, 1992), and Jones and Underwood, 'Beaufort, Margaret, countess of Richmond and Derby (1443–1509)', *Oxford Dictionary of National Biography* (http://www.oxforddnb.com/article/1863).

16. *The English Works of John Fisher*, ed. John E. B. Mayor, EETS e.s. 27 (London: Oxford University Press, 1876), p. 292.

17. Brenda Hosington, '"Dyuers maters of deuocyon": Margaret Beaufort's Translations as Mirrors of Practical Piety', in *Women, Religion, and Text Production, 1500–1625*, ed. Micheline White (Aldershot: Ashgate, forthcoming).

18. See Julia Boffey, 'Berners, Juliana (*fl.* 1460)', *Oxford Dictionary of National Biography* (http://www.oxforddnb.com/view/article/2255, accessed 7 Jan. 2010), for a balanced assessment of the evidence.

19. Printed in *English Hawking and Hunting in the 'Boke of St. Albans'*, ed. Rachel Hands (Oxford: Oxford University Press, 1975) and *Julians Barnes: Boke of Huntyng*, ed. Gunnar Tilander, Cynegetica 11 (Karlshamn: Johansson, 1964).

20. David Scott-Macnab, *A Sporting Lexicon of the Fifteenth Century: The J. B. Treatise*, Ævum Monographs N.S. 23 (Oxford: The Society for the Study of Medieval Languages and Literature, 2003), pp. 2–3.

21. Dean and Boulton, *Anglo-Norman Literature: A Guide to Texts and Manuscripts*, no. 405, p. 222; and by Gunnar Tilander, Cynegetica 2 (Uppsala: Almqvist & Wiksells, 1956).

22. Scott-Macnab, following Hands, argues vigorously that Juliana had nothing to do with the hunting treatise (*A Sporting Lexicon*, pp. 3–4).

23. Helena M. Chew, 'Abbey of Lacock', in *A History of Wiltshire*, ed. R. B. Pugh and Elizabeth Crittall, The Victoria County History of the Counties of England (London, 1956), p. 309.

24. *The Hylle Cartulary*, ed. Robert W. Dunning, Somerset Record Society (1968), pp. xiv, xv.

25. See, for instance, my article, 'Small Latin? The Post-Conquest Learning of English Religious Women', in *Anglo-Latin and its Heritage: Essays in Honour of A. G. Rigg on his 64th Birthday*, ed. Siân Echard and Gernot R. Wieland, Publications of *The Journal of Medieval Latin*, 4 (Turnhout: Brepols, 2001), pp. 51–65.

16
Medieval Women's Letters, 1350–1500

James Daybell

Letters represent one of the most common forms of women's writing that survives for the late-medieval period, and thus an important source for re-examining levels of lay female literacy and for exploring the lives and experiences of a range of women: royal, aristocratic, and mercantile. Perhaps the most probing question that confronts scholars of women's epistolary writing is that of composition. Most medieval women's letters appear not to have been penned in the woman's own hand, raising interesting issues relating to female literacy. Yet, the fact that a woman did not write a letter herself is not necessarily indicative of her inability to write: it is highly likely that medieval tradition dictated use of an amanuensis rather than a pen.[1] Allied to the question of scribal status are issues of female authorship, and the degree to which varying forms of collaboration inflected and mediated *women's* writing. In exploring the category of medieval women's authorship, this essay argues for the relative fluidity of the letter-writing process, the reconstruction of which demands attention to material, scribal, stylistic, intertextual, and historical concerns. It also investigates other issues relating to female epistolarity, assessing the degree to which letters were influenced by the *ars dictaminis* and other conventions, and how far epistolary modes were gendered or marked by social differences. Finally, the essay interrogates the question of 'personal' and 'private' in women's letters, and outlines the nature of correspondence, sketching the uses women made of letters, and the light these documents shed on female activities and relationships.

A substantial corpus of women's letters survives for the late-medieval period – numbering well over 200 individual texts, a fraction of those actually written – among the printed papers of the Paston, Plumpton, Cely, Stonor, and Armburgh families, and the letters of Elizabeth Despenser, Alice de Bryene, and numerous religious and royal women.[2] Unpublished manuscript letters also survive within the class-marks of Ancient Correspondence, Ancient Petitions, and Early Chancery Proceedings held at the National Archives; as copies located in episcopal and monastic registers, and in formularies and 'commonplace books'.[3] The social diversity of female correspondents is wide-ranging, encompassing a breadth of lives and experiences, extending from mercantile women (such as Elizabeth Stonor) at one end of the spectrum to noblewomen and royalty (like Philippa, Queen of Portugal or Margaret Beaufort, mother of Henry VII) at the other. Examples of female letter-writers survive from classical antiquity and earlier medieval periods, their correspondence produced chiefly in Latin and French. The fifteenth century witnessed an explosion in women's letter-writing, coinciding with the rise of the vernacular English letter (a genre appropriated by women) the first specimens of which date from 1392 and 1393 (soon after men began corresponding in English), and by which point the written word had become a favoured and trusted mode of communication.[4] French in addition to English was still utilized for letter-writing by noblewomen and queens from 1400 onwards, and Latin favoured for formal occasions. A letter from the Prioress of Rowney to Henry IV, dating from 1400, survives in Latin.[5] However, the majority of surviving letter texts was rendered in English.

The palaeographical evidence of these letters betrays low levels of female scribal activity in penning or signing correspondence, with scholars conjecturing that only a handful of letters were in fact penned by female signatories.[6] Although interpretations of manuscript letters differ and analysis of handwriting is often highly subjective, current orthodoxy considers that most women's correspondence was ordinarily penned by amanuenses (a neutral term that includes formal secretaries, in the sense of salaried individuals retained for writing services, as well as clerks or scribes and other individuals used in a 'secretarial' capacity for correspondence), either by dictation, from notes or use of templates, with the occasional signatures and postscripts added in an autograph female hand.[7] Linguistic usage can also be ambiguous: Agnes Paston's claim to have written in haste 'in the absence of a good secretary' may indeed indicate her own penmanship, but equally might mean that she was forced to use someone other than a usual trusted secretary.[8] Personal secretaries were, however, not the norm; rather women employed various individuals in their letter-writing, including formal secretaries, sons, husbands and other family members, and professional scribes: Agnes Paston's letters were written in eight different hands, those of Margaret Paston feature twenty-nine hands, while Elizabeth Stonor's thirteen extant missives were penned by at least nine different scribes.[9] Untangling the complex relationship between the skills of penmanship and customary epistolary practice is central to understanding how letters were composed. During the fourteenth and fifteenth centuries most letters (women's and men's) were the work of amanuenses.[10] Writing to Elizabeth Stonor, Thomas Betson, the future husband of her daughter, Katherine, complained of receiving no replies, informing her 'She myght gett a secretary yff she wold, and yff she will nat it shall putt me to lesse labour to answere hir lettres agayn'.[11] Alison Truelove has argued from her study of the Stonor correspondence that women of the Stonor family were more likely than men to dictate their letters than to write with their own hands; it is unclear though whether this reflects a gendered convention or low levels of female lay literacy.[12] Certainly Barbara Harris's statistic that 12 per cent of aristocratic women who wrote wills for the period 1450–1550 either signed them or wrote the whole document themselves attests to some level of practical female literacy during this period.[13] Conceivably personal literacy was reserved for tasks and occasions other than letter-writing. Moreover, illiteracy was not a barrier to epistolary culture; informal letter-writing practices, although sparsely documented for this period, provided semi- or partially literate women access to the world of letter-writing. Indeed, a late-fifteenth-century letter in French sent from a woman to George Cely bears strong signs of having been penned by a professional letter-writer.[14]

The methodological and conceptual problems of defining what constitutes a *woman* writer have recently concerned feminist literary scholars, and these issues clearly extend to women's epistolary writing. Scholars interested in the works of Julian of Norwich and Margery Kempe among others have discussed the 'literary authority' of women's texts that were penned by male secretaries.[15] Julia Boffey has shown the difficulty of reconstructing the processes involved in writing, especially when intermediaries, normally male, were crucial in translating and disseminating women's writings: 'it is difficult', she argues, 'to assess the amount of first-hand contact with any of the texts which English women readers and would-be writers can have enjoyed', although this is not the case with the Paston women, for example.[16] Furthermore, Jennifer Summit has shown that categories of 'authorship' were historically contingent; medieval forms were collaborative, communal, and often anonymous, a far remove from modern egocentric notions of self-expression and creative originators.[17] In her impressive study of the Paston women's letters, Diane Watt highlights the complex and pluralistic nature of the medieval letter-writing process, which complicates our understanding of letters as 'authentic' reflections of 'authorial voices'. Authorship of letters was itself fluid. Secretaries played a significant part in composition; letters were ghosted for women by men ventriloquizing female voices, then copied out in fair by another party. Drafting and redrafting illustrate the measured and calculated nature of what at first glance appear to be spontaneous, reactive texts; individual letters only make sense as a part of an intertextual process or 'conversation' with writers echoing and responding linguistically to the other side of the epistolary exchange, a side often tantalizingly irrecoverable.[18]

Nevertheless, it is worth emphasizing that it was conventional scholarly tradition to employ scribes for the drudgery of writing, an activity separated from the intellectual effort of composition.[19] The task of letter-writing in this instance (which involved the messy and laborious tasks of making ink and cutting quills) should be seen as mechanical. The rudimentary act of putting ink on a page was one of several skills associated with authorship, including composition, communication, memory, imagination, legal and business acumen, and attention to detail. A woman who dictated a letter utilized many of these skills, albeit orally rather than on paper. Furthermore, many individual women (Elizabeth Stonor, Margaret Paston, Margery Brews, and Joan Armburgh) display a discernible stylistic identity consistent across a range of letters indited by various different scribes, suggesting a strong degree of 'authorial' control. Only a relatively broad definition of women's writing incorporates the diversity of compositional methods.

Dictation and scribal input may have imposed some constraints stylistically as well as on privacy, but beyond this letter-writing was also inflected by epistolary conventions. Dominant throughout the period was the *ars dicataminis*, a perennial feature of the pedagogic landscape. Widely taught in cathedral and monastic schools and later in universities, it offered model letters for various situations, outlining correct structure and form for different types of letter, prescribing opening and closural formulae and salutations in a manner that rigidly accentuated social differences between individuals. Recent scholarship, however, has argued that the impact of the *ars dictaminis* declined by the fifteenth century (or was at least indirect), and that most correspondence was in fact modelled on vernacular royal missives and Privy Seal or other official letters. Letter-writing was, therefore, a professional skill requiring legal and business expertise, linked to the legal rhetoric available in the *ars notaria* of common law and royal administration, which further explains women's (and many men's) recourse to scribal assistance.[20] On the whole, surviving letters are divorced from Ciceronian, Erasmian, or even modern models of the 'personal' letter, but rather exhibit traits of more pragmatic, business-related epistolary forms. Model letters specifically tailored for women are extant. In the early-fourteenth century letter-writing guides in French provided models of letters by women, with rules and instructions given in Latin.[21] Furthermore, Christine de Pizan's *The Treasure of the City of Ladies* included 'an example of the sort of letter the wise lady may send to her mistress', while Alice de Bryene maintained a letter-book of diverse correspondence in French for use in educating girls within her household.[22] Such examples suggest that letter-writing skills were a feature of an informal female curriculum outside of male-dominated educational institutions.

How far women's letters in practice adhered to epistolary formulae is a more complex issue, one nuanced by considerations of social status, purpose, and genre. The more formal the occasion of writing, the more closely letters followed templates of protocol. Royal letters and letters of petition, as with other subgenres of officialdom, rigidly conform to the rules of rhetoric in terms of uniform structure. The formality of occasion – a moment of social anxiety in writing – as well as the need for legal exactitude encouraged the adoption of recognized letter-writing conventions. Family correspondence likewise highlights letter-writers' observance of epistolary forms. Watt notes the use of the conventions of the *ars dictaminis* in the salutations of women's letters of the Paston family, and this observation extends to other medieval letter collections.[23] Modes of address employed by wives corresponding with husbands were on the whole formal and impersonal, and narrow in vocabulary, thereby accentuating the apparent distance between spouses. For example, in 1484 Margery Cely wrote to her husband as 'Ryght [re]u*er*[en]d *and* worchupfull Ser'; Jane Stonor, corresponding slightly earlier, addressed her husband Thomas merely as 'Syr'.[24] While medieval epistolary modes of address were almost always formal, a small number of more impersonal forms are evident during the late-fifteenth century – Elizabeth Stonor wrote to her husband as 'Ryght entirely and beste belovyd husbonde', and Margery Paston called her husband 'Myne owyn swete hert' – although such examples are exceptional.[25] How far formality of expression represents or merely masks the emotional quality of women's personal relationships is difficult to infer; yet it also raises further interpretational questions relating to female literacy and conversance with epistolary modes, and to women's social status. By contrast, men's letters appear less restrained by stiff social codes. Indeed, Truelove argues that husbands' letters in the Stonor archive were comparatively more open and relaxed in style, and that the freedom of expression displayed may reflect men's confidence, higher levels of male literacy (men were less likely to employ amanuenses, for example), and familiarity with epistolary mediums.

Scholars have also commented on the orality of late-medieval women's letters: the incidence of colloquialisms, non-standard forms, erratic or phonetic spellings, and the 'oratory didactic tone'.[26] Dictation may have imparted a conversational or speech-like quality; colloquial elements also conceivably indicate greater facility with verbal rather than written media. In general, linguistic and orthographic variants are more pronounced in women's than in men's letters, reflecting men's more formal education and greater familiarity with the written word. While rules of orthography were far from fixed during this period and men's letters also exhibit eccentric spellings, women might still be considered as 'innovators of linguistic forms', in that they were more likely than men to adopt new and unusual linguistic forms apparently found in everyday speech in their letters.[27] However, there is limited evidence of a specifically female style; structure and language was often conditioned more by social status and circumstance than by gender. In studying the Stonor letters Truelove argues that given scribal influence and formal stylistic constraints, the letters of gentlewomen are more formally stylized and less influenced by spoken colloquialisms than those of mercantile women.[28] What marks the correspondence of Elizabeth Stonor (herself of merchant stock) is the lexical richness of her language, often absent in letters of women of higher social standing, who were constrained by dictaminal rhetoric. In writing to her husband, for example, Elizabeth relayed that the duchess of

Suffolk was 'halfindell dysplesyd' at the poverty of his sisters' attire, borrowing an Old English compound rather than the more commonplace 'half'.[29] The balance between oral and literary influence is further explored in Roger Dalrymple's study of the Paston women's correspondence. He argues that the colloquial aspects of the letters are in fact most revealing, unaffected as they are by the rigid formulae of the *ars dictaminis*. Indeed, compared with the literary commonplaces of consolatory piety, he asserts, they permit glimpses of 'reaction', a more emotive, unmeasured mode of writing.[30] Moreover, considerations of the nature of medieval epistolarity illustrate the complex intersection of orality and literacy in the letter form as meaning was generated textually and materially. Letters were not isolated texts, but were conveyed by bearers (corporeal extensions of correspondence who delivered messages in person); and accompanied enclosures (documents, parcels, gifts, books). Elizabeth Stonor, for example, enclosed in a letter to her cousin William, 'a bladyr with powdyr to drynke when ȝe go to bede'.[31] Letters were also often read aloud rather than silently, their reception auricular not textual. The question of whether or not women could read manuscript as opposed to print requires further examination.

Turning from form to function, the overriding purpose of late-medieval women's letter-writing was pragmatic. Characteristically most letters of the period were practical, dealing largely with legal and business affairs, disputes and decision-making. Such missives usefully highlight the diversity of female activities, and emphasize the degree to which women manoeuvred outside of traditionally defined domestic spheres. Jennifer Ward has demonstrated the power of fifteenth-century noblewomen, who employed letters in estate management and as religious patrons and political intermediaries; and letters of women of the Paston, Stonor, Plumpton, and Armburgh families show an overwhelming interest in property and position.[32] The legalistic and technical language employed in women's letters speaks of a conversance and understanding of diverse business matters.[33] This preponderance of legal and business missives may also be symptomatic of archival conditions, since many letters were semi-private, written for posterity and preserved either as legal evidence or in bureaucratic archives, though it would be misleading to imagine a corpus of overtly individualistic and personal epistles having been discarded as ephemera. As Malcolm Richardson importantly points out it is perhaps anachronistic to search for the 'personal' (in the sense of intimate, affective, and self-expressive) in women's letters of late-medieval England. Nonetheless amidst the rhetorical and epistolary conventions and the ubiquitous language of economic advantage reside glimpses of more individualistic elements, occasioned by conflict and circumstance. Standardized prayers and expressions of longing though normative perhaps belie private feelings inaccessible from textual residue; snippets of news and autograph postscripts tangential to the main purpose of communication intimate a degree of personalization of otherwise formulaic correspondence. Through careful reading one can discern individuality of expression from the convention in women's missives. Margery Brews's 'voluntyne' letters to her future husband John Paston III, written in February 1477, the year of their marriage, while respectful and formal nevertheless manage to convey significant amorous feelings: 'I am not in good heele of body ner of herte, nor schall be tyll I here from yowe.'[34] Elizabeth Stonor's letters to her husband William convey 'a detectable undertone of sexual desire'.[35] One striking example is an aggressive letter of invective from Joan Armburgh to John Horell dated 1429/30, goading him with threats of the gallows: 'Yf law wol serue, with the grace of God thu shalt be pullyd out of that nest that thu hast gotyn yn thi trist and labouryd so sore to stroy yt and made to brekyn thy nekke on a perie of galwys', adding 'I can no more at thys but I pray God send the that thu hast deseruyd, that is to say a rope and ladder'.[36]

Letters are thus unrivalled as evidence of the roles and responsibilities of medieval women; their lives, experiences, and relationships; and the degree of power they were able to wield within the family, locality, and occasionally on the wider political stage. Indeed, women corresponded for multifarious reasons, many of which were ancillary to the primary pragmatic impulse to sit with a scribe or in rare instances to put pen to paper. As texts they are intriguingly complex: mostly collaborative, generating meaning textually and materially, with secretarial input in the composition process; intertextually, as part of an epistolary exchange; and orally and corporeally, in that they were presented by bearers in person. Generically and stylistically they are marked by epistolary conventions, and influenced by dictaminal models and protocols, at least indirectly. In reading medieval women's letters one is confronted with a model of letter-writing and authorship that is distinct from modern-day notions of the letter as an intrinsically private and intimate form of interior self-expression. Readers must, therefore, peel away the layers of secretarial intervention, stylistic commonplaces, and social and gender convention, and not labour in vain searching for untrammelled, untainted female *voices*. In so doing, we reorient our expectations of the medieval woman writer within the context of the writing conditions of the period and broaden our conception of epistolary cultures and customs. Through their letters women demonstrated mastery of communal writing practices as well as conversance with the rhetorical, structural, and linguistic demands of letter-writing; they negotiated social and gender hierarchies; understood complex legal and business dealings and were able to marshal all these epistolary skills to powerful effect.

Notes

1. V. M. O'Mara, 'Female Scribal Ability and Scribal Activity in Late Medieval England: The Evidence?', *Leeds Studies in English*, 27 (1996), 87–130 (especially 109–10).

2. *Paston Letters and Papers of the Fifteenth Century*, ed. Norman Davis, 2 vols. (Oxford: Clarendon Press, 1971–6); *The Stonor Letters and Papers, 1290–1483*, ed. C. L. Kingsford, Camden Society, 3rd Series, 29–30, 2 vols. (London: Camden Society, 1919); C. L. Kingsford, 'Supplementary Stonor Letters and Papers (1314–1482)', *Camden Miscellany*, 13, Camden Society, 3rd Series, 34 (London: Camden Society, 1924), pp. i–viii, 1–26; Alison Truelove, 'An Edition of the Stonor Letters and Papers' (unpublished PhD thesis, University of London, 2000); *The Cely Letters, 1472–1488*, ed. Alison Hanham, EETS o.s. 273 (London: Oxford University Press, 1975); *The Plumpton Letters and Papers*, ed. Joan Kirby, Camden Society, 5th Series, 8 (Cambridge: Cambridge University Press, 1996); Paddy Payne and Caroline M. Barron, 'The Letters and Life of Elizabeth Despenser, Lady Zouche (d. 1408)', *Nottingham Medieval Studies*, 41 (1997), 126–56; Ffiona Swabey, 'The Letter Book of Alice de Bryene and Alice de Sutton's List of Debts', *Nottingham Medieval Studies*, 42 (1998), 121–45; *The Armburgh Papers: The Brokholes Inheritance in Warwickshire, Hertfordshire and Essex, c.1417–c.1453*, ed. Christine Carpenter (Woodbridge: Boydell, 1998); Anne Crawford, *Letters of the Queens of England* (Thrupp: Sutton Publishing, 1994); M. A. E. Wood, *Letters of Royal and Illustrious Ladies from the Twelfth Century to the Close of Mary's Reign*, 3 vols. (London: Henry Colburn, 1846), I. See also, Laetitia Lyell, *A Medieval Post-bag* (London: Jonathan Cape, 1934).

3. *Anglo-Norman Letters and Petitions from All Souls MS.182*, ed. M. D. Legge, Anglo-Norman Text Society, 3 (Oxford: Blackwell, 1941).

4. Karen Cherawatuk and Ulrike Wiethaus (eds.), *Dear Sister: Medieval Women and the Epistolary Genre* (Philadelphia: University of Pennsylvania Press, 1993); M. T. Clanchy, *From Memory to Written Record* (London: Edward Arnold, 1979), pp. 288, 231–57.

5. Crawford, *Letters*; Wood, *Letters*, I, p. 73.

6. Josephine Koster Tarvers, 'In a Woman's Hand? The Question of Medieval Women's Holograph Letters', *Post-Script*, 13 (1996), 89–100; Diane Watt, ' "In the Absence of a Good Secretary": The Letters, Lives and Loves of the Paston Women Reconsidered', in *The Paston Women: Selected Letters* (Cambridge: D. S. Brewer, 2004), pp. 134–58 (pp. 136–7).

7. O'Mara, 'Female Scribal Ability'; *Stonor Letters*, ed. Kingsford, I, pp. xlvi–xlvii; James Gairdner, *The Paston Letters, 1422–1509* (London, 1872–5), I, p. 318. Cf. Diane Watt, *Medieval Women's Writing: Works by and for Women in England, 1100–1500* (Cambridge: Polity Press, 2007), p. 12.

8. Watt, *Paston Women*, no.1.

9. *Paston Letters*, ed. Davis; O'Mara, 'Female Scribal Ability', p. 91; Malcolm Richardson, ' "A masterful woman": Elizabeth Stonor and English Women's Letters, 1399–c.1530', in *Women's Letters Across Europe, 1400–1700: Form and Persuasion*, ed. Jane Couchman and Ann Crabb (Aldershot: Ashgate, 2005), pp. 43–62 (p. 50).

10. J. Taylor, 'Letters and Letter Collections in England 1300–1420', *Nottingham Medieval Studies*, 24 (1980), 57–70 (69).

11. *Stonor Letters*, ed. Kingsford, II, p. 185.

12. Alison Truelove, 'Commanding Communications: The Fifteenth-Century Letters of the Stonor Women', in *Early Modern Women's Letter Writing, 1450–1700*, ed. James Daybell (Basingstoke: Palgrave Macmillan, 2001), pp. 42–58.

13. Barbara J. Harris, *English Aristocratic Women, 1450–1550: Marriage and Family, Property and Careers* (New York: Oxford University Press, 2002), p. 34.

14. *Cely Letters*, ed. Hanham, pp. 49–50, 262.
15. Watt, *Medieval Women's Writing*, pp. 118–24; Lynn Stanley Johnson, 'The Trope of the Scribe and the Question of Literary Authority in the Works of Julian of Norwich and Margery Kempe', *Speculum*, 66 (1991), 820–38.
16. Julia Boffey, 'Women Authors and Women's Literacy in Fourteenth- and Fifteenth-Century England', in *Women and Literature in Britain, 1150–1500*, ed. Carol M. Meale (Cambridge: Cambridge University Press, 1993), pp. 159–82.
17. Jennifer Summit, 'Women and Authorship', in *The Cambridge Companion to Medieval Women's Writing*, ed. Carolyn Dinshaw and David Wallace (Cambridge: Cambridge University Press, 2003), pp. 92–108.
18. Watt, *Paston Women*, pp. vii–viii; Watt, *Medieval Women's Writing*, pp. 137, 143, 149–55.
19. Constable, *Letters*, p. 42.
20. Malcolm Richardson, 'The Fading Influence of the Medieval *ars dictaminis* in England after 1400', *Rhetorica*, 19.2 (2001), 225–47.
21. Dorothy Gardiner, *English Girlhood at School: A Study of Women's Education Through Twelve Centuries* (Oxford: Oxford University Press, 1929), p. 63.
22. Christine de Pizan, *The Treasure of the City of Ladies*, trans. Sarah Lawson (1405; London: Penguin, 1985), p. 98; Swabey, 'Letter Book of Alice de Bryene', p. 136.
23. Diane Watt, '"No Writing For Writing's Sake": The Language of Service and Household Rhetoric in the Letters of the Paston Women', in *Dear Sister*, ed. Cherawatuk and Wiethaus, pp. 122–38; Norman Davis, 'The *Litera Troili* and English Letters', *Review of English Studies*, 16.63 (1965), 233–44.
24. *Cely Letters*, ed. Hanham, p. 222; *Stonor Letters*, ed. Kingsford, I, pp. 62–3, 109–10.
25. *Stonor Letters*, ed. Kingsford, II, 18–19; Ralph A. Houlbrooke, *The English Family, 1450–1700* (Harlow: Longman, 1984), p. 104.
26. Watt, *Paston Women*, p. xi.
27. Truelove, 'Commanding Communications', p. 53.
28. Ibid., p. 49–54.
29. Ibid., p. 52; *Stonor Letters*, ed. Kingsford, II, p. 14.
30. Roger Dalrymple, 'Reaction, Consolation and Redress in the Letters of the Paston Women', in *Early Modern Women's Letter Writing*, ed. Daybell, pp. 16–28.
31. *Stonor Letters*, ed. Kingsford, II, p. 15.
32. Jennifer Ward, 'Letter-writing by English Noblewomen in the Early Fifteenth Century', in *Early Modern Women's Letter Writing*, ed. Daybell, pp. 29–41.
33. Malcolm Richardson, 'Women, Commerce and Rhetoric in Medieval England', *Disputatio*, 1 (1996), 123–45.
34. *Paston Letters*, ed. Davis, I, pp. 415, 416.
35. Richardson, 'Elizabeth Stonor', p. 61.
36. *Armburgh Papers*, ed. Carpenter, p. 123.

Part IV
Female Authority

17

Christine de Pizan and Joan of Arc

Nancy Bradley Warren

Throughout her authorial career, Christine de Pizan, though Italian by birth, was identified strongly with the cause of the French royal house, whose rule was challenged in the Hundred Years War by English claimants to the throne and by their Burgundian allies. Indeed, in her *Ditié de Jehanne d'Arc*, composed, according to the poem's final stanza, on 31 July 1429 following Joan of Arc's triumphs in raising the siege of Orléans and in enabling Charles's coronation in Rheims, the English appear in a particularly negative light. Christine calls them, for instance, a 'treacherous lot' and says to the English, 'Go and beat your drums elsewhere, unless you want to taste death, like your companions, whom wolves may well devour' (p. 47).[1] In spite of Christine's anti-English attitudes, her writings were quite popular in England during the fifteenth and sixteenth centuries, a period in which England and France were nearly perennially at odds and in which the legacy of Joan of Arc remained a potent force in the English imagination, as the attention given to Joan in Tudor chronicles makes clear. Thomas Hoccleve translated Christine's *l'Epistre au dieu d'Amours* as the *Letter of Cupid* in 1402. Stephen Scrope translated Christine's *Letter of Othea to Hector* in 1450, and the *Othea* appears in two other English translations over the next hundred years. William Worcester drew on Christine's *Book of the Deeds of Arms and Chivalry* in his *Boke of Noblesse* (which was written in 1450 and then revised in 1475 in connection with Edward IV's efforts to retake English territory in France). And, in 1521, Henry Pepwell published Brian Anslay's translation of the *Book of the City of Ladies*.[2]

This potentially surprising dimension of literary history prompts us to consider the ways in which the French writer Christine de Pizan and the French hero Joan of Arc collaborate in the *Ditié de Jehanne d'Arc* to produce textual and cultural meaning for French and English audiences alike.[3] This pair of French women draws attention to the international dimensions of British textual culture in the later medieval and early modern periods. British writers, men and women alike, focused on topics of international significance; their work was shaped by international political developments;

and their creative processes were influenced by texts in languages other than English. Though Joan of Arc is not generally considered an 'author' in the general sense of the term, she did address texts to English readers, as her letters to King Henry VI and John, duke of Bedford illustrate. Considering Joan of Arc and Christine de Pizan together in a history of British women's writings reminds us that women's writing, including women's writing about other women, played significant roles in the development of nascent national identities as well as in the development of the literary canon.

Given its subject, one might argue that the *Ditié* is a poem fundamentally made of its historical environment, an environment that may have been at least in part shaped by Christine's previous writings. As Benjamin Cornford indicates, Christine's texts quite possibly helped create the phenomenon of Joan of Arc:

> It has been suggested that Christine's decades-long arguments in favour of female authority were so influential that they lay the psychological foundations for Joan's reception. The existence of these recent works and the popular debates they sparked, which produced arguments supporting the possibility of women playing a military role, made the phenomena of Joan of Arc an acceptable one.[4]

Texts, in a sense, may have made the historical Joan possible; at the same time, Christine's textual Joan seeks to make a particular history possible for her current moment and for France's future. The *Ditié* is also therefore a poem that seeks to shape its environment by influencing the actions of members of its audience.

Consisting of 61 *huitains* (eight-line stanzas) in octosyllabic verse rhyming *ababbcbc*, the *Ditié* is organized by a series of apostrophes that follow an introductory section focusing on Christine's personal feelings of happiness at the change in France's fortunes. As Deborah Fraioli observes, stanzas 13 to 20 speak to Charles, the newly crowned monarch, stanzas 21–36 address Joan, and 'stanzas 37–61 announce in different ways to different constituencies the message Christine bears of Joan's divine intervention and its meanings for France'.[5] These constituencies include the French army, the English, the Burgundians, the citizens of Paris, and 'rebel towns'.[6] Thus in its very structure, which gives such a fundamental textual presence to the audience, and in the ways in which this structure underwrites its socio-political aims, the *Ditié* bears witness to the collaborative relationships of text and environment, as well as of text and audience.

A central focus of Christine's efforts to encourage her audience to collaborate with her and with Joan in achieving the future the two women desire for France involves engaging the senses and affective capacities of members of the audience. Christine strives to address her audience's doubts about Joan and to castigate France's enemies through instruction focusing on what may be realized through the senses of sight and hearing. She elucidates indications of the divine plan's revelation in human history and in the material world. After spending the first five stanzas focusing on herself and inserting a stanza celebrating the placement of Charles to the throne, Christine begins her process of instruction. Invoking divine guidance, she states her intention 'to relate how God [...] accomplished all this through His grace' (p. 41). Her concern is in explicating the 'how and why', and the series of stanzas that follow her declaration are filled with imperative verbs concerning sensory, especially visual, perception as well as with other verbal cues directing the audience's intellectual comprehension. For instance, Christine instructs the audience, 'Now *hear*, throughout the whole world, of something which is more wonderful than anything else! *See* if God, in whom all grace abounds, does not in the end support what is right. This is a fact *worthy of note*, given the matter in hand!' (p. 42, my emphasis).

Such a method of persuasion is characteristic of Christine; in many of her texts knowledge proceeds from vision, from observation, and from experiential encounters. Christine's methods in the *Ditié* in helping others to see and understand Joan's deeds, and thus to know the divine truth they convey, are especially reminiscent of her undertaking in the *City of Ladies* to counter antifeminist ideologies (which, indeed, share much with the views of Joan's detractors and opponents during Christine's day and afterward). In the *City of Ladies* three ladies – Lady Reason, Lady Rectitude, and Lady Justice – appear to comfort and enlighten the Christine character who sits in her study, brought to despair by the misogynistic writings of Mathéolus. Lady Reason, the first to instruct Christine, significantly holds a mirror, saying to Christine, 'you see me holding this shiny mirror which I carry in my right hand in place of a scepter. I would thus have you know truly that no one can look into this mirror [...] without achieving clear self-knowledge.'[7] She describes her purpose and that of her companions, Lady Rectitude and Lady Justice, as enabling Christine to 'see clearly' (p. 10). In the *City of Ladies*, sight leads to insight, and the same holds true in the *Ditié*. It is entirely appropriate that the first imagery Christine uses to announce the effects of Joan's coming onto the scene is that of *reverdie*, the return of spring and, specifically, with the return of the sun's light. She writes: 'L'an mil CCCCXXIX / Reprint à luire li soleil' (ll. 17–18) ['In 1429 the sun began to shine again' (p. 41)].

In the *Ditié*, the 'je, Christine' with which the poem opens is collaboratively multi-vocal, blending with the 'je, Christine' of other texts like the *City of Ladies*. Such multi-vocality enhances the extent to which the *Ditié*'s 'je, Christine' is an authoritative, instructive figure who plays a role like Lady Reason. Joan is for her, furthermore, what the women whose lives comprise and populate the City of Ladies are for Ladies Reason, Rectitude, and Justice. That is, Joan is an observable object lesson whose meaning Christine explicates and with whom Christine seeks to shape a new society for France. Christine's exercise of a didactic role is particularly strong in the section of the *Ditié* addressing Charles, where revelation, sight, and insight are again tightly intertwined, as are their necessary relationships to socio-political action. After calling Joan's deeds to Charles's attention with language that focuses on the senses, and particularly on sight, Christine underlines that the knowledge Charles now possesses should result in proper moral, social, and political behaviour:

> I hope that you will be good and upright, and a lover of justice and that you will surpass all others, provided your deeds are not tarnished by pride, that you will be gentle and well-disposed towards your people, that you will always love God who elected you His servant (and you have a first manifestation of this), on condition that you do your duty.
>
> (p. 43)

Christine's inclusion in the *Ditié* of a didactic address concerned with proper governance directed towards Charles is in keeping with her long-term commitment to ameliorating the condition of the body politic by offering instruction to those who lead it. This focus is evident in such texts as her *Book of Peace* and *Book of the Body Politic*. For Christine, proper governance too is a collaborative endeavour, and one in which women properly make important contributions.

That the *Ditié*'s political didacticism is presented by a female speaker and focuses on a woman's life to convey information about divinely approved political theories and practices also recalls Christine's *Letter of Othea to Hector*. In this text addressed to Louis, duke of Orléans, Othea the goddess of prudence sends to the fifteen-year-old Hector of Troy a letter consisting of 'one hundred verse texts describing a mythological figure or moment and prose moral glosses explaining how to read the myth in order to improve human character, followed by allegorical explanations'.[8] In the *Othea* the identity of the 'je, Christine' of the prologue blends with that of Othea in the letter to create a particularly powerful voice of female instruction, much as in the *Ditié* a 'complex relation' exists between Joan and Christine 'in terms of authoritative identity and authorization'.[9] Female figures feature prominently as examples throughout the *Othea*, to the extent that Jane Chance describes it as a 'gynocentric mythography'.[10] Indeed, female figures' lives provide instructive, exemplary material even concerning prowess in arms. For example, the gloss on the text about Minerva reads:

> Minerva was a lady of very great wisdom and invented the art of armor-making [...]. And for the great knowledge which existed in this lady, they

called her goddess. And because Hector could well put armors to work, and this was his right craft, Othea called him the son of Minerva.

(pp. 50–1)

This passage suggests both Christine de Pizan herself as an authoritative voice on knighthood in her 1410 work *The Book of the Deeds of Arms and Chivalry* and the armed and triumphant Joan of the *Ditié*, whom Christine describes as 'a little girl of sixteen [...] who does not even notice the weight of the arms she bears' (p. 46).

As a didactic work directed towards a future ruler, the *Othea* shares much with the genre of the 'Mirror for Princes', a generic affinity that recalls Christine's thoroughgoing emphasis on vision as a means of instruction in the *City of Ladies*. This connection prompts us to consider other generic traditions with which the *Ditié* resonates, traditions in which vision and revelation also have important epistemological functions. Though critics have variously argued for reading the poem as propaganda, as a prophetic work, as a species of chronicle, and as manifestly *not* a chronicle, it seems most useful to treat the poem as a text in which multiple generic traditions converge and collaborate, much as they do in other multi-generic works by Christine de Pizan. The *Ditié* combines elements of propaganda, prophecy, pedagogy, history, hagiography, and visionary literature.

Though the *Ditié* is neither a dream vision like Christine's *The Path of Long Study* nor an account of a divine revelation like that experienced by Christine's name-saint, St Christine, whose life features prominently in Part 3 of the *City of Ladies*, it has affinities with both. Prophecy too is a generic component of the *Ditié*. When Christine speaks of Joan's future, her textual identity blends with the prophetic figure of the Cumaean Sibyl who guides the Christine character in the *Path of Long Study*. As Kevin Brownlee argues, 'Christine has become a new, Christian sibyl with regard to Joan. She speaks with the voice of an authoritative – and authentic – female prophet.'[11] Indeed, one might argue that Christine adopts and extends Joan's own pro-French prophetic voice, countering those of her near contemporaries, St Birgitta of Sweden who attained something of the status of an English patron saint as a result of revelations that seemed to support the English claim to the throne of France, and St Colette of Corbie, whose revelations provided divine support for the Burgundian cause. Christine writes:

For there will be a King of France called Charles, son of Charles, who will be supreme ruler over all Kings. Prophecies have given him the name of 'The Flying Stag', and many a deed will be accomplished by this conqueror (God had called him to this task) and in the end he will be emperor.

(p. 43)

Christine de Pizan adopts not only the voice of a prophet but also that of a hagiographer, and hagiography is another genre much concerned with revelation and exemplarity as well as with the role of the affective in the production of knowledge. As other contributors to this volume also point out, the lives of the saints reveal virtues to be put into practice, delineate spiritual identities to be re-embodied, and recount extraordinary deeds to which one should respond emotionally as well as spiritually and intellectually. As Fraioli indicates, Christine sees Joan as 'already destined for sainthood', adding that Christine demonstrates 'clear understanding of the two requirements needed to meet St Paul's injunction of 1 John 4:1 (*Probate spiritus, si ex Deo sunt*): an examination of the life and the demonstration of a miracle'.[12] Christine provides both, referring to Joan's 'belle vie' (l. 249) and indicating that Joan is sent 'Par miracle' (l. 225). To drive the point home, she also describes Joan's raising of the siege of Orléans as a 'miracle' (l. 260). Furthermore, in the words of Fraioli: 'the Maid is termed "blessed" (*beneurée*) and in wordplay in stanza 22 she is the object of the *double entendre* "born at a propitious hour" and "born of blessedness" (*de bonne heure [bonheur] née*)'.[13]

In her hagiographic account of Joan, Christine claims that the Maid has surpassed Joshua because 'he [...] was a strong and powerful *man*' (p. 42, Kennedy and Varty's emphasis), whereas Joan is 'a *woman* – a simple shepherdess –' (p. 44, Kennedy and Varty's emphasis). Joan also surpasses Gideon, and even outranks the trio of female biblical heroines who so often appear in medieval and early modern texts defending women – Esther, Judith, and Deborah. In emphasizing 'la Pucelle's' extraordinary abilities, Christine de Pizan echoes many virgin martyrs' lives. Indeed, that Joan can do 'something that 5000 *men* could not have done' (p. 46) recalls the life of another shepherdess, St Margaret, one of the saints who features in Joan's voices and whose *vita* appears in Part 3 of the *City of Ladies*. As Christine writes in her version of St Margaret's *Life*, Margaret, while imprisoned, 'feel[s] herself tempted'. She thus

> asked God to be able to see what was causing her so much evil, whereupon a horrible dragon appeared who frightened her terribly and tried to devour her. With the Sign of the Cross, however, she slew the dragon. Afterward she saw in a corner of her prison cell a figure as black as an Ethiopian. Margaret bravely went after him and pinned him down; she placed her foot on his throat and he cried aloud for mercy.[14]

In some versions of the *Life* of St Margaret, though not in Christine de Pizan's, the defeated demon laments having been bested by a girl. For example, in a thirteenth-century English version of the *Life* of St Margaret, discussed by Shari Horner in her contribution to this volume, the bested demon cries out, 'Margaret, maiden, what will become of me? My weapons – alas! – have all been overcome. Now if it had been a man – but it is by a maiden!'[15] His expression of gendered outrage points towards the ways in which, in early modern English engagements with both Joan of Arc and Christine de Pizan, these women's affronts to English chivalric masculine identity play a fundamental role. Joan and Christine continue to collaborate in the English imagination as forces of troubling French female puissance that gall in light of the decline of English fortunes in France.

Christine de Pizan, Joan of Arc, and the state of English fortunes in France have a long history of mutual association, of collaborative meaning-making for English audiences. When Henry VI and Margaret of Anjou married, John Talbot, earl of Shrewsbury, presented Margaret with the gorgeous volume, London, MS British Library Royal 15 E VI, as a wedding gift.[16] This manuscript contains, among other texts, a copy of Christine de Pizan's *Book of the Deeds of Arms and Chivalry*. The illustrations in the manuscript, as I have argued elsewhere, emphasize the importance of passive political roles for women, a message Margaret of Anjou clearly did not take on board, as her political and military activities during civil strife in England make clear. Strikingly, the image in MS British Library Royal 15 E VI that introduces Christine's text is *not* the one typically found in other manuscript versions: the image of Christine conferring with Minerva, who appears clothed in armour (as appears, for instance, in MS British Library Harley 4605 fol. 3). Such an image of an armed female figure associated with a French woman would likely have been far too distressing for Talbot to contemplate, since he would have had an especially personal knowledge of, and likely a particularly sharp animosity towards, Joan of Arc. Talbot was one of the chief commanders at the battle of Patay, where the French army, led by Joan, dramatically defeated the English forces.

Tudor-era English chronicles handle the threats to English chivalric masculinity posed by the figure of an armed French woman by hyper-feminizing Joan in ways that draw on long-established misogynistic stereotypes. Polydore Vergil, in his *English History*, creates from whole cloth an incident in which the captured Joan of Arc, who previously has passionately expressed her commitment to virginity, pleads pregnancy to try to evade execution at the stake. This is a trope taken up by Shakespeare in his *Henry VI, Part I* (see Act 5 scene 6).[17]

Whereas Tudor chronicles and Shakespeare's play depict Joan as a 'puzzel' (a punning transformation of *pucelle*, which means virgin or maid, into an English word for 'whore'), early modern English redactors of Christine's writings take different, though just as strongly gendered, approaches to make less threatening the powerful French female author, and the collaborative spectre of her countrywoman Joan of Arc, who stand behind these texts. One feminizing strategy they adopt is to make Christine's work more properly 'feminine' by subordinating her authorship to the textual work of the English male redactor (as in Anslay's version of the *City of Ladies*). She is also frequently placed in the cloister to remove her from the 'properly' male world of politics and military affairs. In a Latin note written in the margin of Worcester's *Boke of Noblesse*, we are told, for example, that Christine, portrayed as the patron rather than author of the *Book of the Deeds of Arms and Chivalry*, 'manebat in domo religiosarum apud Pasaye prope Parys' [stayed in the nunnery at Poissy, near Paris].[18] Though Christine did spend time at the nunnery of Poissy, she was not, as this text implies, a professed resident there. This note signals the irony of the strategy of 'cloistering' Christine. It is almost certainly precisely *because* Christine spent time at the very politically well-connected nunnery at Poissy, where the king's sister was a nun, that she had access to the detailed information about Joan of Arc that enabled her to compose the *Ditié*.

Notes

1. All citations of the *Ditié* come from Christine de Pizan, *Ditié de Jehanne d'Arc*, ed. Angus J. Kennedy and Kenneth Varty, Medium Aevum Monographs New Series IX (Oxford: Society for the Study of Mediaeval Languages and Literature, 1977). Where appropriate, I cite the original French by line number parenthetically in the text. English translations, unless otherwise noted, are also from Kennedy and Varty's translation included in their edition; I cite translations parenthetically by page number.
2. *The boke of the cyte of ladyes* (London: Henry Pepwell, 1521). On the circulation of Christine's texts in England, and on English attitudes towards Christine's authorship, see Jennifer Summit, *Lost Property: The Woman Writer and English Literary History, 1380–1589* (Chicago: University of Chicago Press, 2000), and Nancy Bradley Warren, *Women of God and Arms: Female Spirituality and Political Conflict, 1380–1600* (Philadelphia: University of Pennsylvania Press, 2001). See, in particular, chapter 3.
3. As Diane Watt observes in *Medieval Women's Writing: Works by and for Women in England, 1100–1500* (Cambridge: Polity Press, 2007), p. 13, 'medieval textual production was primarily collaborative'.
4. Benjamin Cornford, 'Christine de Pizan's *Ditié de Jehanne d'Arc*: Poetry and Propaganda at the Court of Charles VII', *Parergon*, 17 (2000), 76–106 (86).
5. Deborah Fraioli, *Joan of Arc: The Early Debate* (Woodbridge: Boydell, 2000), p. 104.
6. Ibid., p. 49.
7. Christine de Pizan, *The Book of the City of Ladies*, trans. Earl Jeffrey Richards (New York: Persea, 1982), p. 9.
8. *Christine de Pizan's Letter of Othea to Hector*, ed. and trans. Jane Chance (Newburyport: Focus, 1990), 'Introduction', p. 25. All quotations from the *Letter* come from this edition and are cited parenthetically.
9. Kevin Brownlee, 'Structures of Authority in Christine de Pizan's *Ditié de Jehanne d'Arc*', in *The Discourse of Authority in Medieval and Renaissance Literature*, ed. Kevin Brownlee and Walter Stephens (Dartmouth: University Press of New England, 1989), pp. 131–50 (p. 132).
10. *Christine de Pizan's Letter of Othea to Hector*, ed. Chance, p. 8.
11. Brownlee, 'Structures', p. 146.
12. Fraioli, *Joan of Arc*, pp. 112, 115.
13. Ibid., p. 112.

14. *City of Ladies*, ed. Richards, p. 222.
15. Bella Millet and Jocelyn Wogan-Browne (eds.), *Medieval English Prose for Women from the Katherine Group and Ancrene Wisse* (Oxford: Clarendon Press, 1990), p. 71.
16. For an excellent discussion of the contents of this manuscript and its illustrations, see Michel-André Bossy, 'Arms and the Bride: Christine de Pizan's Military Treatise as a Wedding Gift for Margaret of Anjou', in *Christine de Pizan and the Categories of Difference*, ed. Marilynn Desmond (Minneapolis: University of Minnesota Press, 1998), pp. 236–56. Again, I discuss this manuscript at length in chapter 3 of *Women of God and Arms* (see n. 2 above).
17. *Three Books of Polydore Vergil's English History, comprising the reigns of Henry VI, Edward IV, and Richard III: from an early translation, preserved among the mss of the old Royal Library in the British Museum*, ed. Henry Ellis, Works of the Camden Society 19 (London: Bowyer Nichols, 1844), p. 38.
18. William Worcester, *The Boke of Noblesse Addressed to King Edward the Fourth on his Invasion of France in 1475* (1860; reprint New York: Burt Franklin, 1972), pp. 54–5.

18

Marie d'Oignies

Jennifer N. Brown

Marie is widely considered the first of the 'beguines', a movement of women who adopted a semi-religious life and lived in convent-like communities but never took formal vows or answered officially to any church authority.[1] But Marie has also been classified as a mystic, a visionary, and a saint. In truth, she seems to both defy and embody all of these categories at different times. Born in the Liège diocese in the Low Countries *c.*1170 into an aristocratic family, she was married at a young age but soon chose to live in a chaste marriage with her husband and dedicate her life to God. While her many pious activities, including administering to a leper colony and becoming a living holy-mother figure to the brothers at the priory of Oignies, earned her local support, it was Jacques de Vitry's *vita*, the account of her life, which established both fame and support for her cult after her death in 1213.

While the beguine movement was popular on the continent, especially in the Low Countries and France, this way of life never really crossed the Channel. Its women were written about by championing priests and, in some cases, wrote their own texts as well. They needed these authorizing texts because beguines generally had a cloud of suspicion surrounding them. The fact that they took no formal vows and answered to no real authority other than themselves was unsettling to a rigid church hierarchy, and some beguinages (the communities in which they lived) were accused, among other things, of taking in former prostitutes or single mothers.[2] Although little official action was taken against the beguines until the fourteenth century, from the beginning they were held up as models of unorthodox and suspect behaviour just as often as they were seen as devout and pious.[3]

In this environment of suspicion, the *vita* [*Life*] of Marie d'Oignies was written in Latin in the thirteenth century by the bishop of Acre, Jacques de Vitry (*c.*1160–1244). He was Marie's confessor and one of her most devoted followers. Through his championing of her and her cult, Jacques explicitly championed the beguine movement by naming other beguines in his prologue and encouraging other priests to write their lives. He was somewhat successful in his cause, and the beguines' reputation for piety expanded greatly after he penned the *Life* of Marie. In the mid-fifteenth century, this *Life* was translated into Middle English and survives in one codex along with the lives of two other Low Countries beguines,[4] Christina *mirabilis* and Elizabeth of Spalbeek.[5] While extant in only one vernacular manuscript, the Middle English *Life* certainly was disseminated in England among the laity, most attested to in Margery Kempe's *Book* where she recounts being told about Marie's life by her confessor. It also circulated in at least three Latin manuscripts in England, ranging in dates of composition from the late thirteenth to the mid-fifteenth centuries.[6] Throughout the text, Jacques posits Marie as the paradigmatic beguine – both presenting and simultaneously defending her life and its practices.

While this semi-religious life only appears at the margins of medieval English religious experience, the affective and mystical piety the beguines influentially espoused and stood for is reflected in insular anchoritic texts and in many of the formal religious communities, demonstrating their influences, especially in East Anglia with its proximity to the Low Countries. Further, there is record that Robert Grosseteste preached to the Franciscans of Oxford where he 'admitted privately to one of the friars that, although the Franciscans were highly placed on the ladder of poverty because they lived from begging, there was an even higher rung, closer to celestial perfection reached by those' who lived by the work of their own hands'.[7] He continued to say that the beguines achieved this perfection because of their manual labour coupled with their devotion.

In addition to the hagiographies of beguines which had made their way across the Channel, there was also Marguerite Porete's *Mirror of Simple Souls*. Despite the fact that Porete, herself a beguine, had been executed for writing her book in the fourteenth century when the suspicion against beguines reached fever pitch, her book was translated into Middle English and had some English circulation.[8] The beguine and mystical influence that had such a bearing on female piety on the continent was most felt and seen in other forms in England, including the devotional practices of nuns, such as those at Syon Abbey, and in the piety of laywomen.

Marie did not write her own book, as did other prominent beguines like Marguerite Porete and Hadewijch of Brabant, but there is no question that her *Life* by Jacques de Vitry is permeated by her language, visions, and direction. Marie's words are heard throughout the narrative, and she directs many aspects of her life and her legacy through her close relationship with Jacques. Unlike some lives, where the hagiographer is remote in time or knowledge from his subject, Jacques is Marie's close confidant and friend. He is initially drawn to Oignies by Marie's reputation, and upon his arrival there becomes both her spiritual follower and her confessor. Marie is the guiding force in Jacques's life and the *Life* is a narrative of her actions, as with most hagiographies; but this *Life* also serves as a compendious collection of her discourse and advice to Jacques and others. Marie may not have *written* the *Life*, but she did actually *live* it, and the resulting narrative thus forms a kind of collaborative project. In this essay, therefore, I discuss what is 'Jacques' and what is 'Marie' in the Middle English *Life* of Marie, and examine its Middle English context and reading community – what is left out in its translation, and how a reader such as Margery Kempe understands the *Life*. Finally, I will demonstrate what this important translation tells us about the widespread continental tradition of beguine piety and its reception, or lack thereof, on its insular neighbour.

Jacques was not only Marie's follower and friend, he was her confessor, and after her death he makes liberal use of this secret knowledge of Marie in order to convey her life in its entirety. The effect of this is that readers feel intimately invited into Marie's actions and thoughts, just as Jacques was. For example, one of Marie's ascetic practices involved cutting her body. In one particular instance, Marie is disgusted with herself for needing to eat meat and drink wine in order to recover from an illness and, as self-punishment, she cuts off parts of her flesh and buries them. The *Life* reads:

> For with feruour of spirite she, lothinge hir fleshe, cutte awey grete gobettis and for shame hidde hem in the erthe. And for she was enflaumed with houge heet of loue, she sawe on of Seraphyn – that is, a brennynge aungel – standynge by hir in this excesse of mynde. And whan hir body shulde be washen after she was deed, wymmen fonde the places of woundes and hadde mykel maruaile. But thei that knew hir confessyone wiste what it was.[9]

More than articulating a simple cause (shame at eating) and effect (cutting herself), Jacques here describes Marie's innermost emotional response to the events. She is moved by a 'feruour of spirite' and a 'lothinge' of her flesh, but the ascetic practice is not a public one – it is a privately confessed act. Indeed, for 'shame', she hid not only the practice but its evidence, a detail only Jacques would know. The practice is validated by God when she is rewarded with the sight of a Seraph at her side. But it is Jacques's closing words which are the most revealing here: he revels in the knowledge he has of her body, secret knowledge that is revealed after her death. He understands why she bears scars and what prompted her to cause them, but he also knows throughout her life that the scars are there beneath her clothing. It is only after her death that he can relate the story fully.[10]

Jacques relays this kind of knowledge about Marie throughout the *Life*. He explains her motivations, her visions, her encouragements from God and angels, all marshalled to combat all kinds of worldly temptations and troubles. Indeed, these revelations provide the most insight about Marie and who she was. Conversely, when Jacques relays Marie's direct speech, it seems overlaid with Jacques's own theological understandings, perhaps distorting her words to fit what he sees as her meaning. For example, Jacques relates

Marie's encounter with a knight whom she feels has fallen away from God and into avarice. The knight comes upon a weeping Marie and, when he asks her why she sorrows, she responds:

> 'Grete cause haue I,' quod she, 'to make doel for yow and for youre wrecchednesse. My herte is troublid that sythen yee haue bygunen with the spirite, yee purpose wrecchedly to ende and to be consumed with the fleshe. That after yee haue putte youre hande to the ploghe, ye loke byhynd yow, with the wyfe of Loth, and are vnkynde and forgetfyl of the beenfets and ouerabundaunte mercy of Hym that hath delyueryd yow fro the brennynge of this worlde while othere perisshed.'[11]

While the gist of the words is very possibly Marie's – a scolding that the knight has turned from God and towards the temptations of the flesh – the details are most likely not hers. Jacques interpolates into Marie's words with a biblical gloss, a style he maintains throughout the *Life*, alluding to three separate verses: Galatians 3:3, Luke 9:62, and Genesis 19:26. While some references, such as to Lot's wife, would be well known to just about any medieval reader, others would be recognized only by astute ones.

On the one hand, this heavy theological glossing might point to the kind of erasing that can occur in a holy woman's life but, on the other, it can indicate just how collaborative Marie's *Life*, and by extension her 'real' life, is. Certainly Marie, as she is transmitted in the *Life*, is a construction of Jacques's narrative, but it is also evident throughout the text that Marie has had a shaping role in how she is to be written and remembered. Conversely, Marie has, in a sense, simultaneously created Jacques as hagiographer and defender of beguines; she also ultimately defines for Jacques what his own devotional understanding and practice should be, even when he is bishop of Acre: for example, we learn from Thomas of Cantimpré, in his supplement to the *Life* of Marie, that Jacques wears Marie's finger as a reliquary around his neck for much of his life, and that she appears to him post-mortem.[12]

Jacques does not discuss this relic himself in the *Life*, but is otherwise open about his attachment to Marie both during and after her death. His close relationship with Marie demonstrates itself most overtly in his anxiety over her ascetic devotional practices. Very early on in the *Life*, he warns his audience that this is not an *exemplum*, in the sense that Marie cannot be imitated. After describing how Marie wore sharp ropes tied under her dress and slept on boards, he writes:

> I seye not this preisynge the exces, but tellynge the feruoure. In this, and many other that she wroghte by priuelege of grace, lat the discrete reder take hede that priuilege of a fewe makith not a commun lawe. Folowe wee hir vertues; withouten specyal priuelege, folowe maye wee not the workes of hir vertues.[13]

Trying to tread the thin line between holding Marie up as an epitome of pious behaviour while also attempting to discourage imitation, Jacques shows his own concern for Marie's 'exces'. He demonstrates a real empathy for his audience, which includes other beguines in addition to clerical readers, by folding himself into the 'we' who are not capable of following the 'workes of [...] vertues' that Marie manifests.

Later, when writing about her constant fasting and other ascetic practices, he relates how he, with other priests responsible for Marie's care, asks her to eat on Thursdays and Sundays, days she had given to fast. Marie responds:

> 'Sumwhile,' quod she, 'I condescende to myselfe to sensibil thinges, not withouten labour, while I breke ioye of contemplacyone and take bodily mete. Sothly vpon Thursdaye, that is a daye of the Holy Goost, and Sondaye, for ioye of Resurrexione, I am contente with goostly refresshynge and fillyd with euerlastynge metis, and al daye I make a feste, sethen me nedys not to descende lower for any vse of sensible refeccyone of fleshe.' And I, herynge this, helde my pees and ferthermore openyd not my mouthe ageyne hir, and countynge my resoune noon, was sympled in myne owne sighte.[14]

Although Jacques is her spiritual adviser, she turns his admonitions back on to him. By the end of the exchange, Jacques is the one chastened, not Marie. In the defence of her practices, which is not even a real defence but an explanation, she shames Jacques into realizing that his spiritual practice is inadequate in the face of hers. While this passage is ostensibly about how Marie understands, and survives, her extreme fasting practices, it really is about how Jacques feels in the face of Marie's superior spiritual standpoint: 'sympled in [his] owne sighte'.

When Marie is close to death, the reader is again shown how Marie's legacy is very much shaped by her own hand, and also how the narrative is just as much a story about Jacques and his relationship with her. Before Jacques departs on a trip, Marie – having foreseen her own death – lets him know that it will be the last time they see one another, even though she is not ill:

> Soothly, in the yeere that she passed to God – whan I made me redy ageyne heretikes (of offys enioyned to me by the legat of oure Lorde, the pope) to preche and signe whom God enspyred – she asked me whanne I purposed to come ageyne. And whan I answeryd that I shulde tarye longe tyme thann, sythen she hadde no maner sieknesse byfore Lentone, 'I,' quod she, 'leue to yow of testament that I wole yee haue after my dethe.'[15]

Marie takes her very afterlife into her own hands here, telling Jacques where she wants to be buried and how her property should be distributed at her death (she wills to Jacques a belt and a handkerchief, which he claims are 'derrer to me withouten comparysone than golde or siluere').[16] Although not explicitly stated, we can see that Marie's 'testamente' is not only a willing of material goods, but also her story, the shape of the *Life* itself. How she dies and what happens after her death are essential to the hagiographic form, and Marie sets this up perfectly, right down to some of the relics – her clothing – that she will leave behind.

This passage also demonstrates how and why the *Life* would have been translated and rendered interesting to a late-medieval English community, beyond its *de facto* spiritual value. Jacques was instrumental in combating the Cathar heresy, an activity which ultimately earns him the position of bishop. Here, he reminds his readers of that responsibility when he gives the reason why he needs to leave Marie: he must go to fight heretics. It is most likely not a coincidence that the translation of Marie's *Life* corresponds with a time of heightened concern in England about Lollards and what that heresy meant. Many of the heretical views of the Cathars were shared by the later Lollards, in particular the idea that priests were not a necessary intermediary between a person and God; the emphasis in the *Life* on papal obedience, confession, and sacrament would have fit in appropriately with the attempts to combat Lollard beliefs.

This passage also shows how the Middle English translation clips and alters the Latin in order to convey this anti-Lollard sentiment more succinctly. The Latin reads 'In anno autem in quo transsit ad Dominum, cum ego ex officio, mihi a Legato Domini Papæ injuncto, ad prædicandum &ad signandum, quos Deus inspiraret contra hæreticos, me præpararem; ipsa quæsivit a me, quando reverti proponerem',[17] which translates as 'In the year that she passed to the Lord, I was getting ready to preach and to sign those whom God had inspired to fight against the heretics. This office had been placed on me by the Lord's legate – that is to say, the pope – and she asked me when I planned to return.'[18] The Middle English translator has changed the agent of the fight against heretics from those to whom Jacques preached to Jacques himself, drawing a more direct link between Marie and anti-heresy activity than existed in the original Latin *vita*.

The prologue to Marie's *vita* has also been completely excised from the translation. This may be because it specifically deals with the Cathars, a heresy that would be so temporally and geographically remote to its late-medieval English readers as to render it meaningless. But the prologue also acts as a catalogue of marvellous women, listing various beguines and their miraculous behaviour. Addressing Bishop Fulk of Toulouse, to whom Jacques dedicates the Latin *vita*, he reminds him of the wondrous women he has seen living in and around the city of Liège:

They had scorned carnal enticements for Christ, despised the riches of this world for the love of the heavenly kingdom, clung to their heavenly

Bridegroom in poverty and humility, and earned a sparse meal with their hands, although their families abounded in great riches [...]. With what zeal did they preserve their youthful chastity [...] so that their only desire was the heavenly Bridegroom [...]. Many abstained from licit embraces with the assent of their husbands and, leading a celibate – indeed, an angelic – life, they were so much the more worthy of the crown since they did not burn when put in the fire.[19]

The lack of prologue in the translated *Life* makes Marie's case seem unique and perhaps less encouraging therefore for a susceptible readership to embrace. Even though, as mentioned earlier, the Middle English *Life* of Marie appears in a codex with that of two other beguines, there is no sense that these should be true *exempla*. However, this fact may have been somewhat lost on its contemporary audience, especially because these lives stand out so markedly from other vernacular female saints' lives in England, such as those examined by Horner in her essay.

Catherine Sanok has recently argued that the Middle English hagiographical tradition 'overwhelmingly prefers the saints of the early Church and especially the legends of the virgin martyrs',[20] which, as Horner also demonstrates, lends itself to a different reading practice of exemplarity. For a medieval woman reading a virgin martyr's life, the *literal* example is impossible; instead it allows for a metaphorical interpretation. The situational and temporal difference between the reader, hagiographer, and the subject opens them up for reinterpretation. As Sanok explains: 'The expectation that vernacular legends could or should serve as devotional models is, paradoxically, what made them vehicles for thinking about cultural change and ethical variability, as hagiographers and their audiences sought to distinguish the imitable from the inimitable, the transhistorical from the contingent.'[21] The translator of these hagiographies can thus emphasize elements of the saint's faith secure in the knowledge that the reader will be able to read for these elements.

A saint's life like Marie's, however, presents a different set of problems for the reader. Marie is not a virgin martyr nor temporally or geographically distinct from the readers of her *Life*. But her piety is extreme and its example – self-mortification, chaste marriage, religious independence – may not be ideal for widespread imitation. Jacques registers awareness of this fact, and attempts to temper it with frequent warnings to his readers, as discussed above. The translator chooses to excise what he finds too provocative – such as the prologue – for what he may see as susceptible female lay readers, a clearly stated audience in the prologue and coda to the manuscript.

The problems with reading Marie's *Life* too literally are best indicated by the example of Margery Kempe, who does very literally imitate the saints whose lives she knows. Indeed, Kempe's life adheres to the tropes and elements of the lives she has read. For example, in her book she tells of her confessor's change of mind about her devotional practices, especially in regard to her weeping, after reading Marie's *Life*:

> Aftyrward he red of a woman clepyd Maria de Oegines and of hir maner of levyng, of the wondirful swetnesse that sche had in the word of God heryng, of the wondirful compassyon that sche had in hys Passion thynkyng, and of the plentyuows teerys that sche wept, the whech made hir so febyl and so weyke that sche myth not endur to beheldyn the crosse, ne heryn own Lordys Passyon rehersyd, so sche was resolvyd into terys of pyte and compassyon.[22]

Marie's *Life* thus provides a model both for Kempe, through which she can understand her own weeping and devotion, and for her confessor/amanuensis, through which to understand Kempe and his relationship to her. Marie additionally offers a model of a chaste marriage and a link to Mary Magdalene for Margery.[23]

Had the opportunity been open to her, Kempe may have opted to have become a kind of beguine. It would have been a way for her to live her mixture of a lay and religious life without the public reaction she tends to inspire in those around her. In her late-medieval English cultural milieu, Kempe is suspect for the kinds of imitations she enacts, and this especially includes her weeping, her most overt imitation of Marie. These suspicions of mystical female piety and its manifestations may well be a predominant reason why the beguine lifestyle never took hold in England, despite its strong presence such a short distance away in the Low Countries. However, the Middle English *Life* of Marie shows that there was some crucial insular interest in these women and their piety, and its role in Kempe's book shows that her story did indeed reach lay readers.

Notes

1. For the beguines, see Walter Simons, *Cities of Ladies: Beguine Communities in the Medieval Low Countries, 1200–1565* (Philadelphia: University of Pennsylvania Press, 2003).
2. Ibid., pp. 118–37.
3. Jacques never calls Marie a 'beguine' in the *Life*, referring to her as a 'holy woman' instead.
4. Oxford, Bodleian Library, MS Douce 114.
5. I have edited these *Lives* in *Three Women of Liège: A Critical Edition of and Commentary on the Middle English Lives of Elizabeth of Spalbeek, Christina Mirabilis, and Marie of Oignies* (Turnhout: Brepols, 2008). All citations of Marie's *Life* will be taken from this edition.
6. London, British Library, MS Harley 4725; Oxford, Bodleian Library, MS Bodley 240; and Oxford, St Johns College, MS 182.
7. Simons, *Cities of Ladies*, p. 35.

8. See Kathryn Kerby-Fulton's chapter on Marguerite Porete in England in *Books under Suspicion: Censorship and Tolerance of Revelatory Writing in Late Medieval England* (Notre Dame, IN: University of Notre Dame Press, 2006), pp. 272–96.

9. *Three Women of Liège*, p. 97.

10. I have written on confession and eroticism in the *Life* in 'The Chaste Erotics of Marie d'Oignes and Jacques de Vitry', *Journal of the History of Sexuality*, 19.1 (2010), 74–93.

11. *Three Women of Liège*, p. 138.

12. See Hugh Feiss OSB, 'The Supplement to James of Vitry's *Life of Mary of Oignies* by Thomas of Cantimpré', in *Mary of Oignies: Mother of Salvation*, ed. Anneke Mulder-Bakker (Turnhout: Brepols, 2007).

13. *Three Women of Liège*, p. 88.

14. Ibid., p. 145.

15. Ibid., p. 175.

16. Ibid., p. 175.

17. Jacques de Vitry, 'De B. Maria Oigniacensi in Namurcensi Belgii Diocesi', *Acta Sanctorum*, Iun. iv, 636–6 (p. 662).

18. Mulder-Bakker (ed.), *Marie of Oignies*, p. 118.

19. Ibid., pp. 42–3.

20. Catherine Sanok, *Her Life Historical: Exemplarity and Female Saints' Lives in Late Medieval England* (Philadelphia: University of Pennsylvania Press, 2007), p. 25.

21. Ibid., pp. xiv–xv.

22. *The Book of Margery Kempe*, ed. Lynn Staley (Ann Arbor: University of Michigan Press, 1996), p. 149.

23. See Michel Lauwers, ' "Noli Me Tangere": Marie Madeleine, Marie d'Oignies et Le Pénitentes du XIIIe Siècle', *Mélange de l'École Française de Rome. Moyen Âge* (1992), I, 209–68.

19
Bridget of Sweden

Laura Saetveit Miles

Without ever having set foot in the British Isles, St Birgitta, or Bridget, of Sweden was one of the most influential women in late-medieval Britain. Pious lay readers, such as Margery Kempe, could have come across some excerpted part of her majestic book of revelations, the *Liber Celestis Revelationes*, which was certainly familiar to many monastic or enclosed readers – especially women. If they had not read her work, they probably had heard of Syon Abbey. A rich, beautiful monastery where lay people could go to acquire indulgences and hear sermons, Syon was of the Order of St Saviour, founded by Bridget according to a divine vision. To understand why Birgitta became Bridget is to understand the spiritual climate of late-medieval Britain. How did a continental visionary became so immensely popular in this island of readers?

Britain's warm reception for Bridget, her texts, and her Order was in part a matter of timing. Insular spirituality in the fourteenth and fifteenth centuries witnessed a surge of interest in visionary experience, empathetic styles of piety, female-centred devotion, and ecstatic expressions of worship. As Brown has demonstrated in the essay preceding this one, a steady stream of continental texts both fed and satisfied these interests: alongside Bridget, the lives and visions of Catherine of Siena, Marie d'Oignies, Elisabeth of Schonau, and Gertrude the Great of Helfta (to name a few) became well known by means of vernacular translations during this period. These imported holy women in turn influenced generations of home-grown holy women such as Margery Kempe and Julian of Norwich. They also became key exemplars in the world of lay spiritual ambition.

In large part, however, the sheer energy of Bridget's life and the undeniable vivacity of her visions fuelled her popularity. Born in 1302/3 to a royal Swedish family, she married and bore eight children. Soon after the death of her husband she received a 'calling vision' in which God himself proclaimed her new vocation: 'you shall be my bride and my channel [*sponsa mea et canale meum*], and you shall hear and see spiritual things'.[1] After spending some time as a guest at a monastic community in Alvastra, Sweden, Bridget permanently relocated to Rome where she worked tirelessly for social, moral, and ecclesiastical reform. During the course of her lifetime she documented over 700 revelations, many of which were scathing divine rebukes directed towards corrupt worldly leaders. After her death in 1373, she was canonized in 1391.

Early in her career as a visionary, Bridget received a vision from Christ dictating a rule of living for a new monastic order, the *Ordo Sanctissimi Salvatoris*, or Order of St Saviour. The *Regula Salvatoris*, or *Rule of St Saviour* described a type of double monastery centred on sixty nuns, who were assisted by thirteen priests. An abbess led the entire community in temporal affairs, and a confessor general oversaw spiritual affairs. Not without a challenge, however, did the Order secure its existence: it was unheard of for an abbess to have power over men in her monastery, and this reversal in the accepted gender hierarchy met with many detractors.[2] Yet Christ himself proscribed the *Rule* to Bridget, and ultimately the pope agreed, recognizing the Order by a 1378 papal bull as a version of the Order of St Augustine. The founding motherhouse in Vadstena, Sweden, was formally consecrated in 1384 and soon became a locus of literary activity. Nuns at Vadstena were trained as scribes, an extraordinary situation at a time when few women were taught to write. Soon after Vadstena's successful launch Brigittine houses sprang up all across Europe, including a single foundation in England: Syon Abbey.

Syon Abbey was the heart of the English cult of St Bridget. Founded in 1415 by Henry V, the house quickly became a powerhouse of textual production, preaching, liturgy, and prayer. Wealthy and well-connected women joined as nuns and Cambridge-educated clerics became their priests. The nuns of the Order were to lead a life of worship, prayer, and contemplation, while the brethren were to preach a message of moral reform both to the nuns and to the public – reflecting the contemplative and active lives that Bridget herself held in balance. Paradoxically, Bridget did not shape the women of her Order in her image: they were strictly cloistered, with no motherhood, no pilgrimage, no activism, no reforming the corrupt world. They were expected to pray and read, like Mary at the Annunciation, and to bring the spirit of Christ alive in their souls – though visionary experience like Bridget's was not explicitly encouraged. For the nuns, Bridget devised a unique type of divine office (the daily monastic ritual of nine services), based on a series of readings for the service of matins titled the *Sermo Angelicus*, 'The Word of an Angel'. Dedicated to the Virgin Mary, the text was supposedly dictated to Bridget by an angel in 1354. The *Sermo Angelicus* was a radical liturgical innovation. As Katherine Zieman explains, 'the acceptability of reading long, non-biblical texts as lessons during matins allowed Birgitta's visionary experience to be textualized as doctrine'.[3] Indeed, Christ and Mary's speech to Bridget were perceived by some as directly supplementing Scripture. Nuns reading aloud Bridget's text embedded with the Virgin's words constituted a kind of triple threat to the Pauline proscription, 'Let women keep silence in the churches' (1 Corinthians 14:34).

Soon after her death but even before her Order reached England, Bridget's *Revelationes* had become a vital part of the insular devotional culture. Besides many extant Latin copies, two Middle English translations of the entire Latin *Liber Celestis* survive: British Library MS Cotton Julius F ii and British Library MS Cotton Claudius B i (available in a modern edition).[4] Other partial translations feature a selection of chapters or parts of chapters that have been reorganized, while even more partial translations single out individual chapters; these extracts were incorporated into devotional miscellanies and compilations.[5] Passages of prophecy and judgement, often related to Bridget's support of England's side against the French in the Hundred Years War, can be found in many manuscripts.[6] Excerpts concerning the requirements of spiritual life were also popular, being incorporated, for example, into the anonymous text *Contemplations of the Dread and Love of God*, and then recycled over and over again. Most copied, however, were the narrative visions detailing the lives of Christ and the Virgin. If Bridget's visions were not excerpted wholesale, they often heavily influenced native English devotional texts, such as the *Revelation of Purgatory* (as Erler details elsewhere in this volume) and the *Speculum devotorum*, which relied on Bridget's account to portray Christ's life.

In these myriad forms Bridget's writings struck a chord with almost all sectors of the English reading public. The saint had many powerful supporters in the schools, the most prominent among them being Thomas Gascoigne (1404–58), Chancellor of Oxford, who fostered a deep interest in Bridget.[7] Defences of Bridget and her visions were written by three English clerics, among them Adam Easton (*c.*1330–97), a monk at Norwich who served on Bridget's canonization commission.[8] Their works are gathered alongside her *Life*, *Revelationes*, canonization proceedings, and various related texts in the huge and beautiful manuscript London, British Library, MS Harley 612, prepared for Syon.

Wills and other evidence suggest Bridget's abiding popularity among lay female readers. Of the several books dispersed in the remarkable will (*c.*1481) of widow Margaret Purdans, she leaves 'a book called in English St Bridget' to the Benedictine nuns of Thetford, as well as money to Syon.[9] Many women in the generations of royalty leading up to the Dissolution read Bridget's book and fostered close relationships with Syon, usually as visitors, patrons, or recruiters, though sometimes as nuns.[10] Yorkist matriarch Cecily of York (1415–95) read the *Revelationes* as part of her daily routine, and in 1495 she bequeathed her copy to her granddaughter Anne de la Pole (d. 1501), prioress of Syon.[11] Cecily's cousin, Lady Margaret Beaufort, admired *The Fifteen Oes*, devotional prayers memorializing Christ's passion thought to have been written by Bridget; their erroneous attribution to the saint reflects her prominence in devotional culture. Both women, like Henry VIII's wife, Catherine of Aragon, were regular visitors of Syon. Elizabeth Barton (*c.*1506–34), the Benedictine nun and visionary known as the 'Holy Maid of Kent', found support among the community at Syon, where her revelations were likely read. Barton was evidently inspired by Bridget's politically active visionary activity, although the Englishwoman's hard line against Henry VIII's split from Rome and marriage to Anne Boleyn earned her condemnation and execution instead of sainthood.[12]

Perhaps the saint's most well-known devotee was Margery Kempe: wife, mother, visionary, and author, she saw Bridget as a role model. We read in Kempe's *Book* that in a vision, Christ explicitly validates Kempe's vocation in terms of Bridget's: 'rygth as I spak to Seynt Bryde ryte so I speke to þe, dowtyr, & I telle þe trewly, it is trewe euery word þat is wretyn in Brides boke, & be þe it xal be knowyn for very trewth'.[13] On her pilgrimage to Rome, Kempe visited Bridget's house and 'knelyd also on þe ston on þe whech owr Lord aperyd to Seynt Brigypte'.[14] Towards the end of her life, Kempe visited Syon to acquire the 'Pardon of Syon', an indulgence offered to pilgrims to the house. She shocked others in the abbey's church with her 'plentivows teerys of compunccyon & of compassyon'.[15]

Besides its preaching and its pardon, Syon was also well known for printed texts: from the turn of the century until its dissolution in 1539, Syon embraced print technology more heartily than any other English house. Helped by their proximity to London, Brigittine brothers such as Simon Wynter (d. 1448), Thomas Betson (d. 1516), Richard Whytforde (d. 1543?), and John Fewterer (d. 1536) worked in conjunction with printers like Wynken de Worde and Richard Fawkes to print their vernacular treatises aimed at the 'female enclosed market and the lay market'.[16] For the benefit of the nuns, an anonymous brother of Syon translated and explained the sisters' unique Brigittine liturgy in *The Myroure of our Ladye*. This lengthy book circulated in manuscript form until it was printed by Fawkes in 1530 (only one copy, now divided in two parts, survives).[17] The so-called 'logo of the Order' woodcut opened the *Myroure* as well as many other Syon-sponsored printed texts.[18] In this illustration Bridget sits writing at her desk; above her, scenes from her visions play out; at her feet kneel a miniaturized Brigittine brother and nun, the latter identifiable by her distinctive habit. For members of Syon as well as their lay visitors, Bridget loomed larger than life – simultaneously a holy icon of divine authorship and a personal mediatrix between devout Christians and the vivid details of Christian history.

Syon also worked closely with the monks of the neighbouring Carthusian Charterhouse of Sheen to provide manuscripts of reading materials for the nuns. One such book, Cambridge University Library MS Ff.6.33, offers a prime example of *lectio divina*, 'holy reading'. This small vernacular devotional miscellany contains over a dozen mystical and devotional tracts concerning the *via contemplativa*, the contemplative life, including a Middle English version of Bridget's *Rule*. Not only did this *Rule* govern the daily life of the nun who might have read this book, this manuscript suggests it was also studied in private meditation, operating more as a visionary text than a practical text.[19] Nestled among the other works of MS Ff.6.33 is a short extract from Bridget's *Revelationes* describing Christ's message to the pope, commanding him to approve the *Rule*. In reading this book a nun would encounter Bridget in several related positions of female authority: as visionary, wed to Christ; as author, writing both a vision and a rule; and as political force, convincing the most powerful man in Christendom to obey her – Christ's – words. We might wonder what this model meant to a nun at Syon, a house that produced no female visionaries that we know of and very little writing – let alone authored texts – identifiable as a woman's.

By the time Bridget's visionary accounts reached English readers, however, they had gone through many layers of editing. English editors frequently manipulated her texts to suit their own ends, at the expense of Bridget's challenge to the conventional. Critical examination of these extracts proves that they 'often distort her revelations through inept translation, and bowdlerize her spirituality, presenting her as orthodox, pious, sacramental, Christocentric, and minimally scriptural'.[20] Denuded of its revolutionary drive, stripped of its startling originality, some of the power behind Bridget's model of female authority slipped away from English readers. What was left was a multilayered male, clerical voice diluting Bridget's voice through reduction and revision. God and Christ remained the dominant authorities and, while Bridget was upheld as an authentic prophet, it was her piety, morality, and submission which were put forth as exemplary, not her determined character. Even an important tract which asserted that the saint's visions met all the qualifications of authentic divine gift, the *Epistola solitarii ad reges*, was heavily emended by English translators to warn against, instead of encourage, visionary activity; to suppress, rather than promote, the kind of female ecstatic piety which might provide unmediated access to God and offer a rival female authority to the male authority of the Church.[21]

Prior to their arrival in Britain, Bridget's *Revelationes* were in large part transcribed and edited into their final form by a series of confessor-editors. One productive way to think of the relationship between Bridget and her confessors is as a classic example of 'collaborative authorship', as Diane Watt, Jennifer Summit, and Rosalyn Voaden have defined it.[22] In such a collaboration, the 'authors' must negotiate their own working relationship as well as the conflicting concerns of literate culture and orthodoxy. Peter Olofsson (*c.*1307–*c.*1390), then sub-prior of Alvastra, began as Bridget's confessor and continued as the main transcriber of her revelations until her death. Alphonse Pecha (*c.*1327–89), formerly bishop of Jaén in Andalusia, and the author of the *Epistola solitarii ad reges*, was essentially 'editor-in-chief' of the *Revelationes*.

There is some truth to the English woodcut picturing the saint recording her visions in her own hand. Practically speaking, Bridget's aristocratic education enabled her to write in Swedish, and two fragments of her hand-writing survive;[23] she also learned to read and write Latin as an adult. However, her vernacular visionary accounts – whether inscribed or dictated – were usually immediately translated into Latin by one of her confessors. Here is how they describe this mediating process:

> She would call her confessor and a scribe [...] whereupon with great devo-tion and fear of God and sometimes in tears, she spoke the words to him in her native language in a kind of attentive mental elevation, as if she was reading them a book; and then the confessor dictated these words in Latin to the scribe, and he wrote them down there in her presence.[24]

This somewhat idealized scene implies Bridget's constant regulation of the translation of her visions from oral to written account, from Swedish to Latin. In reality, Bridget's editors *did* edit her: they revised, censored, rearranged, and added to her revelations, both before and after her death. Yet this 'interference' reflects a more nuanced view of authorship that acknowl-edges the necessity of collaboration. In a vision from the final years of Bridget's life, Christ himself justifies collaborative authorship: like a car-penter assisted by friends who help paint his carving, 'so I, God, have cut my words from my divine forest, and placed them in your heart. Truly, my friends rendered them into books in accordance with the grace given to them and coloured and decorated them.'[25] Alphonse's extensive edi-torial 'decoration', however much it veiled Bridget's original words, was essentially done with God's blessing; moreover, with his work as liter-ary editor, the *Revelationes* achieved wide circulation and secured Bridget's sainthood. Whether struggle or seamless teamwork shaped the process, ulti-mately the voices of visionary and scribe blend in submission to the original author: God.

God stands as the primary originator or *auctor* of a visionary text and the authority it commands. Bridget functions as a channel, *canale*, of God's words; her confessor-secretaries, as messengers. While Bridget voluntarily submitted herself to the direction of her confessors or 'spiritual fathers' in the humble obedience which defines the saintly life, her direct connection to God as the conduit of divine revelation held them in awe of her power. Kings and potentates, too, came to fear and thus respect (or sometimes condemn) Bridget and her power of prophecy as she sent them copies of her revela-tions in which their moral failings were revealed. Because she is a woman and thus condemned by Eve's weakness, as Summit explains, a visionary writer 'establishes her authority on the basis of her self-effacement, in order to show that her writing issues not from her individual consciousness but from a heavenly source'.[26]

Bridget also saw herself as stepping into a long line of respected female prophets. Despite scriptural citations against women such as 1 Timothy 2:12,

'But I suffer not a woman to teach, nor to use authority over the man, but to be in silence', the Bible offered many important female prophets including Miriam (Micah 6:4), Deborah (Judges 4:4), Anna (Luke 2:36), and even the Virgin Mary (Luke 39–55).[27] Women such as the German visionary Hildegard of Bingen (d. 1179) continued this tradition into the medieval period, where it flourished in the fourteenth and fifteenth centuries. Bridget's insights into not only the future, but also the present (like the corruption of clerical and secular leaders) and the past (details about Christ and Mary not contained in Scripture) placed her firmly in this history of powerful women, so that her voice could not be casually dismissed by male authorities, lest in rejecting her words they rejected the Word of God.

Bridget's developed sense of female authority helps to explain her special appeal to devout women readers like those mentioned above: Margaret Purdans, Cecily of York, Margaret Beaufort, and Margery Kempe. In her *Revelationes*, Bridget's reliance on bodily imagery as a source of female authority reflects a late-medieval trend where compared to men, 'women were more apt to somatize religious experience and to write in intense bodily metaphors', a phenomenon that Carolyn Walker Bynum describes and complicates in her important work on the female body and religious practice, and which can also be seen in the writings of Margery Kempe and Julian of Norwich.[28] As much as Bridget was a channel, *canale* of Christ, she was also his bride, *sponsa*. The most vivid melding of these two roles came in the form of a mystical pregnancy described in the *Revelationes*, when Bridget experienced a great exaltation and felt 'as if a living child were in her heart turning itself around and around'. Mary explains the episode as a parallel of Christ's conception in her own womb at the Incarnation, saying, 'rejoice because that movement which you feel is a sign of the arrival of my son into your heart'.[29] Bridget's previous life as mother of eight finds an unexpected validation in this moment. Her experience of earthly motherhood facilitates a physical metaphor for spiritual fecundity, and the saint's visionary authority recentres itself on a female body that is now an asset instead of a liability. Taken from Mary, like Christ's flesh, Bridget's maternal realization of her visionary calling does not, however, seek nostalgically to recall or to recreate the bearing of human children. Rather, celibate widowhood allows Bridget to repurpose her body as a purified conduit for the spirit of God to take up residence in her soul, and to speak to the world through her mouth.

Dramatic evocations of the maternal made Bridget a likely model for all kinds of British women: lay mothers reading at home, widows dedicated to prayer, even virgin nuns. Many yearned for a devotional discourse that reflected some part of their feminine selves, and the proliferation of copies of the *Revelationes* showing female ownership proves she helped fulfil that need. As we have seen, however, the readership of Bridget's texts was not limited to women: monks, clerics, and laymen also embraced her message.

Between the success of her Order and the far-reaching impact of her texts, Bridget arguably changed the face of late-medieval English religious culture.

Notes

1. Quoted and translated in Bridget Morris, *St Birgitta of Sweden* (Woodbridge: Boydell, 1999), p. 65.
2. Ibid., pp. 163–4.
3. Katherine Zieman, 'Playing *Doctor*: St Birgitta, Ritual Reading, and Ecclesiastical Authority', in *Voices in Dialogue: Reading Women in the Middle Ages*, ed. Linda Olson and Kathryn Kerby-Fulton (Notre Dame, IN: University of Notre Dame Press, 2005), pp. 307–34 (p. 313).
4. *The Liber Celestis of S. Bridget of Sweden*, ed. Roger Ellis, vol. 1, EETS o.s. 291 (Oxford: Oxford University Press, 1987).
5. See Roger Ellis, '*Flores ad Fabricandam . . . Coronam*: An Investigation into the Uses of the Revelations of St Bridget of Sweden in Fifteenth-Century England', *Medium Aevum*, 51 (1982), 163–86; and Dominico Pezzini, 'Brigittine Tracts of Spiritual Guidance in Fifteenth-Century England: A Study in Translation', in *The Medieval Translator II*, ed. Roger Ellis (London: University of London, 1991), pp. 175–207.
6. On Bridget and the Hundred Years War, see Morris, *St Birgitta*, pp. 79–82.
7. F. R. Johnston, 'The English Cult of St. Bridget of Sweden', *Analecta Bollandiana: Revue critique d'hagiographie*, 103.1–2 (1985), 75–93 (80–1).
8. Roger Ellis, 'Text and Controversy: In Defence of St. Birgitta of Sweden', in *Text and Controversy from Wyclif to Bale: Essays in Honour of Anne Hudson*, ed. Helen Barr and Ann M. Hutchinson (Turnhout: Brepols, 2005), pp. 303–21 (pp. 305–6; 318–21).
9. Mary Erler, *Women, Reading, and Piety in Late Medieval England* (Cambridge: Cambridge University Press, 2002), pp. 68–84.
10. Virginia Bainbridge, 'Who Were the English Birgittines? The Brothers and Sisters of Syon Abbey, 1415–1600', in *Saint Birgitta, Syon and Vadstena. Papers from a Symposium in Stockholm 4–6 October 2007*, ed. Claes Gejrot, Sara Risberg, and Mia Åkestam (Stockholm: Kungl. Vitterhets Historie och Antikvitets Akademien, 2010), pp. 37–49 (p. 45).
11. Johnston, 'The English Cult of St. Bridget of Sweden', pp. 86–7; Alexandra Barratt, 'Continental Women Mystics and English Readers', in *The Cambridge Companion to Medieval Women's Writing*, ed. Carolyn Dinshaw and David Wallace (Cambridge: Cambridge University Press, 2003), pp. 240–55 (p. 249).
12. See Diane Watt, 'Barton, Elizabeth (*c*.1506–1534)', *Oxford Dictionary of National Biography* (Oxford: Oxford University Press, 2004), http://www.oxforddnb.com/view/article/1598> [accessed 9 July 2010].
13. *The Book of Margery Kempe*, ed. Sanford Brown Meech and Hope Emily Allen, EETS e.s. 212 (London, 1940; repr. London: Oxford University Press, 1997), p. 47.
14. Ibid., p. 95.
15. Ibid., p. 245.
16. Susan Powell, 'Syon Abbey as a Centre for Text Production', in *Saint Birgitta, Syon and Vadstena*, ed. Gejrot, Risberg, and Åkestam, pp. 50–70 (p. 51).
17. Aberdeen University Library, MS 134 and Oxford, Bodleian Library, Rawlinson MS C.941 (STC 17542); *The Myroure of oure Ladye*, ed. J. H. Blunt, EETS e.s. 19 (London, 1873). See also Anne Hutchison, 'Devotional Reading in the Monastery and in the late Medieval Household', in *De Cella in Seculum: Religious and Secular Life and*

Devotion in Late Medieval England, ed. Michael Sargent (Cambridge: Cambridge University Press, 1989), pp. 215–27.

18. See *The Myroure*, ed. Blunt, p. lxii for a reproduction of this image; for a useful discussion, see Roger Ellis, 'Further Thoughts on the Spirituality of Syon Abbey', in *Mysticism and Spirituality in Medieval England*, ed. William Pollard and Robert Boenig (Cambridge: D. S. Brewer, 1997), pp. 219–43 (pp. 222–4).

19. Laura Saetveit Miles, 'Scribes at Syon: The Communal Usage and Production of Legislative Texts at the English Birgittine House', in *Saint Birgitta, Syon and Vadstena*, pp. 71–88 (p. 71).

20. Vincent Gillespie, 'Religious Writing', in *The Oxford History of Literary Translation in English*, Vol. 1: *To 1550*, ed. Roger Ellis (Oxford: Oxford University Press, 2008), pp. 234–83 (p. 262).

21. Rosalynn Voaden, 'Rewriting the Letter: Variations in the Middle English Translation of the *Epistola solitarii ad reges* of Alfonso of Jaén', in *The Translation of the Works of St Birgitta of Sweden into the Medieval European Vernaculars*, The Medieval Translator, Vol. 7 (Turnhout: Brepols, 2000), pp. 170–85 (p. 178).

22. See, for example, Jennifer Summit's essay 'Women and Authorship', in *The Cambridge Companion to Medieval Women's Writing*, ed. Dinshaw and Wallace, pp. 91–108; as well as the essays by Brown and Watt in this volume.

23. See Morris, *St Birgitta*, plate 1. In Pierpont Morgan, MS 498, fol. 8r., Bridget joins Hildegard of Bingen and Christine de Pizan as one of the few identifiable women depicted writing in medieval manuscripts (i.e. before early printed books); see Lesley Smith, '*Scriba, Femina*: Medieval Depictions of Women Writing', in *Women and the Book: Assessing the Visual Evidence*, ed. Lesley Smith and Jane H. M. Taylor (London: The British Library, 1996), pp. 21–44.

24. Quoted and translated in *The Revelations of S. Birgitta of Sweden: Volume 1, Liber Caelestis, Books I–III*, trans. Denis Searby, with introduction and notes by Bridget Morris (Oxford: Oxford University Press, 2006), p. 12.

25. Claire Sahlin, *Birgitta of Sweden and the Voice of Prophecy* (Woodbridge: Boydell, 2001), p. 32.

26. Summit, 'Women and Authorship', p. 97.

27. See Sahlin, *Birgitta of Sweden*, pp. 6–12, 34–43.

28. Carolyn Walker Bynum, *Fragmentation and Redemption: Essays on Gender and the Human Body in Medieval Europe* (New York: Zone Books, 1991), p. 194.

29. Quoted and translated in Sahlin, *Birgitta of Sweden*, p. 83.

20
Catherine of Siena

C. Annette Grisé

Catherine of Siena's importance to the Middle English devotional canon was early recognized because of the late-medieval interest in her writings at Syon Abbey and other monasteries.[1] Second only to Bridget of Sweden in popularity among continental holy women, Catherine's renown derived from her visionary account, legends, and extracts of her writings and life which were available in the fifteenth and early sixteenth centuries. Born in 1374, Caterina Benincasa, as she was known in her own day, was the twenty-third child of twenty-four children born to her wool-dyer father and her mother, the daughter of a poet. Catherine identified her vocation early and adopted the habit of the Dominican tertiary as a teenager – unusual since it was typically widows who did so. She soon became recognized for her visions of Christ and her extreme asceticism.[2] At first she hardly left her family home, but in 1370 Catherine received a series of visions from God that propelled her into the public sphere, first to work for peace in her homeland and then to seek a resolution to the Great Schism, which had seen two rival popes established in Rome and Avignon respectively. Catherine's textual reputation came from accounts of her holy living as well as the teachings she offered pious lay readers in how to become closer to God through thought, action, and prayer.

Catherine of Siena was a prodigious letter-writer, corresponding with many political figures of her time. She was also the first woman to receive the stigmata, and her spiritual marriage with Christ – though not a unique event for a female mystic – was unusual in that her bridegroom used his foreskin for Catherine's wedding ring. Catherine's followers, intent on achieving her canonization, spent a great deal of time writing for and about her. The account of her visionary experiences, *Il Dialogo* [*The Dialogue*] (or *Il libro della divina dottrina* [*The book of divine doctrine*] Catherine's name for it), detailed the way to God through the allegory of a bridge: the steps needed to prepare for the journey, the process of traversing the bridge, and then achieving union with Christ. Although it is mystical in its finely wrought allegory and emphasis on mystical union, it is also a very practical text following accepted Church practices for spiritual purification and devotion.

The multiple versions of Catherine's legend and its popularity throughout Europe attest to the significance of accounts of her life to the dissemination of her cult. The *Legenda major*, the lengthy account by Raymond of Capua, her most ardent supporter, was quickly translated twice into Italian and abridged by Tomaso Caffarelli as *Legenda minor*, an important version in its own right. These accounts begin predictably with Catherine's early dedication to God and the roadside revelation at the age of seven that began her visionary career. Her family and the local community of Dominican tertiaries play the role of persecutors, misunderstanding her zeal and putting up many obstacles to her desire to be continually with God. Within this hostile environment Catherine developed many strategies for 'guerrilla' mysticism, until she was able to exert more autonomy in the later stages of her life when she gained mobility by moving out of her family home and began her travels. In these stages she started to look outward, both to the plight of the poor and sick and to politics – beginning with regional concerns and moving on to matters of the Great Schism. As her international reputation developed so her cult expanded.

It was shortly after Catherine's death in 1380 that the tradition of continental holy women in late-medieval England gained momentum as part of the sea change in late fourteenth- and early fifteenth-century English devotional culture, something documented by other contributors to this volume. The attention to mysticism, stirred by the Middle English mystics in the late fourteenth century and continuing into the fifteenth, spilled over into an interest in continental mystical traditions, whilst coming at a time of greater commitment to lay participation in devotional practices – including reading religious texts in the vernacular. At a time when writers and readers of vernacular spiritual writings were turning to continental and scholastic sources to enhance Middle English devotional offerings, texts by and about female visionaries made their way from Italy, France, the Low Countries, and Sweden into England. These continental holy women helped meet a demand in England for holy models and devotional texts, a demand which commenced at the end of the fourteenth century, blossomed in the fifteenth century, and continued unabated until the Reformation.

Catherine was recognized in England for both her visionary text and her legends, although her letters and the prayer cycle titled *Orazione* [prayer] seem to have been virtually unknown to the medieval English audience.[3] Her *Dialogo* was translated into Middle English for the Syon nuns in the early fifteenth century and later printed as *The Orcherd of Syon* by Wynkyn de Worde in 1519.[4] Her *Life* was read by nuns at Swine Priory and Dartford, as well as being found in the Syon monks' library.[5] Her works were also owned by Carthusian houses and transmitted in Carthusian-penned manuscript collections. Extracts from her texts were included in Middle

English devotional miscellanies owned by pious lay readers, the most popular extract being 'Clennesse of Sowle', which was copied in eight mostly northern manuscripts. It is only in male monasteries, however, that we find Catherine's texts in Latin; all other extant works and selections are in Middle English, suggesting an effort to disseminate her cult widely to women and vernacular readers. This trend is also confirmed by the popularity of Catherine in the pre-Reformation vernacular devotional print tradition.

Scholarship on Catherine of Siena in late-medieval England follows the lead of Felicity Riddy and Alexandra Barratt in placing her writing in the larger framework of female devotional literary production and reception.[6] Catherine's texts and those of her fellow mystics were the types being read, commissioned, and shared by late-medieval pious and religious women – from nuns and their friends at Syon and Dartford (including Cicely Neville), to Margery Kempe and, in the early sixteenth century, the nun and prophet Elizabeth Barton, the so-called Holy Maid of Kent.[7] In this way they clearly augmented the body of spiritual writings available to the religious and pious vernacular audience. Indeed, the *Orchard of Syon* was an important deluxe production for the Brigittines and survives in three impressive fifteenth-century manuscripts and later printed by Wynkyn de Worde, as mentioned above.[8] This text therefore forms a significant contribution, being the only full-text Middle English translation of Catherine of Siena's revelations.[9] *The Lyf of Katherine of Senis* is also noteworthy: a translation of Catherine's *Legenda minor*, it is extant only in the printed editions of 1492 and 1500 and addressed to an unnamed female religious community. The most substantial of the incunabula in England from the continental holy women, the *Lyf* is the first edition of Catherine's *Life* and/or works to be published outside of Italy.[10] The other major work is found in the Carthusian-owned collection Oxford, Bodleian MS Douce 114, a group of lives of continental holy women, most of them beguines and including an epistolary legend of Catherine by Stefano Maconi,[11] which again confirms Catherine's popularity with religious readers and scribes. Criticism in this area has established the necessary foundations for study of the manuscripts and printed texts and their place within late-medieval devotional literary culture in England, so that further work can now turn towards evaluating Catherine texts in comparison with contemporary devotional translations and Middle English works found in the same or similar textual and situational contexts.

Although female and male religious – notably the Carthusians and Brigittines – were the first wave of Catherine's reception in England and continued to be a significant factor in the transmission of her cult, Catherine's life and works soon moved beyond monastic walls into the homes of pious lay readers, as evidenced by ownership of printed texts and devotional miscellanies and compilations which included Catherine. For example, Elizabeth Strickland, a nun at Syon, gave her copy of the printed *Orcharde* to the wife of her executor, Richard Ashton of Middleton.[12]

Oxford, MS Bodley 131 includes two popular short extracts from Catherine of Siena and Bridget of Sweden in sequence (as well as the Catherine supporter William Flete's *Remedies Against Temptations*), and was owned by John Morton of York, a member (with his wife) of the lay fraternity of the Austin friars. Another important moment in the transmission of Catherine's texts was the selection of extracts printed by Henry Pepwell in 1521, noted early by scholars because it was found with the unique example of printed excerpts from *The Book of Margery Kempe*.

Monastic literary production and vernacular reception of continental ideas and texts were key to expanding the vocabulary for devotional practices in England.[13] For example, Catherine of Siena and Bridget of Sweden lived and had revelations at a time when formulations of contemplative and lay living were being reconsidered.[14] Female visionaries typically experienced revelations in conjunction with their devotional practices, such as praying and meditating, or performing the office.[15] Their visions often were inspired by the world around them and addressed contemporary concerns of their time. These women first and foremost offered models of religious and pious living, much of it occurring outside the monastery or at least being adaptable to lay practice: in fact, Catherine's struggles to devote her life to God outside a monastery were an excellent, if extreme, illustration of the struggles of everyday Christians. Furthermore, extracting 'doctrynes' that could appeal to pious lay readers, Middle English scribes used Catherine's works (and those of other holy continental women) to speak to new ideas about the mixed life and, more generally, the vernacular devotional culture shared by female religious and the lay audiences. The articulation of a shared vernacular devotional culture benefited as well from the translation and transmission of prayers and meditations culled from the works of holy women like Catherine. New exercises stimulated devotional culture by enhancing the canon of vernacular spiritual practices, an area of substantial growth in fifteenth- and early sixteenth-century England. Finally, continental female visionaries and their texts dealt with contemporary concerns of the late-medieval audience, such as the Cult of the Holy Name and the mixed life, so that, by engaging actively with current trends, their readers' devotional practices became relevant and meaningful to them within the new vernacular spirituality of the late Middle Ages.

The limited scholarly interest of the mid-twentieth century in the role of holy women's writings in late-medieval English devotional literature and culture changed in the 1990s when, bolstered by feminist work on women mystics and more sophisticated understandings of both the place of English mysticism within the continental tradition and the ways in which women participated in devotional literary culture, critics began to re-evaluate the cult of visionary women in England.[16] Studies of Catherine of Siena in England now recognize her resemblance to the so-called Middle English mystics: her allegorical bridge reminds us of Julian's extended symbols, for example, while her *legenda* fit well into the mould of the lives emulated by Margery Kempe. It is thus easy to imagine the appeal and importance of Catherine's visions in the late-medieval English context. More recent – and particularly feminist – work thus sets her within the broader context of women's writing and reading in late-medieval England.[17] I would hope that modern theoretical advances in corporeal feminism and feminist materialism will also instigate new avenues of investigation of female mystical bodies and practices, so that Catherine's ascetic practices, for example, can be re-evaluated in this way.[18] Interdisciplinary frameworks will also continue to be important, combining, for example, literary analysis, religious source studies, and historical representations of the body in such areas as late-medieval spiritual practices, contemporary views on the body and soul in a variety of registers from popular to scholastic, and Christian concepts of moderation and discretion developed in both monastic and mystical contexts. Moreover, recent preoccupations with the connections between medieval text and practice may converge well with everyday life theories[19] to influence analysis of how Catherine's practices and everyday experiences translate first into her texts, then into the English context, and finally into her audience's incorporation into their own practices and everyday living. In these ways we will gain a greater understanding of Catherine of Siena's place in the late-medieval English context and the ways in which her life and writings became integrated into English devotional culture – responding to and also shaping its traditions and practices.

Notes

1. It was Edmund Gardner's early monograph which introduced the mystic to English scholars: *Saint Catherine of Siena: A Study in the Religion, Literature and History of the Fourteenth Century in Italy* (New York: Dent, 1907). Suzanne Noffke's English translations have also been integral in establishing Catherine's modern reputation, for which see Catherine of Siena, *The Dialogue*, ed. and trans. Suzanne Noffke, The Classics of Western Spirituality (New York: Paulist Press, 1980); Catherine of Siena, *The Letters of Catherine of Siena*, ed. and trans. Suzanne Noffke, 4 vols. (Tempe, AZ: Arizona Center for Medieval and Renaissance Studies, 2000–8); Catherine of Siena, *The Prayers of Catherine of Siena*, trans. Suzanne Noffke (New York: Paulist Press, 1993). See also Giuliana Cavallini, *Catherine of Siena*, 2nd edn. (London: Continuum, 2005). Other important research on Catherine includes Renate Blumenfeld-Kosinski, *Poets, Saints, and Visionaries of the Great Schism, 1378–1417* (University Park, PA: Pennsylvania State University Press, 2006); Francis Thomas Luongo, *The Saintly Politics of Catherine of Siena* (Ithaca, NY: Cornell University Press, 2006); Gerald Parsons, *The Cult of Saint Catherine of Siena: A Study in Civil Religion* (Aldershot: Ashgate, 2006); John W. Coakley, *Women, Men, and Spiritual Power: Female Saints and Their Male Collaborators* (New York: Columbia University Press, 2006); Heather Webb, 'Catherine of Siena's Heart', *Speculum*, 80 (2005), 802–17; Thomas McDermott, *Catherine of Siena: Spiritual Development in Her Life and Teachings* (New York: Paulist Press, 2008); Jane Tylus, *Reclaiming*

Catherine of Siena: Literacy, Literature, and the Signs of Others (Chicago: University of Chicago Press, 2009).

2. Some scholars have compared her extreme asceticism with that of other female visionaries, drawing connections with their strategies of bodily denial to modern medical theories of anorexia. See, for example, Rudolph M. Bell, *Holy Anorexia* (Chicago: University of Chicago Press, 1987); and Caroline Walker Bynum, *Holy Feast and Holy Fast: The Religious Significance of Food to Medieval Women* (Berkeley: University of California Press, 1987).

3. Catherine of Siena, *Le Orazione*, ed. Giuliana Cavallini, 2nd edn. (Rome: Cateriniane, 1993); Catherine of Siena, *The Prayers of Catherine of Siena*, trans. Suzanne Noffke (New York: Paulist Press, 1993).

4. Catherine of Siena, *The Orcharde of Syon* (Westminster: Wynkyn de Worde, 1519), STC 4815.

5. On the Syon library see, for example, E. A. Jones and Alexandra Walsham (eds.), *Syon Abbey and its Books, Reading, Writing and Religion, c.1400–1700*, Studies in Modern British Religious History 24 (Woodbridge: Boydell and Brewer, 2010); and Vincent Gillespie (ed.), *Syon Abbey with the Libraries of the Carthusians*, Corpus of British Medieval Library Catalogues 9 (London: British Library, 2002).

6. Felicity Riddy, ' "Women Talking About the Things of God": A Late Medieval Sub-culture', in *Women and Literature in Britain, 1150–1500*, ed. Carol M. Meale, Cambridge Studies in Medieval Literature (Cambridge: Cambridge University Press, 1996) pp. 104–27; Alexandra Barratt, *Women's Writing in Middle English* (London: Longman, 1992).

7. See Diane Watt, 'Barton, Elizabeth (c.1506–1534)', *Oxford Dictionary of National Biography* (Oxford: Oxford University Press, 2004), http://www.oxforddnb.com/view/article/1598 [accessed 31 August 2010].

8. London, British Library, Harley MS 3432; Cambridge, St John's Library, MS 75; and New York, Pierpont Morgan, MS 162. For a modern edition, see *The Orcherd of Syon*, ed. Phyllis Hodgson and Gabriel M. Liegey, EETS o.s. 258 (London: Oxford University Press, 1966).

9. For studies of *The Orcherd of Syon* see in particular Mary Denise, 'The Orcherd of Syon: An Introduction', *Traditio*, 14 (1958), 269–93; Phyllis Hodgson, 'The Orcherd of Syon and the English Mystical Tradition', in *Middle English Literature: British Academy Gollancz Lectures*, ed. J. A. Burrow (Oxford: Oxford University Press for the British Academy, 1964), pp. 71–92. See also Denise Despres, 'Ecstatic Reading and Missionary Mysticism: The Orcherd of Syon', in *Prophets Abroad: The Reception of Continental Holy Women in Late-Medieval England*, ed. Rosalynn Voaden (Cambridge: D. S. Brewer, 1996), pp. 141–60; Jane Chance, 'St Catherine of Siena in Late Medieval Britain: Feminizing Literary Reception through Gender and Class', *Annali d'Italianistica*, 13 (1995), 163–203; C. Annette Grisé, 'Catherine of Siena in Middle English Manuscripts: Transmission, Translation, and Trans-formation', in *The Medieval Translator 8*, ed. Rosalynn Voaden, Teresa Sanchez Roura, and René Tixier (Turnhout: Brepols, 2003), pp. 149–59, and 'Holy Women in Print: Continental Female Mystics and the English Mystical Tradition', in *The Medieval Mystical Tradition in England*, ed. E. A. Jones, Exeter Symposium VII (Cambridge: Boydell and Brewer, 2004), pp. 83–95.

10. Ruth Mortimer, 'St. Catherine of Siena and the Printed Book', *The Papers of the Bibliographical Society of America*, 86 (1992), 11–22 (12).

11. For a critical edition of the beguine texts in the manuscript see Jennifer N. Brown, *Three Women of Liege: A Critical Edition of and Commentary on the Middle English*

Lives of Elizabeth of Spalbeek, Christina Mirabilis, and Marie of Oignies, Medieval Women: Texts and Contexts 23 (Turnhout: Brepols, 2008).

12. New York, Public Library, Spencer MS Eng. 1519.

13. The area of vernacular devotional literary production and transmission is a vibrant field of scholarship. See, for example, A. I. Doyle, 'Publication by Members of the Religious Orders', in *Book Production and Publishing in Britain 1375–1475*, ed. Jeremy Griffiths and Derek Pearsall (Cambridge: Cambridge University Press, 1989), pp. 109–23, and 'A Survey of the Origins and Circulation of Theological Writings in English in the Fourteenth, Fifteenth and Early Sixteenth Centuries, with Special Consideration to the Part of the Clergy Therein', PhD thesis (Cambridge University, 1953); J. T. Rhodes, 'Syon Abbey and its Religious Publications in the Sixteenth Century', *Journal of Ecclesiastical History*, 44 (1993), 11–25, and 'Religious Instruction at Syon in the Early Sixteenth Century', in *Studies in St. Birgitta and the Brigittine Order*, ed. James Hogg, 2 vols., Analecta Cartusiana 35.19 (Salzburg: Institut für Anglistik und Amerikanistik; Lewiston, NY: Edwin Mellen Press, 1993), pp. 151–69; Gillespie, *Syon Abbey*, and 'The Book and the Brotherhood: Reflections on the Lost Library of Syon Abbey', in *The English Medieval Book: Essays in Memory of Jeremy Griffiths*, ed. A. S. G. Edwards, Vincent Gillespie, and Ralph Hann (London: British Library, 2000), pp. 185–208.

14. On this see, for example, André Vauchez, *The Laity in the Middle Ages: Religious Beliefs and Devotional Practices*, ed. and intro. Daniel E. Bornstein, trans. Margery J. Schneider (Notre Dame: University of Notre Dame Press, 1993) and *Sainthood in the Later Middle Ages*, trans. Jean Birrell (Cambridge: Cambridge University Press, 1997).

15. For example, Mechthild of Hackeborn often had visions when she was performing the office or contemplating feast days. Elizabeth of Schönau daily enacted Christ's passion in her bedroom by following the schedule of the office.

16. See, for example, Voaden (ed.), *Prophets Abroad*; and Denis Renevey and Christiana Whitehead (eds.), *Writing Religious Women: Female Spiritual and Textual Practices in Late Medieval England* (Cardiff: University of Wales Press, 2000).

17. Some important entries into this field have been Elizabeth A. Petroff (ed.), *Medieval Women's Visionary Literature* (Oxford: Oxford University Press, 1986); Emilie Zum Brunn and Georgette Epiney-Burgard, *Women Mystics in Medieval Europe*, trans. Sheila Hughes (St Paul, MN: Paragon, 1989); and Valerie M. Lagorio, 'The Medieval Continental Women Mystics: An Introduction', in *An Introduction to the Medieval Mystics of Europe*, ed. Paul Szarmach (Albany NY: SUNY Press, 1984), pp. 161–94.

18. For an excellent historical overview of feminist approaches to the major female mystics in England see Nancy Bradley Warren, 'Feminist Approaches to Middle English Religious Writing: The Cases of Margery Kempe and Julian of Norwich', *Literature Compass*, 4 (2007), 1378–96. Amy Hollywood's work is also a compelling example of this kind of research, in particular Amy Hollywood, *Sensible Ecstasy: Mysticism, Sexual Difference, and the Demands of History* (Chicago: University of Chicago Press, 2002).

19. This field follows from the work of theorists such as Walter Benjamin, Henry Lefebvre, and Michel de Certeau. For a good introduction to the topic see Ben Highmore, *Everyday Life and Cultural Theory: An Introduction* (New York: Routledge, 2002).

21
Julian of Norwich

Amy Appleford

Julian of Norwich seems to present an exceptionally unproblematic figure for a book such as this one, which undertakes the difficult task of reconstructing the history of a 'creative female subculture' in the medieval British Isles.[1] Not only is she one of the few women writers of the period we can identify by name, date, and place but, remarkable among medieval vernacular writers of either sex, her works can claim a continuous reading history down to the present. *A Vision Showed to a Devout Woman* and *A Revelation of Love* are respectively the earlier and the much expanded later version of the same description and theological explication of a series of visions Julian experienced in May 1373 at the age of thirty. *A Vision*, which seems to have been written in two stages, is apparently the product of the late 1370s or early 1380s, while *A Revelation*, which Barbara Newman has recently argued may also be a composite, was likely written in the 1390s or early 1400s.[2] Two early copies of parts of this corpus survive from the fifteenth century alongside writings by high-prestige religious figures. One is based on a copy written in 1413, while four manuscript copies of the full text of *A Revelation* made by English recusant nuns and a printed edition of 1670 – all deriving directly or indirectly from at least two lost medieval exemplars – attest to intense interest in the work throughout the seventeenth and early eighteenth centuries. Variously re-edited and modernized on both sides of the Atlantic from the mid-nineteenth century on (the first American edition was published in Boston in 1864), *A Revelation* has in modern times become a focus of attention for poets (including W. B. Yeats and T. S. Eliot), novelists (H. F. M. Prescott and Iris Murdoch), and theologians (Charles Williams and Rowan Williams), as well as for increasing numbers of devout Christians encountering her writing in excerpted form in the dozens of modern anthologies that have been produced.[3] Julian of Norwich is now the best-known Middle English writer apart from Chaucer.

Julian is also the only woman writer working in English in the Middle Ages who seems to answer to Virginia Woolf's paradigm of a 'mother' 'to think back through', presenting a partial answer to the 'problem of antecedents'

that Sheila Delany and others have noted plague both women writers themselves and the project of constructing a continuous feminist literary history.[4]
'Mother Juliana', as her seventeenth-century editor, Serenus Cressy, called
her, has a documented history of influence on women readers and writers in
particular, beginning with the visit in 1413 from Margery Kempe, whose
Book records her conversation with Julian as a known 'expert' in understanding 'wondirful revelacyons', who gave 'good cownsel' to her younger
visionary contemporary.[5] Julian's reputation as an 'expert' in women's religious experience survived the upheavals of the Reformation, as *A Revelation*
became an important text in the spiritual life of English Benedictine nuns
in early seventeenth-century Cambrai and Paris. According to Augustine
Baker, the Cambrai convent's spiritual adviser, *A Revelation* was of especial
interest to the young nun Margaret Gascoigne, whose surviving devotional
writings show an intense engagement with Julian's affective experience of
Christ's presence.[6] In the twentieth century, Julian appears as a figure of
female wisdom and religiosity in the poetry of Denise Levertov, and as a
type of the female artist in the work of Iris Murdoch, and Annie Dillard.
She also plays a key role in contemporary women's spirituality movement,
with a widespread web and print presence as the archetypal 'wise woman'.[7]
As an 'author' whose place in the English literary canon is secure, Julian
thus seems an exception to the paradigm that governs the present volume,
shaped as it is by the perception that 'the modern idea of the author as a single, creative individual holds limited relevance for medieval textual culture,
in which many texts were collaborative, anonymous, or adopted as common
property'.[8]

On closer examination, however, this model of authorship as multiple,
open, and polyvocal proves as useful for understanding Julian's works and
writing strategies as it does for those other figures discussed in this book. The
name 'Julian' itself clearly denotes a single historical figure, the anchoress
enclosed, according to the testimony of several early fifteenth-century wills,
at the church of St Julian's, Conesford in Norwich.[9] Yet the name is not a
personal but a religious one, signifying the choice of the enclosed woman
to become the 'anchor' of a particular East Anglian church, sacrificing her
personal identity to become a metonymic and sacred figure, living a life of
asceticism by 'dying to the world' as an example and as a form of penance
for the entire community. Despite extensive records from late fourteenth-
century East Anglia, we do not and may never know which daughter
of an urban merchant or local gentry family is hidden under the name
'Julian'.

A Vision and *A Revelation* consistently represent themselves as individual responses to revelation and are clearly governed by a single controlling
intelligence. Yet analysis of the literary texture of *A Vision* and *A Revelation* has increasingly pointed to traces of different voices and views in
the texts, urging complementary or alternative understandings of Julian's

experience, or explaining it by way of different theological paradigms and vocabulary sets. Vincent Gillespie has recently described Julian's recurrent mobilization of 'religious and philosophical discourses in tightly controlled tactical ways [...] us[ing] the local velocity of those discourses and registers to project her own text into new and surprising directions'.[10] Later in this essay, I explore an even more local instance of polyvocality, Julian's deployment of 'comune' devotional paradigms – pastoral discourses in the articulation of what is often a difficult and abstract 'imaginative theology'.[11] Such borrowing 'from familiar genres of religious writing' in the articulation of her visionary experience is, I suggest, linked to the larger project of self-effacement and generalization of theological truth to her 'evencristen'.[12] Julian's spiritual authority and canonical status as a literary figure are thus built around a literary as well as a personal ascesis.

Not that literary ascesis appears to have been Julian's first thought when she set out to record and reflect on her revelations. Despite its modest title (derived from its opening manuscript rubric), the account *A Vision Showed to a Devout Woman* offers of the extraordinary visionary sequence Julian experienced over a thirty-hour period when lying in bed, apparently dying, at first seems as singular and personal as the visionary genre appears to make inevitable. *A Vision* begins by conscientiously explaining the background to the revelation in Julian's idiosyncratic desire to experience 'thre graces' – an intensely vivid 'minde of Cristes passion', a 'bodelye syekenes', and three spiritual 'woundes'– and the realization of this desire in the choreographed deathbed scene whose rituals are the revelation's proximate cause, as a cross being held before her face by her 'curate' begins to bleed.[13] We learn circumstantial details about her devotion to Saint Cecilia, her mother's presence at her supposed deathbed, and the exact posture of Julian's dying body, as 'mine handes felle downe on aythere side, and [...] my hede satylde downe on side' while she gazes at the cross.[14] Elsewhere, moments she treats as revelation, such as a period of violent oscillation between a 'soverayne, gastelye likinge in my saule' and a 'hevines and werinesse of myselfe and irkesumnesse of my life', are no more than intimately individual mental impressions.[15] Later episodes bring us back more than once to Julian's personal hopes and anxieties 'before this time' of the revelation. The most celebrated moment in the work, Christ's promise to her that, although 'sinne is behovelye' [fitting, necessary], 'alle shalle be wele, and alle maner of thinge shalle be wele', for example, is represented as an implicit answer to her earlier passionate protests against the coming of 'sin' into the world and what she represents as itself a sinful conviction that, had sin not come, 'alle shulde hafe bene wele'.[16] There are clear traces, here, of the intimate, dialogic visionary relationships Julian's visionary contemporaries, from Bridget of Sweden and Catherine of Siena to Margery Kempe, enjoyed with their lover and Lord, as discussed by other contributors to this volume.

Even in its earliest phases, moreover, the revelation quickly develops such multimedia complexity – as the initial 'bodily sight' of Jesus's bleeding head is supplemented by a 'gastelye sight of his hamly [intimate] lovinge' and other, further manifestations, including words 'formede in mine understandinge'[17] – that attention remains as much on the interpreter and the act of interpretation as on the revelation itself, however careful Julian is to advise readers to 'leve the behaldinge of the wrechid, sinfulle creature' that is herself and 'mightlye, wiselye, lovandlye, and mekelye behalde God', the giver of the revelation.[18] Indeed, the very apologia to which this passage belongs, with its denial that Julian is claiming any role as 'a techere' and notorious assertion that she is nothing more than 'a woman, lewed, febille, and freylle', not only leads us back, yet again, to her individual selfhood but constitutes an implicit instruction to view her as a woman and visionary author, participating in the most significant female literary tradition of the Middle Ages. To term herself 'lewed, febille, and freylle', and to claim that what proceeds from her pen is divine in origin, is to fit a set of qualifications for visionary authorship acknowledged by female visionaries from Hildegard of Bingen on.[19] It may represent an act of self-effacement, but of a kind that encodes both a spiritual state of deep privilege and the literary authority that flows from it.

Yet there are already signs in *A Vision* of the very different mode of self-effacement that will loosen Julian's ties to the visionary genre in *A Revelation*, a work whose primary mode is theological and which depends as little as any visionary work can on the special status of its author. Medieval women's visionary writing in general assumes that it comes into being as a result of the intensity of the visionary's relationship with the divine, blending the *prophetic* role accorded women from the ancient Sibylline tradition onwards with the *saintly* role played by those who find special favour with God and who can hence act both as examples and as intercessors for others. Even in *A Vision*, Julian already partly understands herself neither as prophet nor saint but as a *representative* of her fellow Christians, writing not only for 'ilke man and woman' who 'desires to lyeve contemplatifelye' but for all, and often bringing her experience back to suprapersonal concerns: God's omnipresence ('I sawe God in a pointe [...] by whilke sight I sawe that he es in alle thinge'); his love of creation (which Julian sees as a 'litille thinge the quantite of a haselle nutte', so small it seems it 'might falle sodaynlye to nought for litille' but which is perpetually protected 'thorowe the love of God'); the problem of evil ('A, goode lorde, howe might alle be wele for the grete harme that is comon by sinne to thy creatures?'); and the proper understanding of prayer ('I am grounde of thy besekinge').[20] Despite their mediation through an incessantly visionary language whose key phrase is 'I sawe', such insights are, as Julian puts it, 'generalle', not 'specialle', theological truths, not individual perceptions.[21]

In *A Revelation*, even though 'I sawe' persists, this process of generalization has reached its logical conclusion. The 'lewed' female author figure is
gone, along with all references to the author's femininity, replaced by a new,
genderless voice that belongs to a representative 'simple creature unlettered'
to whom the revelation is now said to have been shown. To emphasize
the impersonality of the revision, there is a new formal division of the
text into 'sixteen revelations', listed at the outset in the third person and
separately rubricated in the manuscripts. Gone are several autobiographical details, some of them apparently replaced by theological ones. We no
longer meet Julian's mother, who in Section 10 of *A Vision* attempts to close
her eyes, thinking she has died. But a new role is found for the Virgin as a
type of religious contemplative, while later Jesus himself becomes a mother,
ministering to the soul's 'sensuality' – its changeable, earthly existence –
even better than an earthly mother ministers to her child: 'The moder may
geve her childe sucke her milke. But oure precious moder Jhesu, he may
fede us with himselfe.'[22] Visionary immediacy has been replaced, sometimes by theological abstraction ('wher Jhesu appireth [in the revelation]
the blessed trinity is understand, as to my sight', reads an early hermeneutic
instruction), sometimes by a self-conscious rhetorical elaboration seemingly
designed not to convey visionary experience but to reproduce a version of it
in the reader: 'The gret droppes of blode felle downe fro under the garlonde
like pelottes, seming as it had comen oute of the veines. And in the coming
oute they were browne rede, for the blode was full thicke. And in the spred-
ing abrode they were bright rede. And whan it came at the browes, ther
they vanished.'[23] Despite how closely *A Revelation* cleaves to *A Vision*, there
are increasing quantities of new materials, designed to give each moment
of revelation its own theological argument and extending, in one instance,
to more than twenty chapters, themselves based on a revelation that is not
found in *A Vision*: a complex parable of a Lord and a Servant that rewrites
the story of the Fall in unequivocally optimistic terms, omitting Eve's
role entirely and giving Julian's project not merely a general but a cosmic
reach.

These substitutions and additions to *A Vision* present a paradox. On the
one hand, their collective effect is to remove attention from the figure of the
visionary and the genre this figure evokes by recasting much of the work,
not as vision but as *exegesis*, a mode of writing medieval thinkers tended to
understand as sub-authorial.[24] On the other hand, however, the additions
A Revelation makes to *A Vision* show a major expansion both of the ambition
of the work and of the theological and rhetorical sophistication of its author.
It is in *A Revelation* that Julian finds formulations that allow her to explain
how sin can be fully a good thing on both personal and cosmic levels, and
to imply, without unorthodoxy, that the group she refers to as 'alle mankind
that shalle be saved' logically includes all humanity.[25] It is also in *A Revelation*

that her ability to evoke and respond to an array of theological discourses is at its most virtuosic, turning the work's account of Julian's visions into something that can read more like a theological encyclopaedia.

The movement of argument in *A Revelation* is so complex that its impersonality as a theological treatise rather than a visionary narrative can create the impression that Julian has substituted one mode of elite discourse for another. As the final note in the Sloane manuscript of the text indicates, Julian's thought might be considered 'hey divinitye and hey wisdam', to be read only by those with a measure of spiritual sophistication. But it is here that Julian's polyvocal writing strategy reveals its intention and efficacy. For *A Revelation* also voices much more 'commene' discourses: the modes of thought and praxis described in pastoral and homiletic literature, that most demotic and socially inclusive category of medieval literature. Moreover, Julian's reference to and inclusion of these widely known devotional modes is not, as Vincent Gillespie has recently argued, a form of 'pastiche', but foundational to her written project and its imperative to efface and generalize her singular experience of the vision to her 'evencristen'.

Throughout both texts, Julian is in dynamic and idiosyncratic interaction not only with liturgical texts and praxis, such as the Middle English deathbed script, the *Visitation of the Sick*, which provides theological and narrative structure for her account, but also with a well-established devotional tradition in which witnessing – in imagination or in reality – the death of the other offers the opportunity for the creation and maintenance of local religious communities. This particular strand of affective piety, which has at its centre the formation of community around any *moriens* or dying individual and her or his interior, subjective experience, was widely taught in pastoralia and in the homiletic discourse, and is on display in the deathbed scene with which both works begin: as Julian's kin, friends, and fellow-parishioners cluster round the bed, through the long days and nights of her illness, to watch her die and, through prayer and witnessing, to assist in the salvation both of her and of their own souls. It is this self-understanding as a participator in a 'comene' experience, not Julian's extraordinary status as a visionary, that is at the root of her self-presentation.

So much becomes clear at the beginning of Chapter 8, after the end of the first 'sight', where Julian presents a review of its contents and the 'six thinges' she 'understood' from them, then reports a sharp desire to communicate to those around her deathbed of her divine communication. This inner urging provides the only justification she gives for her decision to write her revelations down. Yet, in responding to this insistent desire to share her visionary experience, Julian does not describe herself as attempting even the briefest description of the showings to her deathbed attendants, even though she still understands herself as on the point of death. Instead she explicitly assumes the identity of the dying Christian, whose death serves as a heuristic *momento mori* image for the living:

In alle this I was mekille [much] stered in cherite to mine evenchristen, that they might alle see and know the same that I sawe, for I wolde that it were comfort to them. For alle this sight was shewde in generalle. Than saide I to them that were with me: 'It is todaye domesday with me' [...]. This I saide for I wolde they loved God the better, for to make them to have minde that this life is short, as they might se in exsample. For in alle this time I wened to have died. And that was marveyle to me and sweme in perty [partly disturbing], for methought this avision was shewde for them that shuld live. Alle that I say of me, I mene in the person of alle my evencristen.[26]

In this passage, the 'evenchristen' standing at Julian's bedside become the 'evencristen' who now read her book, and who are invited to view her as exemplary, not saintly or prophetic. Her readers should take all she sees as their own, recognize in the singularity of her narrating voice (the 'I' that sees, understands, writes) the utterance of a collective subject, and regard her *metonymically* as a single component of the whole Christian community. Speaking as and for her 'evencristen', Julian further instructs her readers to look past the individual self that experiences the visions to their source, God. She offers her visions, as death pastoralia teaches her to offer her death to others, as an 'ensampille' meant for the whole Christian community and as a mirror in which her readers can see themselves: 'For it is Goddes wille that ye take it with as grete joy and liking as Jhesu had shewde it to you.'[27]

With this instruction to 'leve the beholding' of this 'creature' to 'beholde God' as revealed in the revelation, the revelation replaces Julian as the exemplary dying Christian, and becomes the 'exsample' in which the reader can know for certain of his or her own salvation. Julian the 'author', whose writings find such dazzling language to evoke and analyse the ordinary state of being in the world and the taut, but finally hopeful relationship between sin, suffering, and salvation, offers her insights to her readers as though they were no special revelations at all, and she no visionary, but as a common witness to human experience.

Notes

1. Sandra M. Gilbert and Susan Gubar, *The Madwoman in the Attic: The Woman Writer and the Nineteenth-Century Literary Imagination*, 2nd edn. (New Haven: Yale University Press, 2000), p. 5.
2. See Nicholas Watson, 'The Composition of Julian of Norwich's *Revelation of Love*', *Speculum*, 68 (1993), 637–83; and, more recently, Barbara Newman, 'Redeeming the Time: Langland, Julian, and the Art of Lifelong Revision', *Yearbook of Langland Studies*, 23 (2009), 1–32.
3. On Julian's post-medieval reception, see the recent volume of essays, *Julian of Norwich's Legacy: Medieval Mysticism and Post-Medieval Reception*, ed. Sarah Salih

and Denise N. Baker (New York: Palgrave Macmillan, 2009); for the seventeenth-century interest in her work, see Jennifer Summit's essay, 'Julian of Norwich in 1670' in the same volume, pp. 29–48.

4. Sheila Delany, *Medieval Literary Politics: Shapes of Ideology* (Manchester: Manchester University Press, 1990).

5. *The Writings of Julian of Norwich: A Vision Showed to a Devout Woman and A Revelation of Love*, ed. Nicholas Watson and Jacqueline Jenkins (Turnhout: Brepols, 2006). All references will be to these editions (here at p. 436).

6. For Gascoigne's writings and Cressy's dedication to his edition, see *Writings*, ed. Watson and Jenkins, pp. 437–48 and pp. 448–55; on Baker and Cressy, see Summit, 'Julian of Norwich in 1670', and Elisabeth Dutton, 'The Seventeenth-Century Manuscript Tradition and the Influence of Augustine Baker', in *A Companion to Julian of Norwich*, ed. Liz Herbert McAvoy (Cambridge: D. S. Brewer, 2008), pp. 127–38.

7. On Julian's role in contemporary spirituality movements, see Christiana Whitehead, ' "A Great Woman in our Future": Julian of Norwich's Functions in Late Twentieth-Century Spirituality', in *Julian of Norwich's Legacy*, ed. Salih and Baker, pp. 131–51; and Sarah Salih, 'Julian's Afterlives', in *A Companion to Julian of Norwich*, ed. McAvoy, pp. 208–18.

8. Jennifer Summit, 'Women and Authorship', in *The Cambridge Companion to Medieval Women's Writing*, ed. Carolyn Dinshaw and David Wallace (Cambridge: Cambridge University Press, 2003), pp. 91–108 (p. 91).

9. For a transcript of the wills, see *Writings*, ed. Watson and Jenkins, pp. 431–5.

10. Vincent Gillespie, 'Vernacular Theology', in *Middle English*, ed. Paul Strohm, Oxford Twenty-First Century Approaches to Literature (Oxford: Oxford University Press, 2007), pp. 401–20.

11. Barbara Newman, *God and the Goddesses: Vision, Poetry, and Belief in the Middle Ages* (Philadelphia: University of Pennsylvania Press, 2003), pp. 292–304.

12. Gillespie, 'Vernacular Theology', p. 404.

13. On the relation of Julian's writing to contemporary death rituals, see Amy Appleford, 'The "Comene Course of Prayer": Julian of Norwich and Late Medieval Death Culture', *Journal of English and Germanic Philology*, 107.2 (2008), 190–214.

14. *A Vision*, 2.33–5.

15. Ibid., 9.17, 21–2.

16. Ibid., 13.45, 60, 37.

17. Ibid., 4.1, 72.

18. Ibid., 6, 4–6.

19. On effacement as a visionary trope, see Summit, 'Women and Authorship', pp. 91–108.

20. *A Vision*, 4, 18, 14.

21. Ibid., 7.

22. *A Revelation*, 60; see also Ritamary Bradley, 'Patristic Background of the Motherhood Similitude in Julian of Norwich', *Christian Scholar's Review*, 2 (1978), 101–13.

23. *Revelation*, 4, 7. For the 'hermeneutic instruction', see Nicholas Watson, 'The Trinitarian Hermeneutic in Julian of Norwich's *Revelation of Love*', in *Julian of Norwich: A Book of Essays*, Garland Medieval Casebook 21, ed. Sandra J. McEntire (New York: Garland, 1998), pp. 60–90.

24. On this see Alastair Minnis, *Medieval Theory of Authorship: Scholastic Literary Attitudes in the Later Middle Ages* (Philadelphia: University of Pennsylvania Press, 1988).
25. *A Revelation*, 17.
26. Ibid., 8.22–32.
27. Ibid., 8.32–8.

22
Margery Kempe

Diane Watt

Unlike many other works discussed in this volume, the status of *The Book of Margery Kempe* in the canon of women's writing in English is secure, as is evidenced by its inclusion in the primary textbook in the field, *The Norton Anthology of Literature by Women*.[1] Yet it is by no means immediately obvious why *The Book of Margery Kempe* is so central to the history of women's writing. First, there is a question mark over its authorship. Like many of the medieval English women letter-writers discussed in an earlier chapter of this volume, Kempe was unable to read or write, and she relied on a series of male secretaries to write down her story. Her *Book* is a product of collaboration rather than a work authored solely by a woman. Second, it is not an obviously *literary* text, in terms of its genre or its aesthetic qualities. With its mixture of hagiography, conversion narrative, pilgrimage account, divine revelations, and prayers, the *Book* is not easily categorized, and, with its cumbersome and uneven structure, it reads more like a hurriedly written first draft than the revised and corrected text that it claims to be. Third, the *Book* has had very little discernible impact on later writers. Annotations on the surviving manuscript indicate that the *Book* was read in a monastic context in the century after it was written, and the existence of printed extracts reveal that it was deemed important enough for limited reproduction and wider circulation.[2] Nevertheless, after the Reformation it seems to have fallen into obscurity, where it remained for some five hundred years. And yet, this lively, engaging, and impassioned personal spiritual history has an immediacy that has given it, since its rediscovery in 1934, a growing popularity that has only intensified following the emergence of feminist literary theory and the large-scale inclusion of women's writing on English literature courses since the 1980s.

While there is insufficient space here to survey fully the feminist critical responses to *The Book of Margery Kempe* that have been published since the 1970s, it is possible to identify the main reasons why the *Book* has generated so much attention.[3] A primary aim in the writing of women's literary histories has been the formation of a female tradition, often conceived in reproductive terms as a matrilineage, with considerable attention given to women's influence on other women. Kempe's life and *Book* fit well within such a constructed tradition. The *Book* itself usefully enumerates some of the female saints' lives and books of revelations which Kempe had read to her and which provided her with models for her own 'tretys' (p. 1) and for her religious experiences and forms of expression.[4] As other contributors to this volume have suggested, such exempla include most notably Bridget of Sweden, who, like Kempe, had been married and had had children, and Marie d'Oignies, who shared Kempe's practice of copious weeping. The *Book* also illustrates the extent to which Kempe emulated biblical and legendary saints: in addition to extensive passages which illustrate her personal devotion to the Virgin Mary, clear parallels are drawn between Kempe's experiences and the lives of Katherine of Antioch, Mary Magdalene, and Mary of Egypt. Indeed, while the *Book* may have had only a minimal influence on later mystics, the fact that the *Book* actually records Kempe's visit to her fellow East Anglian visionary and medieval woman writer, Julian of Norwich, seems to confirm only further Kempe's place within women's literary history. While some critical scrutiny has been given to Kempe's relationships with her male spiritual advisers, and the extent to which she relied on them to authorize her controversial piety,[5] other scholars have paid close attention to the ways in which she framed her spirituality around her experiences as a mother.[6] Some, most significantly Kathy Lavezzo, have focused not on biological relationships, but instead examined the importance of female same-sex bonding within the *Book*.[7] Yet a gap remains within feminist scholarship on *The Book of Margery Kempe*: consideration of Kempe's troubled, earthly (though not strictly or narrowly familial or spiritual) relationships with other women. In this essay I will look at two examples of such marginalized female presences in *The Book* – Margery Kempe's daughter-in-law and her maid – which appear in the thematically and structurally foregrounded accounts of her major overseas pilgrimages. My focus is, then, not on the women who love Margery Kempe,[8] but on those who do not.

Kempe's unnamed daughter-in-law features in *Liber* II of the *Book*, which centres on the difficult pilgrimage to Northern Europe that Kempe undertook in her advanced years. Here the daughter-in-law makes her appearance as, quite literally, an answer to Margery Kempe's prayers. The opening chapter of *Liber* II focuses on Kempe's relationship with one of her adult children, her own prodigal son, as it were. This son – who was also the first scribe of her book – travelled abroad on business, where he 'fel in-to þe synne of letchery' and became ill (p. 222). Returning to England, he rather unwillingly sought the intercession of his mother, and was subsequently completely cured. Back in Prussia, he married and had a daughter. Kempe's son, having undergone a conversion of his own, undertook the writing of the first version of his mother's book on a later visit, before setting off on pilgrimage to Rome.[9] Kempe's daughter-in-law is initially represented in positive terms. Hearing the story of her husband's mother's life, the daughter-in-law resolved to 'leeuyn hir fadyr & hir modyr & hir owyn cuntre for to comyn in-to Inglonde & seen hys modyr' (p. 224). When Kempe's son suddenly died only a month after their arrival, shortly after his father had also passed away, his wife remained with his mother for eighteen months. She set off back to Prussia only once she had obtained Kempe's permission.

The decision by Kempe's daughter-in-law to accompany her husband on what might prove to be a perilous trip to England, even when to do so meant leaving their only child in the care of others, has to be understood, at least in part, in terms of the special significance of the relationship between a mother and her son's wife in late-medieval culture. I have argued elsewhere that this bond often proved to be much more resilient than that between a mother and her daughter, and much more mutually supportive than that between a mother and her son.[10] Evidence that backs up this claim can be found in the fifteenth-century correspondence of the Paston women. As the letters of both Agnes and Margaret Paston indicate, from the offset a young man's mother might often play a crucial and diplomatic role in introducing him to his future bride and in negotiating the terms of the marriage.[11] While Kempe was not in a position to find a wife for her son, she does record that she advised him to live in purity while he remained single, and she was relieved when he did marry (pp. 222, 223). But the extent of the closeness that could develop between mother and daughter-in-law can only be understood fully by recognizing that following marriage a woman might well spend more time in the company of her husband's mother than with her husband. For gentry and mercantile families such as the Pastons or the Kempes, the men sometimes spent a great deal of time travelling, either within England or to Europe. In such situations, mother and daughter-in-law might share the management of the household or estate and the upbringing of children, with the mother-in-law instructing her daughter-in-law in her new responsibilities. Mother and daughter-in-law might live together, or near one another; they might work together; and they might attend church together and share their religious devotions. Kempe's daughter-in-law – on hearing the remarkable stories her husband recounted about his mother – evidently felt her absence very strongly. Assuming, as I think we must, that she shared some of her husband's new-found religious zeal, it makes sense that she would have wanted to seek out this remarkable woman early in her marriage in order to learn from her in spiritual matters, and even after her husband's untimely death, she would have felt it appropriate to stay on in England, both women united by their grief and loss.

Discord between Kempe and her daughter-in-law only began to emerge when Kempe, who had offered to accompany her daughter to Ipswich, began to feel called by God to join her on the sea-voyage. Tellingly, many of those who heard of Kempe's intended journey, assumed, positively or negatively, that she was undertaking it on behalf of her daughter-in-law, rather than against her wishes:

> Sum seyd it was a womanys witte & a gret foly for þe lofe of hir dowtyr-in-lawe to putte hir-self, a woman in gret age, to perellys of þe see & for to gon in-to a strawnge cuntre wher sche had not ben be-forn ne not wist how sche xulde come a-geyn. Summe heldyn it was a dede of gret charite for-as-meche as hir dowtyr had be-forn-tyme left hir frendys & hir cuntre & cam wyth hir husbond to visityn hir in þis cuntre þat sche wolde now halpyn hir dowtyr hom a-geyn in-to þe cuntre þat sche cam fro. Oþer whech knewe mor of þe creaturys leuyng supposyd & trustyd þat it was þe wille & þe werkyng of al-mythy God to þe magnifying of hys owyn name.
>
> (pp. 228–9)

While the logic of the narrative structure indicates that only the last reading is correct – that Kempe was motivated to undertake this journey for love of God rather than by human ties – it is clear that Kempe's countrypeople recognized the depth of the bond between a woman and her husband's mother.

Unfortunately, the people were wrong, and Kempe's daughter-in-law did not want Kempe to travel with her. Having failed to gain the permission of her confessor for the journey before she set off, and feeling increasing compelled to undertake it, Kempe sought the authorization of a Grey Friar in Norwich. She then went on to join the ship, with the agreement of the ship's master and of those travelling on it, and her only opposition came from her daughter-in-law 'þat awt most to a ben wyth hir' (p. 228). Much later, after a fraught sea-voyage, Kempe arrived in Danzig, where she remained for a few weeks, and enjoyed the hospitality of the Prussian people. Once again, however, the woman who should have been closest and most obliged to her, and supported her, let her down: 'Þer was non so meche a-geyn hir as was hir dowtyr-in-lawe, þe whech was most bowndyn & beholdyn to a comfortyd hir yf sche had ben kende' (p. 231). The discomfort of Kempe's daughter-in-law seems to stand as a reminder throughout the first half of this journey that Kempe was travelling without the permission of her spiritual guide, and consequently would find herself subject to the disapproval of many when she returned to England. At the same time, perhaps, the narrative of Kempe's voyage to Prussia resonates with the biblical story of Naomi, Orpah, and Ruth and the journey to Judah following the death of the sons of the widow Naomi (Ruth 1), but in Kempe's account her daughter-in-law, rather than vowing to remain with her as Ruth promised Naomi, did all she could to leave Kempe behind. Kempe's daughter-in-law signifies the limited understanding of people of the world for Kempe's spiritual mission, and also the extent to which Kempe was disappointed by earthly relationships on which she should have been able to rely.

In the chapters devoted to her pilgrimages to Jerusalem and Rome (*Liber I*, chapters 26–43), which form the devotional heart of the *Book*, a different kind of bond between women, that between the mistress and her maid, takes on a similar meaning. Kempe's troubled relationship with her anonymous maidservant signifies, in part, the extent to which Kempe finds herself ostracized and eventually abandoned by her fellow English pilgrims. Rather than find herself part of a spiritual community of like-minded penitents, who share her religious enthusiasm, Kempe is spiritually – and at times literally – isolated. Kempe's maid is, however, the only one of her original group of travelling companions to be identified as an individual. The narrative that emerges is one of disloyalty, breach of contract, and a reversal of social norms and hierarchies. The problems first arise early on in the journey across mainland Europe – Kempe's companions reprimand her for her fasting, weeping, and constantly talking about God, and when the disagreement escalates 'summe of þe cumpany on whech sche trostyd best', including her maidservant, 'seyden sche xuld no lengar gon in her felaschep, & þei seyden þei woldyn han a-wey hyr mayden fro hir þat sche xuld no strumpet be in hyr cumpany' (pp. 61–2). Sharon Farmer has argued that maidservants might be associated with promiscuity, and were sometimes accused of corrupting their mistresses by talking about men.[12] Here these expectations are reversed. It is Kempe, with her exuberant exhibitions of piety, who is seen to be sexually transgressive and it is Kempe's presence that threatens the reputation of her maid, rather than vice versa.

Although Kempe and her maid, together, are not explicitly associated with accusations of prostitution or sexual excess in any later passages, Kempe does subsequently liken herself to the woman taken in adultery (John 8:3–11), and prays to God 'Lord, as þow dreve a-wey hir enmys, so dryfe a-wey myn enmys, & kepe wel my chastite' (p. 65). Kempe's prayer reflects anxieties concerning sexual assault and rape that recur throughout the *Book*. Such anxieties were reasonable on the part of a woman who often found herself travelling alone or with a single male companion, although the threat of sexual defilement is also central to the lives of many legendary female saints, such as Agatha or Lucy. Nevertheless, in identifying with the woman taken in adultery, Kempe also associates herself still further with sexual transgression. This is consistent with elsewhere in the *Book* where she is likened, for example, to Mary Magdalene and Mary of Egypt (p. 49), and thus with prostitution, adultery, and uncontrollable sexuality. Indeed Kempe's excessive piety is balanced by – and intrinsically linked to – the excessive sexual desire that characterizes her life in the years following her conversion.

Although the first conflict between Kempe and her companions is temporarily resolved, following the intervention of one of the other members of the pilgrimage group, on reaching the city of Constance the situation escalates further. When Kempe gains the support of an English papal legate, her fellow pilgrims reject her completely, and one of them steals some of her money, '& þei wythheldyn also hir mayden & wolde not letyn hir gon wyth hir maystres, not-wythstondyng sche had behestyd [promised] hir maystres & sekyrd [assured] hir þat sche xulde not forsake hir for no nede' (p. 64). Here it is the breach of the oath taken by the maidservant to Kempe as her mistress that is stressed – Kempe, we are told, was then forced to take leave of her pilgrimage companions '& also of hir mayden whech was *bown-dyn* to a gon wyth hir' (p. 65, my italics). The cyclical pattern of desertion, reconciliation, and desertion is repeated again in the next stage of the pilgrimage. Half way through a protracted wait for a boat at Venice, Kempe was forced by her companions to retreat to her room, where she became ill, '& al þe tyme hir mayden let hir a-lone & mad þe cumpanyes mete & wesch her cloþis, & to hir maystres, whom sche had *behestyd* servyse, sche wolde no dele attende' (p. 66, my italics). It is clear that Kempe's maidservant does more than simply stand for the pilgrim group, although she is closely linked to it. The point being stressed is that the relationship between maidservant and mistress is, or should be, much stronger than the bonds between members of a pilgrim company. The breaking of the bond of service is a serious act of disloyalty.

While Kempe's conflicts with her fellow pilgrims continue on the journey to Jerusalem, and throughout her stay in the Holy Land, her maid is only encountered again – within the narrative, at least – following Kempe's return to Italy, during her extended visit to Rome. Here the maid's much improved situation represents the inverse of Kempe's own experience:

> Than fond sche [Kempe] þer hir þat was hir mayden be-fore-tyme, & wyth ryght schulde a be so stylle, dwellyng in þe Hospital [of St Thomas] in meche welth & prosperyte, for sche was kepar of her wyn. And þis crea-tur went sumtyme to hir for cawse of mekenes & preyd hir of mete & drynke, & þe mayden ʒaf hir wyth good wyl, & sumtyme a grote þerto. Þan sche compleyned to hir mayden & seyd þat sche thowt gret swem [felt great sorrow] of her departyng & what slawndir & euyl wordys men seyd of hir for þei wer a-sundyr, but wold sche neuyr þe raþar be a-geyn wyth hir.
>
> (p. 95)

Their fortunes have been reversed. Kempe, the former mistress, had to seek alms from her former maid. Indeed Kempe's impoverishment was such that she was comforted by a vision of the Virgin Mary – God's own handmaiden – begging on her behalf (p. 93). The account of the former maid's newfound position and success follows an earlier description of how Kempe's confessor in Rome required her, as an act of penance, to serve an impoverished old woman (pp. 85–6). However, these episodes not only provide an example of the extent to which a formerly proud and haughty woman chose to humble herself. Rather they follow and adapt a hagiographical model. That Kempe, in embracing a life of voluntary poverty in Rome, was following a divine path in emulation of Bridget of Sweden, is made explicit in the passages surrounding the discussion of her maid. Not only is this prefaced with a story about a woman, who had known St Bridget, who asked Kempe to be godmother to her child, but it is immediately followed by Kempe's personal encounter with one of St Bridget's former maidservants, who described her mistress as one who 'was goodly & meke to euery creatur' and who 'had a lawhyng cher [laughing demeanour]' (p. 95). In imitating St Bridget, Kempe also outdid her in adversity, for whereas St Bridget shared her life in Rome with her servants, Kempe was abandoned by her maid, who then prospered in her new position. Whereas Kempe's former maid showed no concern for Kempe's reputation, the saint's maid continued to speak favourably of St Bridget.

Finally, it is worth briefly considering *The Book of Margery Kempe* alongside the anonymous female-authored fifteenth-century English epistolary treatise, *A Revelation of Purgatory* (the subject of the next chapter in this volume). This treatise also focuses on a troubled relationship between women – in this case that between the anonymous lay anchoress visionary from Winchester and her deceased friend, a nun whom she saw suffering for her sins in purgatory. In important respects, however, the two texts differ. The contrasts can be seen in an example that also illustrates some of the generic differences between the two texts. Like the Winchester anchoress, Kempe was also blessed with revelations concerning the dying and the dead, and indeed she was often asked to advise individuals on how they might help their deceased friends and relatives. On one occasion a widow asked about her husband, and Kempe warned her that his soul would remain in purgatory for thirty years, and recommended that she 'don almes for hym iij pownd, er iiij in messys & almes-ʒeuyng to powyr folke' (pp. 46–7). Clearly this was not the answer the widow had been looking for, because she 'toke lytyl hede at hir wordys & let it pasyn forth' (p. 47). Whereas the Winchester anchorite represented herself as an intercessor, closely involved in the fate of her dead friend in order to hasten her passage to heaven, even going on pilgrimage on her behalf, Kempe emphasizes instead her own status as one with access to the secrets of God and of people's hearts. Furthermore, whereas within the *Book of Margery Kempe* many of Kempe's associates, including the maid and daughter-in-law, remain anonymous, the visionary of *A Revelation of Purgatory* gives a name as well as a voice to the nun Margaret. Nevertheless, for Kempe, her troubled earthly relationships with other women *were* in many ways as important as her devout role models and her spiritual supporters. In forging her route to heaven, Kempe presents herself as having negotiated her way through the resistance, even hostility, of family, servants, and friends. In so doing, Kempe emphasizes her replacement of her earthly ties with a new heavenly kin group.

What does this consideration of Margery Kempe's troubled relationships contribute to a history of women's writing? Because the study of women's writing tends to focus on maternal and sexual relationships, and on influence and tradition, non-familial, non-reproductive and disruptive relationships can be overlooked, and those that are characterized by discord are seldom explored. However, an understanding of kinship in terms of bonds that are not primarily biological or reproductive, combined with a focus on points of disagreement, can offer new insights that might better reflect the social reality of extended medieval households. Likewise an understanding of influence and tradition that can accommodate discord and disagreement may give us a more nuanced sense of how texts such as *The Book of Margery Kempe* negotiate the problem of female authority in an age when authority was the prerogative of men. If the recuperation of lost women's 'voices' is still central to a feminist literary project, and if *The Book of Margery Kempe* is acknowledged as a key text in the early history of British women's writing, then the recuperation of the marginalized female presences within the *Book* – presences against which those of Margery Kempe and her God are pitted – has to be part of that project.

Notes

1. Sandra M. Gilbert and Susan Gubar (eds.), *The Norton Anthology of Literature by Women: The Traditions in English*, 3rd edn, 2 vols. (New York: W. W. Norton, 2007), I.
2. Diane Watt, *Secretaries of God: Women Prophets in Late Medieval and Early Modern England* (Cambridge: D. S. Brewer, 1997), pp. 155–8.
3. For an annotated bibliography of secondary criticism, see Diane Watt, *Medieval Women's Writing: Works by and for Women in England, 1100–1500* (Cambridge: Polity Press, 2007), pp. 193–8.
4. All in-text references are to *The Book of Margery Kempe*, ed. Sanford Brown Meech and Hope Emily Allen, EETS o.s. 212 (Oxford: Oxford University Press, 1940).
5. See, for example, Rosalynn Voaden, *God's Words, Women's Voices: The Discernment of Spirits in the Writing of Late-Medieval Women Visionaries* (York: York Medieval Press, 1999), pp. 109–54.
6. For example, Liz Herbert McAvoy, *Authority and the Female Body in the Writings of Julian of Norwich and Margery Kempe* (Cambridge: D. S. Brewer, 2004).
7. Kathy Lavezzo, 'Sobs and Sighs Between Women: The Homoerotics of Compassion in *The Book of Margery Kempe*', in *Premodern Sexualities*, ed. Louise Fradenburg and Carla Freccero (New York and London: Routledge, 1996), pp. 175–98.
8. Ibid., p. 182.
9. Nicholas Watson 'The Making of *The Book of Margery Kempe*', in *Voices in Dialogue: Reading Women in the Middle Ages*, ed. Linda Olson and Kathryn Kerby-Fulton (Notre Dame, IN: University of Notre Dame Press, 2005), pp. 395–434 (pp. 399–400).

10. Diane Watt, 'Afterword', in *Women and Experience in Later Medieval Writing: Reading the Book of Life*, ed. Anneke B. Mulder-Bakker and Liz Herbert McAvoy (Basingstoke and New York: Palgrave Macmillan, 2009), pp. 169–75 (p. 173).

11. See *The Paston Women: Selected Letters*, ed. Diane Watt (Cambridge: D. S. Brewer, 2004), pp. 148–9.

12. Sharon Farmer, ' "It Is Not Good That [Wo]man Should Be Alone": Elite Responses to Singlewomen in High Medieval Paris', in *Singlewomen in the European Past, 1250–1800*, ed. Judith M. Bennett and Amy M. Froide (Philadelphia: University of Pennsylvania Press, 1999), pp. 82–105 (pp. 90–1). See also Cordelia Beattie, *Medieval Single Women: The Politics of Social Classification in Late Medieval England* (Oxford: Oxford University Press, 2007), especially pp. 39–61.

23
A Revelation of Purgatory

Mary C. Erler

In a three-part vision that began on the night of 10 August 1422, an anonymous woman saw a nun named Margaret suffering in purgatory and eventually entering the gate of paradise.[1] Afterwards, the revelation was either recounted personally by the visionary or sent as a dictated letter to six men, her spiritual directors and members of her circle. All of them can be identified, as can the visionary herself.[2] Recent work has situated her as a member of the large and famous abbey of St Mary Winchester, or Nunnaminster, in Hampshire – an Anglo-Saxon women's foundation.[3] Scholars have thought it likely that she was either a nun there or an 'unattached holy woman', but it seems most probable that she was the unnamed Winchester anchoress consulted by Richard Beauchamp, earl of Warwick, in another connection the year before the vision. In January 1421 the earl had sent two men, one of them the anchorite chaplain of Guy's Cliff, a hermitage patronized by the earls of Warwick, to visit this woman, paying their expenses of 13s 4d. Several months later in May of the same year the Winchester anchoress was brought to London to meet with the earl while Parliament was in session. This time Warwick's accounts show that he spent £2 6s 8d for the anchoress's transportation, for her three-day maintenance in London, and for a reward.[4] It seems likely that the Winchester anchoress whom Warwick consulted twice in 1421 was the author of *A Revelation of Purgatory* in 1422. Her narrative in that year refers to previous visions: 'I saw al þe peynes whiche wer showed to me many tymes before as ȝe, fadyr, knew wel by my tellynge' (p. 59). This latest revelation is presented as one among many and her earlier visions have, in the approved manner, been submitted to the oversight of a clerical adviser. Such a spiritual adept might well have been consulted by an aristocrat like Warwick, the king's trusted councillor and diplomat, whose interest in anchoritism was shared by both his father and his wife. A visionary anchorite with a substantial contemporary reputation and elevated connections, this woman is present in the historical record but anonymous to us. That there would have been two such women in Winchester simultaneously seems unlikely.

Members of the coterie who received the account are likewise known. Four of the men lived in or near Winchester. The visionary says that she personally took the news at least to two, probably all four: 'And on þe morow when I risse vp, I went to Maister Fforest, my gostly fadyr and told hym [...]. I went to Sir John Wynbourne, my oþer gostly fadyr and told hym' (p. 66). John Forest was the man responsible for the day-to-day administration of the diocese, as vicar-general to Henry Beaufort, bishop of Winchester at the time of the vision, later cardinal and several times royal chancellor. The second son of John of Gaunt, half-brother to Henry IV and uncle to Henry V, Beaufort was an ardent promoter of his dynasty's interests. His connections with Syon and Sheen, the reforming foundations favoured by his royal nephew, were many. Nevertheless these involvements seem rather attributable to his sense of family than to any particular religious position. Though he commissioned an investigation of Lollardy in his Winchester diocese, his biographer says that for him 'Lollardy was principally dangerous as a threat to civil society', and his opening speech at Henry V's second parliament (Leicester 1414) underlined the tie between heresy and sedition.[5]

This speech was surely recalled in Leicester just three years later in 1417, when Margery Kempe's visit to that city provoked a response of alarm from Leicester's civil and ecclesiastical authorities. In Margery's case the connection made between female visionary authority and political dissent was explicit. Given this history, surely Forest, the bishop's vicar-general, would have apprised the bishop of the local Winchester revelations Forest was now receiving if he thought them politically or religiously troublesome. (Forest's own orthodoxy is demonstrated by his considerable financial support of Lincoln College, Oxford, founded expressly to train preachers to combat the Lollard heresy.)[6] The subsequent written spread of the Nunnaminster vision (three surviving manuscripts) demonstrates the apparent latitude allowed to criticism in this elevated milieu.

A second recipient whom the visionary also identified as her spiritual director, the Augustinian canon John Wynbourne, belonged to the house of Christchurch, Twinham, in the southwest corner of Hampshire about thirty miles from Winchester. In the year of the vision, however, it seems likely he was in the cathedral city, since the visionary says that she 'went' to him. He too was a Beaufort family dependant. In 1416 he had been chaplain to Henry Beaufort's younger brother Thomas, duke of Exeter (and perhaps was so still) and had been admitted to confraternity at Winchester's cathedral priory, St Swithun.[7] The text's connection with the Beauforts through trusted members of their staffs thus places the vision beyond heterodoxy – although perhaps the real significance of such ties is not theological but political, situating the text as it does at a level within the Lancastrian dynasty just below the royal.

We know less about the remaining two Winchester priests to whom the revelation was given: John Pury or Pery, a monk of St Swithun, the cathedral priory, and Richard Bone, attached to Nunnaminster when he was ordained, later in 1426 and 1431 rector of the Winchester parish of St Michael outside King's Gate. He was bookish: his will leaves a copy of *Florarium Bartolomaei* to Winchester College.[8] The circle's Winchester members are thus notably diverse: an Augustinian canon, a Benedictine member of the cathedral clergy, and two secular priests. All share, nevertheless, a thoroughgoing orthodoxy. The visionary also sent the message to London. The surviving text is her letter; after an introductory paragraph, probably added later by someone else, the second paragraph opens, 'My der fadyr, I do ȝe to witte...' and the dictated letter is full of speech signals ('and þan, fadyr', 'Now fadyr'). Its addressee, the recluse of Westminster, was either William Alnwick or John London. The former has been favoured, based on a passage in the St Albans chronicle identifying Alnwick as 'a recluse monk of Westminster' who was given charge of the Syon nuns at the abbey's foundation.[9] The Westminster muniments, however, do not mention him at all, and he does not appear in the Syon martyrology.[10] That the recluse monk of Westminster who took charge of the new Syon foundation for a year or so was John London seems more likely, since London is recorded as enclosed at Westminster and appears as a special benefactor in the Syon martyrology. The letter also instructed its recipient to tell the vision to Don Petrus Combe, a Benedictine monk of Westminster who died soon after, probably in 1422/3.

If it was indeed John London, with his experience in advising female religious life, to whom the Winchester author sent her account, not only Winchester and Westminster were associated with the vision, but perhaps, and more distantly, Syon – all three important centres of monastic life intimately tied to royal power. The message's course reveals the connections within this orthodox network and it argues for the acceptability in these circles of ecclesiastical criticism and (implicitly) reform.

In the year before the vision Henry V had taken two notable initiatives towards the renewal of institutional religious life. At Westminster on 5 May 1421 he assembled a meeting of all Benedictines in England – 'as gret nombre as is goodly possible', the announcement specified – and gave an address urging return to a purer, earlier monasticism and repudiation of modern neglect and lukewarmness. The Benedictine meeting belonged to the same intention that founded Syon and Sheen, both intended to offer a vision of possibility for the English church in their example of an elevated religious life. Despite the critical perspectives enunciated by the founder of its order, St Bridget of Sweden, and perhaps partly because of its royal sponsorship, Syon's purist perspectives were never allowed a challenging formulation and it remained both sympathetic to reform, and orthodox.

In its circulation to a mainstream clerical audience of a text excoriating failure in the lives of professed religious, *A Revelation of Purgatory* speaks strongly from this historical context. Though Henry V had at least partly brought the moment into being, royal initiative here joined a wider interest in reform within the church, as well as outside its boundaries. *A Revelation* can be seen as participating in such an internal movement towards a purified institution, while Forest, Wynbourne, and London were part of an audience for such change.

Although the central interest of *A Revelation* is the passage of the Winchester nun Margaret through purgatory to heaven, Margaret does not suffer alone, and to the criticisms of female religious life embodied in her story must be added the presentation of other sins and sinners who surround her. Lechery, particularly clerical, is especially condemned.

Between nine and ten in the evening while sleeping on St Lawrence's day, the visionary viewed the pains of purgatory that she had seen on other occasions: three great fires and in them the spirit of Margaret, whom she knew. She awoke and prayed with her 'lytel mayde child', then fell asleep about eleven p.m. Again Margaret appeared, accompanied by a dog and cat, identified herself as a spirit of purgatory and requested specific masses, psalms, and hymns to be said for her by the six named priests. The worm of conscience, she said, constituted her greatest pain. The dreamer woke at one a.m. and next morning delivered the vision's messages.

The second night revealed the most intense sufferings of purgatory, both for Margaret and for others. Margaret was hideously tortured for her interest in dress and gnawed by her pets for her immoderate attachment to them. She was further tormented for gluttony, sloth, covetousness, and lechery, the latter sin receiving the heaviest punishment in all sinners, male and female, lay and clerical. The centrepiece of night two was the torture of priests and nuns, though married and single people were also punished for lechery.

Margaret appeared black on the third night, but when thrown into the middle fire she turned red, then passed through the third fire and emerged white and fair. She explained the three forms of punishment: the purgatory of righteousness, the purgatory of mercy, constituted by suffering in this world, and the purgatory of grace which allowed souls to appear to the living and appeal for help. Margaret was weighed in the balance with the worm of conscience and was awarded to the Virgin. Led over a bridge to a white chapel, she was washed in a well, crowned with grace, and escorted to the gate of paradise.

The similarity of *A Revelation* to Bridget of Sweden's *Revelations* has been noticed since Harley pointed out the three-part division of purgatory in both works.[11] Their purgatorial imagery shares the same spirit of horror, full of snakes and bodily deformity. Here is Bridget describing a woman in purgatory:

> Hir hert was drawen oute. Hir lippis were cutt awai. Hir chin tremeled; hir tethe chattird [...]. Hir forhed was dimpled in and þere was a mirke hole,

and in þe shede of hir braine was wellinge lede and pike. Hir neke was wreþen all abute, hir breste was opyn and full of wormes.

(VI, lii, 441)[12]

Compare the nun Margaret:

[a devil] toke [...] a lange grete addyr and put al about hyr hede [...] and one pulled out hyr tonge, and anoþer pulled out hyr hert, and me þoȝt þay raked hit with iren rakes [....]. [Another devil] pared away al hyr lyppis, and he toke a grete hoke of iren and smote þroȝ-out hyr hert.

(pp. 66–7)

The similarity in the two works' imagery of purgatory, however, is incidental to the thematic emphases that they share. For Bridget, purgatory demonstrates a theology of mutuality. In a famous vision she intercedes at the particular judgement for the soul of her wayward son, Charles. When she wins, an angel tells her: 'þis reuelacion is noght oneli for þe, bot þat Christes freendes mai wit [...] what he will do for teris and praiers of his frendes' (VII.xiv.479). This is, of course, the whole point of *A Revelation*, as Margaret's thanks make clear when she acknowledges that without the help of the visionary and her circle she would have had to suffer for three years more (p. 79).

In this mutuality, female ties, in particular, are central to both writers. Bridget's *Life*, which sometimes accompanied her *Revelations* in manuscript, tells how the saint experienced a vision much like that of the Winchester anchoress. Appearing to Bridget from purgatory, her sister-in-law tells her, 'I want to inform you of my situation, for it thus pleases God that as we have loved each other while both living in the flesh, so we should now love each other in spirit.' The dead woman is being punished for a tendency to anger and 'that I was not content with the things that I had'. Like Margaret, she appears three times, asks for masses and prayers, and in the final vision specifies her release: 'What I longed for, I now have.'[13] In its purgatorial locus, its tripartite structure moving towards resolution, and above all in its stress on the power of female connection, Bridget's vision of a beloved dead woman foreshadows and may have influenced the Winchester recluse's.

Equally important to both writers is the necessity for reform of religious life and, in both, purgatory provides the imagery of disgust that allows this perspective its powerful sway. Christ tells Bridget that no one had so far forgotten his words as much as had the rulers of the holy church, due to their pride, covetousness, and lusty living. Because of their 'euell ensampill to oþer' they will be put out of the book of life (VII.xii.476). Similarly in *A Revelation*, prelates' crowns, fingers, and lips are cut off for refusal to chastise sin in themselves, their households, and their subjects, and snakes are put in prelates' ears for their refusal to hear correction (pp. 71–2). Priestly unchastity too is excoriated by both Bridget and the anchoress. Bridget's assumption of the prophetic role certainly aided the Winchester visionary in formulating her own critical assessment of English life, an assessment whose reception must owe something to clerical regard for visionary prophecy, or as Jeremy Catto puts it, clerics' 'awareness of forms of divine guidance alternative to their own'.[14]

The anchoress was writing well after Bridget's work began to be circulated in England, her English readership perhaps beginning slightly before her death in 1373, hence almost half a century earlier.[15] Most tellingly, a copy of Bridget's revelations was present in Winchester, listed in an inventory from the fellows' library at Winchester College. The 1421/2 book-list entry reads 'liber celestium revelationem beatae Brigittae ex dono magister Johannis Campedum' [book of divine revelation of the blessed Bridget from the gift of master John Campeden], that is, the master of the Winchester hospital of Saint Cross and a connection of William of Wykeham (WCM MS 21865).[16] Two slightly later book-lists also carry Brigittine titles.

Though Bridget's visionary work is strongly recalled in *A Revelation*, an English purgatorial visionary tradition existed as well, and the Winchester anchoress knew some of its components, two Middle English works in particular. Harley pointed out several resemblances between *A Revelation* and *The Gast of Gy*, originally a Latin account of a 1323 French apparition. Both its Middle English prose and poetic forms survive in manuscripts early enough to have been known by the anchoress. The same prayers precipitate each vision. In *Gast*, the visionary prior 'hedde a deuocion to seye þe seuen psalmes wiþ þe letanye. And whon þei come to Agnes dei þey herden a mer vois & a small as of a child, seyinge Amen' ($\overline{YW\ 296}$).[17] In *A Revelation*, 'I rose vp, and a lytel mayd child with me, and we two seiden þe vij psallmes and þe lytany. And by, we had seid out Agnes dei, I was so heuy of slep I [. . .] bade my child go to bedde, and so did I' (p. 80). In both works, the spirit appears immediately and is asked whether it is good or bad. The list of masses recommended for souls in purgatory is identical, and Marian intercession is presented in similar terms. *Gast* is centrally a *disputatio* or dialogue, and remnants of that format remain in *A Revelation*, as the first and second nights each conclude with questions put to the ghost, and its instructive answers.

Even stronger are the reminiscences of the second in Guillaume de Deguilleville's trilogy of visions, *Le pelerinage de l'ame*, translated into Middle English in 1413 according to five of its manuscripts. The similarities between *The Pilgrimage of the Soul* and *A Revelation* are strong indeed and it seems likely that the visionary encountered this extremely popular, extremely traditional work within ten years of its translation – if she read it in English and not in its original French. Both visions occur on St Lawrence's day at night, 10 August. In both, the worm of conscience is prominent. *Pilgrimage* names it Sinderesis (interior self-judgement or remorse), a monster consisting only of a head and tail. The worm appears as the soul's accuser in both *Pilgrimage* and *A Revelation*, and in both works plays a dramatic part in the final weighing scene where she crawls into the balance scale, but is outweighed in the scale by Mercy or the Virgin, and vanishes with a cry. This last scene in the vision is likely to have had a visual antecedent. Since all ten extant manuscripts of *Pilgrimage* are illustrated, the Winchester anchoress was probably introduced to this narrative visually as well as verbally. Two illustrations appear in almost all the manuscripts. Both show the lady and the worm confronting each other across the balance scale, and are likely to have influenced the anchoress's imagining of her vision's final scene.

Finally, the most popular poem of the middle ages, the *Pricke of Conscience*, may also have left its traces on *A Revelation*, since it too features a worm of conscience and in its sixth book the pains of purgatory include the alternation of fire and ice, the gnawing of worms, and beating with diabolic hammers, all found in the vision.[18]

A Revelation thus allows us to see something of the reading of another visionary woman, and to observe that it differs considerably from what we know of Margery Kempe's, despite their common perusal of Bridget. To some extent clerically directed, Margery's reading illustrates what might be called a formal study of mystical practice; it is certainly more ambitious (the Bible with commentaries, Hilton, Bonaventure, *Stimulus Amoris*, *Incendium Amoris*). The anchoress's reading demonstrates another approach to spiritual experience: narrative, experiential, accessible (*Pricke of Conscience*, *Gast of Gy*, Deguilleville). We need not see these reading choices as representing more and less elevated paths to visionary experience. Nicholas Watson has pointed to elements in Julian of Norwich's visions that may spring from the same sort of reading as the Winchester visionary's. Julian's hope for a bodily glimpse of the Virgin, her desire for 'ful syte' of hell or purgatory, and her enquiry about the spiritual destiny of a woman friend, represent elements familiar in the literature of visions, and integral to the Winchester woman's account.

This account supplements – and indeed challenges – our slender knowledge of women's writing in Middle English. Watson has emphasized that Julian of Norwich's *Revelation of Love* must be seen as strongly influenced by a like-minded group of readers and hearers, and has suggested ways of defining that community, using evidence both inside and outside its text.[19] *A Revelation of Purgatory* shows us the membership of such a group and to some extent, their beliefs. The response of its first six readers or hearers – conventional, well-placed, two connected with the Lancastrian dynasty – suggests a degree of toleration for this unfamiliar English employment of the female prophetic voice, particularly in the rapid consent given by all of them to the spirit's detailed commands. Then too, the absence of anxiety or hesitation in the author's narrative and its reception-account (so unlike Margery Kempe's stance) indicates that both she and her substantial circle saw her violent and explicit attack on the religious life as well within the bounds of acceptability. The vision's general criticism of the ecclesiastical milieu includes an implicit local impulse as well, since she condemns the practice she knows best, that of Winchester's famous, ancient, female religious house, and this criticism of women by a woman calls implicitly for reform of one of England's oldest monastic foundations. In its adaptation of a female prophetic voice (like Bridget's, like Margery Kempe's) to an English tradition of otherworld writing, *A Revelation* provides a singular example of a woman's critique which does not come from below and is not, apparently, met with resistance.

The transmission of this text between the important houses of Winchester and Westminster (and, more speculatively, Syon) suggests some channels for exchange of reading and ideas among those near to centres of spiritual and temporal power. Henry V's intentions regarding reform of the church were so emphatically truncated by his early death that it is impossible to guess what might have followed. Yet it may be right to read *A Revelation* as joining a collective and elevated concern about religious reform in the last years of the reign.

Notes

1. For a longer account of the vision, the identities of the visionary and her circle, her reading and influences, with fuller documentation see Mary C. Erler, ' "A Revelation of Purgatory" (1422): Reform and the Politics of Female Visions', *Viator*, 38 (2007), 321–47.
2. This essay relies on the almost-simultaneous work of two earlier scholars: S. J. Ogilvie-Thomson, 'An Edition of the English Works of MS Longleat 29, Excluding "The Parson's Tale" ' (DPhil thesis, Oxford University 1980) and Marta Powell Harley, *A Revelation of Purgatory by an Unknown, Fifteenth-Century Woman Visionary: Introduction, Critical Text and Translation*, Studies in Women and Religion 18 (Lewiston, NY: Edwin Mellen Press, 1985), based on her 1981 Columbia University dissertation. There are three manuscripts: MS Longleat 29; Lincoln Cathedral MS 91; Bodleian MS Eng.Th.c.58. In this essay the text has been cited from Harley.
3. Eileen Power, *Medieval English Nunneries, c.1275 to 1535* (Cambridge: Cambridge University Press, 1922), p. 151; and see *Victoria County History* (hereafter *VCH*), *Hampshire*, 7 vols. (London: Institute for Historical Research, rev. edn. 1973) II, pp. 123–6; David Knowles and R. Neville Hadcock, *Medieval Religious Houses, England and Wales* (London: Longmans, Green, 1953), p. 221; Diana K. Coldicott, *Hampshire Nunneries* (Chichester, Sussex: Phillimore and Co., 1989), passim.
4. Charles Ross, 'The Estates and Finances of Richard Beauchamp, Earl of Warwick', *Dugdale Society Occasional Papers*, 12 (1956), 3–22 (15).
5. G. L. Harriss, *Cardinal Beaufort: A Study in Lancastrian Ascendancy and Decline* (Oxford: Oxford University Press, 1988), p. 377; Richard Rex, *The Lollards* (Basingstoke: Palgrave Macmillan, 2002), p. 87, citing Edward Powell, *Kingship, Law and Society: Criminal Justice in the Reign of Henry V* (Oxford: Clarendon Press, 1989), pp. 162, 165, 168–9.

6. Margaret Toynbee, 'Lincoln College', *VCH Oxfordshire*, 7 vols. (London, 1954), III, p. 163.

7. Joan Greatrex, *The Register of the Common Seal of the Priory of St Swithun, Winchester 1345–1497*, Hampshire Record Series 2 (Trowbridge, 1979), no. 149.

8. Harley discovered the ordination dates of both: 1389 and 1394 (see *Revelation of Purgatory*, p. 35). For Pery/Pury, see Joan Greatrex, *Biographical Register of the English Cathedral Priories of the Province of Canterbury, c.1066 to 1540* (Oxford: Clarendon Press, 1997), p. 24; for Bone, see Derek Keene, *Survey of Medieval Winchester*, 2 vols. (Oxford: Oxford University Press, 1985), II, pp. 987, 999. For his bequest, see W. H. Gunner, 'Catalogue of Books Belonging to the College of St Mary, Winchester in the Time of Henry VI', *Archaeological Journal*, 15 (1858), 62–74 (70).

9. David Knowles, *The Religious Orders of England*, 3 vols. (Cambridge: Cambridge University Press, 1948–59), II, p. 368, and see Appendix 2, 'Henry V and the Westminster Recluse'.

10. Margaret Deanesly, *The Incendium Amoris of Richard Rolle of Hampole* (Manchester: Manchester University Press, 1913), pp. 118, 121, 123–4, 125. A. I. Doyle points out that the St Albans chronicle was probably compiled a good deal later than these events and its attribution to John Amundesham is uncertain (private communication, 14 August 2003).

11. *Revelation of Purgatory*, p. 16, and see George R. Keiser, 'More Light on the Life and Milieu of Robert Thornton', *Studies in Bibliography*, 36 (1983), 111–19; and Jonathan Hughes, *Pastors and Visionaries: Religious and Secular Life in Late Medieval Yorkshire* (Woodbridge: Boydell, 1988), p. 342.

12. References from *The Liber Celestis of St Bridget of Sweden*, ed. Roger Ellis, 2 vols., EETS o.s. 291 (Oxford: Oxford University Press, 1987), vol. 1.

13. *Birgitta of Sweden: Life and Selected Revelations*, ed. Marguerite Tjader Harris, trans. Albert Ryle Kezel (Mahwah, NJ: Paulist Press, 1990), pp. 84–5.

14. Review of Claire Sahlin, *Bridget of Sweden and the Voice of Prophecy* in *English Historical Review*, 108 (April 2003), 486–7.

15. Roger Ellis, ' "Flores ad Fabricandam Coronam": An Investigation into the Uses of the Revelations of St Bridget of Sweden in Fifteenth-Century England', *Medium Aevum*, 51 (1982), 163–86. For specific information on Brigittine manuscripts in England pre-1422, see F. R. Johnston, 'The English Cult of St. Bridget of Sweden', *Analecta Bollandiana*, 103 (1985), 75–93 (79); *Bodleian Summary Catalogue* V.682; Kathleen L. Scott, *Later Gothic Manuscripts, 1390–1490*, 2 vols. (London: Harvey Miller, 1996), vol. 2I, pp. 119–20; Ellis, *Liber*, ix.

16. Walter Oakeshott, 'Winchester College Library before 1750', *The Library*, 5th series, 9 (1954), 1–16 (14–15).

17. References from *Yorkshire Writers: Richard Rolle of Hampole ... and His Followers*, ed. Carl Horstmann (London and New York: S. Sonnenschien, 1895–6).

18. *The Pricke of Conscience (Stimulus Conscientiae), A Northumbrian Poem by Richard Rolle de Hampole*, ed. Richard Morris (New York: AMS Press, repr. 1973).

19. Nicholas Watson, 'Julian of Norwich', in *The Cambridge Companion to Women's Writing*, ed. Carolyn Dinshaw and David Wallace (Cambridge: Cambridge University Press, 2003), pp. 211, 218–20.

Select Bibliography

Primary printed sources

Ælfric of Eynsham, *Lives of Saints*, ed. Walter W. Skeat, EETS o.s. 76, 82 and 94, 114 (London and Oxford: Trübner and Kegan Paul, Trench and Trübner, 1881, 1885 and 1890, 1900; repr. as 2 vols., London: Oxford University Press, 1966)

Ælred of Rievaulx, 'Rule of Life for a Recluse (*De institutione inclusarum*)', in *Treatises and Pastoral Prayer*, by Ælred of Rievaulx (Kalamazoo, MI: Cistercian Publications, 1995), pp. 41–102

Aldhelm: The Poetic Works, trans. Michael Lapidge and James Rosier (Woodbridge: Boydell and Brewer, 1985)

Aldhelm: The Prose Works, trans. Michael Lapidge and Michael Herren (Woodbridge: Boydell and Brewer, 1979)

Anchoritic Spirituality: Ancrene Wisse and Associated Works, ed. and trans. Anne Savage and Nicholas Watson (New York: Paulist Press, 1991)

Ancrene Wisse: A Corrected Edition of the Text in Cambridge, Corpus Christi College, MS 402 with Variants from other Manuscripts, 2 vols., ed. Bella Millet, EETS o.s. 325 and o.s. 326 (Oxford: Oxford University Press, 2005)

Barnes, Juliana, *Juliana Barnes: Boke of Huntyng*, ed. Gunnar Tilander, Cynegetica 11 (Karlshamn: Johansson, 1964)

Barratt, Alexandra, ed., *Women's Writing in Middle English*, 2nd edn. (London: Pearson, 2010)

Bartlett, Anne Clark and Thomas H. Bestul, eds., *Cultures of Piety: Medieval English Devotional Literature in Translation*, I (Ithaca: Cornell University Press, 1999)

Bede, *Ecclesiastical History of the English People*, ed. and trans. B. Colgrave and R. A. B. Mynors (Oxford: Clarendon Press, 1969)

Blamires, Alcuin with Karen Pratt and C. W. Marx, eds., *Woman Defamed and Woman Defended: An Anthology of Medieval Texts* (Oxford: Clarendon Press, 1992)

Bokenham, Osbern, *A Legend of Holy Women: A Translation of Osbern Bokenham's Legends of Holy Women*, ed. and trans. Sheila Delany (Notre Dame, IN: University of Notre Dame Press, 1992)

—— *Legendys of Hooly Wummen*, ed. Mary S. Serjeantson, EETS o.s. 206 (London: Oxford University Press, 1938; repr. New York: Kraus Reprint Co., 1971)

Bridget of Sweden, *Birgitta of Sweden: Life and Selected Revelations*, ed. Marguerite Tjader Harris, trans. Albert Ryle Kezel, The Classics of Western Spirituality (Mahwah, NJ: Paulist Press, 1990)

—— *The Liber Celestis of St Bridget of Sweden*, ed. Roger Ellis, 2 vols., EETS o.s. 291 (Oxford: Oxford University Press, 1987)

—— *The Word of the Angel: Sermo Angelicus*, trans. with introduction and notes by John E. Halborg (Toronto: Peregrina Publishing, 1996)

Brown, Jennifer N., *Three Women of Liège: A Critical Edition of and Commentary on the Middle English Lives of Elizabeth of Spalbeek, Christina Mirabilis, and Marie d'Oignies* (Turnhout: Brepols, 2008)

The Cely Letters, 1472–1488, ed. Alison Hanham, EETS o.s. 273 (London: Oxford University Press, 1975)

Charnell-White, Cathryn A., ed., *Beirdd Ceridwen: Blodeugerdd o Ganu Menywod hyd tua 1800* (Llandybïe: Cyhoeddiadau Barddas, 2005)

The Chastising of God's Children and the Treatise of Perfection of the Sons of God, ed. J. Bazier and E. Colledge (Oxford: Oxford University Press, 1957)

Chaucer, Geoffrey, *The Riverside Chaucer*, 3rd edn., ed. Larry D. Benson (Boston: Houghton Mifflin, 1991)

Christine de Pizan, *The boke of the cyte of ladyes* (London: Henry Pepwell, 1521)

—— *The Book of the City of Ladies*, trans. Earl Jeffrey Richards (New York: Persea, 1982)

—— *Book of the Deeds of Arms and of Chivalry*, trans. Charity Cannon Willard (College Park: Pennsylvania State University Press, 1999)

—— *Christine de Pizan's Letter of Othea to Hector*, ed. and trans. Jane Chance (Newburyport: Focus, 1990)

—— *Ditié de Jehanne d'Arc*, ed. Angus J. Kennedy and Kenneth Varty, Medium Aevum Monographs New Series IX (Oxford: Society for the Study of Mediaeval Languages and Literature, 1977)

—— *The Selected Writings of Christine de Pizan*, trans. Renate Blumenfeld-Kosinski and Kevin Brownlee (New York: W. W. Norton, 1997)

Clemence of Barking, *The Life of St. Catherine by Clemence of Barking*, ed. William MacBain, Anglo-Norman Text Society 18 (Oxford: Blackwell, 1964)

—— *The Life of St Catherine*, in *Virgin Lives and Holy Deaths: Two Exemplary Biographies for Anglo-Norman Women*, trans. Jocelyn Wogan-Browne and Glyn S. Burgess (London: Dent, 1996)

Contemplations on the Dread and Love of God, ed. Margaret Connell, EETS 303 (Oxford: Oxford University Press, 1987)

Crawford, Anne, ed., *Letters of the Queens of England* (Thrupp: Sutton Publishing, 1994)

Dafydd ap Gwilym, *Dafydd ap Gwilym*, ed. Dafydd Johnston *et al.*, Swansea University, http://www.dafyddapgwilym.net

The Early South English Legendary or Lives of Saints, ed. Carl Horstman, EETS O.S. 87 (London: N. Truebner and Co., 1887)

Elene, ed. P. O. E Gradon, Exeter Medieval Texts and Studies (Exeter: University of Exeter Press, 1958, rev. edn. 1977)

Encomium Emmae Reginae, ed. A. Campbell (London: Offices of the Royal Historical Society, 1949; repr. with supplementary introduction by Simon Keynes, Cambridge: Cambridge University Press for the Royal Historical Society, 1998)

The English Text of the Ancrene Riwle: Cotton Cleopatra C.VI, ed. E. J. Dobson EETS 267 (Oxford: Oxford University Press, 1972)

Epistolae: Medieval Women's Letters, http://epistolae.ccnmtl.columbia.edu/letter/374.html

The Floure and the Leafe; The Assembly of Ladies; The Isle of Ladies, ed. Derek Pearsall (Kalamazoo: Medieval Institute Publications, 1990)

Geoffroy La Tour Landry, *The Book of the Knight of La Tour-Landry*, ed. Thomas Wright, rev. edn., EETS O.S. 33 (London: Kegan Paul, Trench, Trübner & Co., 1906)

Gilbert, Sandra M. and Susan Gubar, eds., *The Norton Anthology of Literature by Women: The Traditions in English*, 3rd edn. (New York: W. W. Norton, 2007)

Gilte Legende, 2 vols., ed. Richard Hamer and Vida Russell, EETS O.S. 327, 328 (Oxford: Oxford University Press, 2006, 2007)

The Good Wife Taught Her Daughter, The Good Wyfe Wold a Pylgremage, The Thewis of Gud Women, ed. Tauno F. Mustanoja (Helsinki: Suomalaisen Kirjallisuuden Scu, 1948)

Goscelin of St Bertin, *The Book of Encouragement and Comfort: Goscelin's Letter to the Recluse Eva*, ed. Monika Otter (Cambridge: D. S. Brewer, 2004)

—— 'La Legende de Ste Edith', ed. A. Wilmart, *Analecta Bollandiana*, 56 (1938), 5–101, 265–307

—— *Writing the Wilton Women: Goscelin's* Legend of Edith *and* Liber confortatorius, ed. Stephanie Hollis *et al.* (Turnhout: Brepols, 2004), pp. 17–93

Gramich, Katie and Catherine Brennan, eds., *Welsh Women's Poetry, 1460–2001* (Llandybïe: Honno, 2003)

Harries, Leslie, ed., *Gwaith Huw Cae Llwyd ac Eraill* (Caerdydd: Gwasg Prifysgol Cymru, 1953)

Howells, Nerys Ann, ed., *Gwaith Gwerful Mechain ac Eraill* (Aberystwyth: Canolfan Uwchefrydiau Cymreig a Cheltaidd Prifysgol Cymru, 2001)

Hull, Eleanor, *The Seven Psalms: A Commentary on the Penitential Psalms translated from French into English by Dame Eleanor Hull*, ed. Alexandra Barratt, EETS o.s. 307 (Oxford: Oxford University Press, 1995, repr. 2001)

Huws, Bleddyn O., ed., *Detholiad o Gywyddau Gofyn a Diolch* (Caernarfon: Cyhoeddiadau Barddas, 1998)

Jacobus de Voragine, *Jacobus de Voragine: The Golden Legend. Readings on the Saints*, ed. and trans. W. Granger Ryan, 2 vols. (Princeton, NJ: Princeton University Press, 1993)

Jacques de Vitry, *The* Exempla *or Illustrative Stories from the* Sermones Vulgares *of Jacques de Vitry*, ed. Thomas Frederick Crane (London: David Nutt, 1890) http://www.archive.org/stream/theexempla00vitruoft#page/n9/mode/2up

Judith, ed. Mark Griffith, Exeter Medieval Texts and Studies (Exeter: University of Exeter Press, 1997)

Julian of Norwich, *The Writings of Julian of Norwich: A Vision Showed to a Devout Woman and A Revelation of Love*, ed. Nicholas Watson and Jacqueline Jenkins (Turnhout: Brepols, 2006)

Kempe, Margery, *The Book of Margery Kempe*, ed. Sanford Brown Meech and Hope Emily Allen, EETS o.s. 212 (Oxford: Oxford University Press, 1940; repr. London: Oxford University Press, 1997)

Kerrigan, Catherine, ed., with Gaelic translations by Meg Bateman, *An Anthology of Scottish Women Poets* (Edinburgh: Edinburgh University Press, 1991)

Khanna, Lee Cullen, ed., *Early Tudor Translators: Margaret Beaufort, Margaret More Roper and Mary Basset*, The Early Modern Englishwoman: A Facsimile Library of Essential Works Series I: Printed Writings, 1500–1640, Part 2 (Aldershot: Ashgate, 2001)

Kingsford, C. L., 'Supplementary Stonor Letters and Papers (1314–1482)', in *Camden Miscellany* 13, Camden Society, 3rd series, 34 (London, 1924), pp. i–viii; 1–26

The Knowing of Woman's Kind in Childing: A Middle English Version of Material Derived from the Trotula and Other Sources, ed. Alexandra Barratt (Turnhout: Brepols, 2001)

The Life of Christina of Markyate: A Twelfth Century Recluse, ed. and trans. C. H. Talbot (Toronto: University of Toronto Press, 2001)

Þe Liflade and te Passium of Seinte Iuliene, ed. S. R. T. O. D'Ardenne, EETS o.s. 248 (London: Oxford University Press, 1961)

Love, Nicholas, *Mirror of the Blessed Life of Jesus Christ*, ed. Michael G. Sargent (Exeter: Exeter University Press, 2004)

Marie, *The Life of Saint Audrey: A Text by Marie de France*, trans. and ed. June Hall McCash and Judith Clark Barban (Jefferson, NC and London: McFarland, 2006)

—— *La Vie seinte Audree, poème anglo-normand du XIIIe siècle*, ed. Östen Södergård (Uppsala: Lundenquistska Bokhandeln, 1955)

Marie de France, *Fables*, ed. and trans. Harriet Spiegel (Toronto: University of Toronto Press, 1994)

—— *Lais*, ed. Alfred Ewert (Oxford: Blackwell, 1944; repr. 1978)

—— *The* Lais *of Marie de France*, trans. Glyn S. Burgess and Keith Busby, 2nd edn. (Harmondsworth: Penguin, 1999)

—— *Saint Patrick's Purgatory: A Poem by Marie de France*, trans. Michael J. Curley (Binghamton: NY: Medieval and Renaissance Texts and Studies, 1993)

McCarthy, Conor, ed., *Love, Sex and Marriage in the Middle Ages: Sourcebook* (London: Routledge, 2004)

Millet, Bella and Jocelyn Wogan-Browne, eds., *Medieval English Prose for Women from the Katherine Group and Ancrene Wisse* (Oxford: Clarendon Press, 1990)

Morton, Vera, ed., with an introduction by Jocelyn Wogan-Browne, *Guidance for Women in Twelfth-Century Convents* (Cambridge: D. S. Brewer, 2003)

Mulder-Bakker, Anneke, ed., *Mary of Oignies: Mother of Salvation* (Turnhout: Brepols, 2007)

The Myroure of our Ladye, ed. John Blunt, EETS E.S. 19 (London: Oxford University Press, 1873)

Nun of Barking, *La Vie d'Edouard le confesseur: poème anglo-normand du XIIe siècle*, ed. Östen Södergård (Uppsala: Almqvist and Wiksells, 1948)

The Old English Lives of St. Margaret, ed. Mary Clayton and Hugh Magennis (Cambridge: Cambridge University Press, 1994)

The Paston Women: Selected Letters, ed. Diane Watt (Cambridge: D. S. Brewer, 2004)

Payne, Paddy and Caroline M. Barron, eds., 'The Letters and Life of Elizabeth Despenser, Lady Zouche (D. 1408)', *Nottingham Medieval Studies*, 41 (1997), 126–56

The Plumpton Letters and Papers, ed. Joan Kirby, Camden Society, 5th Series, 8 (Cambridge: Cambridge University Press, 1996)

Reames, Sherry L., ed., *Middle English Legends of Women Saints* (Kalamazoo: TEAMS, 2003)

A Revelation of Purgatory by an Unknown, Fifteenth-Century Woman Visionary: Introduction, Critical Text, and Translation, ed. Marta Powell Harley, Studies in Women and Religion 18 (Lewiston, NY: Edwin Mellen Press, 1985)

Rolle, Richard, *Richard Rolle: The English Writings*, ed. and trans. Rosamund S. Allen (New York: Paulist Press, 1988)

Scrope, Stephen, *The Epistle of Othea translated from the French Text of Christine de Pisan by Stephen Scrope*, ed. C. F. Bühler, EETS 264 (London: Oxford University Press, 1970)

Seinte Katerine, ed. Bella Millet and E. J. Dobson, EETS s.s. 7 (London: Oxford University Press, 1981)

Seinte Marherete: Þe Meiden ant Martyr, ed. Frances M. Mack, EETS O.S. 193 (London: Oxford University Press, 1934; repr. with corrections 1958)

The South English Legendary, ed. Charlotte D'Evelyn and Anna J. Mill, EETS O.S. 235, 236 (London: Oxford University Press, 1956)

Spearing, Elizabeth, ed., *Medieval Writings on Female Spirituality* (Harmondsworth: Penguin, 2002)

Stevenson, Jane and Peter Davidson, eds., *Early Modern Women Poets: An Anthology* (Oxford: Oxford University Press, 2001)

The Stonor Letters and Papers, 1290–1483, ed. C. L. Kingsford, 2 vols., Camden Society, 3rd Series (London, 1919)

Swabey, Ffiona, 'The Letter Book of Alice de Bryene and Alice de Sutton's List of Debts', *Nottingham Medieval Studies*, 42 (1998), pp. 121–45

Treharne, Elaine, ed., *Old and Middle English: An Anthology* (Oxford: Blackwell, 2000)

Winstead, Karen A., ed. and trans., *Chaste Passions: Medieval English Virgin Martyr Narratives* (Ithaca and London: Cornell University Press, 2000)

Þe Wohunge of Ure Lauerd, ed. W. Meredith Thompson, EETS O.S. 241 (London: Oxford University Press, 1958)

Secondary sources

Abbot, Christopher, *Julian of Norwich: Autobiography and Theology* (Cambridge: D. S. Brewer, 1999)

Aers, David, *Community, Gender, and Individual Identity: English Writing, 1360–1430* (New York: Routledge, 1988)

—— and Lynn Staley, *Powers of the Holy: Religion, Politics, and Gender in Late Medieval English Culture* (University Park, PA: Pennsylvania State University Press, 1996)

Altmann, Barbara K. and Deborah L. McGrady, eds., *Christine de Pizan: A Casebook* (New York: Routledge, 2002)

Amtower, Laurel, *Engaging Words: The Culture of Reading in the Later Middle Ages* (New York: Palgrave Macmillan, 2000)

Arnold, John and Katherine J. Lewis, eds., *A Companion to The Book of Margery Kempe* (Cambridge: D. S. Brewer, 2004)

Ashley, Kathleen M. and Robert L. A. Clark, eds., *Medieval Conduct* (Minneapolis: University of Minnesota Press, 2001)

—— and Pamela Sheingorn, *Interpreting Cultural Symbols: Saint Anne in Late Medieval Society* (Athens, GA and London: University of Georgia Press, 1990)

Astell, Ann and Bonnie Wheeler, eds., *Joan of Arc and Spirituality* (New York: Palgrave Macmillan, 2003)

Atkinson, Clarissa, *Mystic and Pilgrim: The Book and the World of Margery Kempe* (Ithaca: Cornell University Press, 1983)

—— *The Oldest Vocation: Christian Motherhood in the Middle Ages* (Ithaca: Cornell University Press, 1991)

Baker, Denise Nowakowski, *Julian of Norwich's "Showings": From Vision to Book* (Princeton: Princeton University Press, 1994)

Bartlett, Anne Clark, *Male Authors, Female Readers: Representation and Subjectivity in Middle English Devotional Literature* (Ithaca: Cornell University Press, 1995)

Bauerschmidt, Frederick Christian, *Julian of Norwich and the Mystical Body Politic of Christ* (Notre Dame, IN: University of Notre Dame Press, 1999)

Bell, David N., *What Nuns Read: Books and Libraries in Medieval English Nunneries* (Kalamazoo, MI: Cistercian Publications, 1995)

Bennett, Judith M., *History Matters: Patriarchy and the Challenge of Feminism* (Philadelphia: University of Pennsylvania Press, 2006)

Bernau, Anke, *Virgins: A Cultural History* (London: Granta, 2007)

—— Ruth Evans, and Sarah Salih, eds., *Medieval Virginities* (Cardiff: University of Wales Press, 2003)

Betella, Partizia, *The Ugly Woman: Transgressive Aesthetic Models in Italian Poetry from the Middle Ages to the Baroque* (Toronto: University of Toronto Press, 2005)

Blamires, Alcuin, *The Case For Women in Medieval Culture* (Oxford: Clarendon Press, 1997)

Blanton, Virginia, *Signs of Devotion: The Cult of St. Aethelthryth in Medieval England, 695–1615* (University Park, PA: Pennsylvania State University Press, 2007)

Bloch, R. Howard, *The Anonymous Marie de France* (Chicago: University of Chicago Press, 2003)

—— *Medieval Misogyny and the Invention of Western Romantic Love* (Chicago: University of Chicago Press, 1991)

Bond, Gerald A., *The Loving Subject: Desire, Eloquence, and Power in Romanesque France* (Philadelphia: University of Pennsylvania Press, 1995)

Bornstein, Diane, *The Lady in the Tower: Medieval Courtesy Literature for Women* (Hamden, CT: Archon Books, 1983)

Boss, Sarah Jane, ed., *Mary: The Complete Resource* (Oxford: Oxford University Press, 2007)

Bradbury, Nancy, *Writing Aloud: Storytelling in Fourteenth Century England* (Urbana and Chicago: University of Illinois Press, 1998)

Bradley, Ritamary, *Julian's Way: A Practical Commentary on Julian of Norwich* (London: HarperCollins, 1992)

Brantley, Jessica, *Reading in the Wilderness: Private Devotion and Public Performance in Late Medieval England* (Chicago: University of Chicago Press, 2007)

—— *Symbolic Stories: Traditional Narratives of the Family Drama in English Literature* (Woodbridge: D. S. Brewer, 1980)

Brozyna, Martha A., ed., *Gender and Sexuality in the Middle Ages: A Medieval Source Documents Reader* (Jefferson: McFarland, 2005)

Bryan, Jennifer, *Looking Inward: Devotional Reading and the Private Self in Late Medieval England* (Philadelphia: University of Pennsylvania Press, 2008)

Bullough, Vern L. and James A. Brundage, eds., *Handbook of Medieval Sexuality* (New York: Garland Publishing, 1996)

Bynum, Caroline Walker, *Fragmentation and Redemption: Essays on Gender and the Human Body in Medieval Religion* (New York: Zone Books, 1991)

Cadden, Joan, *Meanings of Sex Difference in the Middle Ages: Medicine, Science, and Culture* (Cambridge: Cambridge University Press, 1993)

Calin, William, *The French Tradition and the Literature of Medieval England* (Toronto: University of Toronto Press, 1994)

Cartwright, Jane, *Feminine Sanctity and Spirituality in Medieval Wales* (Cardiff: University of Wales Press, 2008)

Chance, Jane, ed., *Gender and Text in the Later Middle Ages* (Gainesville: University Press of Florida, 1996)

—— *Woman as Hero in Anglo-Saxon Literature* (Syracuse, NY: Syracuse University Press, 1986)

Cherawatuk, Karen and Ulrike Wiethaus, eds., *Dear Sister: Medieval Women and the Epistolary Genre* (Philadelphia: University of Pennsylvania Press, 1993)

Coldicott, Diana K., *Hampshire Nunneries* (Chichester, Sussex: Phillimore and Co., 1989)

Coleman, Joyce, *Public Reading and the Reading Public in Late Medieval England and France* (Cambridge: Cambridge University Press, 1996)

Constable, Giles, *Letters and Letter Collections*, Typologie des Sources du Moyen Âge Occidental, facs. XVII (Turnhout: Brepols, 1976)

Coss, Peter, *The Lady in Medieval England, 1000–1500* (Stroud: Sutton Publishing Limited, 1998)

Crane, Susan, *Insular Romance: Politics, Faith, and Culture in Anglo-Norman and Middle English Literature* (Berkeley: University of California Press, 1986)

Cré, Marleen, *Vernacular Mysticism in the Charterhouse: A Study of London, British Library, MS Additional 37790*, The Medieval Translator 9 (Turnhout: Brepols, 2006)

D'Arcens, Louise and Juanita Feros Ruys, eds., *Maistresse of My Wit: Medieval Women, Modern Scholars* (Turnhout: Brepols, 2004)

Davidson, Clifford, *Festivals and Plays in Medieval Britain* (Aldershot: Ashgate, 2007)

Davis, Isabel, *Writing Masculinity in the Later Middle Ages* (Cambridge: Cambridge University Press, 2007)

Daybell, James, ed., *Early Modern Women's Letter Writing* (Basingstoke: Palgrave Macmillan, 2001).

Delaney, Sheila, *Impolitic Bodies: Poetry, Saints, and Society in Fifteenth-Century England: The Work of Osbern Bokenham* (Oxford: Oxford University Press, 1998)

—— *Writing Woman: Women Writers and Women in Literature, Medieval to Modern* (New York: Shocken Books, 1983)

Desmond, Marilynn, ed., *Christine de Pizan and the Categories of Difference* (Minneapolis: University of Minnesota Press, 1998)

Dinshaw, Carolyn, *Chaucer's Sexual Poetics* (Madison: University of Wisconsin Press, 1989)

—— *Getting Medieval: Sexualities and Communities, Pre- and Postmodern* (Durham, NC: Duke University Press, 1999)

—— and David Wallace, eds., *The Cambridge Companion to Medieval Women's Writing* (Cambridge: Cambridge University Press, 2003)

Dobson, Eric J., *The Origins of Ancrene Wisse* (Oxford: Clarendon Press, 1976)

Duckett, Eleanor, *Women and their Letters in the Early Middle Ages* (Baltimore: Barton-Gillet, 1965)

Dunnigan, Sarah M., C. Marie Harker, and Evelyn S. Newlyn, eds., *Woman and the Feminine in Medieval and Early Modern Scottish Writing* (Basingstoke: Palgrave Macmillan, 2004)

Dutton, Elizabeth, *Julian of Norwich: The Influence of Late-Medieval Devotional Compilations* (Cambridge: D. S. Brewer, 2008)

Edwards, R. R. and S. Spector, eds., *The Olde Daunce: Love, Friendship, Sex, and Marriage in the Medieval World* (Albany: State University of New York Press, 1991)

Elliot, Dyan, *Fallen Bodies: Pollution, Sexuality, and Demonology in the Middle Ages* (Philadelphia: University of Pennsylvania Press, 1999)

—— *Proving Women: Female Spirituality and Inquisitional Culture in the Later Middle Ages* (Princeton: Princeton University Press, 2004)

Ellis, Roger, *Viderunt eam Filie Syon: The Spirituality of the English House of a Medieval Contemplative Order from its Beginnings to the Present Day*, Analecta Cartusiana, 68 (Salzburg: Institut für Anglistik und Amerikanistik, 1984)

Erler, Mary C., *Women, Reading, and Piety in Late Medieval England* (Cambridge: Cambridge University Press, 2002)

—— and Maryanne Kowaleski, eds., *Gendering the Master Narrative: Women and Power in the Middle Ages* (Ithaca: Cornell University Press, 2003)

Ewan, Elizabeth and Maureen M. Meikle, eds., *Women in Scotland, c.1100–c.1750* (Edinburgh: Tuckwell, 1999)

Ezell, Margaret J. M., *Writing Women's Literary History* (Baltimore: Johns Hopkins University Press, 1993)

Fanous, Samuel and Henrietta Leyser, eds., *Christina of Markyate: A Twelfth-Century Holy Woman* (Abingdon: Routledge, 2005)

Farina, Lara, *Erotic Discourse and Early English Religious Writing* (New York: Palgrave Macmillan, 2006)

Fell, Christine E., with Cecily Clark and Elizabeth Williams, eds., *Women in Anglo-Saxon England* (Oxford: Blackwell, 1984)

Felski, Rita, *Literature after Feminism* (Chicago: University of Chicago Press, 2003)

Fenster, Thelma S., ed., *Arthurian Women: A Casebook*, Arthurian Characters and Themes 3 (New York: Garland 1996)

Ferrante, Joan M., *To the Glory of her Sex: Women's Roles in the Composition of Medieval Texts* (Bloomington: Indiana University Press, 1997)

Finke, Laurie A., *Women's Writing in English: Medieval England* (Harlow: Longman, 1999)

Fisher, Sheila and Janet E. Halley, eds., *Seeking the Woman in Late Medieval and Renaissance Writings: Essays in Feminist Contextual Criticism* (Knoxville: University of Tennessee Press, 1989)

Fradenburg, Louise and Carla Freccero, eds., with Kathy Lavezzo, *Premodern Sexualities* (New York and London: Routledge, 1996)

Fraioli, Deborah, *Joan of Arc: The Early Debate* (Woodbridge: Boydell, 2000)

Frese, Dolores Warwick and Katherine O'Brien O'Keeffe, *The Book and the Body* (Notre Dame, IN: University of Notre Dame Press, 1997)

Gaunt, Simon, *Gender and Genre in Medieval French Literature* (Cambridge: Cambridge University Press, 1995)

—— and Sarah Kay, eds., *The Cambridge Companion to Medieval French Literature* (Cambridge: Cambridge University Press, 2008)

Geddes, Jane, *The St Albans Psalter: A Book for Christina of Markyate* (London: The British Library, 2005)

Georgianna, Linda, *The Solitary Self* (Cambridge, MA: Harvard University Press, 1981)

Gibson, Gail McMurray, *The Theatre of Devotion: East Anglian Drama and Society in the Late Middle Ages* (Chicago: University of Chicago Press, 1989)

Gies, F. and J. Gies, *Women in the Middle Ages: The Lives of Real Women in a Vibrant Age of Transition* (New York: Harper & Row, 1978)

Gifford, Douglas and Dorothy McMillan, eds., *A History of Scottish Women's Writing* (Edinburgh: Edinburgh University Press, 1997)

Gillespie, Vincent, ed., *Syon Abbey with the Libraries of the Carthusians*, Corpus of British Medieval Library Catalogues 9 (London: British Library in association with the British Academy, 2001)

Goldberg, P. J. P., *Women in England, c.1275–1515* (Manchester: Manchester University Press, 1995)

Goodman, Anthony, *Margery Kempe and Her World* (London: Longman, 2002)

Green, D. H., *Women Readers in the Middle Ages* (Cambridge: Cambridge University Press, 2007)

Gregg, Joan Young, *Devils, Women, and Jews: Reflections of the Other in Medieval Sermon Stories* (Albany: State University of New York Press, 1997)

Gunn, Cate, *Ancrene Wisse: From Pastoral Literature to Vernacular Spirituality* (Cardiff: University of Wales Press, 2008)

Hamburger, Jeffrey F. and Susan Marti, eds., *Crown and Veil: Female Monasticism from the Fifth to the Fifteenth Centuries* (New York: Columbia University Press, 2008)

Hamel, Christopher de, *The Library of the Bridgettine Nuns and their Peregrinations after the Reformation* (Roxburghe Club, 1991)

Hansen, Elaine Tuttle, *Chaucer and the Fictions of Gender* (Berkeley, CA: University of California Press, 1992)

Harris, Barbara J., *English Aristocratic Women, 1450–1550: Marriage and Family, Property and Careers* (New York: Oxford University Press, 2002)

Hirsch, John C., *The Revelations of Margery Kempe: Paramystical Practices in Late Medieval England*, Medieval and Renaissance Authors 10 (Leiden: E. J. Brill, 1989)

Hogg, J., ed., *Studies in St. Birgitta and the Bridgettine Order*, 2 vols., Analecta Cartusiana 35.19 (Salzburg: Institut für Anglistik und Amerikanistik; Lewiston, NY: Edwin Mellen Press, 1993)

Hollis, Stephanie, *Anglo-Saxon Women and the Church: Sharing a Common Fate* (Woodbridge: Boydell and Brewer, 1992)

Horner, Shari, *The Discourse of Enclosure: Representing Women in Old English Literature* (Albany: State University of New York Press, 2001)

Jacquart, Danielle and Claude Thomasset, *Sexuality and Medicine in the Middle Ages*, trans. Matthew Adamson (Princeton, NJ: Princeton University Press, 1988)

Jantzen, Grace M., *Julian of Norwich: Mystic and Theologian* (New York: Paulist Press, 1988)

—— *Power, Gender, and Christian Mysticism* (Cambridge: Cambridge University Press, 1995)

Jenkins, Jacqueline and Katherine J. Lewis, eds., *St. Katherine of Alexandria: Texts and Contexts in Western Medieval Europe* (Turnhout: Brepols, 2003)

Johns, Susan M., *Noblewomen, Aristocracy, and Power in the Twelfth-Century Anglo-Norman Realm* (Manchester: Manchester University Press, 2003)

Jones, E. A. and Alexandra Walsham, eds., *Syon Abbey and its Books: Reading, Writing and Religion, c.1400–1700*, Studies in Modern British Religious History 24 (Woodbridge: Boydell and Brewer, 2010)

Jones, Michael K. and Malcolm G. Underwood, *The King's Mother: Lady Margaret Beaufort, Countess of Richmond and Derby* (Cambridge: Cambridge University Press, 1992)

Karras, Ruth Mazo, *From Boys to Men: Formations of Masculinity in Late Medieval Europe* (Philadelphia, PA: University of Pennsylvania Press, 2002)

—— *Sexuality in Medieval Europe: Doing Unto Others* (New York: Routledge, 2005)

Kelly, Kathleen Coyne, *Performing Virginity and Testing Chastity in the Middle Ages* (New York: Routledge, 2000)

Kerby-Fulton, Kathryn, *Books Under Suspicion: Censorship and Tolerance of Revelatory Writing in Late Medieval England* (Notre Dame, IN: University of Notre Dame Press, 2006)

Klein, Stacy S., *Ruling Women: Queenship and Gender in Anglo-Saxon Literature* (Notre Dame, IN: University of Notre Dame Press, 2006)

Krug, Rebecca, *Reading Families: Women's Literate Practice in Late Medieval England* (Ithaca: Cornell University Press, 2002)

Larrington, Carolyne, *King Arthur's Enchantresses: Morgan and her Sisters in Arthurian Tradition* (London: I. B. Tauris, 2006)

Leech, Kenneth and Benedicta Ward, *Julian Reconsidered*, Fairacres Publications 106 (Oxford: SLG Press, 1988)

Lees, Clare A. and Gillian R. Overing, *Double Agents: Women and Clerical Culture in Anglo-Saxon England* (Philadelphia: University of Pennsylvania Press, 2001; repr. with new preface, Cardiff: University of Wales Press, 2009)

Lewis, Katherine J., *The Cult of St Katherine of Alexandria in Late Medieval England* (Woodbridge: Boydell, 2000)

Lochrie, Karma, *Margery Kempe and Translations of the Flesh* (Philadelphia: University of Pennsylvania Press, 1991)

—— Peggy McCracken, and James A. Schultz, eds., *Constructing Medieval Sexuality* (Minneapolis: University of Minnesota Press, 1997)

LoPrete, Kimberley A., *Adela of Blois: Countess and Lord, c.1067–1137* (Dublin: Four Courts Press, 2007)

Mann, Jill, *Feminizing Chaucer*, rev. edn. (Cambridge: D. S. Brewer, 2002)

Mannion, Margaret M. and Bernard J. Muir, eds., *The Art of the Book: Its Place in Medieval Worship* (Exeter: Exeter University Press, 1998)

Marks, Richard, *Image and Devotion in Late Medieval England* (Stroud: Sutton Publishing Limited, 2004)

Marshall, Simone Celine, *The Female Voice in* The Assembly of Ladies (Cambridge: Cambridge Scholars Publishing, 2008)

Martin, Priscilla, *Chaucer's Women: Nuns, Wives and Amazons* (London: Macmillan 1990, repr. 1996)

McAvoy, Liz Herbert, *Authority and the Female Body in the Writings of Julian of Norwich and Margery Kempe* (Cambridge: D. S. Brewer, 2004)

—— ed., *A Companion to Julian of Norwich* (Cambridge: D. S. Brewer, 2008)

McCarthy, Conor, ed., *Love, Sex, and Marriage in the Middle Ages: A Sourcebook* (London: Routledge, 2004)

McCash, June Hall, ed., *The Cultural Patronage of Medieval Women* (Athens, GA: University of Georgia Press, 1996)

McDonald, Nicola, ed., *Pulp Fictions of Medieval England: Essays in Popular Romance* (Manchester: Manchester University Press, 2004)

McEntire, Sandra J., ed., *Julian of Norwich: A Book of Essays*, Garland Medieval Casebook 21 (New York: Garland, 1998)

—— ed., *Margery Kempe: A Book of Essays* (New York: Garland, 1992).

McSheffrey, Shannon, *Gender and Heresy: Women and Men in Lollard Communities, 1420–1530* (Philadelphia: University of Pennsylvania Press, 1995)

Meale, Carol M., ed., *Women and Literature in Britain, 1150–1500*, Cambridge Studies in Medieval Literature 17 (Cambridge: Cambridge University Press, 1993, 2nd edn., 1996)

Morris, Bridget, *St Birgitta of Sweden* (Woodbridge: Boydell, 1999)

Mulder-Bakker, Anneke, ed., *Mary of Oignies: Mother of Salvation* (Turnhout: Brepols, 2007)

—— and Liz Herbert McAvoy, eds., *Women and Experience in Later Medieval Writing: Reading the Book of Life* (Basingstoke and New York: Palgrave Macmillan, 2009)

Nuth, Joan M., *Wisdom's Daughter: The Theology of Julian of Norwich* (New York: Crossroad, 1991)

Olson, Linda and Kathryn Kerby-Fulton, eds., *Voices in Dialogue: Reading Women in the Middle Ages* (Notre Dame, IN: University of Notre Dame Press, 2005)

Pasternack, Carol Braun and Sharon Farmer, eds., *Gender and Difference in the Middle Ages* (Minnesota: University of Minnesota Press, 2003)

—— and Lisa M. C. Weston, eds., *Sex and Sexuality in Anglo-Saxon England: Essays in Memory of Daniel Gillmore Calder* (Tempe, AZ: Arizona Center for Medieval and Renaissance Studies, 2004)

Payer, Pierre J., *The Bridling of Desire: Views of Sex in the Later Middle Ages* (Toronto: University of Toronto Press, 1993)

Petroff, Elizabeth, ed., *Medieval Women's Visionary Literature* (Oxford: Oxford University Press, 1986)

Phillips, Kim, *Medieval Maidens: Young Women and Gender in England, 1270–1540* (Manchester: Manchester University Press, 2003)

Power, Eileen, *Medieval English Nunneries, c.1275 to 1535* (Cambridge: Cambridge University Press, 1922)

Quilligan, Maureen, *The Allegory of Female Authority: Christine de Pizan's* Cité des dames (Ithaca: Cornell University Press, 1991)

Radway, Janice A., *Reading the Romance: Women, Patriarchy, and Popular Literature* (Chapel Hill and London: University of North Carolina Press, 1991)

Renevey, Denis and Christiania Whitehead, eds., *Writing Religious Women: Female Spiritual and Textual Practices in Late Medieval England* (Cardiff: University of Wales Press, 2000)

Richards, Earl Jeffrey, *Reinterpreting Christine de Pizan* (Athens, GA: University of Georgia Press, 1991)

Riches, Samantha J. E. and Sarah Salih, eds., *Gender and Holiness: Men, Women, and Saints in Late Medieval Europe* (London: Routledge, 2002)

Riddy, Felicity, ed., *Prestige, Authority, and Power in Late-Medieval Manuscripts and Texts* (Woodbridge: York Medieval Press, 2000)

Roberts, Enid Pierce, *Dafydd Llwyd o Fathafarn*, Darlith Lenyddol Eisteddfod Genedlaethol Cymru, Maldwyn a'i Chyffiniau (1981)

Robertson, Elizabeth, *Early English Devotional Prose and the Female Audience* (Knoxville: University of Tennessee Press, 1990)

Rubin, Miri, *Emotion and Devotion: The Meaning of Mary in Medieval Religious Cultures* (Budapest: Central European University Press, 2009)

Sahlin, Claire L., *Birgitta of Sweden and the Voice of Prophecy* (Woodbridge: Boydell, 2001)

Salih, Sarah, *Versions of Virginity in Late Medieval England* (Cambridge: D. S. Brewer, 2001)

—— and Denise Baker, eds., *Julian of Norwich's Legacy: Medieval Mysticism and Post-Medieval Reception* (New York: Palgrave Macmillan, 2009)

Salisbury, Joyce E., *Church Fathers, Independent Virgins* (London: Verso, 1991)

—— *Medieval Sexuality: A Research Guide* (London: Garland, 1990)

Sanok, Catherine, *Her Life Historical: Exemplarity and Female Saints' Lives in Late Medieval England* (Philadelphia: University of Pennsylvania Press, 2007)

Saunders, Corinne, *Rape and Ravishment in the Literature of Medieval England* (Cambridge: D. S. Brewer, 2001)

Saupe, Karen, ed., *Middle English Marian Lyrics* (Kalamazoo, MI: Medieval Institute Publications, 1998)

Scheck, Helene, *Reform and Resistance: Formations of Female Subjectivity in Early Medieval Ecclesiastical Culture* (Albany, NY: State University of New York Press, 2008)

Simons, Walter, *Cities of Ladies: Beguine Communities in the Medieval Low Countries, 1200–1565* (Philadelphia: University of Pennsylvania Press, 2003)

Siraisi, Nancy G. *Medieval and Early Renaissance Medicine: An Introduction to Knowledge and Practice* (Chicago: University of Chicago Press, 1990)

Skemer, Don C., *Binding Words: Textual Amulets in the Middle Ages* (University Park, PA: Pennsylvania State University Press, 2006)

Sponsler, Claire, *Drama and Resistance: Bodies, Goods, and Theatricality in Late Medieval England* (Minneapolis: University of Minnesota Press, 1997)

Stafford, Pauline, *Queen Emma and Queen Edith: Queenship and Women's Power in Eleventh-Century England* (Oxford: Blackwell, 1997)

Staley, Lynn, *Margery Kempe's Dissenting Fictions* (Pennsylvania: Pennsylvania State University Press, 1994)

Summit, Jennifer, *Lost Property: The Woman Writer and English Literary History, 1380–1589* (Chicago: University of Chicago Press, 2000)

Taylor, Jane H. M. and Lesley Smith, eds., *Women and the Book: Assessing the Visual Evidence* (London and Toronto: The British Library and University of Toronto Press, 1997)

—— *Women, the Book, and the Godly: Selected Proceedings of the St. Hilda's Conference 1993*, vol. 1 (Woodbridge: Boydell and Brewer, 1995)

—— *Women, the Book, and the Worldly: Selected Proceedings of the St. Hilda's Conference 1993*, vol. 2 (Woodbridge: Boydell and Brewer, 1995)

Voaden, Rosalynn, *God's Words, Women's Voices: The Discernment of Spirits in the Writing of Late-Medieval Women Visionaries* (York: York Medieval Press, 1999).

—— ed., *Prophets Abroad: The Reception of Continental Holy Women in Late-Medieval England* (Cambridge: D. S. Brewer, 1996)

Wada, Yoko, ed., *A Companion to Ancrene Wisse* (Cambridge: D. S. Brewer, 2003)

Warner, Marina, *Alone of All Her Sex: The Myth and Cult of the Virgin Mary* (London: Picador, 2nd edn. 1985)

Warren, Ann K., *Anchorites and Their Patrons in Medieval England* (Berkeley: University of California Press, 1985)

Warren, Nancy Bradley, *Women of God and Arms: Female Spirituality and Political Conflict, 1380–1600* (Philadelphia: University of Pennsylvania Press, 2001)

Watt, Diane, *Medieval Women's Writing: Works by and for Women in England, 1100–1500* (Cambridge: Polity Press, 2007)

—— *Secretaries of God: Women Prophets in Late Medieval and Early Modern England* (Cambridge: D. S. Brewer, 1997)

Wheeler, Bonnie, ed., *Fresh Verdicts on Joan of Arc* (New York: Routledge, 1999)

—— and Fiona Tolhurst, eds., *On Arthurian Women: Essays in Memory of Maureen Fries* (Dallas, TX: Scriptorium Press, 2001)

Winstead, Karen A., *Virgin Martyrs: Legends of Sainthood in Late Medieval England* (Ithaca and London: Cornell University Press, 1997)

Wogan-Browne, Jocelyn, *Saints' Lives and Women's Literary Culture, c.1150–1300: Virginity and its Authorizations* (Oxford: Oxford University Press, 2001)

—— Rosalynn Voaden, Arlym Diamond, Ann Hutchison, Carol Meale, and Lesley Johnson, eds., *Medieval Women: Text and Contexts in Late Medieval Britain* (Turnhout: Brepols, 2000)

—— Nicholas Watson, Andrew Taylor, and Ruth Evans, eds., *The Idea of the Vernacular: An Anthology of Middle English Literary Theory, 1280–1520* (University Park, PA: Pennsylvania State Press, 1999)

Zimmermann, Margarete and Dina De Rentiis, eds., *The City of Scholars: New Approaches to Christine de Pizan* (Berlin: Walter de Gruyter, 1994)

Index